— THE —

GLOBAL
ECONOMY

AS YOU'VE NEVER SEEN IT

— THE —
GLOBAL ECONOMY
AS YOU'VE NEVER SEEN IT

Thomas Ramge and Jan Schwochow

with Adrian Garcia-Landa

THE EXPERIMENT

NEW YORK

The Experiment, LLC
220 East 23rd Street, Suite 600
New York, NY 10010-4658
theexperimentpublishing.com

Library of Congress Control Number: 2018949520

ISBN 978-1-61519-517-6

Cover design by Sarah Smith
Cover infographic by Infographics Group
Translation by Jonathan Green
Adaptation by Adrian Garcia-Landa, Camembert Communication
Photograph of Jan Schwochow by Infographics Group
Photograph of Thomas Ramge by Stefan Ostermeier

Manufactured in China

First printing October 2018
10 9 8 7 6 5 4 3 2 1

INTRODUCTION

The goal of this book is to inspire you to explore the complex world of the economy.

We want to provide understandable and entertaining access to it through the medium of the infographic. *The Global Economy as You've Never Seen It* is for everyone who finds it impossible to work their way through the business section of *The New York Times* each morning and who missed—or slept through—their Business and Econ 101 classes.

Our expedition through the economic world begins with the smallest economic unit: the individual. Then, the perspective becomes progressively broader with each chapter. We'll take a look at companies, the national economy, and the world economy. We'll seek insights from the greatest minds of economic theory, and then think about how—if we avoid the dangers of greed—profits can be made without throwing the planet off balance and destroying the environment. Finally, we'll look into the future and speculate about new ways of thinking and new technologies that might make possible a new economy focused on the human being.

This is no easy undertaking. The economic world is not only complex, but also enormous. At each way station of our journey, we have tried to translate into graphic form a broad spectrum of terms, contexts, concepts, and facts that seem essential to us. At many points we had to make decisions and accept trade-offs. *The Global Economy as You've Never Seen It* cannot, therefore, claim to be comprehensive—like an atlas that fully maps out Earth. Instead, the aim of our book is to arouse curiosity about intellectual terrain that is worth further exploration, not only because this territory is home to so many fascinating stories that have excited us—a journalist and a graphic designer—for two decades; but because, above all, economics connects everyone around the world.

And that's precisely why it's so important to understand the global economy, and to see it as you've never seen it before.

—Thomas Ramge and Jan Schwochow

CONTENTS

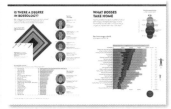

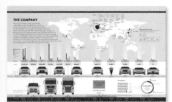

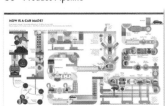
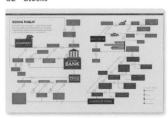
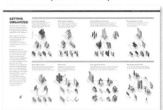
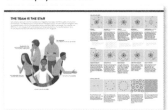

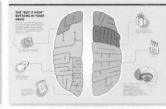

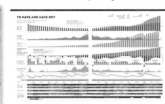
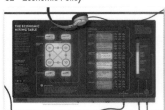
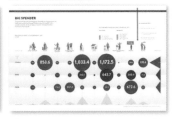
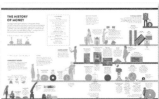

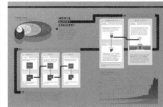
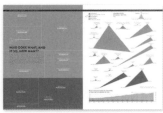
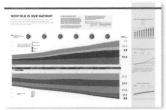

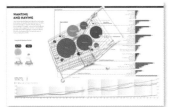

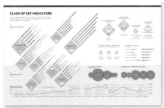
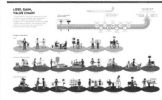
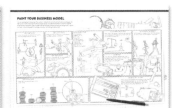

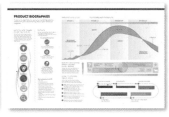

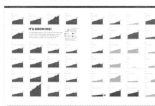

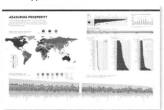

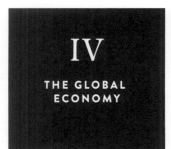 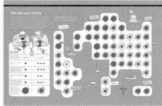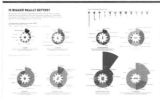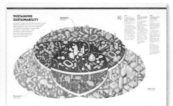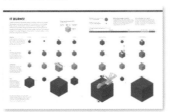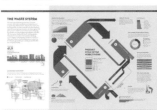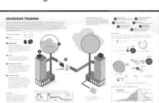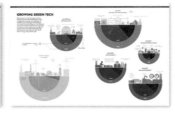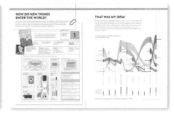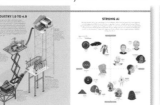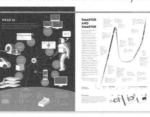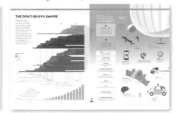

WORLD TRADE

96 • Flows of People and Goods

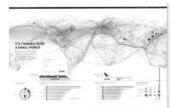

98 • Trade Agreements

100 • Imports and Exports

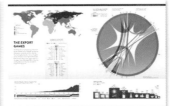

ILLEGAL GLOBAL MARKETS

102 • Organized Crime

104 • Modern Slavery

TALENT DISTRIBUTION AND LABOR MIGRATION

116 • The Water Market

117 • US Migration

118 • Global Migration

J. M. KEYNES

130 • Countercyclical Economic Policy

MILTON FRIEDMAN

132 • Money Matters

AMARTYA SEN

134 • An Economy for Human Beings

FARMING AND THE FOOD INDUSTRY

146 • Agricultural Commodities

148 • Biological   149 • Genetic

BUSINESS ETHICS

150 • Open and Honest

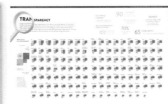

152 • Pseudo-Sustainable

DIGITALIZATION

170 • Top Innovators

172 • Elon Musk

174 • The Everything Company

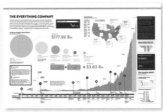

176 • Unicorns

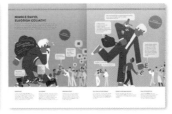

178 • Disruption / Transformation

THE FUTURE OF WORK

190 • How Do We Want to Work?

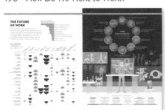

THE FUTURE OF FINANCE

192 • Fintech

194 • Bitcoin   195 • Blockchain

SAVING THE BEST FOR LAST

196 • Luxury Communism

I

THE
INDIVIDUAL

HOW WE WORK

Our work determines our lives. The framework in which we carry out our jobs determines how we work. These six categories make up the bulk of the labor force in the USA.

Labor Force
In the US, in millions of workers (2016)

Women   12.8

Men   9.1

34.2

38.7

40.7

39.8

IN EDUCATION

Undergo training to enter the labor force.

Apprentices, students enrolled in on-the-job training: 500,000.

Sub-baccalaureate training, 1–2 years schooling: 6.9 million.

Colleges and universities, 4 to 5 years: 13.5 million.

SALARIED EMPLOYEE

Receive a fixed amount of money by an employer for his or her work.

Exempt employees must accomplish their tasks regardless of hours worked. If non-exempt, they must work for specific hours.

Benefits: guaranteed minimum pay, and full pay for partial-day absences. No overtime pay if an exempt position.

Salaried employees usually earn more than workers paid hourly.

HOURLY EMPLOYEE

Paid by an employer for the amount of hours worked.

Usually lower income jobs, often physically intensive, with less potential for advancement. Typically in construction or hospitality.

Hourly workers receive a minimum wage and are entitled to overtime pay if working more than 40 hours a week.

Benefits like paid vacation and health insurance depend on company policy.

PART-TIME

27.7 million people worked fewer than 35 hours per week in 2016, the threshold set by the Bureau of Labor Statistics for part-time employment. Of the 21.4 million people working part-time, 29.1% are still at school and 20.5% are taking care of their families. Average weekly pay: $230 for men, and $252 for women (who are twice as likely to work part-time).

INEQUALITY

The demographics of the US population are not mirrored in its jobs: 90% of CEOs are white and 97.7% of preschool teachers are women. The job with the highest proportion of African Americans is postal work (38.4%). Hispanic and Latino workers comprise 27.3% of construction jobs and 22.3% of leisure and hospitality jobs. Asian American employees make up 62.3% of personal appearance work.

JOBS, GENDER, AND RACE

Jobs with highest rates of women and people of color, in percent (2016)

Total Population		Preschool Teachers	CEOs	Postal Workers	Appearance Workers	Drywall Installers
46.8	Female	97.5	27.3	42.4	86.1	1.1
78.8	White	81.0	88.8	53.4	30.4	88.7
11.9	Black	12.5	3.4	34.3	9.5	6.7
6.1	Asian	3.4	6.0	7.5	57.8	0.5
16.7	Hispanic or Latino	13.3	5.6	9.7	9.2	62.7

GENDER PAY GAP

It's not a myth, it's 81.8%. That's the average percentage of a man's weekly salary that women earned in 2016. In 1980, the percentage was 64.2. Although the gender pay gap is smaller with millennials at 93%, it is much bigger by race. For every dollar a white male makes, Black women earn 60 cents and Hispanic women 55 cents.

Precise figures for this category are not systematically tracked.

CIVIL SERVANT

Civilians working for US government departments and agencies.

Selected on merit and cannot be fired by elected officials, to guard them from political patronage.

A complex set of pay systems distinguishes between white-collar, blue-collar, and executive employees, among others.

Cannot engage in political activities when performing their duties.

SELF-EMPLOYED

Working for several employers and not on a payroll.

Offers highly skilled services; i.e., doctors, or construction contractors.

About 1/3 of the self-employed have turned their passions or expertise into a company. If they choose to incorporate, their business becomes a separate legal entity with tax and liability advantages.

Risks include a lack of job security.

ALTERNATIVE WORK FORMS

Holds several temporary or on-call jobs.

Estimates range from 6 to 35% of the workforce.

The rise of digital companies in need of an ad hoc work force, also called the gig economy, has increased this category.

Some experts see this flexibility as a factor of the US economy's strength. Others see this as a loss of stable, full-time employment with benefits.

THE BOSS

What must a good boss be able to do? To put it abstractly: The boss has to guide other people toward producing added economic value in the value-creation process. To accomplish this, a boss has to combine both expert knowledge and leadership. He or she has to make decisions with foresight, set goals, set the right tone, and put up with conflicts of all kinds. To combine all of that in one person is difficult. Presumably, that's why there are so many unloved bosses. On the other hand, one could argue that what's expected from leaders is often ratcheted up to unattainable levels.

HOW GOOD LEADERSHIP WORKS

The Balcony and the Dance Floor
Bosses have to simultaneously dance while also observing themselves and their teams from the balcony. That's how Ronald Heifetz, professor of leadership at Harvard University, sees it.

The Myth of Motivation
A boss cannot motivate employees, especially not with financial bonuses. A boss can only create the context in which employees can continue to develop personally so that they are self-motivated to achieve at a high level. So says the management consultant Reinhard K. Sprenger.

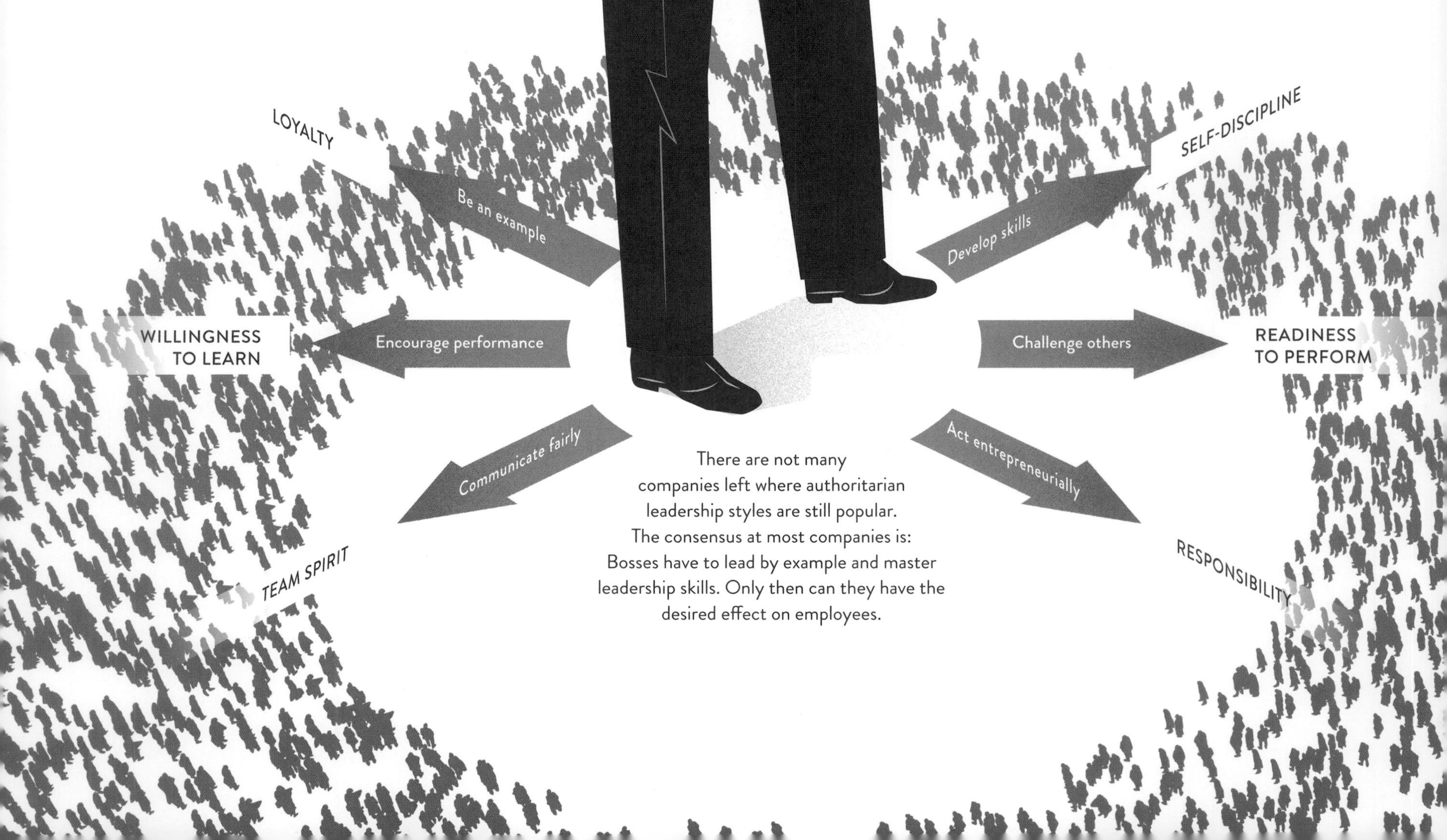

LOYALTY

SELF-DISCIPLINE

Be an example

Develop skills

WILLINGNESS TO LEARN

Encourage performance

Challenge others

READINESS TO PERFORM

Communicate fairly

Act entrepreneurially

TEAM SPIRIT

RESPONSIBILITY

There are not many companies left where authoritarian leadership styles are still popular. The consensus at most companies is: Bosses have to lead by example and master leadership skills. Only then can they have the desired effect on employees.

LEADERSHIP STYLES

Management changed tremendously during the twentieth century. At the beginning of the century, the sociologist Max Weber recognized four types of authoritarian leadership styles. Beginning in the 1950s, bosses in the USA increasingly led their companies by using target agreements. Management theorists referred to this style as "transactional." Modern team leadership today is usually founded on the concept of transformational leadership, a model developed in the late 1970s by James MacGregor Burns.

Charismatic leadership: "Charisma" means "gift of grace." Charismatic bosses lead with a radiance that sets them above others. Bosses can demand any sacrifice of those they lead without the bosses incurring any obligation toward them.

Bureaucratic leadership style: Management is administration. Precise descriptions of the authority and work procedures for each employee's position regulate the creation of value. There is no person who controls everything. The boss is the system.

Patriarchal leadership: The boss has a father's authority and kindness. Subordinates have access at any time to the patriarch and are obligated to obey him.

Autocratic leadership style: The autocrat possesses a great amount of power and makes use of a strictly organized leadership apparatus. Subordinates are obligated to unconditionally obey. Autocracy lacks both patriarchy's warmth and the enthusiasm of charismatic leadership.

Transactional leadership is based on the principle of exchange. A leader and an employee establish a goal. If the employee accomplishes it, they are rewarded financially or otherwise. The fundamental idea derives from the economist Peter F. Drucker's concept of "management by objectives" from 1954.

Transformational leadership capitalizes on the values of trust, respect, loyalty, and appreciation. When managers succeed in making these values the foundation of their relationships with employees, individuals and teams achieve above-average results. A common mission is often the focus of this leadership style. The mission is supposed to lift the behavior and consciousness of the employees to a higher level—to "transform" them.

IS THERE A DEGREE IN BOSSOLOGY?

What college major do I need to make my way to the top of a company? A Harvard MBA raises the statistical probability. But academic sidetracks or even dead ends can also lead to the stratosphere.

Degrees of the 30 CEOs of Dow Jones Companies*
2018

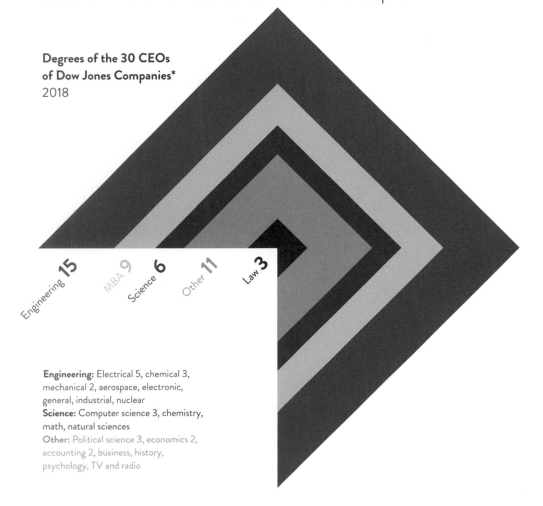

Engineering **15** MBA **9** Science **6** Other **11** Law **3**

Engineering: Electrical 5, chemical 3, mechanical 2, aerospace, electronic, general, industrial, nuclear
Science: Computer science 3, chemistry, math, natural sciences
Other: Political science 3, economics 2, accounting 2, business, history, psychology, TV and radio

Big minds, small colleges

GER

Herbert Hainer (born 1954)
CEO of
adidas AG (2001–2016)

Economics
University of Applied
Sciences, Landshut

USA

Randall L. Stephenson (born 1960)
Chairman and CEO
of AT&T (since 2007)

Accounting
University of Central Oklahoma
and University of Oklahoma

GER

Joe Kaeser (born 1957)
CEO of
Siemens AG (since 2013)

Business administration
Regensburg University of Applied Sciences

NL

Paul Polman (born 1956)
CEO of consumer goods giant
Unilever (since 2009)

Economics and business administration
University of Groningen and
University of Cincinnati

International elite universities
Fortune 500 alma mater index (top 20), number of CEO graduates, 2013

USA	Harvard University	25
JPN	University of Tokyo	13
FRA	École Polytechnique	12
USA	Stanford University	11
FRA	HEC Paris	9
FRA	ENA, École Nationale d'Administration	9
USA	University of Pennsylvania	8
JPN	Keio University	8
KOR	Seoul National University	8
USA	Massachusetts Institute of Technology	7
FRA	INSEAD (European Institute of Business Administration)	7
CHN	Tsinghua University	7
USA	Cornell University	6
USA	University of Chicago	6
USA	Northwestern University	6
USA	Columbia University	6
FRA	MINES ParisTech	6
JPN	Kyoto University	6
USA	Yale University	6
JPN	Waseda University	6

Elite universities, but no diploma

USA

Mark Zuckerberg (born 1984)
CEO of Facebook Inc.
(since 2004)

Psychology and computer science
Harvard University

IND

Azim Premji (born 1945)
Chairman of the giant software
firm Wipro (since 1966)

Engineering
Stanford University

* The total number of degrees is more than 30 because many of these CEOs hold more than one each.

WHAT BOSSES TAKE HOME

Hock Tan, the CEO of Broadcom, earned $103.2 million in 2017, making him the highest paid manager worldwide. How much does your boss make? Or if you *are* a boss, do you get more or less than what's usual in your sector?

Gender pay gap at the top
in US$ thousands, 2016

Pay of women vs. men in %

	♀	♂	
69.9%	81.7	116.8	Chief Executives
86.8%	79.5	91.6	IT Systems Managers
71.2%	67.6	95.0	Human Resources Managers
67.5%	58.6	86.8	Financial Managers

Pay of senior managers in the US
by occupation in US$, 2018

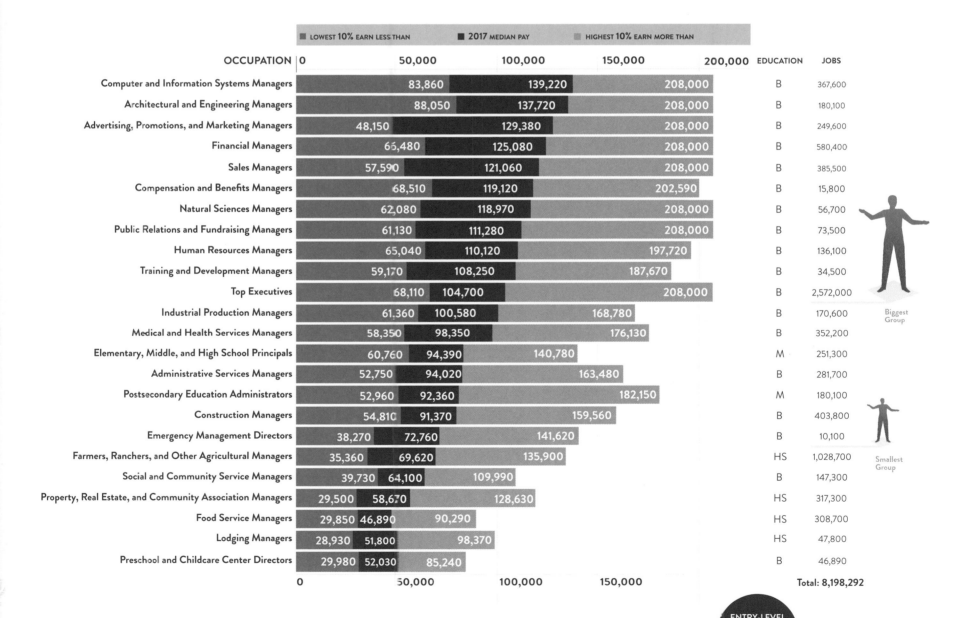

■ LOWEST 10% EARN LESS THAN   ■ 2017 MEDIAN PAY   ■ HIGHEST 10% EARN MORE THAN

OCCUPATION	LOWEST 10%	MEDIAN	HIGHEST 10%	EDUCATION	JOBS
Computer and Information Systems Managers	83,860	139,220	208,000	B	367,600
Architectural and Engineering Managers	88,050	137,720	208,000	B	180,100
Advertising, Promotions, and Marketing Managers	48,150	129,380	208,000	B	249,600
Financial Managers	66,480	125,080	208,000	B	580,400
Sales Managers	57,590	121,060	208,000	B	385,500
Compensation and Benefits Managers	68,510	119,120	202,590	B	15,800
Natural Sciences Managers	62,080	118,970	208,000	B	56,700
Public Relations and Fundraising Managers	61,130	111,280	208,000	B	73,500
Human Resources Managers	65,040	110,120	197,720	B	136,100
Training and Development Managers	59,170	108,250	187,670	B	34,500
Top Executives	68,110	104,700	208,000	B	2,572,000
Industrial Production Managers	61,360	100,580	168,780	B	170,600
Medical and Health Services Managers	58,350	98,350	176,130	B	352,200
Elementary, Middle, and High School Principals	60,760	94,390	140,780	M	251,300
Administrative Services Managers	52,750	94,020	163,480	B	281,700
Postsecondary Education Administrators	52,960	92,360	182,150	M	180,100
Construction Managers	54,810	91,370	159,560	B	403,800
Emergency Management Directors	38,270	72,760	141,620	B	10,100
Farmers, Ranchers, and Other Agricultural Managers	35,360	69,620	135,900	HS	1,028,700
Social and Community Service Managers	39,730	64,100	109,990	B	147,300
Property, Real Estate, and Community Association Managers	29,500	58,670	128,630	HS	317,300
Food Service Managers	29,850	46,890	90,290	HS	308,700
Lodging Managers	28,930	51,800	98,370	HS	47,800
Preschool and Childcare Center Directors	29,980	52,030	85,240	B	46,890

Biggest Group

Smallest Group

Total: 8,198,292

ENTRY-LEVEL DEGREE
HS - HIGH SCHOOL
B - BACHELOR'S
M - MASTER'S

BS AT THE OFFICE

People talk a lot at the office. What's said and what's really meant often have little to do with each other, and that goes for the boss just as much as it does for employees. There's a name for the fake outward surface that hides the real meaning of office talk: BS. Most bosses and employees are fluent speakers.

I have no clue what I'm supposed to praise him for.

Of course you know how valuable an employee you are . . .

I'd also like to ask the rest of the team for feedback.

Save your breath. If worse comes to worst, I'm going to the union rep.

WANTING AND HAVING

Consumption refers to the purchase of goods for private use by private persons. At least that's how economists see it. For them, consumer sentiment is an important factor for predicting economic growth. For shoppers, consumption means happiness, frustration, status, compensation, restriction to the essentials, passing the time, a shared experience, or many hours alone on the couch while shopping online. This is what we spend our money on (all numbers in US$):

Average Monthly Spending per Household

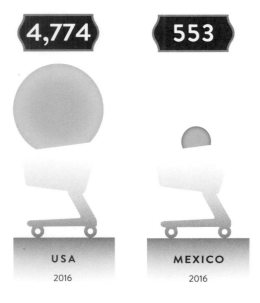

4,774   553

USA
2016

MEXICO
2016

Evolution of Yearly Spending per Person
1970–2015, in US$

— China — Germany — United Kingdom — Japan — USA

Apparel and Services

Tobacco and Alcohol

Health Care

Personal Insurance and Pensions

569

68

Housing

150

Transportation

152

119

926

157

Utilities, Fuel, and Public Services

Telephone Services

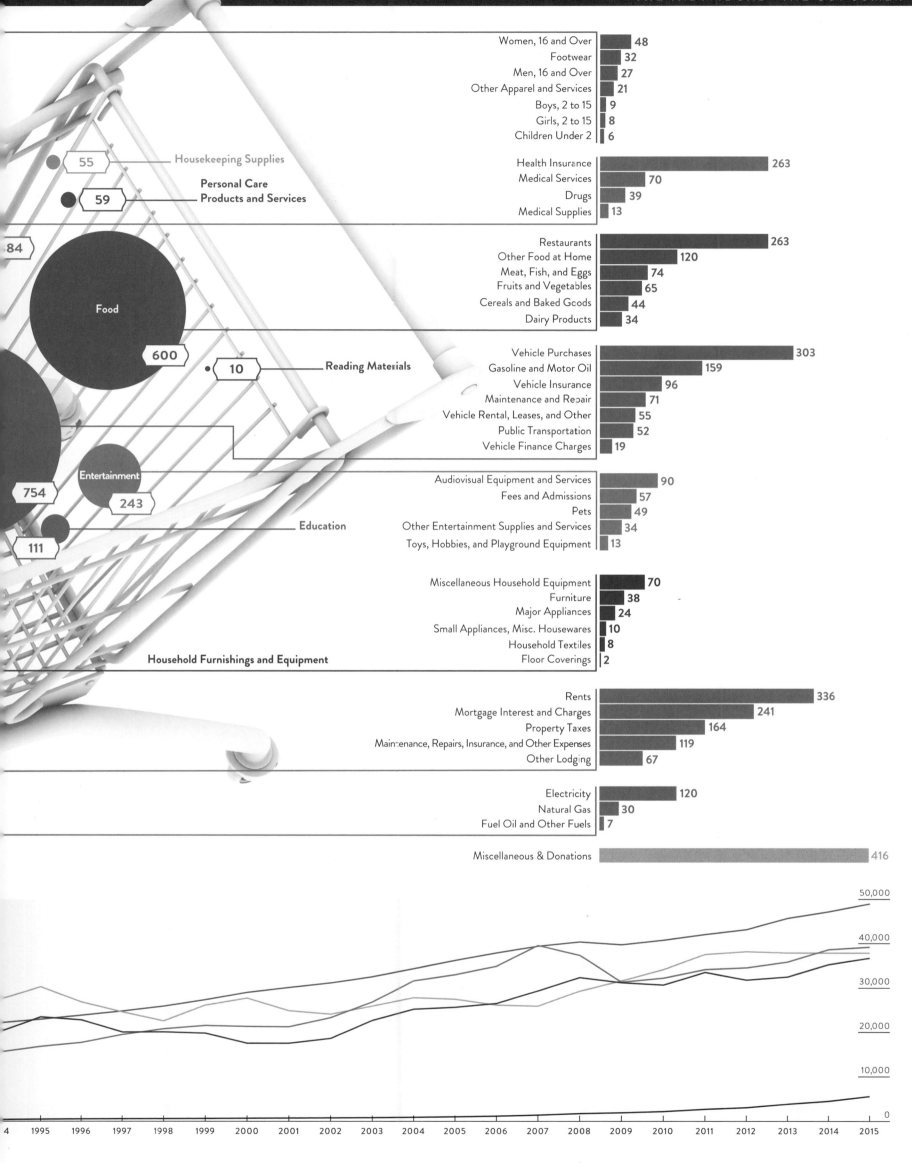

Women, 16 and Over — 48
Footwear — 32
Men, 16 and Over — 27
Other Apparel and Services — 21
Boys, 2 to 15 — 9
Girls, 2 to 15 — 8
Children Under 2 — 6

Housekeeping Supplies — 55
Personal Care Products and Services — 59

Health Insurance — 263
Medical Services — 70
Drugs — 39
Medical Supplies — 13

84
Food — 600

Restaurants — 263
Other Food at Home — 120
Meat, Fish, and Eggs — 74
Fruits and Vegetables — 65
Cereals and Baked Goods — 44
Dairy Products — 34

Reading Materials — 10

Vehicle Purchases — 303
Gasoline and Motor Oil — 159
Vehicle Insurance — 96
Maintenance and Repair — 71
Vehicle Rental, Leases, and Other — 55
Public Transportation — 52
Vehicle Finance Charges — 19

Entertainment — 754
243
Education — 111

Audiovisual Equipment and Services — 90
Fees and Admissions — 57
Pets — 49
Other Entertainment Supplies and Services — 34
Toys, Hobbies, and Playground Equipment — 13

Miscellaneous Household Equipment — 70
Furniture — 38
Major Appliances — 24
Small Appliances, Misc. Housewares — 10
Household Textiles — 8
Floor Coverings — 2

Household Furnishings and Equipment

Rents — 336
Mortgage Interest and Charges — 241
Property Taxes — 164
Maintenance, Repairs, Insurance, and Other Expenses — 119
Other Lodging — 67

Electricity — 120
Natural Gas — 30
Fuel Oil and Other Fuels — 7

Miscellaneous & Donations — 416

50,000
40,000
30,000
20,000
10,000
0

4 1995 1996 1997 1998 1999 2000 2001 2002 2003 2004 2005 2006 2007 2008 2009 2010 2011 2012 2013 2014 2015

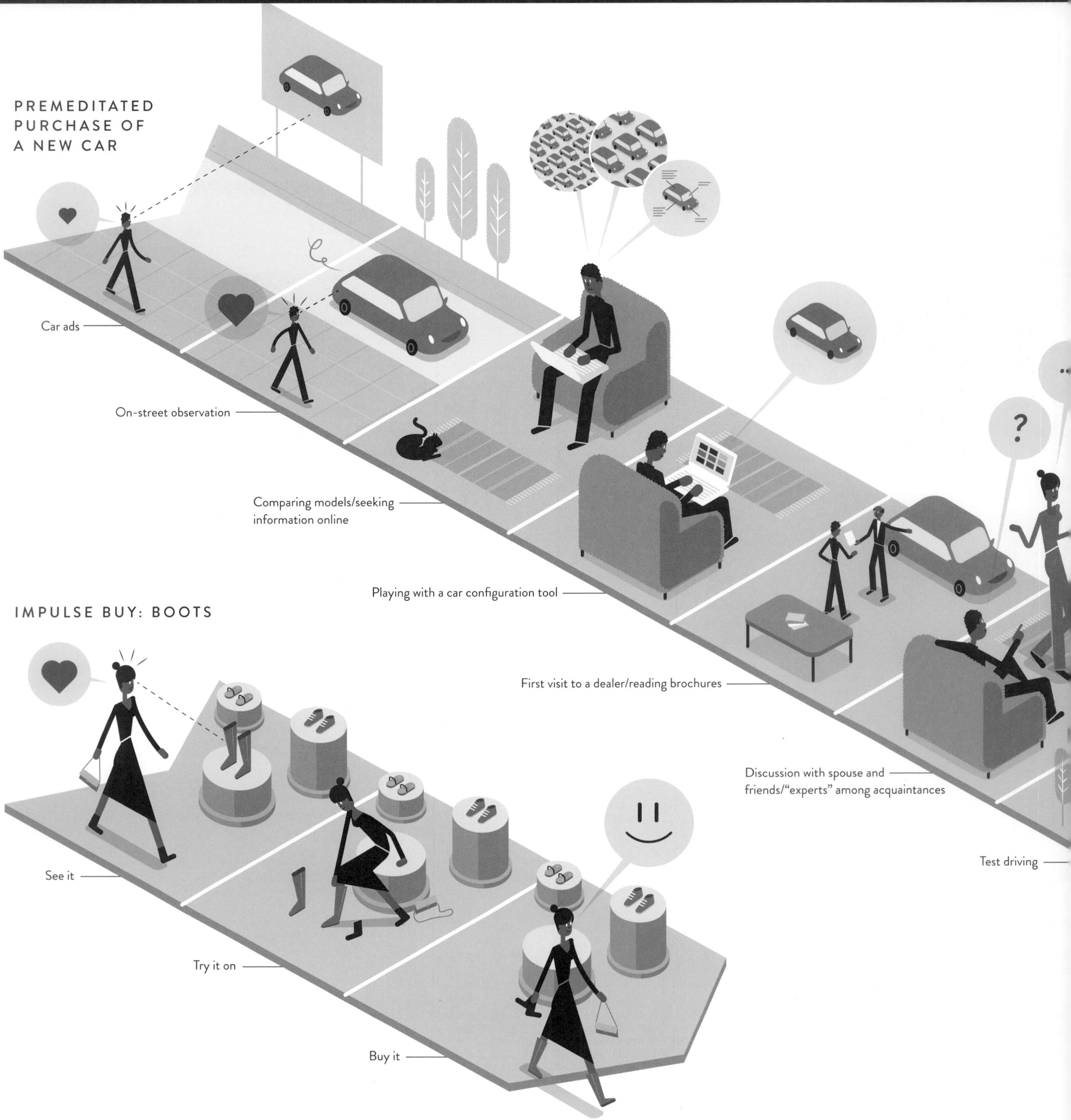

PREMEDITATED
PURCHASE OF
A NEW CAR

Car ads

On-street observation

Comparing models/seeking
information online

Playing with a car configuration tool

First visit to a dealer/reading brochures

Discussion with spouse and
friends/"experts" among acquaintances

Test driving

IMPULSE BUY: BOOTS

See it

Try it on

Buy it

THE PATH TO A PURCHASE

As customers, we go through various phases before deciding to buy something. Marketing experts talk
about the "customer journey." Customers' pathways to purchase vary from the first contact ("touchpoint")
with a product, a brand, or a service. A rule of thumb applies: The more expensive and complex a product is,
the more stages in the journey. At every point of contact, marketers try to make the transition to the next
phase of decision-making easier.

FOLLOW YOUR HEAD OR GO WITH YOUR GUT?

The customer's brain is the point of sale. Various elements of the limbic system take part in the purchase decision. Rational, emotional, and physical reactions to purchase stimuli lay the groundwork for the decision. Current consumer research points to this conclusion: We make the best purchase decisions when we consider many rational factors, sleep on it for a few nights, and then decide intuitively.

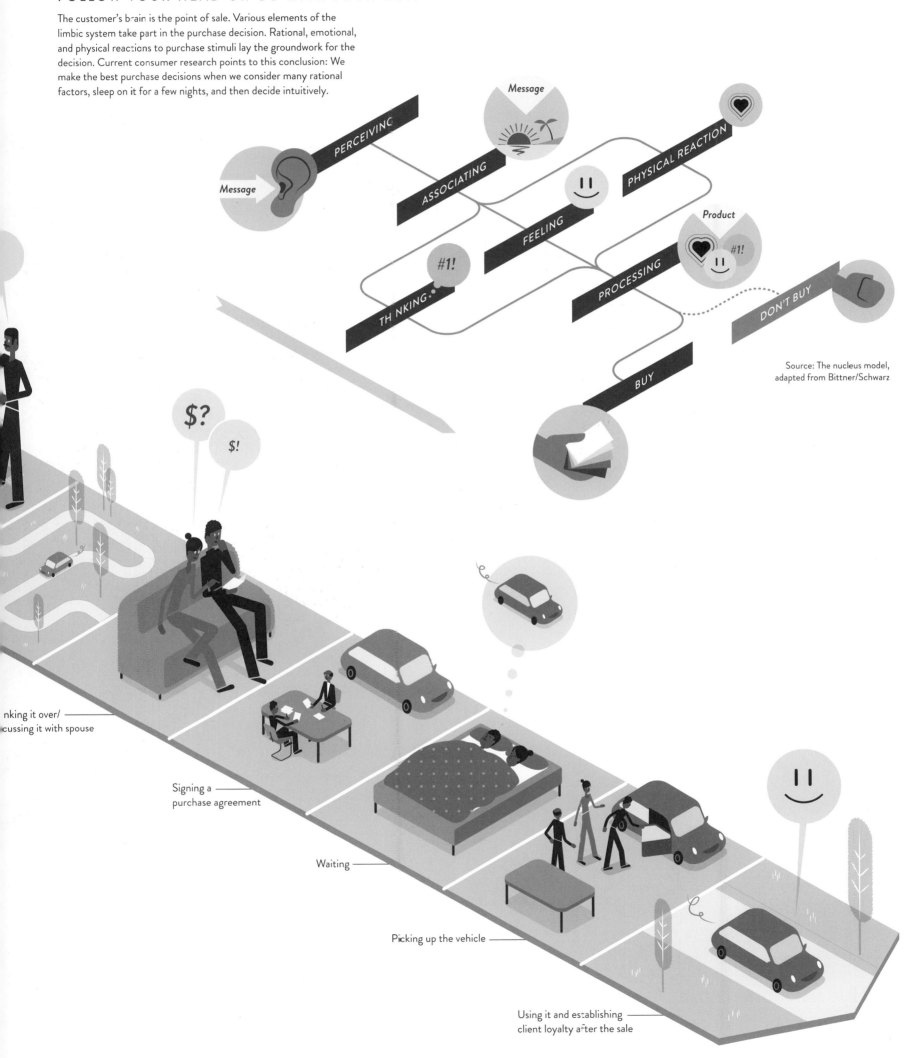

Source: The nucleus model, adapted from Bittner/Schwarz

Thinking it over/ discussing it with spouse

Signing a purchase agreement

Waiting

Picking up the vehicle

Using it and establishing client loyalty after the sale

EVERYTHING SUPER AT THE MARKET?

Why is the entrance to grocery stores always on the right? Because consumer research has discovered that most customers are more comfortable when their shopping tour takes a counterclockwise course. Feeling more comfortable means buying more. And selling more is the goal of every supermarket design.

1 SIZE DOES MATTER

No, you didn't shrink. Shopping carts are getting larger. If you double the size of a standard shopping cart, customers will buy 40% more on average.

2 NO TURNING BACK

The automatic entrance doors are not to prevent shoplifters from escaping. They're to force honest customers to make their way without fail all the way to the checkout line.

3 A SENSUAL START

Fruits and vegetables in the entry area attract more customers into the store. They stimulate the senses, and during the rest of the shopping trip we'll have a greater tendency to purchase recklessly.

4 THE BREAKFAST ALLIANCE

Coffee is shelved near the jam and English muffins because sales are higher together than when it's every breakfast product for itself.

5 SHELVES AS SALES FUNNELS

On the shelves at the ends of aisles (known as "endcaps"), you'll find high-margin articles because customers look at these shelves especially frequently.

6 AT EYE LEVEL

Shelf space at eye level is expensive. Not only for customers, but also for the manufacturers behind the brand names. They often have to pay high "placement fees" to stores if they want their products to be located there.

7 FRESH BREAD MAKES YOU HUNGRY

Even bargain stores have learned by now that the scent of fresh bread makes people hungry, and hungry customers load their carts to the top.

8 ACTION ALLEY

Short-term bargains in a central aisle always give the impression: You'll find some great deals here. Sometimes it's even true.

9 THE LONG WALK FOR MILK

You'll typically find bread and butter in the back of the store. On the long trip there, you'll have many opportunities to make impulse buys.

10 THE CHEESE IS ON THE HOUSE

Free samples can be very expensive. Because whether or not we think the bite of cheese tastes good, it gives us a guilty conscience. And we assuage our guilt by buying something.

11 FLAGSHIP BRANDS

Coca-Cola, Heinz Ketchup, and Wonder Bread are located in the middle of their aisles. We use them as orientation markers spatially and in terms of price.

12 THE STORE INSIDE THE STORE

Cosmetic and wine sections often seem like their own worlds. And in another world, we accept unearthly prices.

13 SPECIAL OFFERS

Competitive prices lure frugal customers into the store. For most customers, however, their only function is to signal: This is a low-price store; pay no attention to the prices!

14 THE CHECKOUT LINE

In front of the register, it's not only children we calm by buying them something. We also like to reward ourselves for the great accomplishment of having finished our shopping.

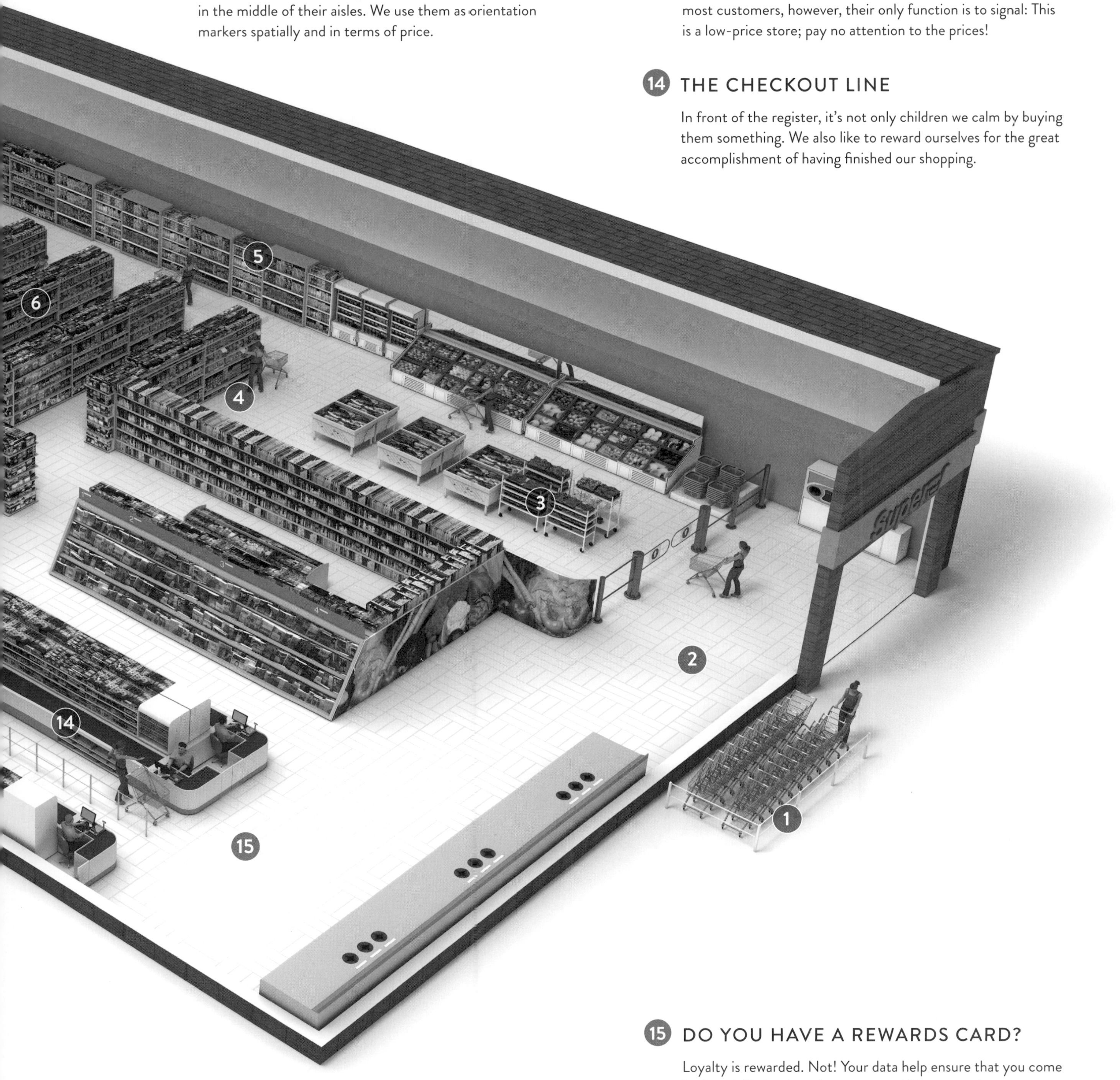

15 DO YOU HAVE A REWARDS CARD?

Loyalty is rewarded. Not! Your data help ensure that you come back and fill the shopping cart even higher next time.

THE POOR

Who is poor? There are more rigorous definitions for poverty than for individual wealth. Economists make a fundamental distinction between absolute and relative poverty. In wealthy countries, absolute poverty primarily includes homeless people and those who slip through the social safety net. Relative poverty is based on average income. The good news is that according to United Nations figures, absolute poverty has been continuously decreasing for years.

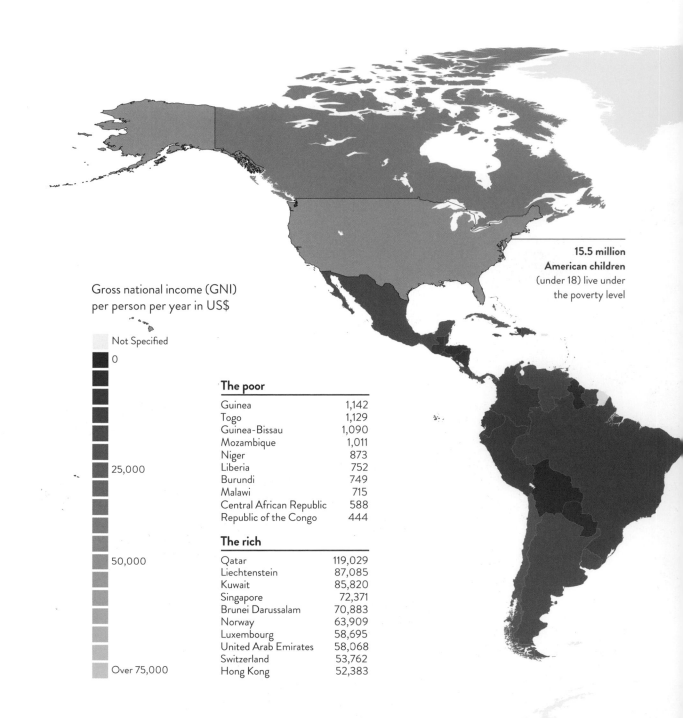

15.5 million American children (under 18) live under the poverty level

Gross national income (GNI) per person per year in US$

Not Specified
0

25,000

50,000

Over 75,000

The poor

Guinea	1,142
Togo	1,129
Guinea-Bissau	1,090
Mozambique	1,011
Niger	873
Liberia	752
Burundi	749
Malawi	715
Central African Republic	588
Republic of the Congo	444

The rich

Qatar	119,029
Liechtenstein	87,085
Kuwait	85,820
Singapore	72,371
Brunei Darussalam	70,883
Norway	63,909
Luxembourg	58,695
United Arab Emirates	58,068
Switzerland	53,762
Hong Kong	52,383

How are absolute and relative poverty defined?

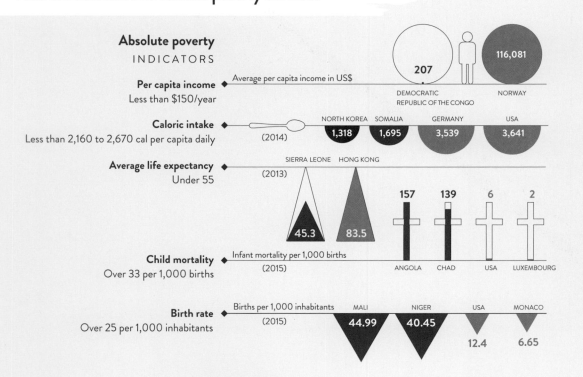

Absolute poverty
INDICATORS

Per capita income
Less than $150/year

Average per capita income in US$

207 DEMOCRATIC REPUBLIC OF THE CONGO

116,081 NORWAY

Caloric intake
Less than 2,160 to 2,670 cal per capita daily

(2014)   NORTH KOREA 1,318   SOMALIA 1,695   GERMANY 3,539   USA 3,641

Average life expectancy
Under 55

(2013)   SIERRA LEONE 45.3   HONG KONG 83.5

Child mortality
Over 33 per 1,000 births

Infant mortality per 1,000 births
(2015)   ANGOLA 157   CHAD 139   USA 6   LUXEMBOURG 2

Birth rate
Over 25 per 1,000 inhabitants

Births per 1,000 inhabitants
(2015)   MALI 44.99   NIGER 40.45   USA 12.4   MONACO 6.65

Relative poverty
DEFINITION

Poverty in quantitative comparison to the social environment (prosperity and standard of living) of a person

A single person lives in relative poverty if he or she has to live on less than 60% of the median of the weighted net equivalent income.

	USA	Germany
Threshold	$12,064	$13,612
Affected Population	14.8%	16.7%

Migrant workers in Qatar
Portion of the entire population

Residents
12%

Approx. **88%**
migrant workers

Homelessness in Germany
(estimate)

284,000 Without permanent residence

24,000 Entirely without shelter

including around **2,500** Women

How economically unjust is the world?

	Wealth per person in US$		Distribution of average household income by country (as a Gini coefficient)*	
	Median	Average		
MEXICO	8,737	22,346		0.459
CHILE	20,141	52,829		0.454
TURKEY	5,087	20,061		0.398
UNITED STATES	55,876	388,585		0.39
LITHUANIA	17,931	27,507		0.381
RUSSIA	3,919	16,733		0.376
UNITED KINGDOM	102,641	278,038		0.36
ISRAEL	78,244	198,406		0.36
LATVIA	17,828	27,631		0.35
NEW ZEALAND	147,593	337,441		0.349
ESTONIA	43,185	27,522		0.346
SPAIN	63,369	129,578		0.344
GREECE	54,665	111,684		0.339
PORTUGAL	38,242	89,437		0.338
AUSTRALIA	195,417	402,603		0.337
JAPAN	123,724	225,057		0.33
ITALY	124,636	223,572		0.326
CANADA	91,058	259,271		0.313
NETHERLANDS	94,373	204,045		0.303
IRELAND	84,592	248,466		0.298
POLAND	10,502	28,057		0.298
SWITZERLAND	229,059	537,599		0.297
FRANCE	119,720	253,399		0.297
KOREA	67,934	160,609		0.295
GERMANY	47,901	203,946		0.289
HUNGARY	30,111	39,813		0.288
LUXEMBOURG	167,664	313,687		0.284
AUSTRIA	57,534	221,456		0.274

*The Gini coefficient measures equality in distribution of wealth and ranges from 0 to 1. One is maximum inequality, and zero is perfect equality of wealth.

Is there a way out of debt?
How does personal bankruptcy work?

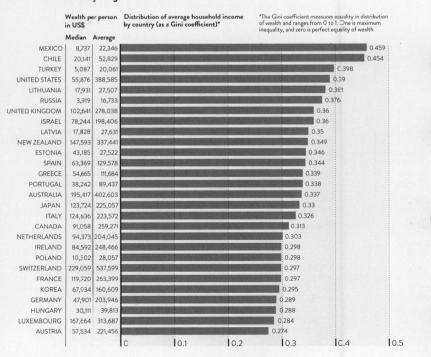

Debt overload
Monthly income insufficient to cover living expenses, and reduction of the standard of living does not help matters.

Filing a petition in court for relief
Typically filed under Chapter 7 (liquidation) or Chapter 13 (reorganization) of the Bankruptcy Code.

Seizure of property or repayment plans
In a liquidation bankruptcy, any seizable nonexempt property is collected and sold to pay creditors. In a reorganization bankruptcy, secured debt can be restructured, property kept, and monthly payments made toward debt within three to five years. The amount of each payment depends on the debtor's monthly income.

Debt free
After property is liquidated or regular payment obligations are successfully met, the debtor is considered to be debt-free.

THE RICH

Who is rich? There is no universally valid answer to this question. The trade union–affiliated Hans Böckler Foundation considers rich anyone who earns more than $42,000 annually. For many American private bankers, wealth begins at $1 million in investible assets; at that level, people are categorized as high-net-worth individuals (HNWIs) in customer databases. Very-high-net-worth individuals have over $5 million in investible capital, and ultra-high-net-worth individuals have over $30 million. And yet, as American comedian W. C. Fields said: "A rich man is nothing but a poor man with money."

Billionaires per million inhabitants

- Over 80
- 50–80
- 25–50
- 20–25
- 15–20
- 10–15
- 5–10
- 3–5
- 2–3
- 1.5–2
- 1–1.5
- 0.5–1
- 0.1–0.5
- 0.01–0.1
- 0

Countries with the highest density of billionaires per million inhabitants

Number of billionaires

	Number	Country		Number	Country
1	3	MONACO	6	29	SWITZERLAND
2	1	ST. KITTS & NEVIS	7	19	SINGAPORE
3	1	GUERNSEY	8	1	ICELAND
4	55	HONG KONG	9	23	SWEDEN
5	5	CYPRUS	10	17	ISRAEL

The Super Rich

US$ in Billions, 2017

Type of wealth: ■ inherited ■ inherited and multiplied ■ self-made

The Richest Men in the World

Jeff Bezos USA		112	Amazon
Bill Gates USA		90	Microsoft
Warren Buffett USA		84	Berkshire Hathaway
Bernard Arnault FRA		72	LVMH
Mark Zuckerberg USA		71	Facebook
Amancio Ortega ESP		70	Inditex
Carlos Slim MEX		67.1	Telecom
Charles Koch USA		60	Koch Inds.
David Koch USA		60	Koch Inds.
Larry Ellison USA		58.5	Oracle

The Richest Women in the World

Alice Walton USA		46	Walmart Inc.
Françoise Bettencourt Meyers FRA		42.2	L'Oréal
Susanne Klatten GER		25	BMW, pharmaceuticals
Jacqueline Mars USA		23.6	Candy, pet food
Yang Huiyan CHN		21.9	Real estate
Laurene Powell Jobs USA		18.8	Apple, Disney
Gina Rinehart AUS		17.4	Mining
Iris Fontbona CHI		16.3	Mining
Abigail Johnson USA		15.9	Money management
Charlene de Carvalho-Heineken NL		15.8	Heineken

The Richest People in the USA

Jeff Bezos		112	Amazon
Bill Gates		90	Microsoft
Warren Buffett		84	Berkshire Hathaway
Mark Zuckerberg		71	Facebook
Charles Koch		60	Koch Inds.
David Koch		60	Koch Inds.
Larry Ellison		58.5	Oracle
Michael Bloomberg		50	Bloomberg
Larry Page		48.8	Google
Sergey Brin		47.5	Google

Top 10 countries with the most billionaires

1	**>600** USA	**6**	**55** HONG KONG	
2	**213** CHINA	**7**	**54** BRAZIL	
3	**103** GERMANY	**8**	**53** UNITED KINGDOM	
4	**90** INDIA	**9**	**47** FRANCE	
5	**88** RUSSIA	**10**	**39** CANADA	**39** ITALY

How do you become rich?

INHERITING

Rockefeller's heirs

John D. Rockefeller was worth more than $300 billion in today's dollars, by some estimates, making him the richest American to have ever lived. But while his Standard Oil fortune made his last name synonymous with wealth, none of today's Rockefellers are anywhere near the top of the list of the world's richest people. It's true that no money-making family business ever replaced Standard Oil, but the primary reason the family fortune doesn't still tower over all others is that there are simply too many Rockefellers. It's estimated that there are more than 150 living blood relatives of John D., and with every marriage, child, and remarriage, the money is further divided. Robert Frank, writing for *The Wall Street Journal,* reports that "many members of the latest generation of the family . . . aren't likely to be able to live off their dwindling family trusts."

INHERITING AND INCREASING

Susanne Klatten (born 1962)

Susanne Klatten is an heir to the family-owned German carmaker BMW, holding 19.2% of its shares, with her brother holding 23.7%. That makes her the richest woman in Germany and the third richest in the world. Among the top 10 richest women, she's the first to have increased her wealth by her own work. The holder of an MBA, she did not become part of BMW management. Rather, she turned Altana AG, a company inherited by her grandfather, into one of the top pharmaceutical and chemical companies worldwide, generating sales of $2.5 Bn annually.

SELF-MADE

Jeff Bezos (born 1964)

There are many people in the USA who have built colossal fortunes in their own right. We singled out Amazon's CEO, Jeff Bezos, because he is the richest man on Earth, having surpassed longtime frontrunner Bill Gates in 2017. Bezos has not only the largest, but also the fastest-growing fortune: From 2017 to 2018 his wealth increased by a record $39 Bn, reaching $112 Bn. His wealth mirrors the exponential growth of Amazon's stock, of which he holds 16%. His company was founded less than 30 years ago in a garage. It is now on track to reach $1 trillion in market capitalization by the end of 2018, making it the most valuable firm in history.

Multimillionaires* worldwide	48	18	34	27,465 women
Share in percent				
* Wealth above $35 Mn	13	19	68	183,810 men

FLOWWWWWWWW!

When do we experience flow as we work? When we don't fear excessive demands and are not bored by having nothing to challenge us. When we forget the time as we lose ourselves in our task. When our limbic system, which controls our emotions, is in harmony with the neocortex, which controls rational thought. When all of this comes together, work is fun and the results are first-rate.

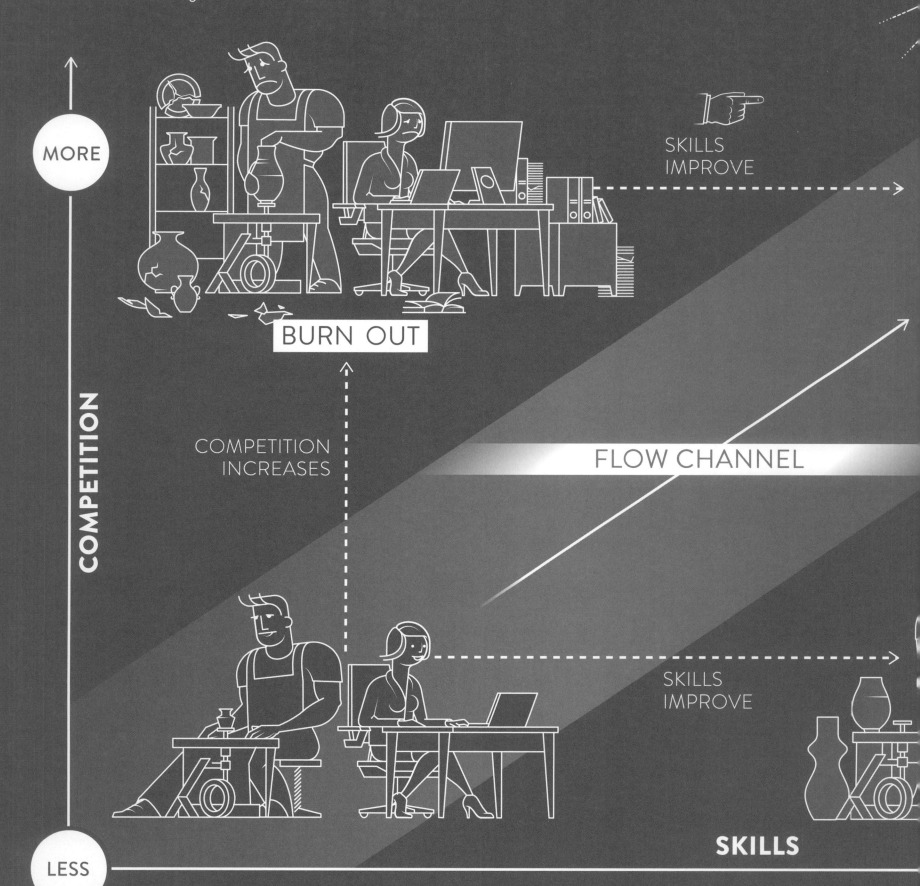

MORE

SKILLS IMPROVE

BURN OUT

COMPETITION

COMPETITION INCREASES

FLOW CHANNEL

SKILLS IMPROVE

SKILLS

LESS

COMPETITION
INCREASES

BORE OUT

MORE

Source: The concept of flow according to Mihály Csíkszentmihályi

The 10 most dangerous industries in the US
Injuries and illnesses at work per 100 employees, 2016

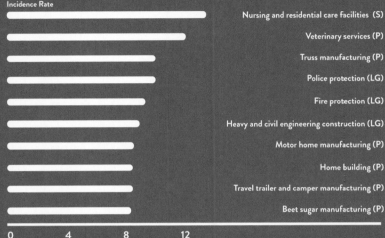

Incidence Rate

Nursing and residential care facilities (S)
Veterinary services (P)
Truss manufacturing (P)
Police protection (LG)
Fire protection (LG)
Heavy and civil engineering construction (LG)
Motor home manufacturing (P)
Home building (P)
Travel trailer and camper manufacturing (P)
Beet sugar manufacturing (P)

0   4   8   12

Legend:

P = Private Industry | S = State Industry | LG = Local Government

Number of sick leave days taken in the US by age group, 2016

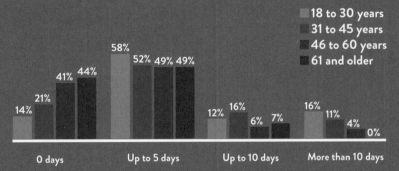

18 to 30 years
31 to 45 years
46 to 60 years
61 and older

58% 52% 49% 49%

14% 21% 41% 44%   12% 16% 6% 7%   16% 11% 4% 0%

0 days   Up to 5 days   Up to 10 days   More than 10 days

Main sources of stress at work
Survey among US employees, 2017

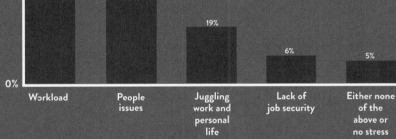

40%

39%
31%
19%
6%
5%

0%

Workload   People issues   Juggling work and personal life   Lack of job security   Either none of the above or no stress

Revenue of corporate wellness service industry
In the USA, in US$ Mn, 2007–2017

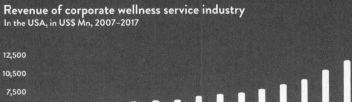

12,500
10,500
7,500
5,000
2,500
0

2007 2008 2009 2010 2011 2012 2013 2014 2015 2016 2017 2018 2019 2020 2021

BATTLE TO THE TOP, THEN YOGA

What needs do we have as human beings? In 1943, the American psychologist Abraham Maslow organized human needs as a pyramid. The core concept: Our needs give us an impetus for economic success. As soon as individuals or societies have reached one level, they start eyeing the next one up.

SELF-ACTUALIZATION

INDIVIDUAL NEEDS

SOCIAL NEEDS

SAFETY NEEDS

BASIC NEEDS

II

THE
COMPANY

MANUFACTURING
·
INVESTMENTS
·
PROFITS
·
BUSINESS MODELS
·
THE PRODUCT
·
THE ORGANIZATION
·
THE TEAM
·
FINANCES
·
THE CUSTOMERS

THE COMPANY

The history of Volkswagen—today a quintessentially multinational corporation with a global reach—parallels the history of Germany. The company was founded because Hitler wanted an affordable car for the people, and it was placed under British military administration after World War II. The VW Bug became the engine of German postwar economic expansion and the symbol of the "economic miracle" of the 1950s. Volkswagen pioneered the German model of economic success through social partnership between a company and its employees. The company took advantage of opportunities for globalization early on and became the largest automobile manufacturer in the world. But a few virtues—in the areas of technical engineering and business ethics—were apparently forgotten along the way. The exhaust emissions scandal that has rocked Volkswagen since 2015 has been very costly for the company, and the management had to hit the road.

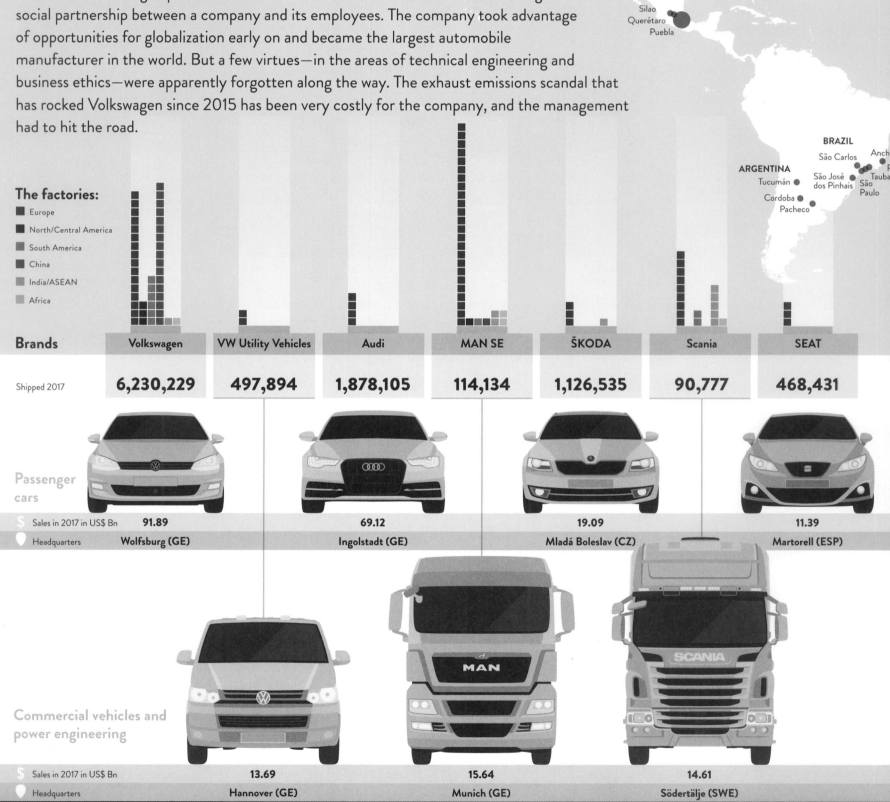

UNITED STATES
Chattanooga, TN

MEXICO
Silao
Querétaro
Puebla

BRAZIL
São Carlos
Anchieta
Rese
Taubaté
São
Paulo

ARGENTINA
Tucumán
São José
dos Pinhais
Cordoba
Pacheco

The factories:
- Europe
- North/Central America
- South America
- China
- India/ASEAN
- Africa

Brands	Volkswagen	VW Utility Vehicles	Audi	MAN SE	ŠKODA	Scania	SEAT
Shipped 2017	6,230,229	497,894	1,878,105	114,134	1,126,535	90,777	468,431

Passenger cars

	Volkswagen		Audi		ŠKODA		SEAT
$ Sales in 2017 in US$ Bn	91.89		69.12		19.09		11.39
Headquarters	Wolfsburg (GE)		Ingolstadt (GE)		Mladá Boleslav (CZ)		Martorell (ESP)

Commercial vehicles and power engineering

	VW Utility Vehicles	MAN SE	Scania
$ Sales in 2017 in US$ Bn	13.69	15.64	14.61
Headquarters	Hannover (GE)	Munich (GE)	Södertälje (SWE)

The scandal:

| **20 times** HIGHER NITRIC OXIDE | as the allowed limits (VW Passat in tests under realistic conditions) | **11 million** DIESEL VEHICLES | affected worldwide (in the US, around 500,000) | **$12** PER VEHICLE | for replacement of the affected component (current transformer) | **$30 Bn** MARKET LOSSES | between September 18 and 29, 2015 (Drop in share price: over 22%) |

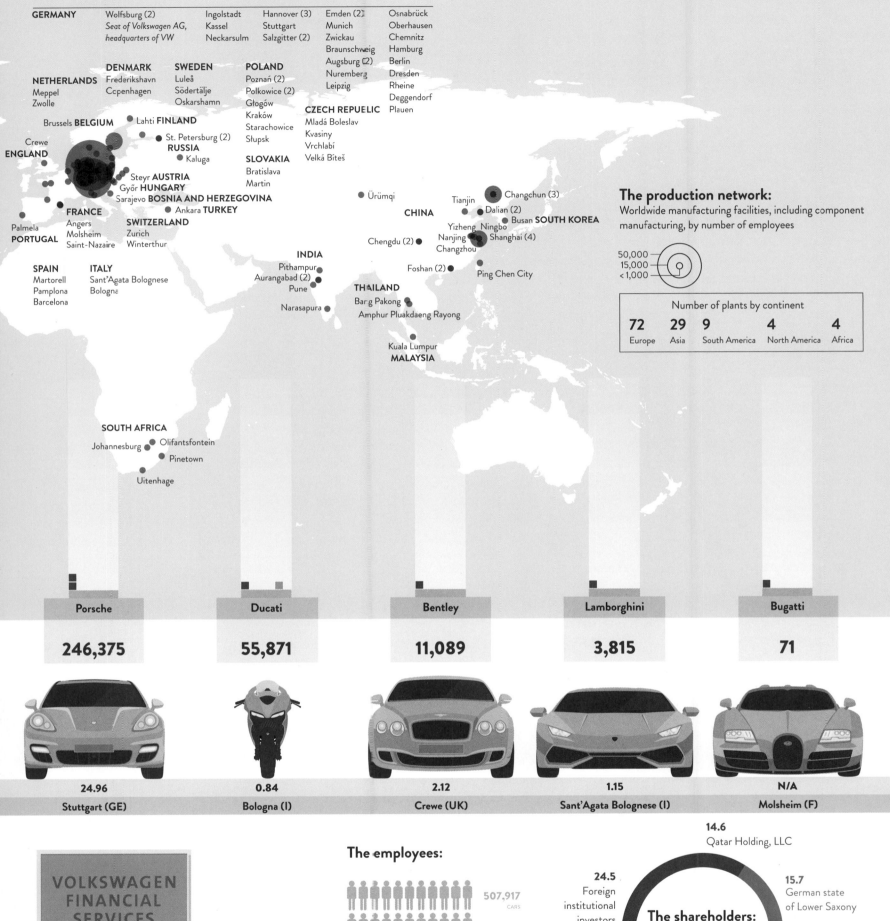

GERMANY
Wolfsburg (2) — Ingolstadt — Hannover (3) — Emden (2) — Osnabrück
Seat of Volkswagen AG, — Kassel — Stuttgart — Munich — Oberhausen
headquarters of VW — Neckarsulm — Salzgitter (2) — Zwickau — Chemnitz
Braunschweig — Hamburg
Augsburg (2) — Berlin
Nuremberg — Dresden
Leipzig — Rheine
Deggendorf
Plauen

NETHERLANDS — **DENMARK** — **SWEDEN** — **POLAND**
Meppel — Frederikshavn — Luleå — Poznań (2)
Zwolle — Copenhagen — Södertälje — Polkowice (2)
Oskarshamn — Głogów
Kraków
Brussels **BELGIUM** — Lahti **FINLAND** — Starachowice
Słupsk
Crewe — St. Petersburg (2) — **CZECH REPUELIC**
ENGLAND — **RUSSIA** — Mladá Boleslav
Kaluga — **SLOVAKIA** — Kvasiny
Steyr **AUSTRIA** — Bratislava — Vrchlabí
Győr **HUNGARY** — Martin — Velká Bíteš
Sarajevo **BOSNIA AND HERZEGOVINA**
Ankara **TURKEY**
Palmela — **FRANCE**
PORTUGAL — Angers — **SWITZERLAND**
Molsheim — Zurich
Saint-Nazaire — Winterthur

SPAIN — **ITALY**
Martorell — Sant'Agata Bolognese
Pamplona — Bologna
Barcelona

INDIA
Pithampur
Aurangabad (2)
Pune

Narasapura

CHINA
Ürümqi — Tianjin — Changchun (3)
Dalian (2)
Yizheng Ningbo — Busan **SOUTH KOREA**
Chengdu (2) — Nanjing — Shanghai (4)
Changzhou
Foshan (2) — Ping Chen City

THAILAND
Bang Pakong
Amphur Pluakdaeng Rayong

Kuala Lumpur
MALAYSIA

SOUTH AFRICA
Johannesburg — Olifantsfontein
Pinetown
Uitenhage

The production network:
Worldwide manufacturing facilities, including component manufacturing, by number of employees

50,000
15,000
<1,000

Number of plants by continent				
72	**29**	**9**	**4**	**4**
Europe	Asia	South America	North America	Africa

	Porsche	Ducati	Bentley	Lamborghini	Bugatti
Employees	**246,375**	**55,871**	**11,089**	**3,815**	**71**
	24.96	0.84	2.12	1.15	N/A
	Stuttgart (GE)	Bologna (I)	Crewe (UK)	Sant'Agata Bolognese (I)	Molsheim (F)

VOLKSWAGEN
FINANCIAL
SERVICES

Financial services, 2017

$50.23 Bn Sales

$0.61 Bn Operating profit

Braunschweig (GE)

The employees:

507,917 CARS
101,673 UTILITY VEHICLES
16,553 ENGINEERING
16,149 FINANCIAL SERVICES

= 15,000 employees (as of December 2017)

The shareholders:
Who owns the Volkswagen company?

14.6 Qatar Holding, LLC
15.7 German state of Lower Saxony
2.7 German institutional investors
30.8 Porsche Automobil Holding SE
24.5 Foreign institutional investors

Distribution of voting rights in percent (as of December 2017)

| **$3.9 Bn** OPERATING LOSSES | in the 3rd quarter 2015 (first loss in 15 years) | **$21.73 Bn** SPECIAL LOANS | loaned by 13 banks in order to cushion resulting costs | **6 models** SALES HALTED | in the USA (November 2015) | **$15 billion** SETTLEMENT IN THE USA | after agreement with US authorities and plaintiffs |

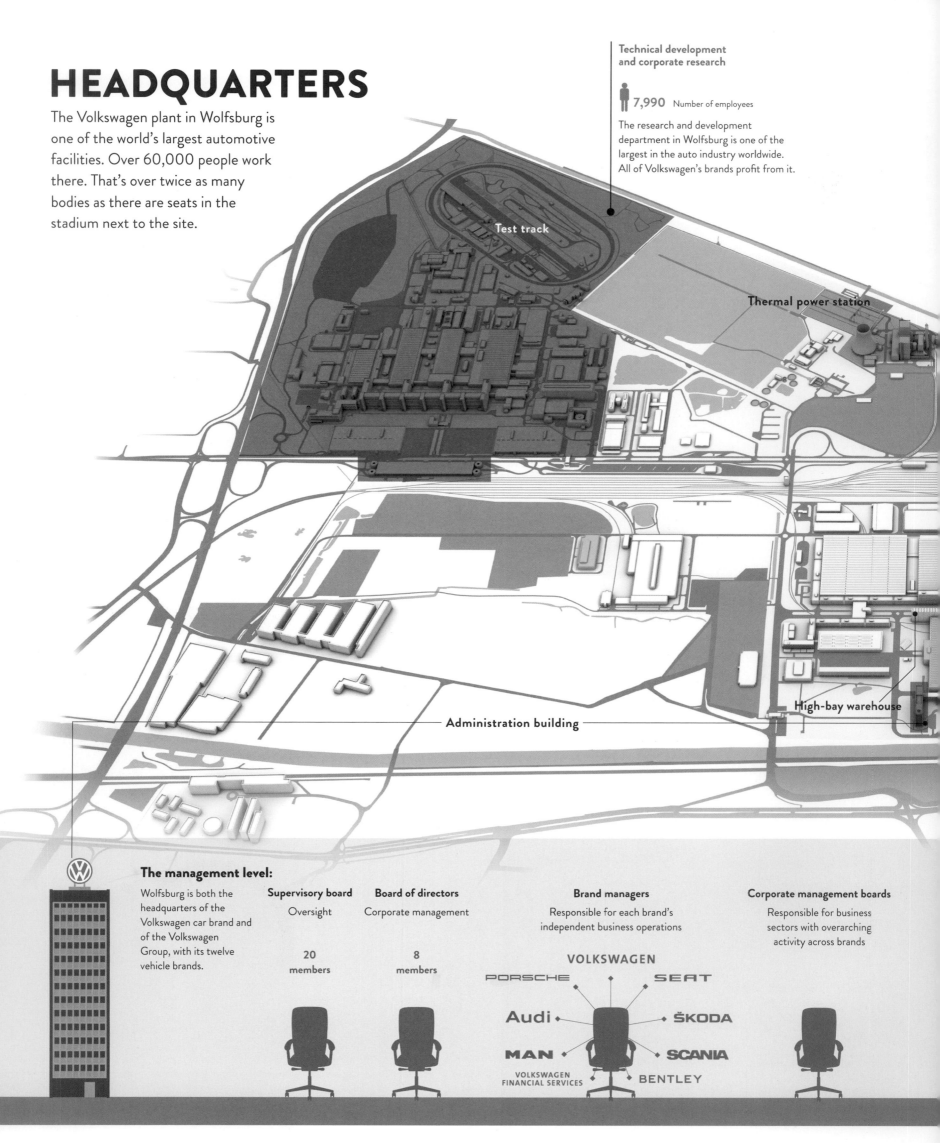

HEADQUARTERS

The Volkswagen plant in Wolfsburg is one of the world's largest automotive facilities. Over 60,000 people work there. That's over twice as many bodies as there are seats in the stadium next to the site.

Technical development and corporate research

👤 **7,990** Number of employees

The research and development department in Wolfsburg is one of the largest in the auto industry worldwide. All of Volkswagen's brands profit from it.

Test track

Thermal power station

High-bay warehouse

Administration building

The management level:

Wolfsburg is both the headquarters of the Volkswagen car brand and of the Volkswagen Group, with its twelve vehicle brands.

Supervisory board
Oversight

20
members

Board of directors
Corporate management

8
members

Brand managers
Responsible for each brand's independent business operations

Corporate management boards
Responsible for business sectors with overarching activity across brands

VOLKSWAGEN

PORSCHE   SEAT

Audi   ŠKODA

MAN   SCANIA

VOLKSWAGEN
FINANCIAL SERVICES   BENTLEY

The layout:

2.5 mi²
Total area

consisting of:

.5 mi²
Area for research and development

76
Employees of the factory fire safety office ensure the safety of the grounds.

.6 mi²
Plant areas

consisting of ft²

840,000	Pressing plant
2.6 Mn	Chassis construction
587,000	Paint shop
2.2 Mn	Assembly
600,000	Testing stations
2.2 Mn	Component manufacturing

Inside the halls, approx. **6,000 bicycles** are a popular means of transport.

43.5-mile
rail network

7
locomotives

2
robotic shunting locomotives

1
rail traverser

The factory railway employs **88 staff members.**

46.6-mile
road network

Three bus lines shuttle the employees on the grounds from building to building.

The workforce:

62,000
employees

The production:

Models
Golf, Golf Sportsvan, e-Golf, Tiguan, and Touran

Number of vehicles produced

3,020
per working day

790,000
per year

2017

8 million
currywurst

The most-produced product in 2017 wasn't a car, but rather the sausage the company makes itself.

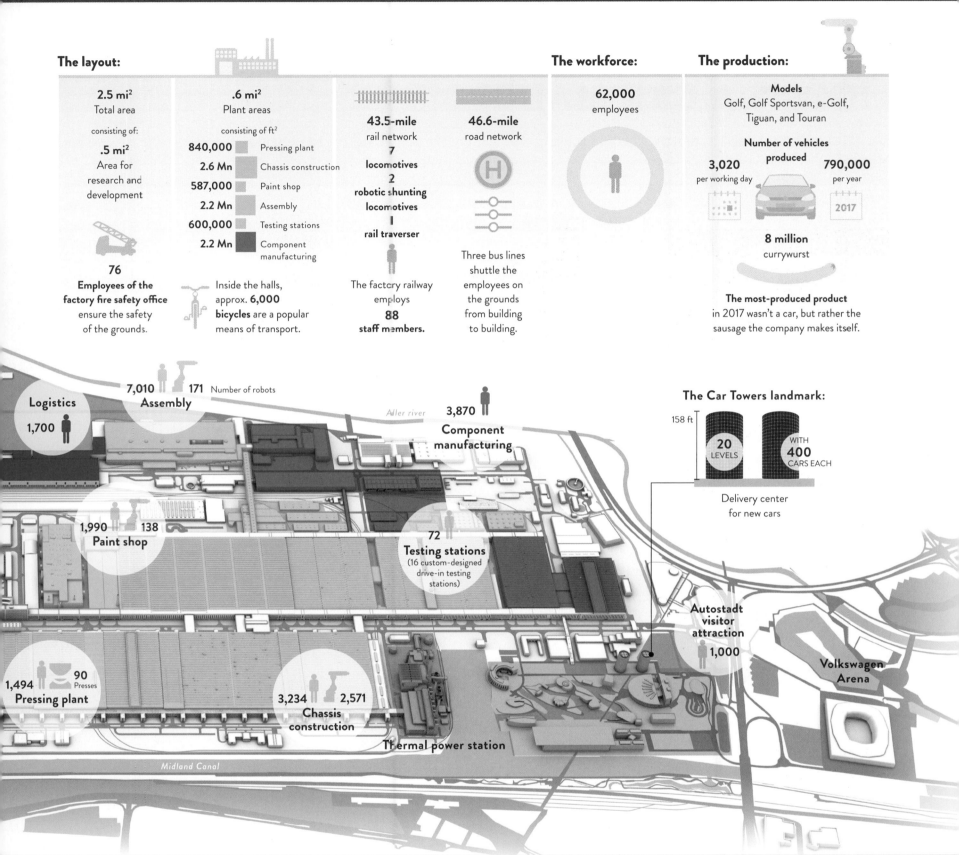

Logistics
1,700

7,010 · **171** Number of robots
Assembly

Aller river

3,870
Component manufacturing

1,990 · **138**
Paint shop

72
Testing stations
(16 custom-designed drive-in testing stations)

1,494 · **90** Presses
Pressing plant

3,234 · **2,571**
Chassis construction

Thermal power station

Midland Canal

The Car Towers landmark:

158 ft

20 LEVELS

WITH **400** CARS EACH

Delivery center for new cars

Autostadt visitor attraction
1,000

Volkswagen Arena

The city:

Without Volkswagen, there would be no Wolfsburg. The city and the manufacturing facility were built from the ground up by the Nazis starting in 1938. Until May 1945, the factory housing areas officially bore the name "City of the 'Strength Through Joy' Car near Fallersleben." During World War II, war matériel was initially produced by numerous forced laborers, among others. Series production of the Bug started after the war, under British leadership.

Population Growth of Wolfsburg
(1998–2014)

124,481

6,797

1939 · 1980 · 2014

The partnership:

Wolfsburg AG

There has been a public-private partnership between Volkswagen and the city of Wolfsburg since 1999. It has the goal of increasing the location's appeal, and is above all active in promoting employment and structural development.

The energy:

VW Kraftwerk GmbH

Two thermal power stations provide the facility with energy and generate heat and electricity for the city of Wolfsburg.

The soccer team:

As a business entity, Wolfsburg's soccer team is a 100% subsidiary of Volkswagen. Volkswagen is the main sponsor of the team and its arena.

HOW IS A CAR MADE?

It takes three to seven years from strategic deliberations to the delivery of a new model. The exact sequence of this complex process is a little different with each manufacturer. The prototypical process looks like this:

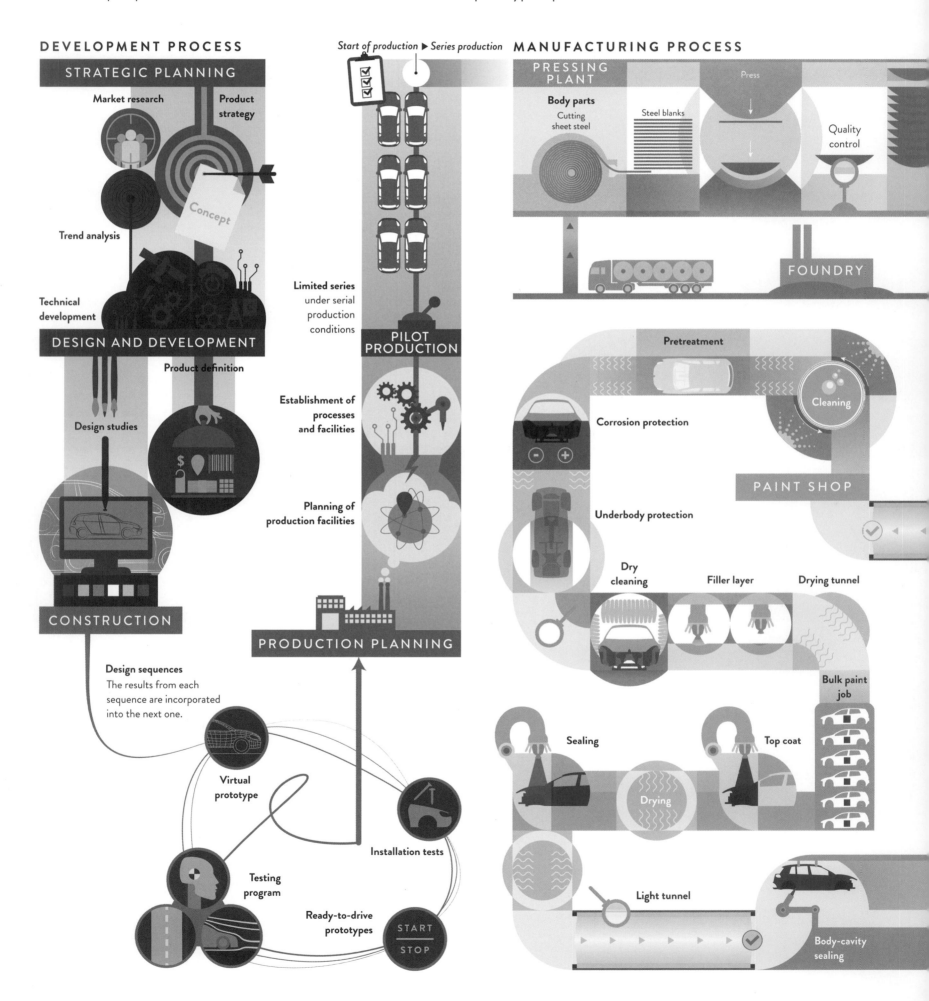

DEVELOPMENT PROCESS

Start of production ▶ Series production

MANUFACTURING PROCESS

STRATEGIC PLANNING

Market research

Product strategy

Trend analysis

Concept

Technical development

DESIGN AND DEVELOPMENT

Product definition

Design studies

CONSTRUCTION

Design sequences
The results from each sequence are incorporated into the next one.

Virtual prototype

Testing program

Installation tests

Ready-to-drive prototypes

START
STOP

Limited series
under serial production conditions

PILOT PRODUCTION

Establishment of processes and facilities

Planning of production facilities

PRODUCTION PLANNING

PRESSING PLANT

Body parts
Cutting sheet steel

Steel blanks

Press

Quality control

FOUNDRY

Pretreatment

Cleaning

Corrosion protection

PAINT SHOP

Underbody protection

Dry cleaning

Filler layer

Drying tunnel

Bulk paint job

Sealing

Drying

Top coat

Light tunnel

Body-cavity sealing

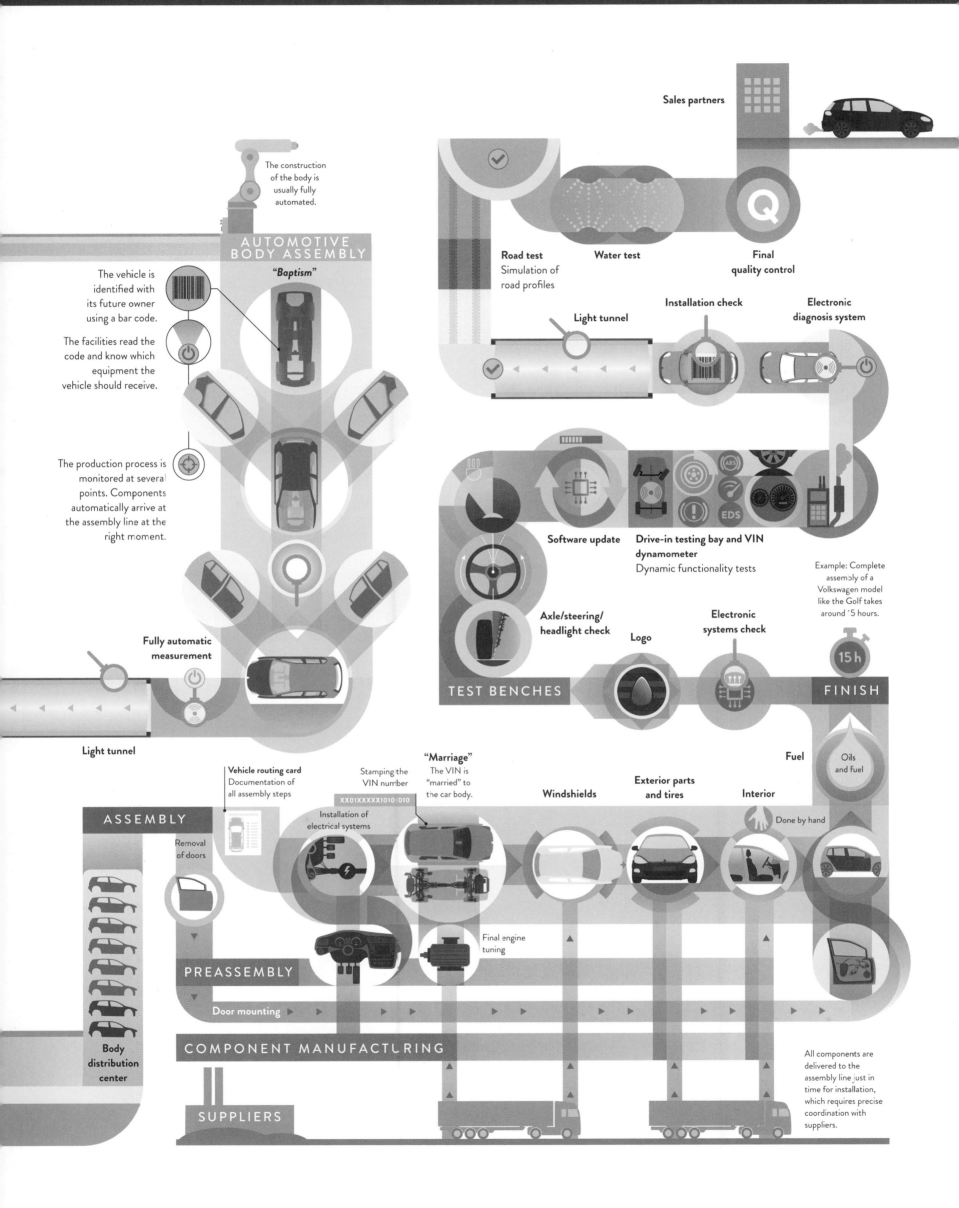

Sales partners

The construction of the body is usually fully automated.

AUTOMOTIVE BODY ASSEMBLY
"Baptism"

Road test
Simulation of road profiles

Water test

Final quality control

The vehicle is identified with its future owner using a bar code.

The facilities read the code and know which equipment the vehicle should receive.

Light tunnel

Installation check

Electronic diagnosis system

The production process is monitored at several points. Components automatically arrive at the assembly line at the right moment.

Software update

Drive-in testing bay and VIN dynamometer
Dynamic functionality tests

Example: Complete assembly of a Volkswagen model like the Golf takes around 15 hours.

Fully automatic measurement

Axle/steering/ headlight check

Logo

Electronic systems check

15 h

Light tunnel

TEST BENCHES

FINISH

Fuel

Oils and fuel

Vehicle routing card
Documentation of all assembly steps

Stamping the VIN number

"Marriage"
The VIN is "married" to the car body.

Windshields

Exterior parts and tires

Interior

ASSEMBLY

XX01XXXXX1010·010

Installation of electrical systems

Done by hand

Removal of doors

Final engine tuning

PREASSEMBLY

Door mounting

Body distribution center

COMPONENT MANUFACTURING

All components are delivered to the assembly line just in time for installation, which requires precise coordination with suppliers.

SUPPLIERS

GOING PUBLIC

Someone who buys stock purchases shares in a company. A business owner sells shares in order to obtain capital. Typically, the owner wants to use the money to continue developing the company. Sometimes the owner wants to buy an island in the South Pacific, too. Before the owner can do that and before new shareholders can make a profit (or a loss), the owner has to make many decisions . . .

You're a **COMPANY** and want to raise equity capital?

Are you a joint-stock company?

Do you want to **INCREASE CAPITAL?**

Then exchange one share for several small ones. The effect is purely psychological and makes the share easier to trade.

no — yes

You cannot raise equity this way. But you can conduct a **STOCK SPLIT!**

no

yes — no

Only joint-stock companies are permitted to issue shares.

no

Do you want to learn more about stocks?

yes — no

Do you want to found **A JOINT-STOCK CORPORATION?**

no

Do you want to transform your company into a **JOINT-STOCK CORPORATION?**

yes

yes

Then consult with an **INVESTMENT BANK** It serves as an intermediary and receives a share of the proceeds.

Then just answer yes.

yes

Then skip over these pages.

no

What should the **PRICE PER SHARE** be?

no

BOOK BUILDING PROCESS?

no

AUCTION PROCESS?

no

FIXED PRICE PROCESS?

yes

I'd rather not

yes

I'd rather not

yes

The investment bank feels out investors and sets a price range. Investors submit bids. The issue price (closing) results from the submissions. Those who bid under that level do not receive any shares. All others are able to purchase shares at the issue price.

Hold an auction and sell to the highest bidders.

Then pick a good price. But if it's too high, no one will buy. And if it's too low, you're giving away money.

yes

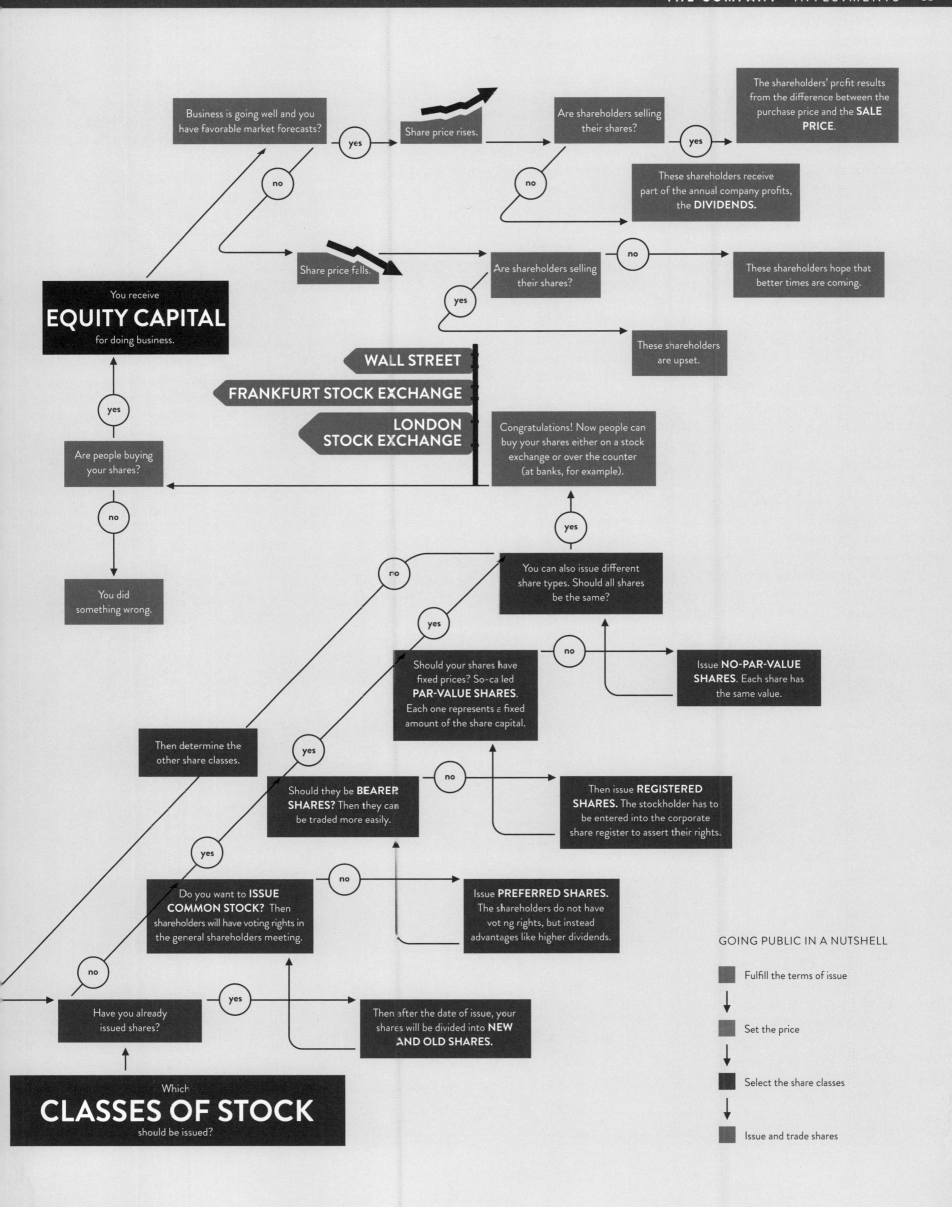

Business is going well and you have favorable market forecasts?

yes

Share price rises.

no

Are shareholders selling their shares?

yes

The shareholders' profit results from the difference between the purchase price and the **SALE PRICE**.

no

These shareholders receive part of the annual company profits, the **DIVIDENDS**.

Share price falls.

Are shareholders selling their shares?

no

These shareholders hope that better times are coming.

yes

These shareholders are upset.

EQUITY CAPITAL
for doing business.

You receive

yes

Are people buying your shares?

no

You did something wrong.

WALL STREET

FRANKFURT STOCK EXCHANGE

LONDON STOCK EXCHANGE

Congratulations! Now people can buy your shares either on a stock exchange or over the counter (at banks, for example).

yes

no

You can also issue different share types. Should all shares be the same?

yes

no

Issue **NO-PAR-VALUE SHARES**. Each share has the same value.

Should your shares have fixed prices? So-called **PAR-VALUE SHARES**. Each one represents a fixed amount of the share capital.

Then determine the other share classes.

yes

Should they be **BEARER SHARES?** Then they can be traded more easily.

no

Then issue **REGISTERED SHARES**. The stockholder has to be entered into the corporate share register to assert their rights.

yes

Do you want to **ISSUE COMMON STOCK?** Then shareholders will have voting rights in the general shareholders meeting.

no

Issue **PREFERRED SHARES**. The shareholders do not have voting rights, but instead advantages like higher dividends.

no

Have you already issued shares?

yes

Then after the date of issue, your shares will be divided into **NEW AND OLD SHARES.**

Which
CLASSES OF STOCK
should be issued?

GOING PUBLIC IN A NUTSHELL

Fulfill the terms of issue

Set the price

Select the share classes

Issue and trade shares

CLASH OF KEY INDICATORS

Steve Jobs described his goal for Apple: "We're here to put a dent in the universe."
It's hard to say how our economy looks from another galaxy. But here on Earth, the
keys to grasping the economy are figures.

◆ **Top 5 Companies in the World**
2017

MARKET CAP
$
US$ in Billions
(as of June 2018)

- APPLE INC. — 945.77
- AMAZON.COM INC. — 830.37
- ALPHABET INC. — 787.91
- MICROSOFT CORP. — 775.39
- FACEBOOK INC. — 554.44

SALES
US$ in Billions

- WALMART INC. — 485.9
- STATE GRID CORP. OF CHINA — 315.2
- SINOPEC — 267.5
- CHINA NATL. PETROLEUM — 262.6
- TOYOTA MOTOR CORP. — 254.7

NET PROFIT
US$ in Billions

- 45.7
- 41.9
- 34.8
- 27.7
- 24.

EMPLOYEES
Number

- WALMART INC. — 2,300,000
- CHINA NATIONAL PETROLEUM CORP. — 1,512,048
- STATE GRID CORP. OF CHINA — 926,067
- FOXCONN — 724,772
- SINOPEC — 713,288

MOST PROFITABLE COMPANIES
Return on sales in %
%

- ICBC (banking) — 28.4%
- CHINA CONSTRUCTION BANK (banking) — 25.8%
- AGRICULTURAL BANK OF CHINA (banking) — 23.6%
- JPMORGAN CHASE & CO. (banking) — 23.4%
- WELLS FARGO (banking) — 23.3%

SALES
US$ in Billions

- WALMART INC. — 500.3
- BERKSHIRE HATHAWAY INC. — 241.4
- APPLE INC. — 238.8
- EXXON MOBIL CORP. — 220.4
- UNITEDHEALTH GROUP — 207.6

NET PROFIT
US$ in Billions

- APPLE INC. — 50.5
- BERKSHIRE HATHAWAY INC. — 44.9
- VERIZON COMMUNICATIONS INC. — 30.1
- AT&T INC. — 29.5
- JPMORGAN CHASE & CO — 26.5

◆ **Top 5 Companies in the US**
2017

EMPLOYEES
Number

- WALMART INC. — 2,300,000
- US POSTAL SERVICE — 574,349
- THE KROGER CO. — 443,000
- IBM CORP. — 414,400
- HOME DEPOT — 406,000

**Bankruptcies of Businesses
and Individuals 1980–2017**

— Business Filings for Chapter 11
— Non-Business Filings for Chapter 11

100,000
1,000,000

50,000
500,000

0
0

43,694 286,444 81,235 872,438 52,374 1,350,118

1980 1982 1984 1986 1988 1990 1992 1994 1996 1998

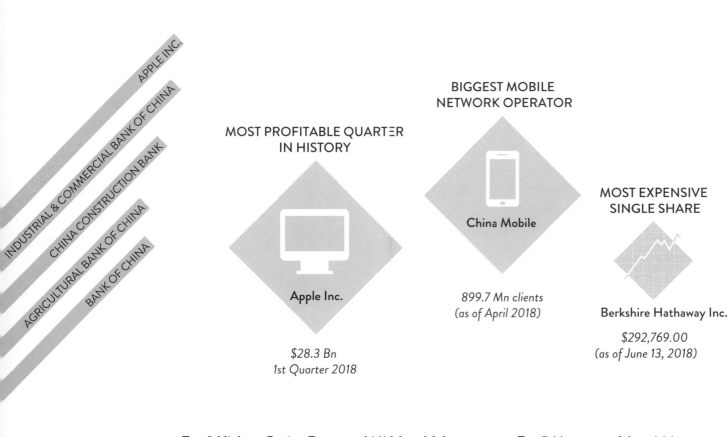

APPLE INC.

INDUSTRIAL & COMMERCIAL BANK OF CHINA

CHINA CONSTRUCTION BANK

AGRICULTURAL BANK OF CHINA

BANK OF CHINA

MOST PROFITABLE QUARTER IN HISTORY

Apple Inc.

$28.3 Bn
1st Quarter 2018

BIGGEST MOBILE NETWORK OPERATOR

China Mobile

899.7 Mn clients
(as of April 2018)

MOST EXPENSIVE SINGLE SHARE

Berkshire Hathaway Inc.

$292,769.00
(as of June 13, 2018)

OLDEST COMPANY IN ACTIVITY

Nishiyama Onsen Keiunkan

Founded in **705 CE**;
hotel run by the same
family for **52** generations

Top 3 Highest-Paying Entry- and Mid-Level Jobs
Median Annual Gross Salary Including Bonuses

$105,000
Investment
Banking Analyst

$105,000
Associate Brand
Manager

$79,500
Equity Research
Analyst

Top 5 Mergers and Acquisitions
US$ in Billions

Vodafone buys **Mannesmann**	2000	180
AOL buys **Time Warner**	2000	164
Verizon buys **Verizon Wireless**	2013	130.1
Dow Chemical buys **Dupont**	2017	130
Anheuser-Busch InBev buys **SABMiller**	2015	104.3

Top 5 Bankruptcies Worldwide
US$ in Billions

Top 5 Bankruptcies in the US by Number of Employees

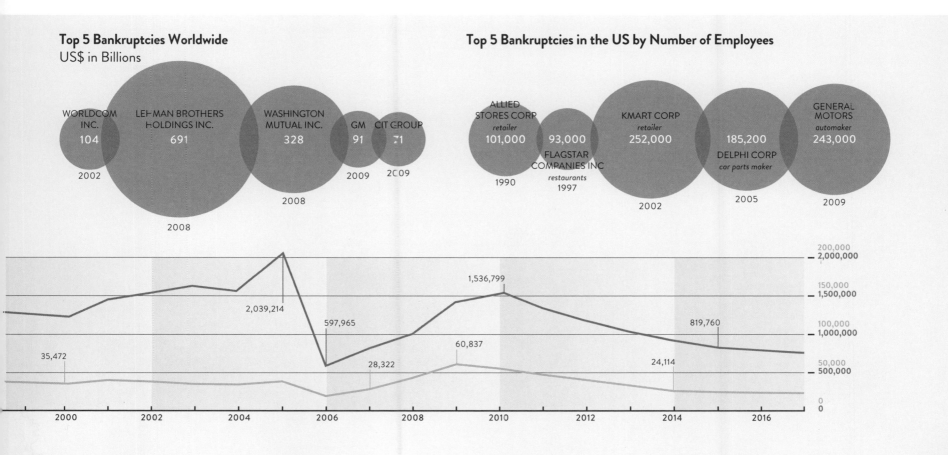

WORLDCOM INC.
104
2002

LEHMAN BROTHERS HOLDINGS INC.
691
2008

WASHINGTON MUTUAL INC.
328
2008

GM
91
2009

CIT GROUP
71
2009

ALLIED STORES CORP
retailer
101,000
1990

FLAGSTAR COMPANIES INC
restaurants
93,000
1997

KMART CORP
retailer
252,000
2002

DELPHI CORP
car parts maker
185,200
2005

GENERAL MOTORS
automaker
243,000
2009

2,039,214

1,536,799

597,965

819,760

35,472

28,322

60,837

24,114

200,000 — 2,000,000
150,000 — 1,500,000
100,000 — 1,000,000
50,000 — 500,000
0 — 0

2000   2002   2004   2006   2008   2010   2012   2014   2016

LOSS, GAIN, VALUE CHAIN

Companies create value. To do this, they consume resources. If they are successful, there will ultimately be a profit. To systematically describe the combined activities performed by companies, management experts use the model of the value chain (or value-added chain). Harvard professor Michael E. Porter introduced it in 1985. Analyzing the value chain helps companies optimize business processes and enhance competitive advantages.

Value-chain model as defined by Michael E. Porter

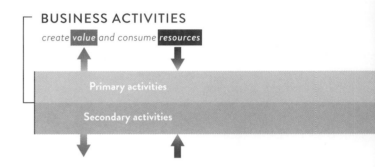

Examples of Value Chains

BANK

| Product Development | Marketing | Sales | Transaction Processing |

DETERGENT MANUFACTURER

| Research and Development | Procurement | Production | Packaging |

ADVERTISING AGENCY

| Project Acquisition | Sales Order | Project Management | Initial Concept |

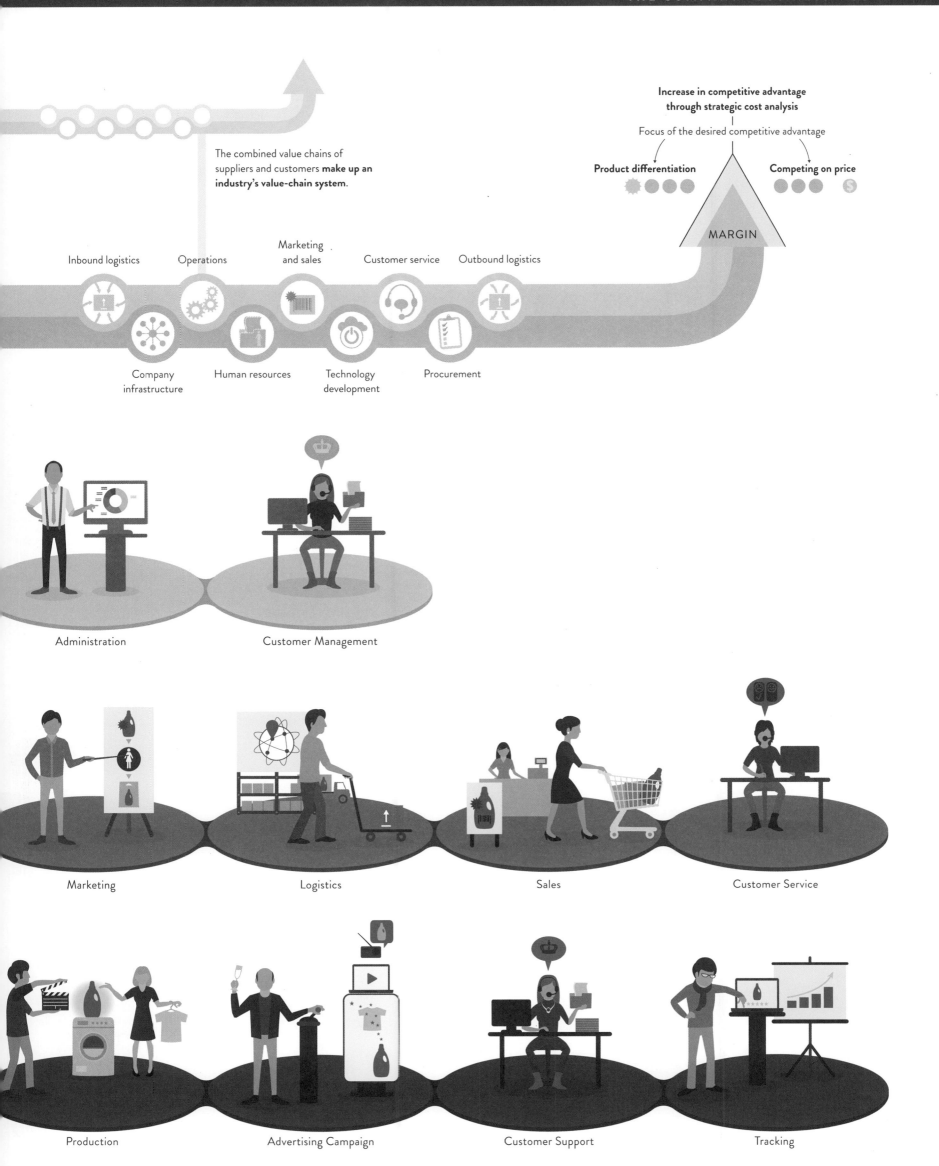

The combined value chains of suppliers and customers **make up an industry's value-chain system.**

Increase in competitive advantage through strategic cost analysis

Focus of the desired competitive advantage

Product differentiation

Competing on price

MARGIN

Inbound logistics

Operations

Marketing and sales

Customer service

Outbound logistics

Company infrastructure

Human resources

Technology development

Procurement

Administration

Customer Management

Marketing

Logistics

Sales

Customer Service

Production

Advertising Campaign

Customer Support

Tracking

PAINT YOUR BUSINESS MODEL

How are we going to earn any money? That question is always on the minds of start-up founders. Searching for the right business model is easier with the Business Model Canvas, a tool Alex Osterwalder developed for his 2004 doctoral thesis in Switzerland. Today it's used worldwide by business founders and seasoned managers alike—anyone who needs a common language for visualizing, evaluating, and modifying business models.

KEY PARTNERS
List all the resources and external suppliers that the start-up/company relies on.

KEY ACTIVITIES
What activities are necessary so the company can offer a product or service?

KEY RESOURCES
Resources and (technical) infrastructure that are essential to be able to offer a product or service

VALUE PROPOSITION
Each customer segment has its own value proposition: a product and/or service that brings value to the customer and is tailored to the needs of the segment.

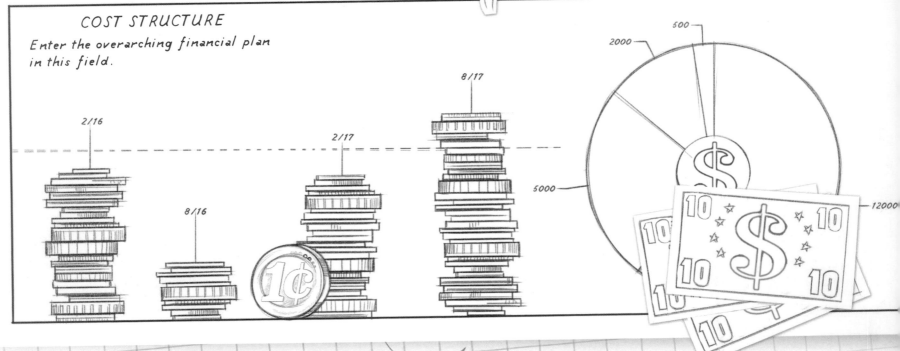

COST STRUCTURE
Enter the overarching financial plan in this field.

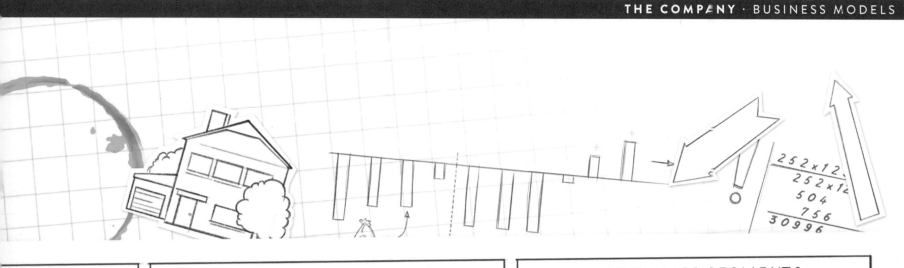

CUSTOMER RELATIONS

How should the company interact with customers? In a community? Through personalized service? Or via digital automation?

CUSTOMER SEGMENTS

All the people or organizations that the company wants to reach with its products or services

CHANNELS

How does the company communicate with its customers? What do the points of contact look like? How does it deliver its value proposition to the customer?

SOURCES OF INCOME

Which groups of customers are prepared to pay how much for which products or services? The various payment methods such as buying versus leasing, a flat rate versus individual statements, etc.

TOP VS. FLOP

The Volkswagen Golf. Pampers diapers. McDonald's Big Mac. Bestsellers dominate our image of the world of consumer goods. It's only logical; they sell so well, after all. But around two thirds of all market launches fail within a year, and even apparently popular products can be real flops economically. Just look at the Segway.

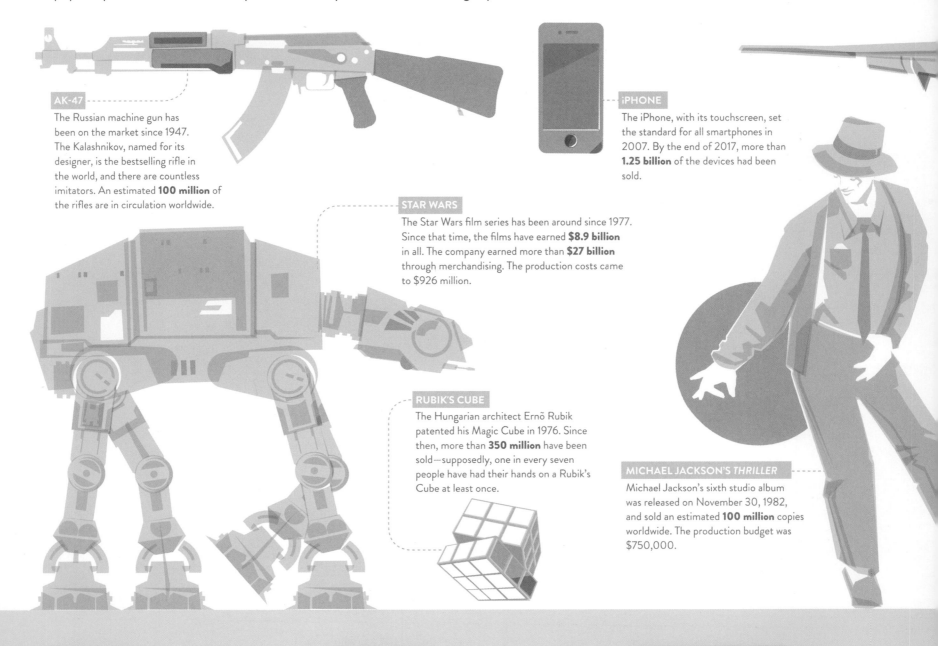

AK-47
The Russian machine gun has been on the market since 1947. The Kalashnikov, named for its designer, is the bestselling rifle in the world, and there are countless imitators. An estimated **100 million** of the rifles are in circulation worldwide.

iPHONE
The iPhone, with its touchscreen, set the standard for all smartphones in 2007. By the end of 2017, more than **1.25 billion** of the devices had been sold.

STAR WARS
The Star Wars film series has been around since 1977. Since that time, the films have earned **$8.9 billion** in all. The company earned more than **$27 billion** through merchandising. The production costs came to $926 million.

RUBIK'S CUBE
The Hungarian architect Ernö Rubik patented his Magic Cube in 1976. Since then, more than **350 million** have been sold—supposedly, one in every seven people have had their hands on a Rubik's Cube at least once.

MICHAEL JACKSON'S *THRILLER*
Michael Jackson's sixth studio album was released on November 30, 1982, and sold an estimated **100 million** copies worldwide. The production budget was $750,000.

CLEAR COLAS
In 1992, Pepsi introduced a caffeine-free cola that looked like mineral water. Coca-Cola followed a year later with the diet soda "Tab Clear." Both soft drinks were clear, and both flopped.

MICROSOFT ZUNE
The music player was on the market from 2006 to 2011. At the end of 2008, a particular model of first-generation devices crashed in droves—and rebooting was impossible.

COLGATE KITCHEN ENTRÉES
In 1982, Colgate entered the market for groceries with frozen entrées. But the corporation kept the world-famous toothpaste logo. The frozen meals disappeared from the shelves the same year.

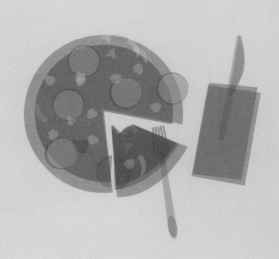

BOEING 737

ranks as the bestselling commercial aircraft in the world. By March 2018, 10,000 of the **14,600** aircraft ordered had been delivered.

SUPER MARIO

The video game series, one of the most extensive in gaming history, has been on the market since September 1985. More than **550 million** units have been sold up to now.

COFFEE PODS AND CAPSULES

were developed in 2001 and brought to market by Douwe Egberts/Philips and by Senseo in 2002. Sales are steadily climbing each year, and in 2015 coffee capsules by themselves were estimated to generate sales of **$4.4 billion**.

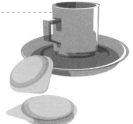

SONY PLAYSTATION

The PS1 was released in Japan in 1994. Over **524 million** have been sold since.

TOYOTA COROLLA

has been coming off the assembly lines through eleven generations of models since 1966 and is the bestselling car in the world: **43 million** vehicles.

iPAD

The tablet was launched in 2010. By June 2017, more than **360 million** had been sold.

SONY AIBO

The robotic dog had its debut in 1999. By 2006, Sony had sold at least 150,000 copies worldwide. The problem: Warranty service proved expensive for the company. Customer service was suspended eight years after production had ended.

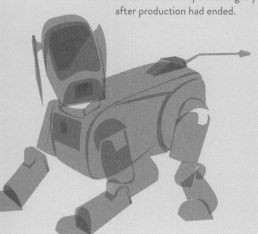

ARCH DELUXE

The gourmet burger from McDonald's was intended to mark the beginning of a product line for sophisticated palates. McDonald's poured more than $300 million for research, development, and marketing down the drain.

ISDN VIDEOPHONE

was sold by Deutsche Telekom for 998 deutsche marks ($600 at the time, around $900 today) beginning in 1997. The purchase price was high, and the picture quality was poor. People preferred to wait for Skype to come along.

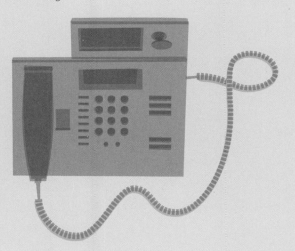

PRODUCT BIOGRAPHIES

Products are like people. They're born, grow up, have a period of high productivity, and then at some point it's time for them to go. Business experts call it life cycle management.

HOW DO NEW THINGS ENTER THE WORLD?

Different innovation methods help creators better understand users/customers and find new (product) solutions. Most methods proceed iteratively. That means that they work on the basis of many loops in which ideas, approaches to a solution, and prototypes are gradually refined. This is also the approach of Design Thinking.

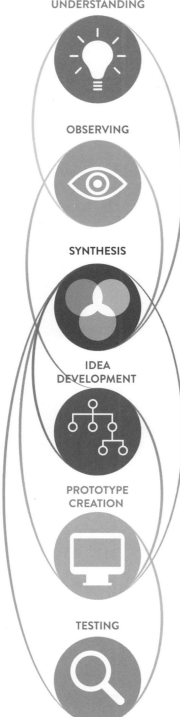

UNDERSTANDING

OBSERVING

SYNTHESIS

IDEA DEVELOPMENT

PROTOTYPE CREATION

TESTING

PATENTS

Innovation is expensive. Patents (and other rights) are meant to prevent new products from being immediately copied. Otherwise no one would invest in technological advancement.

The requirements for a patent are:

1. Novelty
An idea that doesn't already belong to the current state of technology.

2. Inventive activity
The idea may not emerge in an obvious way from current technology.

3. Commercial application
Ideas that are not feasible and/or commercially usable cannot be patented. Medical procedures are considered not commercially usable for social and ethical reasons.

What cannot be patented in the US?

- abstract ideas
- laws and products of nature
- scientific theories and mathematical methods
- software performing mathematical operations
- physical phenomena occurring in nature
- new plants sexually reproduced by breeding
- human genes, since 2013; a Supreme Court ruling invalidated 4,300 existing gene patents
- genetically engineered living animals or bacteria
- biological substances if they are not sufficiently transformed
- inventions if they are totally incapable of achieving a useful result
- inventions or processes if they use illegal material or substances
- business ideas

PRODUCT LIFE CYCLE

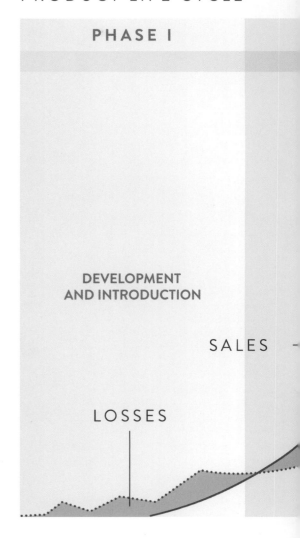

PHASE I

DEVELOPMENT AND INTRODUCTION

SALES

LOSSES

MARKET GROWTH

BOSTON CONSULTING GROUP GROWTH-SHARE MATRIX

Managers need to keep an eye on the life cycles of their entire product portfolio. The matrix of the Boston Consulting Group helps them understand the health of their products (individually and as a whole)— and thus the future health of the company as well.

QUALITY CONTROL DMAIC CYCLE

Quality is often a decisive competitive advantage. Quality management systems are supposed to ensure that it's you and not your competitors with the advantage.

1. **Define:** Define the problem and scope, identify customers' requirements, conduct a stakeholder analysis, determine a measurable project result, create a work plan

2. **Measure:** Create a data collection plan, analyze statistics, determine the current status, understand customer needs, calculate process capability

3. **Analyze:** Map the process, analyze root causes, filter out influence factors and determine their relationship

4. **Improve:** Find solutions for the most important root causes, evaluate the solutions and choose the best one, create a plan for change, start a pilot project

5. **Control:** Develop a process management plan, establish a control plan, document and monitor improvement

(FOR CONSUMER PRODUCTS)

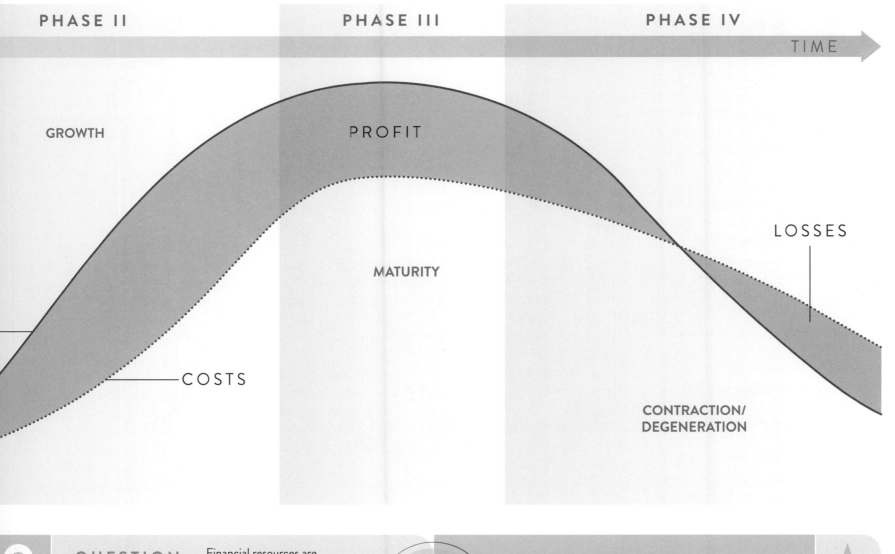

PHASE II   PHASE III   PHASE IV

TIME

GROWTH

PROFIT

COSTS

MATURITY

LOSSES

CONTRACTION/
DEGENERATION

?	QUESTION MARKS	Financial resources are needed, uncertain market development				Strong growth, high stability, investments made	STARS	★
🐕	POOR DOGS	Low revenue, instability, loss of profits, sale or spin-off				High stability, slow growth, high productivity	CASH COWS	🐄

MARKET SHARE

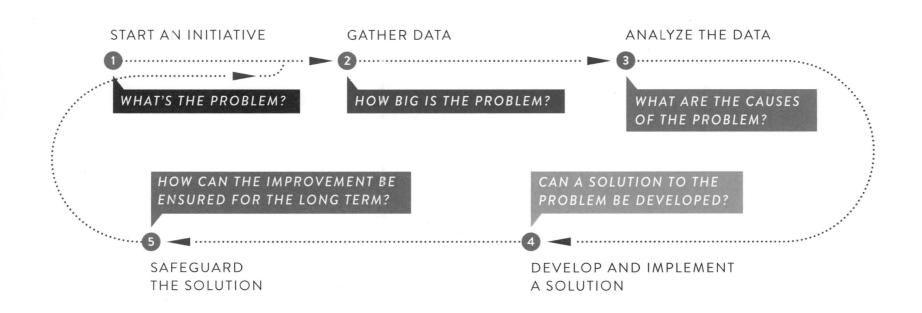

START AN INITIATIVE   GATHER DATA   ANALYZE THE DATA

1   **2**   **3**

WHAT'S THE PROBLEM?   *HOW BIG IS THE PROBLEM?*   *WHAT ARE THE CAUSES OF THE PROBLEM?*

HOW CAN THE IMPROVEMENT BE ENSURED FOR THE LONG TERM?   *CAN A SOLUTION TO THE PROBLEM BE DEVELOPED?*

5   **4**

SAFEGUARD THE SOLUTION   DEVELOP AND IMPLEMENT A SOLUTION

GETTING ORGANIZED

Who decides what in a company? Who directs which processes, using what resources, and how? Who has which rights and responsibilities? The organizational structure regulates it.

Modern organizational theory is about as complex as particle physics. It approaches companies—and other organizations such as bureaucracies—from two different perspectives: looking at structure, or at processes.

The organizational structure describes the hierarchical framework of a company. It determines which tasks are to be dealt with by which people and with what material resources. The process organization, on the other hand, governs how work and information processes take place within the structural framework—or, more precisely, how they are ideally supposed to happen. Because the company organization, of course, has a third, informal level. Not everything is done as envisioned by the hierarchy. That's just as true in line organizations, in which individual employees take orders from only one place, as in multiline organizations where the individual often has many bosses, which does not necessarily simplify the organizational structure.

Functional line organization

Below the management level, organizational tasks are divided according to functions—for example, development, production, and distribution. Small and mid-sized companies with a modest range of products often have a functional structure.

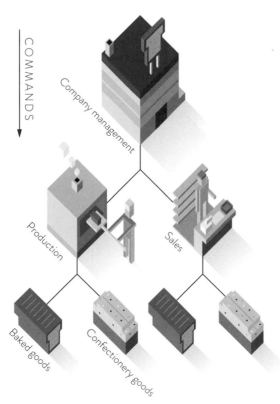

Departmental line organization

Division according to sectors or areas of business, typically on the second management level. A goal of this structure is typically to combine similar technologies, products, services, or even regions or customer groups into one organizational unit wherever possible.

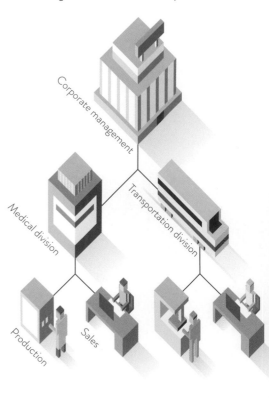

Simple multiline structure

Also known as the functional system. Responsible specialists are authorized to issue commands in various directions. This reduces decision-making processes and procedures. Handicraft and smaller technology operations are often organized this way.

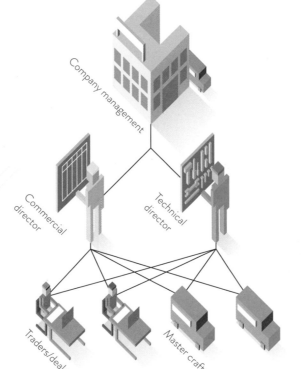

Matrix structure

Management functions are distributed across two independent and equal dimensions, such as product groups and activities. The goal of the matrix structure is to solve problems while taking different perspectives into account.

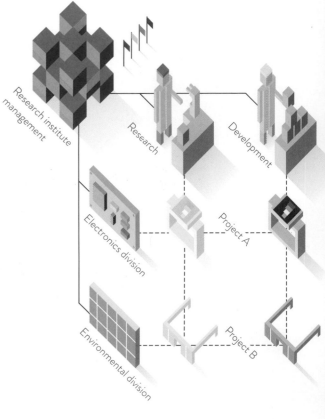

Line and staff organizational structure

A functional organization complemented by staff positions. The staff has an advisory function and is intended to relieve the burden on management. This organizational principle was adopted for corporate structures from religious institutions and the military. The staff and line management are often in conflict.

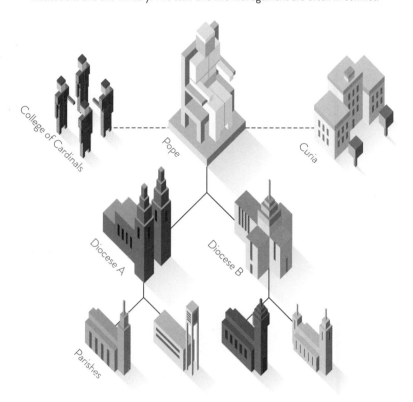

Holding organizational structure

A special form of organization by area of business or corporate division. The business sectors of the subsidiaries are run as independent organizational units under an overarching parent company (a holding company).

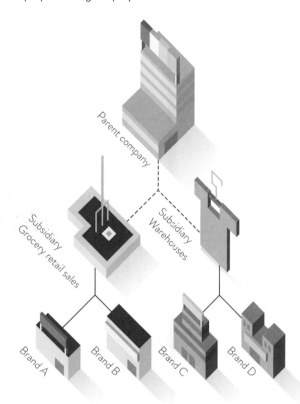

Tensor organizational structure

A further development of the matrix structure in which not two, but rather three or more organizational principles are combined—for example, function, product, and region. This is, among other things, advantageous for international enterprises that offer a diversified range of products in heterogeneous markets.

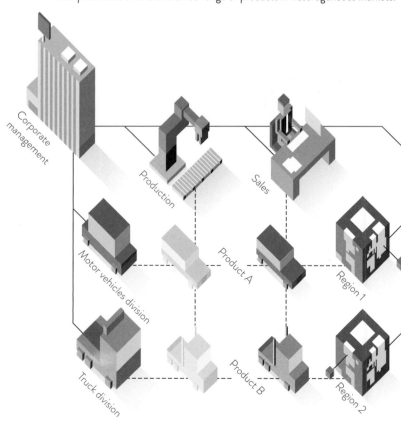

Network organizational structure

Individual areas, products, and business units enjoy a high level of autonomy. Headquarters is often tasked only with coordinating the various units and reminding them of their common long-term goals.

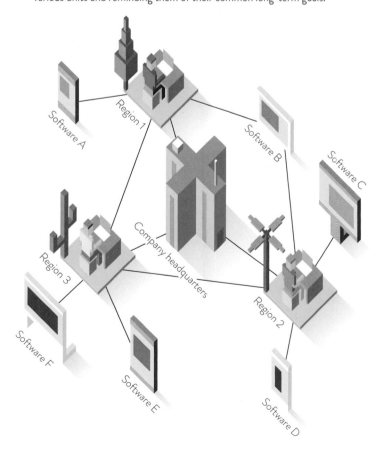

THE TEAM IS THE STAR

Value creation is a team sport. In business, it's just like in soccer: A good team needs players with different qualities and personalities. Almost all studies of team effectiveness point in the same direction. Heterogeneous groups have better results than homogeneous teams. The prerequisite, however, is that the various personalities cooperate and are able to agree on common goals. That's inherently more difficult than in a team of people who all march to the same beat. Consequently, that means: The more heterogeneous a team is, the more competence the team leader needs in team development and conflict management.

THE ORGANIZER,
WHO KEEPS AN EYE ON THE BIG PICTURE

THE CREATIVE TYPE,
RESPONSIBLE FOR GOOD IDEAS
AND FLASHES OF BRILLIANCE

THE CONSULTANT TYPE, WHO
INFORMS AND CONVINCES

THE ARTICULATE **SALESMAN**

THE PRACTICAL-MINDED **DOER**

TEAM DEVELOPMENT

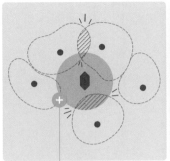
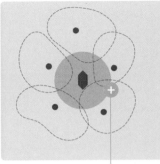
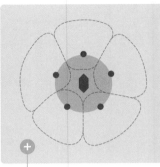
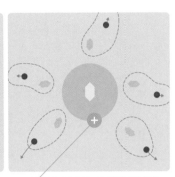

FORMING
(TEST PHASE)

The formation phase is a time of slowly feeling your way through and getting to know each other. It's marked by caution and politeness. Little communication among team members occurs and everyone tries to find their purpose and role on the team.

Clear expectations: Supervisors must ensure that the team members understand the team's purpose.

STORMING (HAND-TO-HAND COMBAT PHASE)

In the phase of hand-to-hand combat, the first conflicts and rivalries arise between team members and subgroups and against the task. This phase is necessary so that a team can develop a high level of maturity.

A lot of communication between equals about the status and progress of projects is required. That's because often, the different personalities aren't the problem, but rather uncertainty about processes.

NORMING
(ORGANIZING PHASE)

In the third phase, the team develops new ways to behave and communicate. Common goals and tasks are worked out through dialogue and the work is organized. A feeling of common identity arises, so power struggles are resolved constructively.

Variety and fun play a role: A feeling of common identity is strengthened by members taking part in events outside of work as a team.

PERFORMING
(WORKING PHASE)

In the fourth phase, the team is full of ideas, flexible, united, and capable. Energy flows toward solving problems, and the team demonstrates its autonomy and viability over a longer period of time.

Just let the team run. Build small elements of fun into the work day, such as loosening up meetings.

TRANSFORMING (SEPARATION AND TRANSFER PHASE)

In the last phase, the team looks back at the team process and takes stock: How can the team process be optimized in the future? What insights can be applied to future situations? Continuing activities are planned.

Consciously create space for reflection. And then go party together!

CONFLICTS

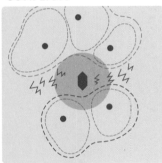
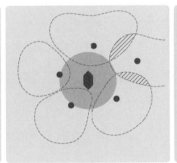
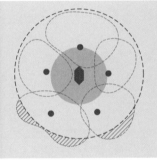
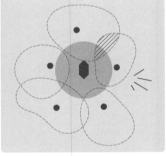
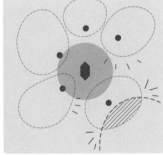

SUBGROUP CONFLICTS

Subgroups mutually exclude each other from information and then work against each other. Early and decisive intervention is often necessary, as the danger is high that the team will completely fall apart.

RANK CONFLICTS

Especially prevalent among newly forming teams and when new members are added. They are inherently part of the team formation process. They often resolve on their own once an informal hierarchy is established.

NORM CONFLICTS

Crop up after violations of the team's official or unofficial rules (norms). Often it's enough to identify the offense. The last resort: punishment of the misconduct. That increases the willingness to reintegrate the "perpetrator" into the team.

SUBSTITUTION CONFLICTS

A battle is waged not at the site of the actual problem, but rather on a secondary battlefield. Substitution conflicts can be resolved only if the actual problem is identified.

LOYALTY CONFLICTS

A team member faces an attack from the outside, but is not supported by other team members. It often marks the onset of decay in a team, as the termination of loyalty quickly runs rampant in all directions.

OPTIMAL TEAM SIZE

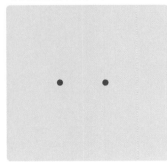
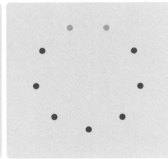
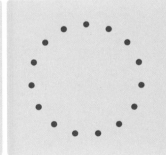
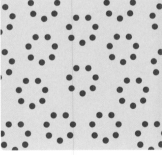
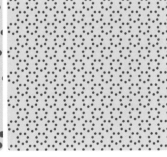

2

The smallest team is a duo. In start-ups, two-person teams enjoy higher than average success. Google founders Sergey Brin and Larry Page showed how it's done.

7 +/− 2

Project teams with five to nine members having complementary skills are the most effective. If they are organized democratically, the number of members should be odd for the sake of forming majorities.

15

Small businesses with up to 15 employees can be managed with relative ease. Everyone knows and can talk to everyone else. There's no need for a second level of management.

150

The anthropologist Robin Dunbar determined that people can keep track of up to 150 names and the essential relationships between them. For businesses, that means: Once you get to more than 150 coworkers, it gets confusing for everyone.

1,500 + X

How can many small, elective teams form a large unit? That's the reason business management invented the organizational structure.

COUNTING BEANS

What's the scoop on a company's assets and earnings? Shareholders, creditors, rating agencies, and tax officials find the answer in the company's balance sheet as well as its profit and loss statement. The balance sheet juxtaposes the company's assets with its liabilities and owner's equity as of a reporting date. The company's economic growth and financial stability can be discerned from a comparison of the balance sheets at various times.

Assets

Anything with commercial value that is owned by a business.

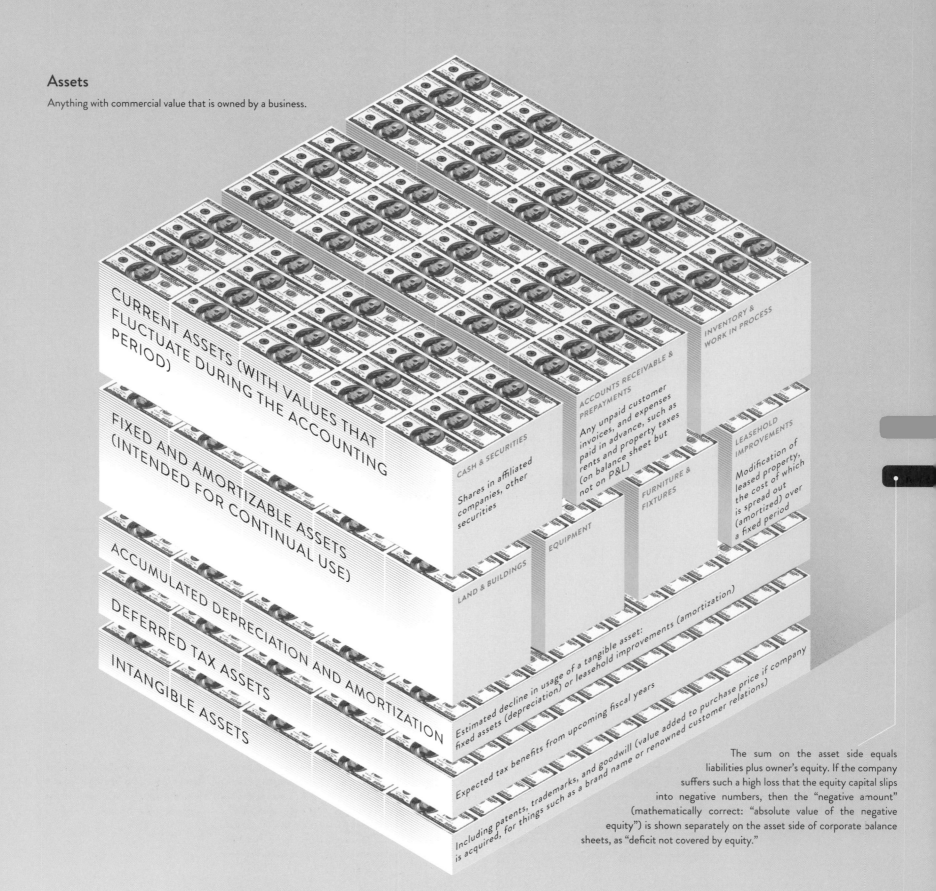

CURRENT ASSETS (WITH VALUES THAT FLUCTUATE DURING THE ACCOUNTING PERIOD)

FIXED AND AMORTIZABLE ASSETS (INTENDED FOR CONTINUAL USE)

ACCUMULATED DEPRECIATION AND AMORTIZATION

DEFERRED TAX ASSETS

INTANGIBLE ASSETS

CASH & SECURITIES

Shares in affiliated companies, other securities

ACCOUNTS RECEIVABLE & PREPAYMENTS

Any unpaid customer invoices, and expenses paid in advance, such as rents and property taxes (on balance sheet but not on P&L)

INVENTORY & WORK IN PROCESS

LAND & BUILDINGS

EQUIPMENT

FURNITURE & FIXTURES

LEASEHOLD IMPROVEMENTS

Modification of leased property, the cost of which is spread out (amortized) over a fixed period

Estimated decline in usage of a tangible asset: fixed assets (depreciation) or leasehold improvements (amortization)

Expected tax benefits from upcoming fiscal years

Including patents, trademarks, and goodwill (value added to purchase price if company is acquired, for things such as a brand name or renowned customer relations)

The sum on the asset side equals liabilities plus owner's equity. If the company suffers such a high loss that the equity capital slips into negative numbers, then the "negative amount" (mathematically correct: "absolute value of the negative equity") is shown separately on the asset side of corporate balance sheets, as "deficit not covered by equity."

THE THREE MOST IMPORTANT FUNCTIONS

Determining profits
The company's profit is the excess of revenues over expenses within an accounting period. There are two methods for determining profit, and they differ in the timing of their record-keeping. Under the accrual system, anticipated revenues and related expenses are tied together, while the cash system records when cash actually changes hands.

Documenting the day-to-day company actions
The balance sheet is a listing of the items making up the two sides of the equation below: Assets on one side, liabilities and owner's equity on the other. It's a snapshot of a business's accounting records at a particular moment.

A more detailed overview
A profit and loss statement (P&L) is a summary of a company's revenues, costs, and expenses during an accounting period. Offering a more detailed portrait of a company's finances, it shows the results of operations over a fixed period of time.

Liabilities and Owner's Equity

Liabilities are claims on the assets of a company. Owner's equity is the value of the business, represented by the difference between assets and liabilities.

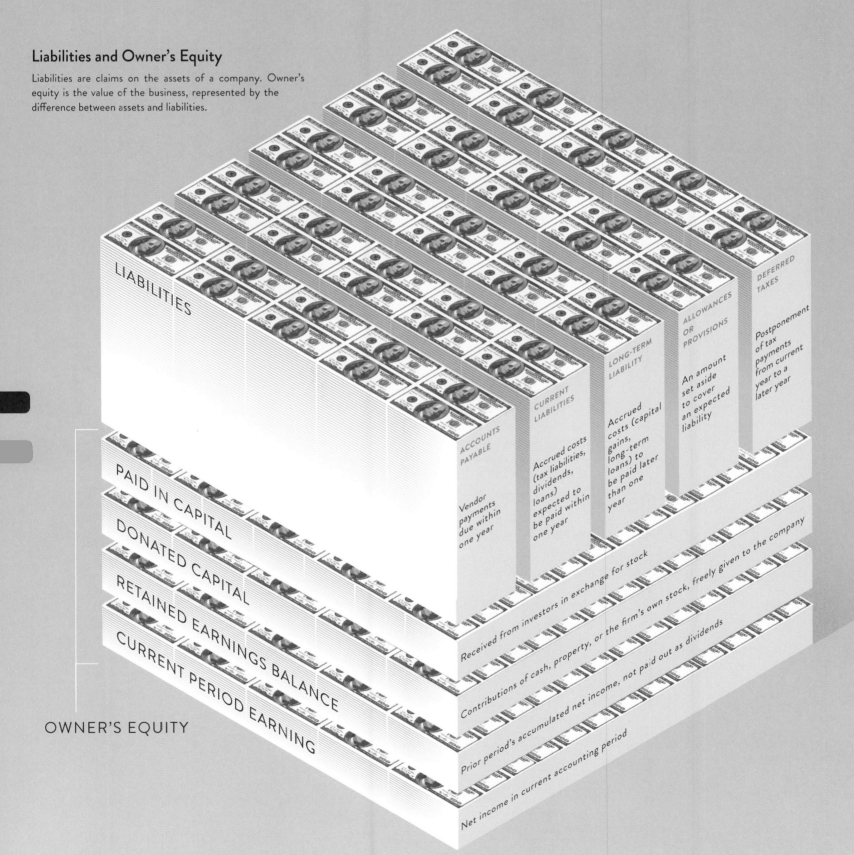

LIABILITIES

ACCOUNTS PAYABLE
Vendor payments due within one year

CURRENT LIABILITIES
Accrued costs (tax liabilities, dividends, loans) expected to be paid within one year

LONG-TERM LIABILITY
Accrued costs (capital gains, long-term loans) to be paid later than one year

ALLOWANCES OR PROVISIONS
An amount set aside to cover an expected liability

DEFERRED TAXES
Postponement of tax payments from current year to a later year

OWNER'S EQUITY

PAID IN CAPITAL — Received from investors in exchange for stock

DONATED CAPITAL — Contributions of cash, property, or the firm's own stock, freely given to the company

RETAINED EARNINGS BALANCE — Prior period's accumulated net income, not paid out as dividends

CURRENT PERIOD EARNING — Net income in current accounting period

FUNNELED IN!

Marketing is preparing to sell. Many marketing strategies build on the concept of a sales funnel. Advertising attracts attention. Targeted marketing activities then lead potential customers step by step (or from one point of contact to the next) to make a purchase. The more effective the advertising is, the more customers finally buy the product. A multistage model has been used in advertising for over a century, called AIDA. It was originally used primarily for the design of individual advertisements. AIDA remains the mother of all forms of push marketing up to the present.

Awareness
The customer's attention is aroused.

Interest
The customer begins to take interest in the product. Marketing offers its support—with additional information, for example.

The four P's are the basic principles of marketing. They help to position a product or a service in the marketplace. Companies who don't master them seldom go far.

Desire
Interest turns into the desire to own something. Marketing intensifies this emotion.

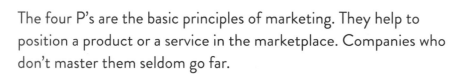

PRODUCT
The basis of all success in business. If the quality isn't good, it had better be cheap.

PRICE
Expensive can be bad and cheap can be good for a company. The crucial point is: How well does a company know its customers' willingness to pay?

PLACE
Where does a product reach its customers? Today, the place can also be on the Internet.

PROMOTION
How and with whom does a company communicate, and in which channel, and with what message?

EXTENSIONS OF AIDA

AIDA**S**   **Satisfaction** (The customer's desire is satisfied.)
AID**C**A   **Conviction** (The product is convincing compared to other products.)

ALTERNATIVES TO AIDA

DAGMAR assumes that advertising must be able to do more than sell things. It emphasizes that advertising only has an effect if it penetrates various hierarchical levels of the consumer's consciousness.

DEFINING **A**DVERTISING **G**OALS FOR **M**EASURED **A**DVERTISING **R**ESULTS

Contact: Is the advertising noticed?
Uptake: Is the advertising information recognized quickly?
Understanding: Is the advertising message immediately understood by the target audience?
Internalization: Is the core message easily absorbed?
Attitude: Is the advertising message delivered credibly, sympathetically, and in a visually memorable way?
Action: It ends with the sale.

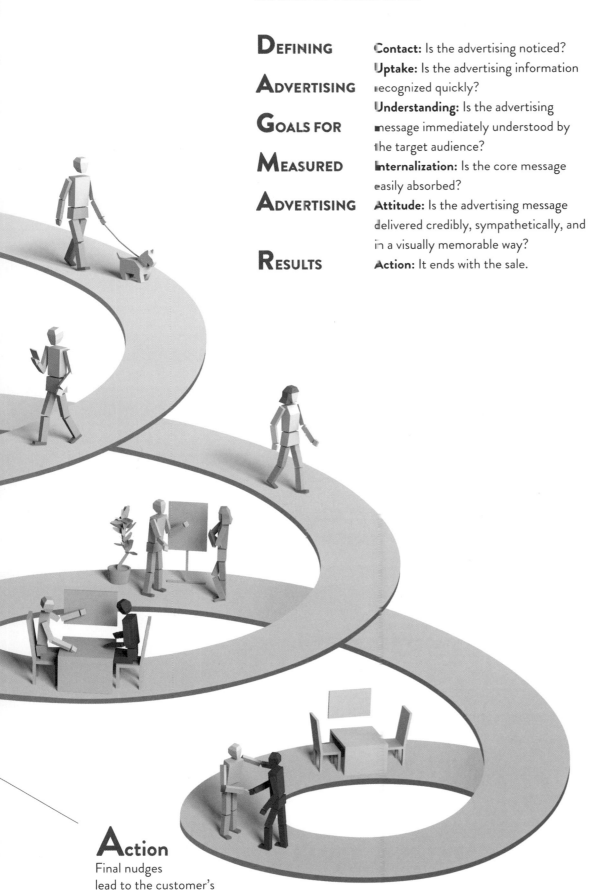

Action
Final nudges lead to the customer's action. Action means sales.

STAGES OF DEVELOPMENT IN MARKETING
according to Manfred Bruhn

1950 Product orientation in the 1950s (mere production, due to the enormous demand during the postwar period)

1960 Sales orientation in the 1960s (from production to distribution)

1970 Market orientation in the 1970s (market segmentation; specializing in individual needs)

1980 Competitive orientation in the 1980s (emphasis on unique selling points)

1990 Context orientation in the 1990s (in response to ecological, political, technological, or social changes)

2000 Dialogue orientation since 2000 (interactivity of Internet and email communication)

2010 Network orientation since 2010 (Web 2.0, social networks, word of mouth)

THE 10 BIGGEST ADVERTISING BUDGETS IN THE USA
Based on 2016 US ad spending (in US$ Mn)

Geico	1,400
Verizon	1,100
Chevrolet	926
AT&T	905
Ford	892
Apple	750
Toyota	743
T-Mobile	741
Samsung	733

THE "BUY IT NOW" BUTTONS IN YOUR HEAD

Why do we buy something? The field of neuromarketing builds on the assumption that many purchase decisions are caused by emotional triggers in the brain. Psychology describes these triggers as key stimuli. Advertising and marketing try to systematically appeal to deep emotional needs—in order to repress the role of reason in the purchase decision process.

Love is stronger than greed. So don't haggle with someone selling roses, even if one flower costs $5.

Yes, status consumption is embarrassing. Funny how the allure of "premium" works so well, no matter what product category.

Old-age poverty? Disability? A break-in at home? Not for you. You have insurance policies and door locks that are so advanced you can't tell if they're worth the money.

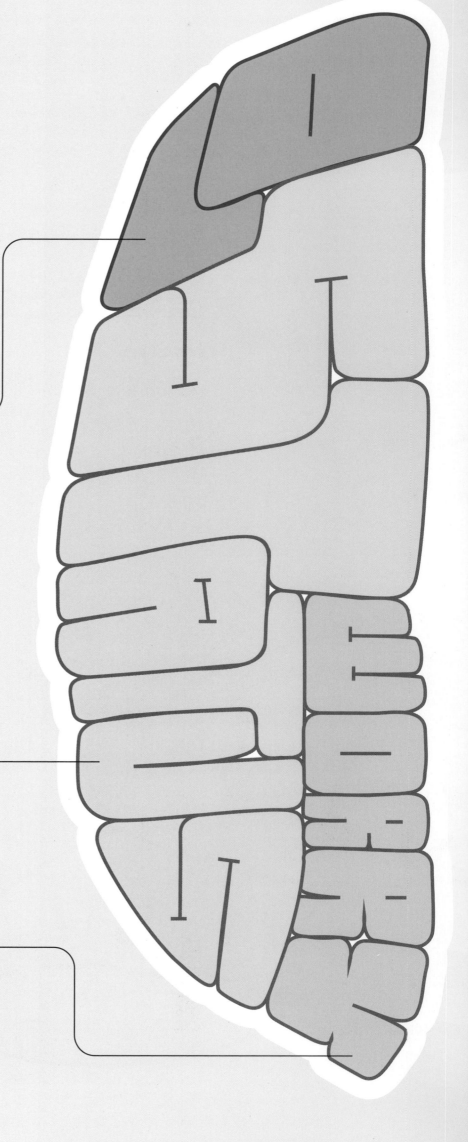

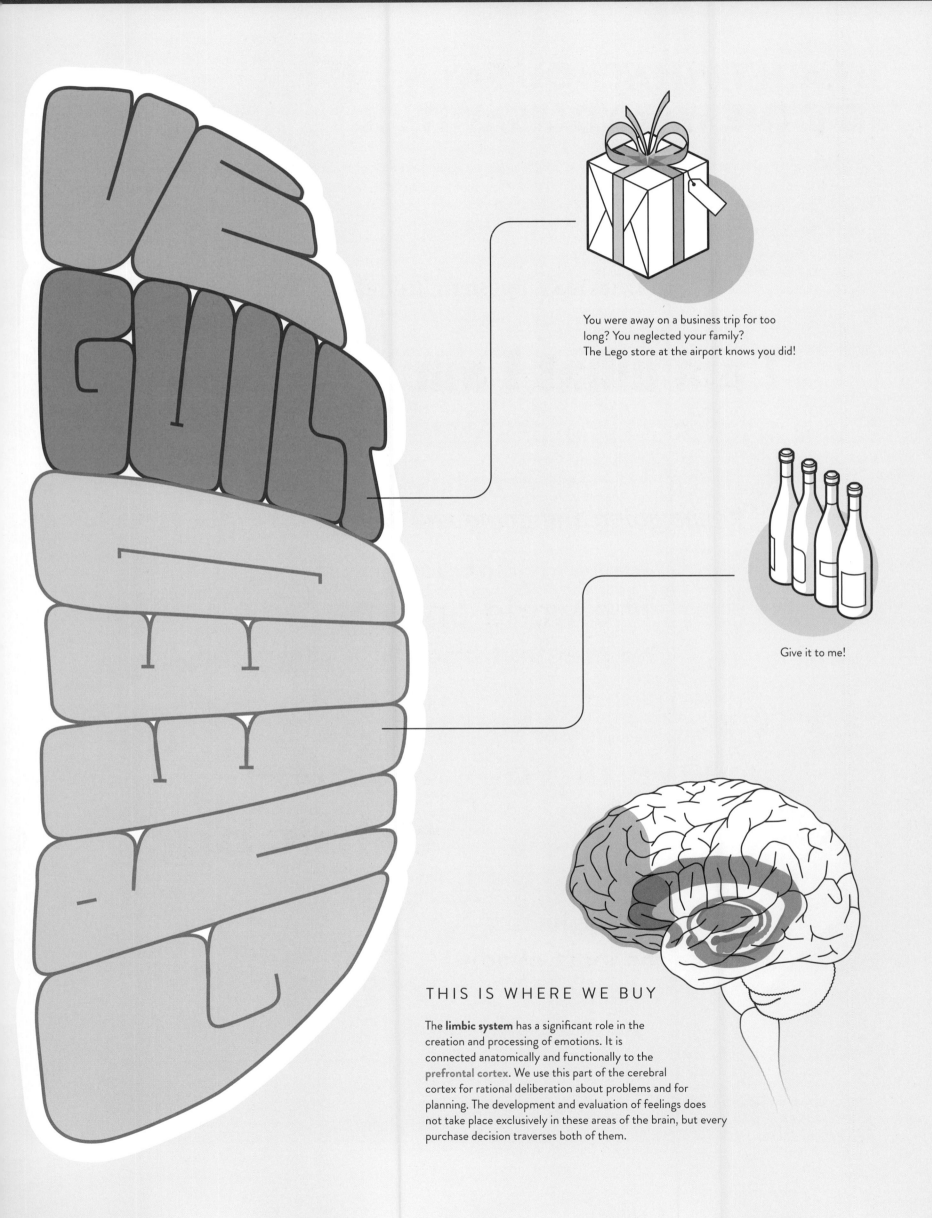

You were away on a business trip for too long? You neglected your family?
The Lego store at the airport knows you did!

Give it to me!

THIS IS WHERE WE BUY

The **limbic system** has a significant role in the creation and processing of emotions. It is connected anatomically and functionally to the **prefrontal cortex**. We use this part of the cerebral cortex for rational deliberation about problems and for planning. The development and evaluation of feelings does not take place exclusively in these areas of the brain, but every purchase decision traverses both of them.

IT AIN'T WHAT YOU SAY, IT'S THE WAY YOU SAY IT . . .

"Our product is great—please buy it." If this line worked, companies could save a lot of money. But it's not that simple—so advertising has evolved into a highly specialized industry, crafting sophisticated messages to attract attention and entice people to buy. In 2016, total ad spending represented 1% of the US GDP. To paraphrase jazz legend Ella Fitzgerald: it's not what you say—it's the way you say it—that gets results.

American by Birth. Rebel by Choice. [1]

Think small [2]

The Happiest Place on Earth [3]

I am what I am [4]

QUALITY NEVER GOES OUT OF STYLE [5]

IMPOSSIBLE IS NOTHING [6]

JUST DO IT. [7]

Innovation [8]

Finger Lickin' Good. [9]

Keeps going and going and going [10]

HAVE IT YOUR WAY. [11]

make.believe [12]

The world on time. [13]

The greatest tragedy is indifference. [14]

When you care enough to send the very best. [15]

FOR THE MEN IN CHARGE OF CHANGE. [16]

LIVE IN YOUR WORLD. PLAY IN OURS. [17]

Let your fingers do the walking. [18]

think big. [19]

Challenge Everything [20]

Taste the feeling [21]

Melts in your mouth, not in your hands. [22]

make the most of now [23]

Think different. [24]

1 Harley-Davidson 2 Volkswagen 3 Disneyland 4 Reebok 5 Levi's 6 Adidas 7 Nike 8 3M 9 KFC 10 Energizer 11 Burger King 12 Sony 13 FedEx 14 Red Cross 15 Hallmark 16 Fortune 17 PlayStation 18 Yellow Pages 19 IMAX 20 Electronic Arts 21 Coca-Cola 22 M&M's 23 Vodafone 24 Apple

Global Ad Spending 2017

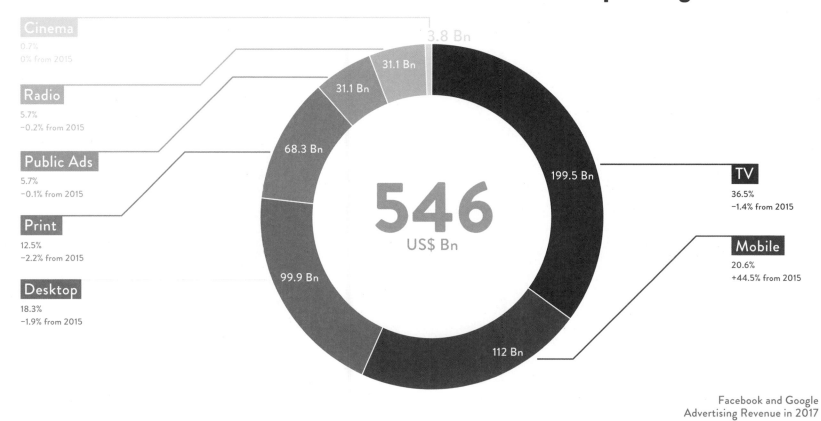

Cinema
0.7%
0% from 2015

3.8 Bn

31.1 Bn

31.1 Bn

Radio
5.7%
−0.2% from 2015

Public Ads
5.7%
−0.1% from 2015

68.3 Bn

Print
12.5%
−2.2% from 2015

199.5 Bn

546
US$ Bn

TV
36.5%
−1.4% from 2015

Mobile
20.6%
+44.5% from 2015

Desktop
18.3%
−1.9% from 2015

99.9 Bn

112 Bn

Facebook and Google
Advertising Revenue in 2017

133.2
US$ Bn

World's 5 Largest Advertisers

Total Ad Spending

Who	What	Where	Amount (US$ Bn)
Procter & Gamble	Personal Care & Housekeeping	USA	10.4
Unilever	Personal Care & Housekeeping	UK-NL	8.9
L'Oréal	Cosmetics	France	8.2
Volkswagen	Cars	Germany	6.6
Comcast	Media	USA	5.9

Ad Spending by Region

In US$ Bn

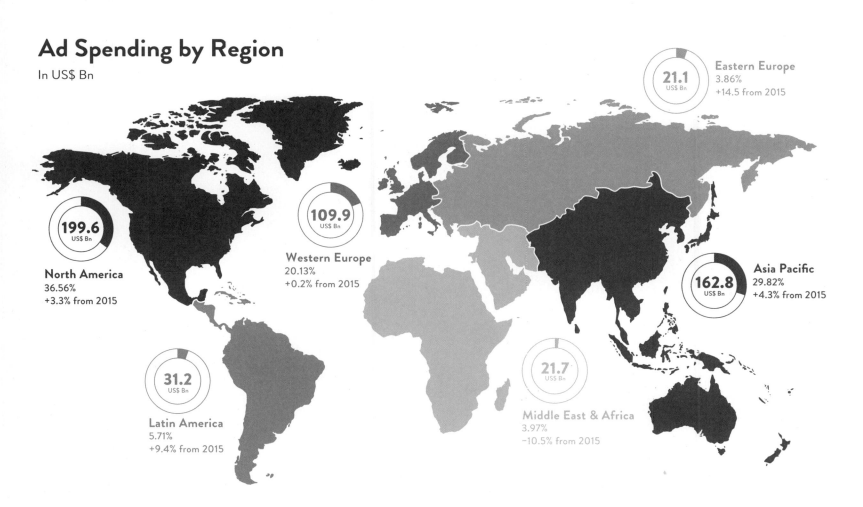

21.1 US$ Bn
Eastern Europe
3.86%
+14.5 from 2015

109.9 US$ Bn
Western Europe
20.13%
+0.2% from 2015

199.6 US$ Bn
North America
36.56%
+3.3% from 2015

162.8 US$ Bn
Asia Pacific
29.82%
+4.3% from 2015

31.2 US$ Bn
Latin America
5.71%
+9.4% from 2015

21.7 US$ Bn
Middle East & Africa
3.97%
−10.5% from 2015

III

THE NATIONAL ECONOMY

LET'S ADD IT ALL UP . . .

The gross domestic product describes how productive a national economy is. It's calculated from the total value of goods and services that are produced in a national economy in a year. Dividing it by the size of the population yields an important factor (GDP per capita) for comparing a country's prosperity.

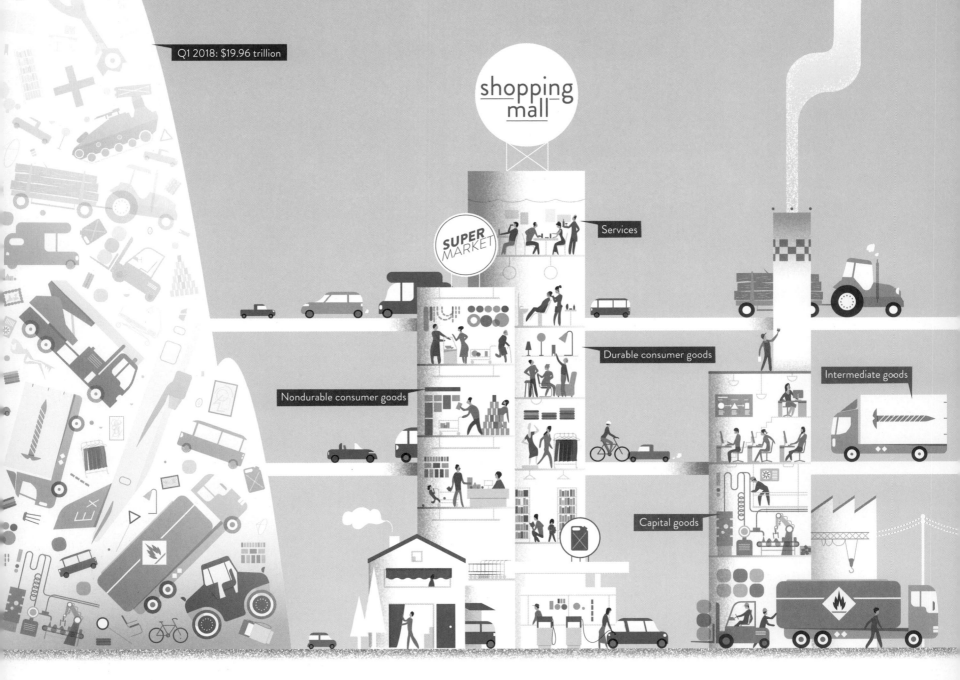

Q1 2018: $19.96 trillion

shopping mall

SUPER MARKET

Services

Nondurable consumer goods

Durable consumer goods

Intermediate goods

Capital goods

$$GDP = C + I +$$

At market prices, the gross domestic product is calculated from . . .

. . . personal consumption expenditures . . .

. . . plus private investment . . .

Collective consumption

Export goods

Import goods

Individual consumption

$$G + (Ex - Im)$$

... plus government spending (government consumption, public investment, social transfers, subsidies, transfers to intergovernmental organizations) ...

... taking into account the net exports, or the difference between exports and imports.

TO HAVE AND HAVE NOT

The economic history of the United States is one of growth:
of general wealth and of federal debt.

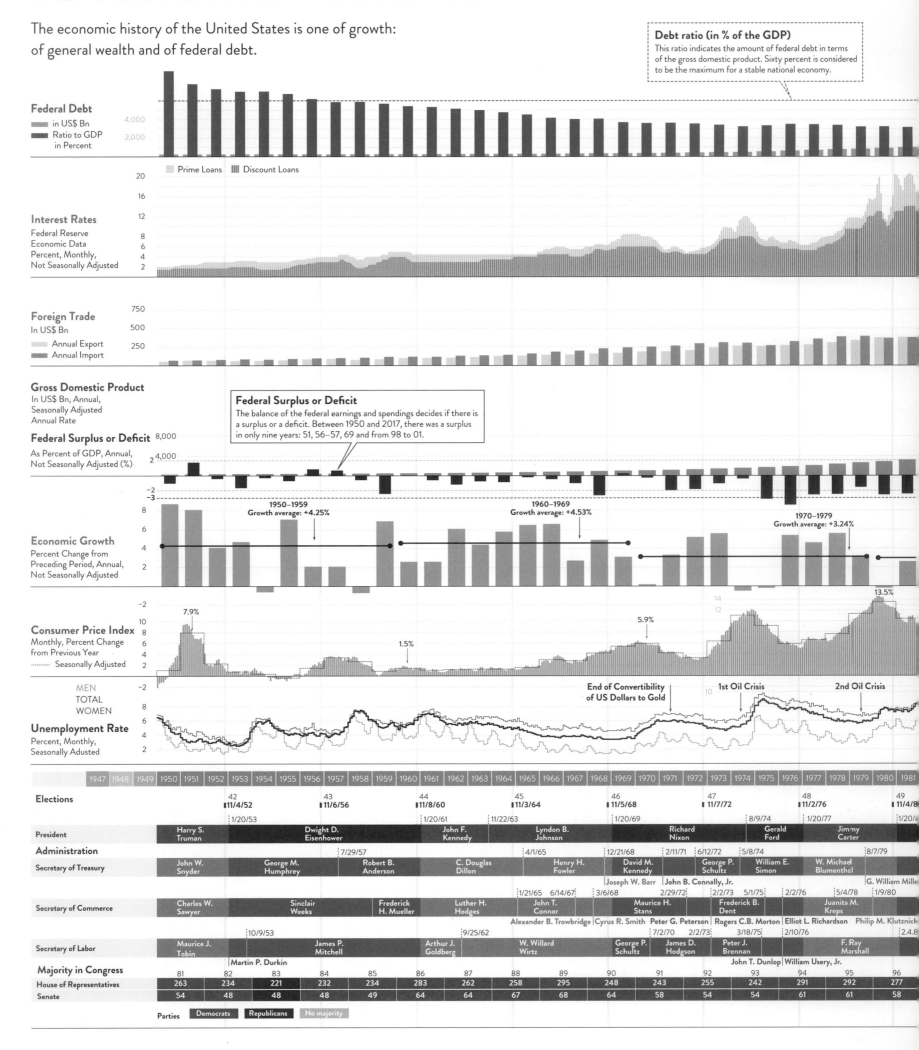

Debt ratio (in % of the GDP)
This ratio indicates the amount of federal debt in terms
of the gross domestic product. Sixty percent is considered
to be the maximum for a stable national economy.

Federal Debt
in US$ Bn
Ratio to GDP
in Percent

4,000
2,000

Prime Loans   Discount Loans

Interest Rates
Federal Reserve
Economic Data
Percent, Monthly,
Not Seasonally Adjusted

20
16
12
8
6
4
2

Foreign Trade
In US$ Bn
Annual Export
Annual Import

750
500
250

Gross Domestic Product
In US$ Bn, Annual,
Seasonally Adjusted
Annual Rate

Federal Surplus or Deficit
The balance of the federal earnings and spendings decides if there is
a surplus or a deficit. Between 1950 and 2017, there was a surplus
in only nine years: 51, 56–57, 69 and from 98 to 01.

Federal Surplus or Deficit
As Percent of GDP, Annual,
Not Seasonally Adjusted (%)

8,000
4,000
-2
-3

Economic Growth
Percent Change from
Preceding Period, Annual,
Not Seasonally Adjusted

8
6
4
2

1950–1959
Growth average: +4.25%

1960–1969
Growth average: +4.53%

1970–1979
Growth average: +3.24%

Consumer Price Index
Monthly, Percent Change
from Previous Year
------- Seasonally Adjusted

7.9%
1.5%
5.9%
13.5%
14
12
10
8
6
4
2
-2

Unemployment Rate
Percent, Monthly,
Seasonally Adusted

MEN
TOTAL
WOMEN

End of Convertibility
of US Dollars to Gold
1st Oil Crisis
2nd Oil Crisis

8
6
4
2
10

	1947	1948	1949	1950	1951	1952	1953	1954	1955	1956	1957	1958	1959	1960	1961	1962	1963	1964	1965	1966	1967	1968	1969	1970	1971	1972	1973	1974	1975	1976	1977	1978	1979	1980	1981

Elections
42 ■11/4/52
43 ■11/6/56
44 ■11/8/60
45 ■11/3/64
46 ■11/5/68
47 ■11/7/72
48 ■11/2/76
49 ■11/4/8

1/20/53
1/20/61   11/22/63
1/20/69
8/9/74   1/20/77
1/20/

President
Harry S. Truman
Dwight D. Eisenhower
John F. Kennedy
Lyndon B. Johnson
Richard Nixon
Gerald Ford
Jimmy Carter

Administration
7/29/57
4/1/65
12/21/68 2/11/71 6/12/72 5/8/74
8/7/79

Secretary of Treasury
John W. Snyder
George M. Humphrey
Robert B. Anderson
C. Douglas Dillon
Henry H. Fowler
David M. Kennedy
George P. Schultz
William E. Simon
W. Michael Blumenthal
G. William Mille
Joseph W. Barr | John B. Connally, Jr.
1/21/65 6/14/67   3/6/68 2/29/72   2/2/73   5/1/75   2/2/76   5/4/78   1/9/80

Secretary of Commerce
Charles W. Sawyer
Sinclair Weeks
Frederick H. Mueller
Luther H. Hodges
John T. Connor
Maurice H. Stans
Frederick B. Dent
Juanita M. Kreps
Philip M. Klutznick
Alexander B. Trowbridge   Cyrus R. Smith   Peter G. Peterson   Rogers C.B. Morton   Elliot L. Richardson
10/9/53   9/25/62   7/2/70   2/2/73   3/18/75   2/10/76   2.4.8

Secretary of Labor
Maurice J. Tobin
James P. Mitchell
Arthur J. Goldberg
W. Willard Wirtz
George P. Schultz
James D. Hodgson
Peter J. Brennan
F. Ray Marshall
Martin P. Durkin
John T. Dunlop | William Usery, Jr.

Majority in Congress

	81	82	83	84	85	86	87	88	89	90	91	92	93	94	95	96
House of Representatives	263	234	221	232	234	283	262	258	295	248	243	255	242	291	292	277
Senate	54	48	48	48	49	64	64	67	68	64	58	54	54	61	61	58

Parties   Democrats   Republicans   No majority

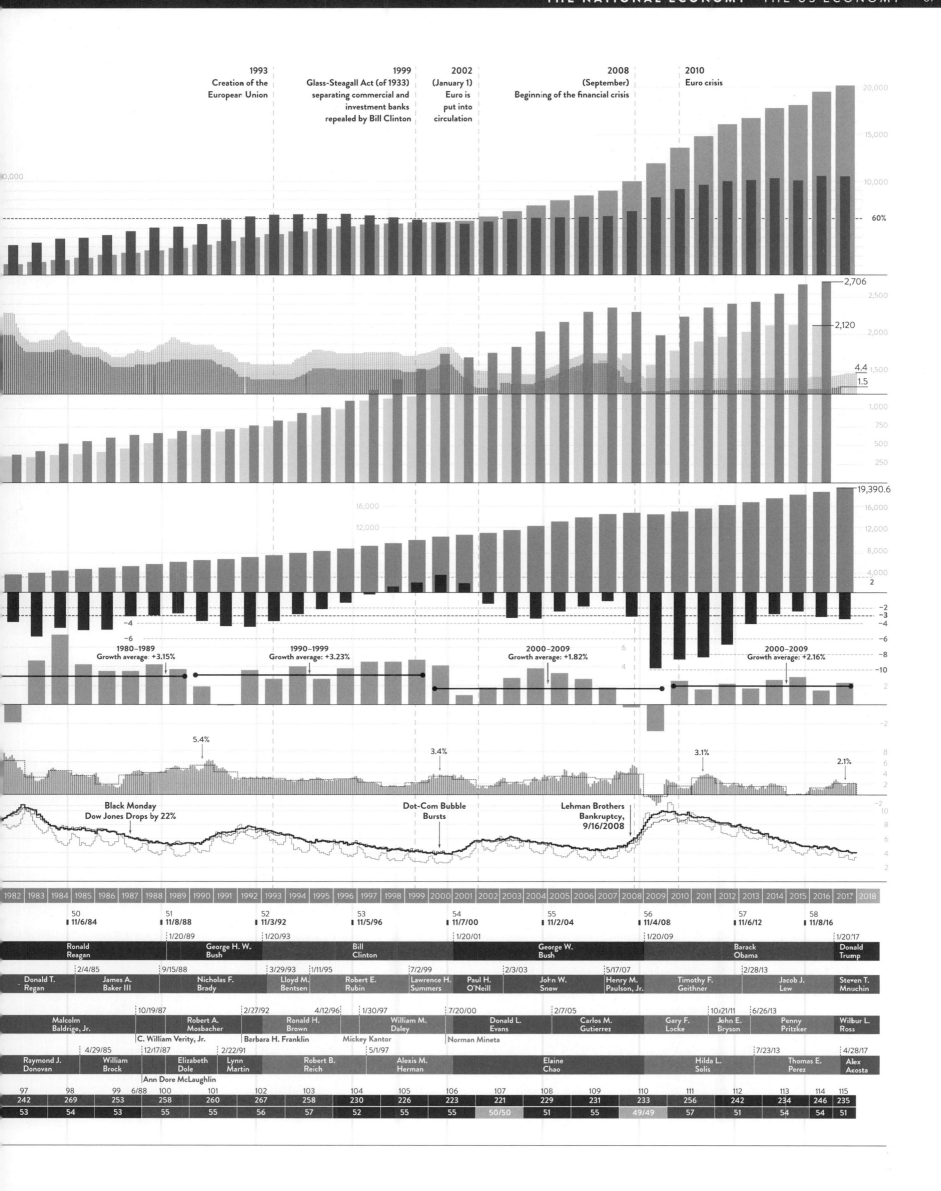

1993
Creation of the
European Union

1999
Glass-Steagall Act (of 1933)
separating commercial and
investment banks
repealed by Bill Clinton

2002
(January 1)
Euro is
put into
circulation

2008
(September)
Beginning of the financial crisis

2010
Euro crisis

2,706

2,120

4.4
1.5

19,390.6

1980–1989
Growth average: +3.15%

1990–1999
Growth average: +3.23%

2000–2009
Growth average: +1.82%

2000–2009
Growth average: +2.16%

5.4%

3.4%

3.1%

2.1%

Black Monday
Dow Jones Drops by 22%

Dot-Com Bubble
Bursts

Lehman Brothers
Bankruptcy,
9/16/2008

| 1982 | 1983 | 1984 | 1985 | 1986 | 1987 | 1988 | 1989 | 1990 | 1991 | 1992 | 1993 | 1994 | 1995 | 1996 | 1997 | 1998 | 1999 | 2000 | 2001 | 2002 | 2003 | 2004 | 2005 | 2006 | 2007 | 2008 | 2009 | 2010 | 2011 | 2012 | 2013 | 2014 | 2015 | 2016 | 2017 | 2018 |

50
11/6/84

51
11/8/88

52
11/3/92

53
11/5/96

54
11/7/00

55
11/2/04

56
11/4/08

57
11/6/12

58
11/8/16

1/20/89   1/20/93   1/20/01   1/20/09   1/20/17

Ronald
Reagan

George H. W.
Bush

Bill
Clinton

George W.
Bush

Barack
Obama

Donald
Trump

2/4/85   9/15/88   3/29/93   1/11/95   7/2/99   2/3/03   5/17/07   2/28/13

Donald T.
Regan

James A.
Baker III

Nicholas F.
Brady

Lloyd M.
Bentsen

Robert E.
Rubin

Lawrence H.
Summers

Paul H.
O'Neill

John W.
Snow

Henry M.
Paulson, Jr.

Timothy F.
Geithner

Jacob J.
Lew

Steven T.
Mnuchin

10/19/87   2/27/92   4/12/96   1/30/97   7/20/00   2/7/05   10/21/11   6/26/13

Malcolm
Baldrige, Jr.

Robert A.
Mosbacher

Ronald H.
Brown

William M.
Daley

Donald L.
Evans

Carlos M.
Gutierrez

Gary F.
Locke

John E.
Bryson

Penny
Pritzker

Wilbur L.
Ross

C. William Verity, Jr.   Barbara H. Franklin   Mickey Kantor   Norman Mineta

4/29/85   12/17/87   2/22/91   5/1/97   7/23/13   4/28/17

Raymond J.
Donovan

William
Brock

Elizabeth
Dole

Lynn
Martin

Robert B.
Reich

Alexis M.
Herman

Elaine
Chao

Hilda L.
Solis

Thomas E.
Perez

Alex
Acosta

Ann Dore McLaughlin

97	98	99	6/88	100	101	102	103	104	105	106	107	108	109	110	111	112	113	114	115
242	269	253		258	260	267	258	230	226	223	221	229	231	233	256	242	234	246	235
53	54	53		55	55	56	57	52	55	55	50/50	51	55	49/49	57	51	54	54	51

THE ECONOMIC MIXING TABLE

Economic policy regulates and affects things. That is to say, it defines economic goals. It creates the legal framework within which primarily private participants act. And it intervenes in the economy through a series of business-cycle policy measures. And when that doesn't help? Then the music stops and the political DJs get voted out of office. . . .

MAIN DIRECTIONS IN ECONOMIC POLICY

ON · OFF

Supply-side economics
(supply-oriented economic policy) puts the yield expectations of investors at the center of its analysis. Its instruments therefore primarily relate to the economic policy framework (monetary stability, wages, regulations governing working hours, taxes, etc.).

ON · **OFF**

Demand-side economics
(demand-oriented economic policy) focuses on stabilizing overall economic development. Its tools are countercyclical fiscal policy (such as boosting spending if private-sector demand is weak or reducing spending in cases of excess demand), as well as expansionary and/or contractionary monetary policy.

MEASURED VARIABLES

COST OF LIVING INFLATION RATE, INDEX

UNEMPLOYMENT RATE

"MAGIC SQUARE"

QUANTITATIVE TARGETS

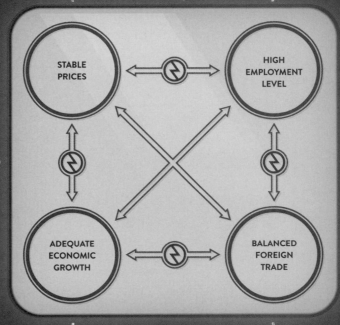

STABLE PRICES

HIGH EMPLOYMENT LEVEL

ADEQUATE ECONOMIC GROWTH

BALANCED FOREIGN TRADE

MEASURED VARIABLES

GROSS NATIONAL INCOME/ GROSS DOMESTIC PRODUCT

NET EXPORT RATIO*

 *CONFLICTING GOALS*

The economic theory of the "magic square" was developed by the economist Nicholas Kaldor. The word "magic" hints at its element of fantasy: The government, central bank, and social partners would have to be magicians to attain a perfectly balanced economy, especially since some objectives compete against one another. Growth and high employment typically lead to higher prices, for example. In addition to the quantitative goals of the magic square, there are also qualitative ones, like equitable income distribution or environmental conservation.

*Net exports (exports minus imports of goods and services) divided by nominal GDP times 100

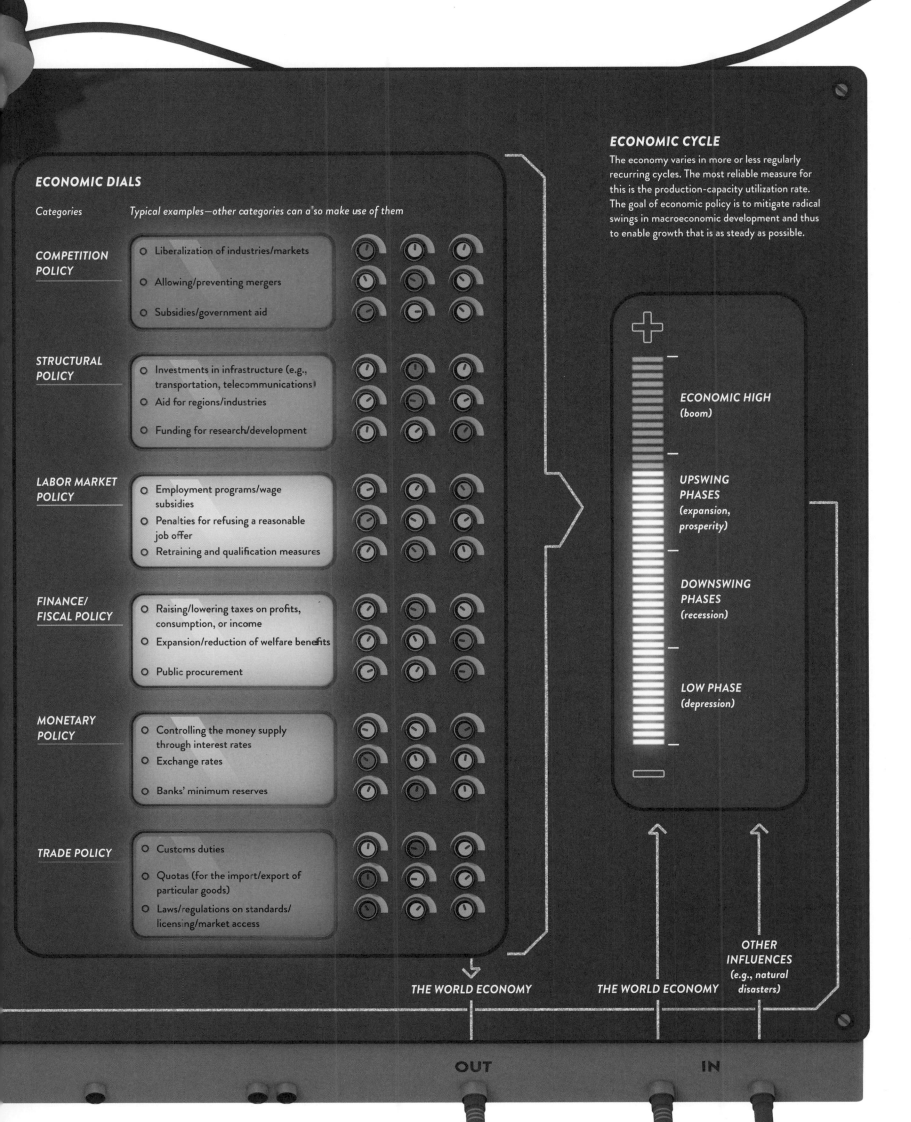

ECONOMIC DIALS

Categories   Typical examples—other categories can also make use of them

COMPETITION POLICY
- Liberalization of industries/markets
- Allowing/preventing mergers
- Subsidies/government aid

STRUCTURAL POLICY
- Investments in infrastructure (e.g., transportation, telecommunications)
- Aid for regions/industries
- Funding for research/development

LABOR MARKET POLICY
- Employment programs/wage subsidies
- Penalties for refusing a reasonable job offer
- Retraining and qualification measures

FINANCE/ FISCAL POLICY
- Raising/lowering taxes on profits, consumption, or income
- Expansion/reduction of welfare benefits
- Public procurement

MONETARY POLICY
- Controlling the money supply through interest rates
- Exchange rates
- Banks' minimum reserves

TRADE POLICY
- Customs duties
- Quotas (for the import/export of particular goods)
- Laws/regulations on standards/ licensing/market access

ECONOMIC CYCLE

The economy varies in more or less regularly recurring cycles. The most reliable measure for this is the production-capacity utilization rate. The goal of economic policy is to mitigate radical swings in macroeconomic development and thus to enable growth that is as steady as possible.

ECONOMIC HIGH (boom)

UPSWING PHASES (expansion, prosperity)

DOWNSWING PHASES (recession)

LOW PHASE (depression)

THE WORLD ECONOMY

THE WORLD ECONOMY

OTHER INFLUENCES (e.g., natural disasters)

OUT

IN

BIG SPENDER

The government has power. Purchasing power. Combined, the US government at the federal, state, and local levels buys goods and services worth roughly $7 trillion annually. Economists use the term "gross investment." Some say that certain investments will even pay off.

SPENDING BY THE US GOVERNMENT, 2017
In US$ Bn

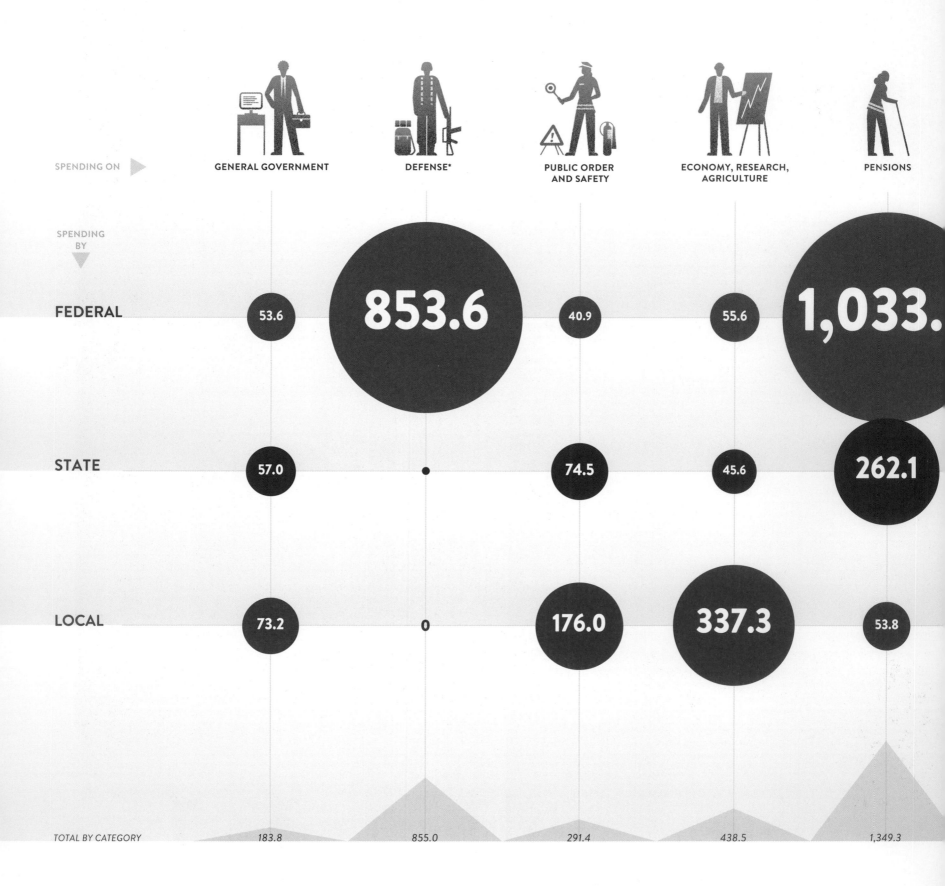

SPENDING ON ▶

	GENERAL GOVERNMENT	DEFENSE*	PUBLIC ORDER AND SAFETY	ECONOMY, RESEARCH, AGRICULTURE	PENSIONS
FEDERAL	53.6	853.6	40.9	55.6	1,033.
STATE	57.0	•	74.5	45.6	262.1
LOCAL	73.2	0	176.0	337.3	53.8
TOTAL BY CATEGORY	183.8	855.0	291.4	438.5	1,349.3

SPENDING BY ▼

Gross domestic product: $19.8 Tn

13.65   Personal consumption expenditures

3.41   Government consumption expenditures
and gross investment

3.30   Gross private domestic investment

−0.60   Net export of goods and services

GOVERNMENT REVENUE AND SPENDING, 2017

Revenue: $3.3 Tn

Spending: $4 Tn

1.6   Income taxes
1.2   Payroll taxes
0.3   Corporate income taxes
0.3   Other taxes & revenues

0.94   Social security
0.61   Nondefense
0.59   Medicare
0.59   Defense**
0.38   Medicaid
0.26   Interest of Debt
0.61   Other

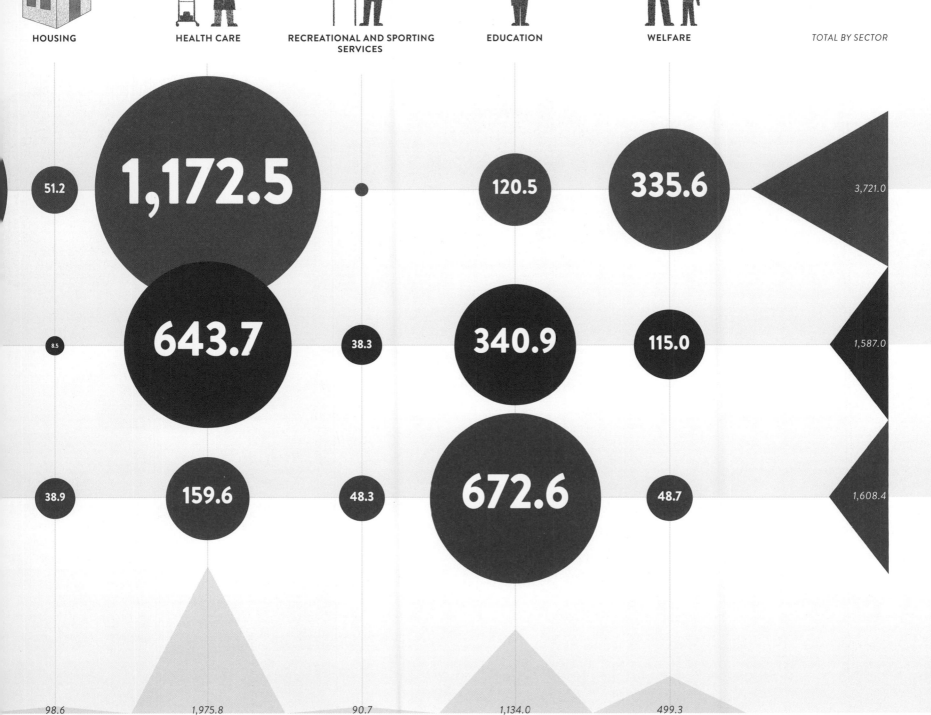

HOUSING   **HEALTH CARE**   **RECREATIONAL AND SPORTING SERVICES**   **EDUCATION**   **WELFARE**   *TOTAL BY SECTOR*

51.2   1,172.5   •   120.5   335.6   3,721.0

8.5   643.7   38.3   340.9   115.0   1,587.0

38.9   159.6   48.3   672.6   48.7   1,608.4

98.6   1,975.8   90.7   1,134.0   499.3

*Including foreign economic and military aid, veterans. **Without foreign economic and military aid, veterans.*

MONEY FLOWS

Companies produce. To do so, they use labor, land, and capital. Private households consume. To do so, they have to sell labor, lease land, and loan money. In this way, two money flows with equivalent value are created. The economist Herbert Sperber represents them as two inverse cycles. Interaction takes place on the "factor markets" and "consumer goods markets."

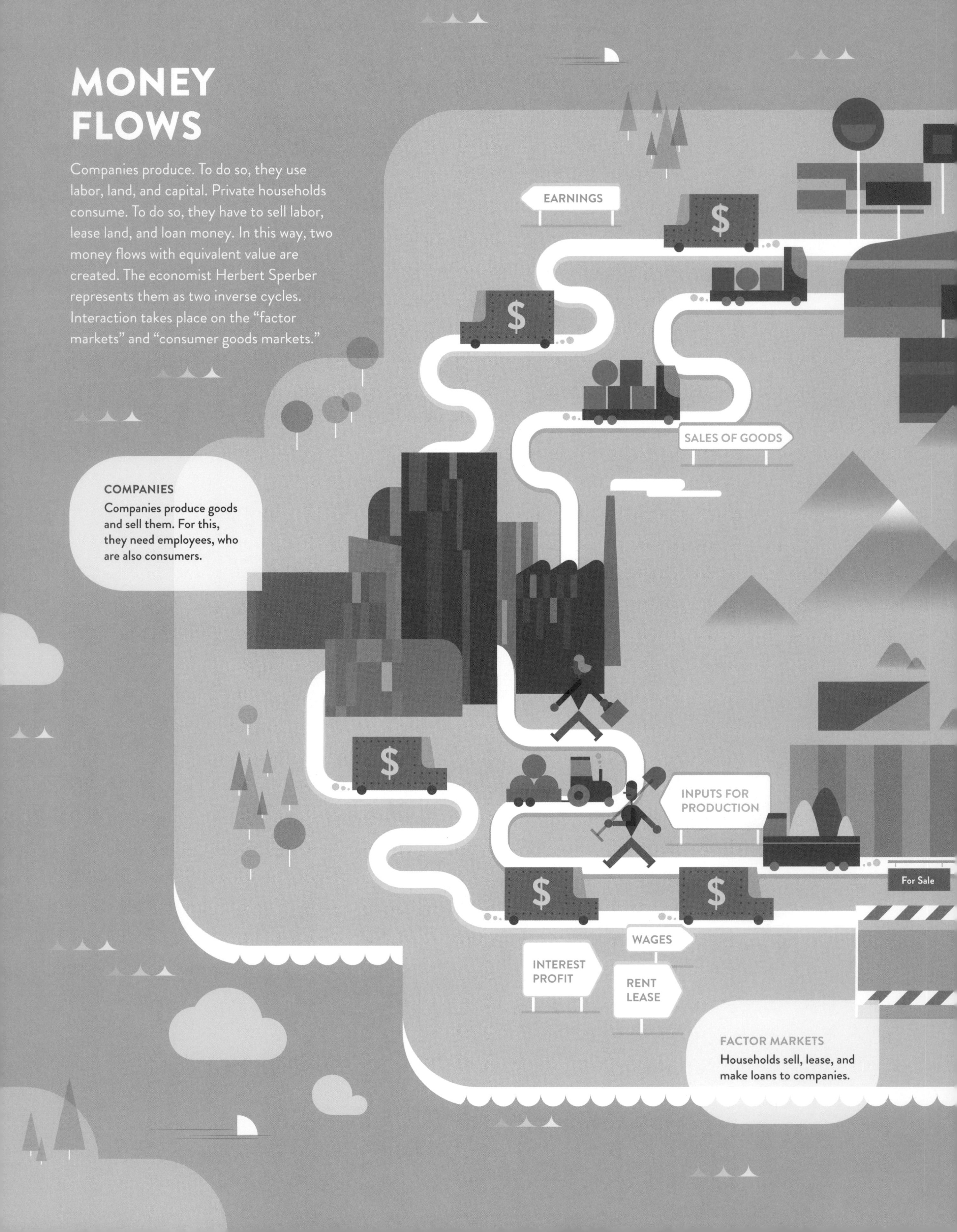

EARNINGS

$

$

SALES OF GOODS

COMPANIES
Companies produce goods and sell them. For this, they need employees, who are also consumers.

$

$

INPUTS FOR PRODUCTION

$

$

For Sale

WAGES

INTEREST PROFIT

RENT LEASE

FACTOR MARKETS
Households sell, lease, and make loans to companies.

CONSUMER GOODS MARKETS
Companies sell.
Households buy.

EXPENSES

PURCHASE OF GOODS

HOUSEHOLDS
Private households sell "factor services" (primarily their labor). With the proceeds, they then buy companies' goods (in whose production they take part).

For Lease

WORK
LAND
CAPITAL

For Lease

For Loan

For Sale

INCOME

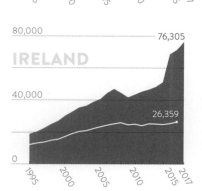

ICELAND
80,000
40,000
53,518
26,021
0
1995 2000 2005 2010 2015 2017

DENMARK
80,000
40,000
50,541
31,972
0
1995 2000 2005 2010 2015 2017

NORWAY
80,000
60,978
40,000
38,302
0
1995 2000 2005 2010 2015 2017

SWEDEN
80,000
40,000
50,069
32,508
0
1995 2000 2005 2010 2015 2017

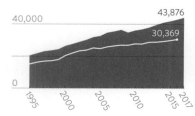

IRELAND
80,000
76,305
40,000
26,359
0
1995 2000 2005 2010 2015 2017

IT'S GROWING!

Is the world getting better or worse? It's hard to say. But statistically it's clear: In most countries, people are becoming more and more wealthy—at least on average. That's what World Bank and OECD data on gross domestic product and available household income per capita show.

GDP per capita in US$

Household disposable income per capita in US$ (if data available)

Europe	Africa
North America	Asia
South America	Australia

*Not a member state of the OECD (Organization for Economic Cooperation and Development)

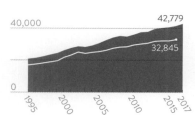

UNITED KINGDOM
80,000
40,000
43,876
30,369
0
1995 2000 2005 2010 2015 2017

NETHERLANDS
80,000
52,941
40,000
31,633
0
1995 2000 2005 2010 2015 2017

CZECH REPUBLIC
80,000
40,000
36,916
20,000
22,495
0
1995 2000 2005 2010 2015 2017

POLAND
80,000
40,000
29,291
20,000
20,295
0
1995 2000 2005 2010 2015 2017

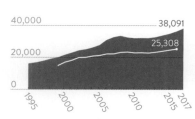

FRANCE
80,000
40,000
42,779
32,845
0
1995 2000 2005 2010 2015 2017

GERMANY
80,000
40,000
50,716
36,871
0
1995 2000 2005 2010 2015 2017

AUSTRIA
80,000
40,000
52,557
35,282
0
1995 2000 2005 2010 2015 2017

SLOVAKIA
80,000
40,000
32,110
20,000
21,566
0
1995 2000 2005 2010 2015 2017

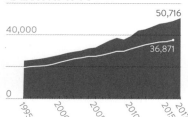

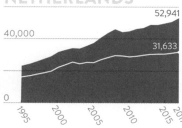

SPAIN
80,000
40,000
38,091
20,000
25,308
0
1995 2000 2005 2010 2015 2017

BELGIUM
80,000
40,000
47,561
32,364
2017
2015
0
1995 2000 2005 2010 2015 2017

SWITZERLAND
80,000
65,007
40,000
39,441
0
1995 2000 2005 2010 2015 2017

HUNGARY
80,000
40,000
28,375
20,000
17,226
0
1995 2000 2005 2010 2015 2017

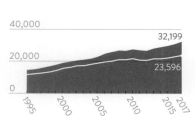

PORTUGAL
80,000
40,000
32,199
20,000
23,596
0
1995 2000 2005 2010 2015 2017

LUXEMBOURG
103,662
80,000
40,000
41,396
0
1995 2000 2005 2010 2015 2017

ITALY
80,000
40,000
39,817
29,044
0
1995 2000 2005 2010 2015 2017

SLOVENIA
80,000
40,000
34,802
20,000
22,403
0
1995 2000 2005 2010 2015 2017

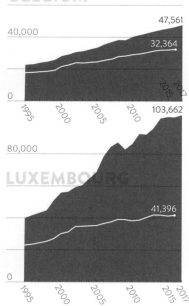
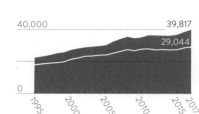
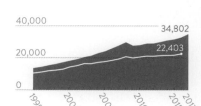
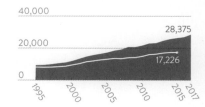
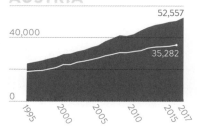
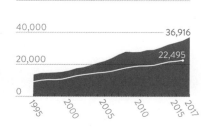
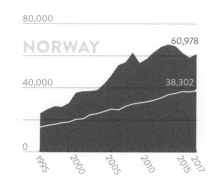
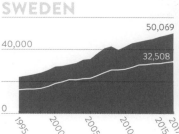
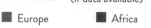
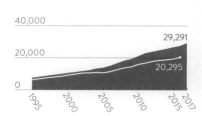
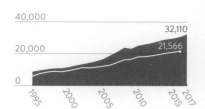
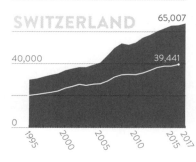

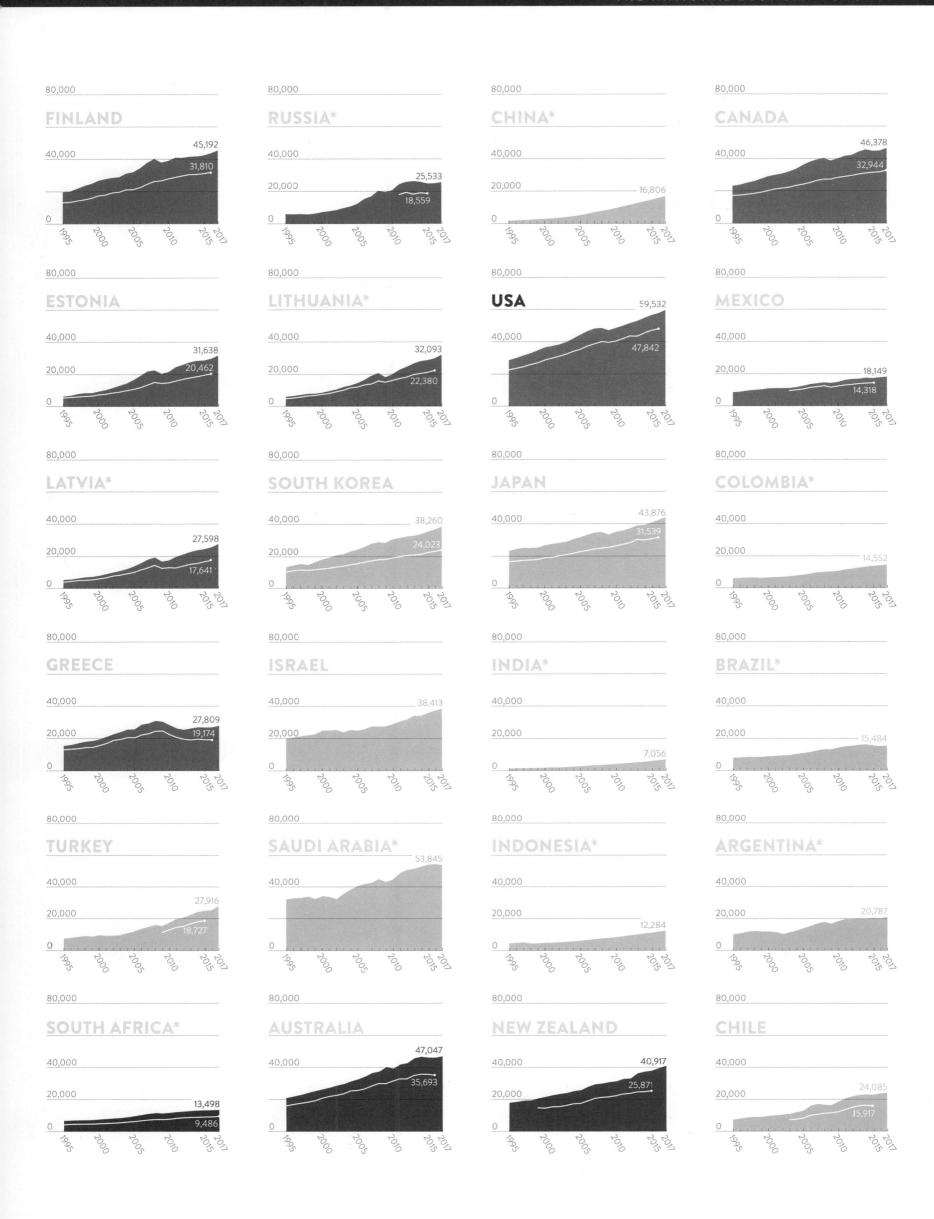

FINLAND
80,000
40,000
0
45,192
31,810
1995 2000 2005 2010 2015 2017

RUSSIA*
80,000
40,000
20,000
0
25,533
18,559
1995 2000 2005 2010 2015 2017

CHINA*
80,000
40,000
20,000
0
16,806
1995 2000 2005 2010 2015 2017

CANADA
80,000
40,000
0
46,378
32,944
1995 2000 2005 2010 2015 2017

ESTONIA
80,000
40,000
20,000
0
31,638
20,462
1995 2000 2005 2010 2015 2017

LITHUANIA*
80,000
40,000
20,000
0
32,093
22,380
1995 2000 2005 2010 2015 2017

USA
80,000
40,000
0
59,532
47,842
1995 2000 2005 2010 2015 2017

MEXICO
80,000
40,000
20,000
0
18,149
14,318
1995 2000 2005 2010 2015 2017

LATVIA*
80,000
40,000
20,000
0
27,598
17,641
1995 2000 2005 2010 2015 2017

SOUTH KOREA
80,000
40,000
20,000
0
38,260
24,023
1995 2000 2005 2010 2015 2017

JAPAN
80,000
40,000
0
43,876
31,539
1995 2000 2005 2010 2015 2017

COLOMBIA*
80,000
40,000
20,000
0
14,552
1995 2000 2005 2010 2015 2017

GREECE
80,000
40,000
20,000
0
27,809
19,174
1995 2000 2005 2010 2015 2017

ISRAEL
80,000
40,000
20,000
0
38,413
1995 2000 2005 2010 2015 2017

INDIA*
80,000
40,000
20,000
0
7,056
1995 2000 2005 2010 2015 2017

BRAZIL*
80,000
40,000
20,000
0
15,484
1995 2000 2005 2010 2015 2017

TURKEY
80,000
40,000
20,000
0
27,916
18,727
1995 2000 2005 2010 2015 2017

SAUDI ARABIA*
80,000
40,000
0
53,845
1995 2000 2005 2010 2015 2017

INDONESIA*
80,000
40,000
20,000
0
12,284
1995 2000 2005 2010 2015 2017

ARGENTINA*
80,000
40,000
20,000
0
20,787
1995 2000 2005 2010 2015 2017

SOUTH AFRICA*
80,000
40,000
20,000
0
13,498
9,486
1995 2000 2005 2010 2015 2017

AUSTRALIA
80,000
40,000
20,000
0
47,047
35,693
1995 2000 2005 2010 2015 2017

NEW ZEALAND
80,000
40,000
20,000
0
40,917
25,871
1995 2000 2005 2010 2015 2017

CHILE
80,000
40,000
20,000
0
24,085
15,917
1995 2000 2005 2010 2015 2017

HEALTHY COMPETITION

A market economy is based on competition. This means: At least two market players are striving for the same goal. The more successful one is, the worse off the other is. That sounds grim, but it's healthy for economies. Economics distinguishes between the **ECONOMIC** (static and dynamic) and *SOCIOPOLITICAL* functions of competition.

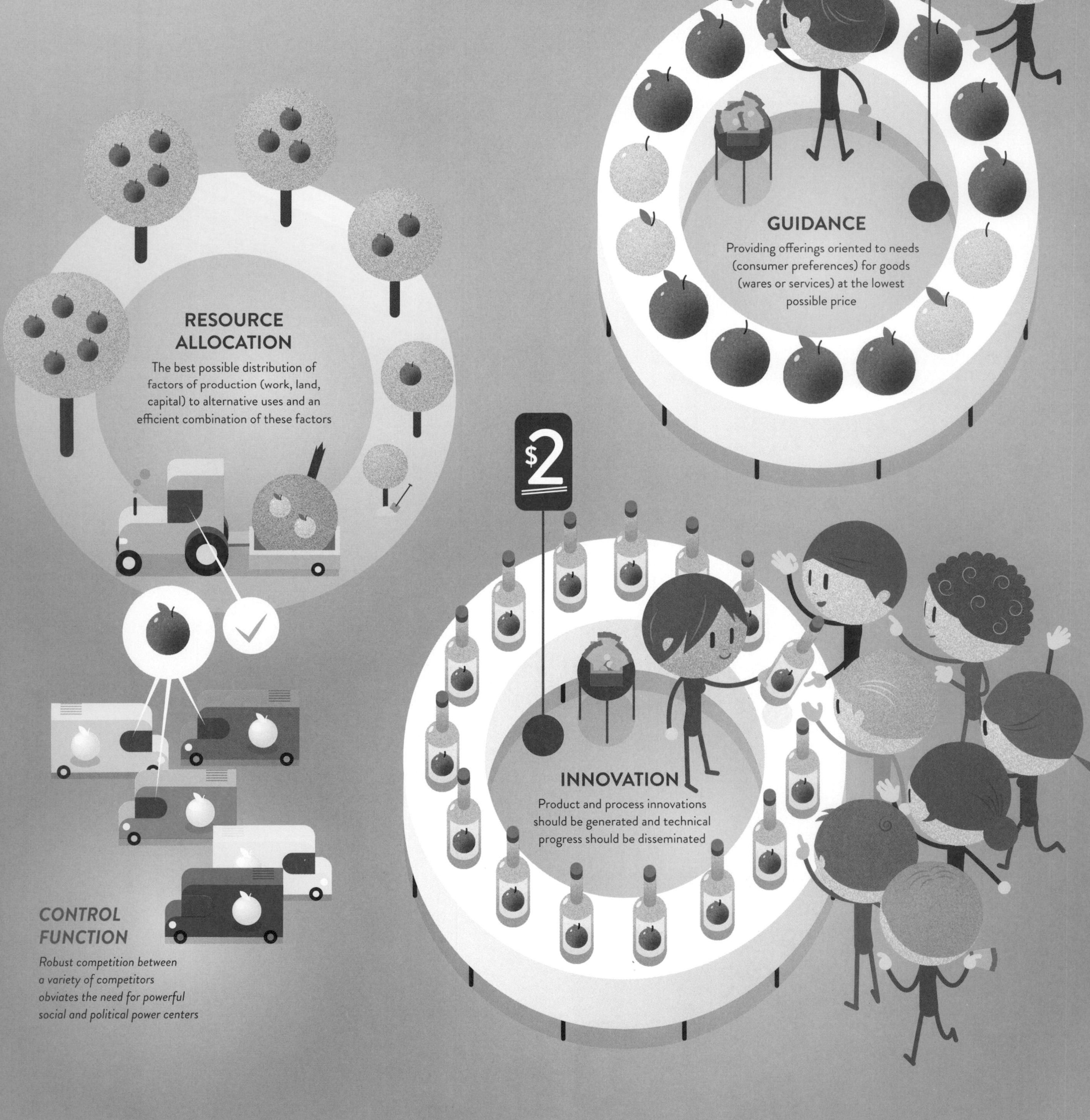

$1

GUIDANCE

Providing offerings oriented to needs (consumer preferences) for goods (wares or services) at the lowest possible price

RESOURCE ALLOCATION

The best possible distribution of factors of production (work, land, capital) to alternative uses and an efficient combination of these factors

$2

INNOVATION

Product and process innovations should be generated and technical progress should be disseminated

CONTROL FUNCTION

Robust competition between a variety of competitors obviates the need for powerful social and political power centers

DISTRIBUTION

Primary income distribution
(market income) according to the
principle of rewards commensurate
with performance

FREEDOM OF CHOICE

Consumers have a choice between
different offers, and workers have a
chance to change their employment

ADAPTATION

Quick reaction to
constantly changing data

FREEDOM OF ACTION

Market participants should be able to take action in
the marketplace without restrictions on competition;
governmental competition watchdogs will step in,
however, if the market's control function fails

FAILURE OF THE PLAN

The pioneers of the socialist command economy believed that economic
management by the state could control production better than the market.
The historical experiment in economic central planning failed spectacularly.
But why?

LACK OF INFORMATION

Economic processes are complex. Economic planners are much too far
away to be able to sensibly direct economic processes on the basis
of sufficient information.

LACK OF FLEXIBILITY

The decisions of the planners are binding. If things turn out
differently than planned, all the gears grind to a halt. Or they
work against each other.

LACK OF FREEDOM

Self-determination and personal responsibility promote economic
ambition and productivity. Communist dictatorships stifled both.

What are trusts?

A trust designates cooperation among large companies to dominate a market. They can use their combined power to undermine competition by fixing prices, output, or market share, which is illegal—at least since the Sherman Act of 1890, which gave the US government the right to examine if market-distorting cooperation exists and the power to dismantle it. Hence its more common name, antitrust or trust-buster legislation. Companies forming a trust usually agree behind closed doors on . . .

Limiting supply

Prices for the goods and services offered

A geographic, product-related, or other division of the market

Pooling profits

COMPANY B

COMPANY B

COMPANY B

CARTEL EDUCATION

COMPANY A

COMPANY A

TRUSTS

Competition is good for business.
In other words: Competition drives companies to be more client-centered, to lower prices, to innovate more, and to improve the quality of their products and services. Conversely, trusts or monopolies throttle competition or eliminate it entirely.

LAW BY ANTITRUST

CONVICTED

BANKING
2017

MOBILE WEB
2017

TELEVISIONS
2012

INTEREST RATE AGREEMENT
2013

ELEVATORS & STAIRS
2007

AIR TRAFFIC
2010

Citicorp, JPMorgan Chase & Co., Barclays, and others

Fined 5.70 US$ Bn

Fined 2.78 US$ Bn

Google

Fined 1.92 US$ Bn

LG Electronics, Philips

Fined 1.75 US$ Bn

Deutsche Bank, Société Générale, Royal Bank of Scotland, and others

Fined 0.98 US$ Bn

ThyssenKrupp, Otis, Schindler, and others

Fined 0.84 US$ Bn

Air France-KLM, British Airways, and others

Busted Trusts

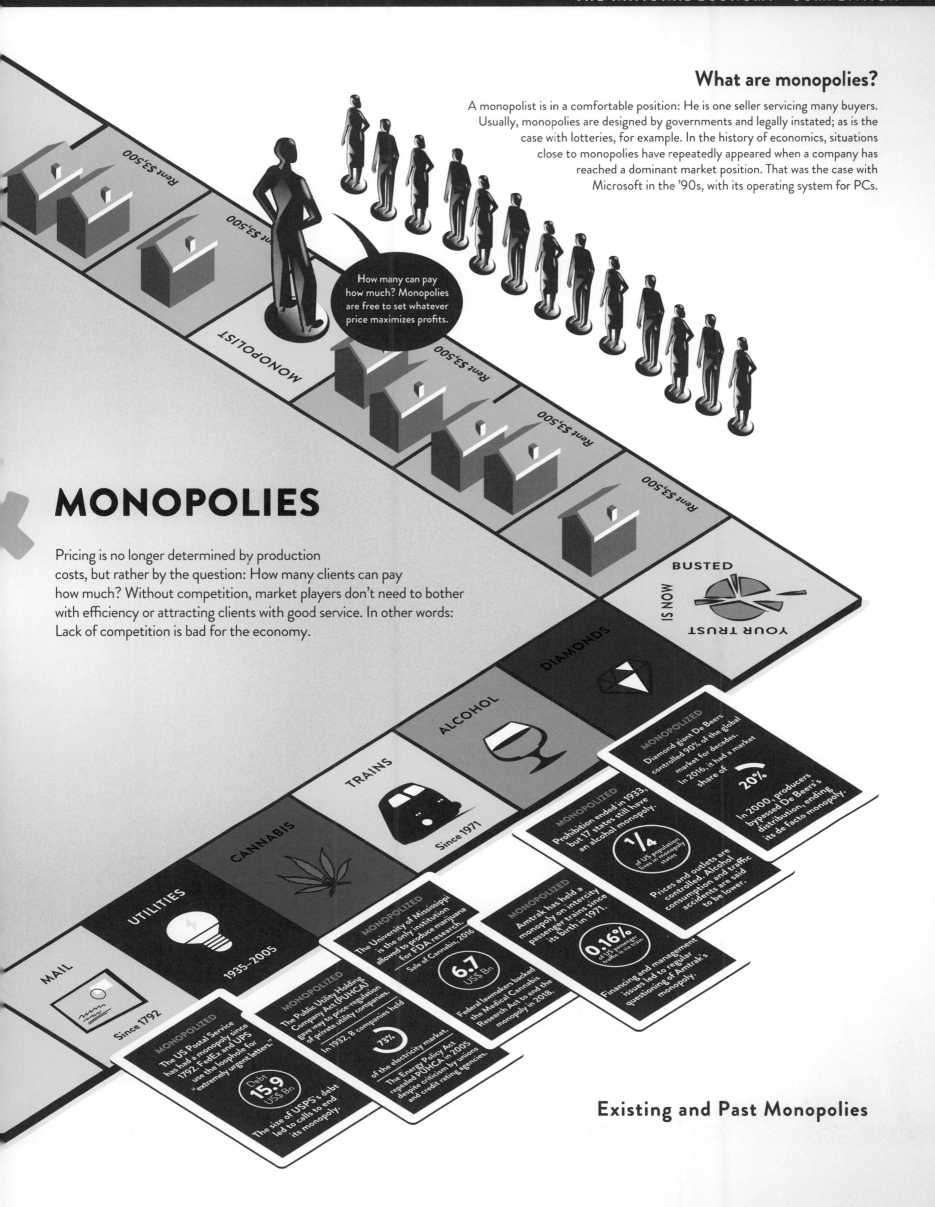

What are monopolies?

A monopolist is in a comfortable position: He is one seller servicing many buyers. Usually, monopolies are designed by governments and legally instated; as is the case with lotteries, for example. In the history of economics, situations close to monopolies have repeatedly appeared when a company has reached a dominant market position. That was the case with Microsoft in the '90s, with its operating system for PCs.

How many can pay how much? Monopolies are free to set whatever price maximizes profits.

MONOPOLIST

Rent $3,500

MONOPOLIES

Pricing is no longer determined by production costs, but rather by the question: How many clients can pay how much? Without competition, market players don't need to bother with efficiency or attracting clients with good service. In other words: Lack of competition is bad for the economy.

YOUR TRUST IS NOW BUSTED

DIAMONDS

MONOPOLIZED
Diamond giant De Beers controlled 90% of the global market for decades. In 2016, it had a market share of

20%

In 2000, producers bypassed De Beers's distribution, ending its de facto monopoly.

ALCOHOL
Since 1971

MONOPOLIZED
Prohibition ended in 1933, but 17 states still have an alcohol monopoly.

¼
of US population lives in monopoly states

Prices and outlets are controlled. Alcohol consumption and traffic accidents are said to be lower.

TRAINS

MONOPOLIZED
Amtrak has held a monopoly on intercity passenger trains since its birth in 1971.

0.16%
of US passenger traffic is via train

Financing and management issues led to regular questioning of Amtrak's monopoly.

CANNABIS
1935–2005

MONOPOLIZED
The University of Mississippi is the only institution allowed to produce marijuana for FDA research.

Sale of Cannabis, 2016

6.7
US$ Bn

Federal lawmakers backed the Medical Cannabis Research Act to end the monopoly in 2018.

UTILITIES

MONOPOLIZED
The Public Utility Holding Company Act (PUHCA) gave way to price-regulation of private utility companies. In 1932, 8 companies held

73%
of the electricity market.

The Energy Policy Act repealed PUHCA in 2005 despite criticism by unions and credit rating agencies.

MAIL
Since 1792

MONOPOLIZED
The US Postal Service has had a monopoly since 1792. FedEx and UPS use the loophole for "extremely urgent letters."

Debt 15.9
US$ Bn

The size of USPS's debt led to calls to end its monopoly.

Existing and Past Monopolies

THE HISTORY OF MONEY

Exchanging sheep for grain is impractical in the long term. All early civilizations recognized this and created the first currencies that distinguished between wares and value and developed into general means of payment. The word "dollar" is derived from the German word *thaler*—a reference to the 16th-century silver coins called "Joachim's thalers"—coming out of a mine in Sankt Joachimsthal, in the present-day Czech Republic.

FUNCTIONS OF MONEY

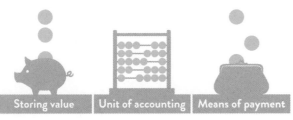

| Storing value | Unit of accounting | Means of payment |

GLOSSARY

Fiat money
Money without an intrinsic value (from the Latin *fiat*, "let it be so") that is not backed by precious metals. Money issued today by central banks, like the euro or dollar, is fiat money.

Currency money
The face value matches the metal content.

Token coins
The face value is significantly higher than the metal content.

Gold and silver standard
A uniform currency standard in which every banknote has a fixed value in precious metals.

Deposit money
Intangible money that is listed only in banks' account books.

Electronic money
Digital monetary value stored on digital media.

Cryptocurrency
Digital currency secured by the principles of cryptography.

PAPER MONEY

Around 1000 AD, Chinese regional rulers begin to issue paper money. The new form of payment is easier to transport and more difficult to counterfeit.

A HISTORY OF MONEY

COMMODITY MONEY

Until around 5000 BC, people exclusively exchanged goods directly. So-called **commodity money** (also known as primitive money) marks the first major developmental leap in the history of money. Nonperishable goods such as rice, shellfish, and metals were popular. But livestock also served as an early form of money.

Commodity money is divided into:

| Natural currency | Usage money | Decorative money |

COINS

In India, China, and Asia Minor, the first coins are used. Beginning around 700 BC, the Lydians (in present-day Turkey) mint the first **currency money** from a naturally occurring gold-silver alloy with a fixed size and value. Coins no longer have to be tediously weighed.

Around 650 BC, Lydia
Minting of first uniform gold coins

400 BC, China
Bronze coins ("cash coins")

1st century AD, Roman Empire
Coinage with minting rights (emperor: silver and gold; senate: brass and copper)

The Roman goddess Moneta. Coins are produced in her temple.

Around 1000 BC, China
Spade and knife coins made of bronze

| Au | Ag | Fe | Cu | Pb | Sn |

The rarer, the more valuable. Metals are suitable as a medium of exchange due to their inherent value.

Around 2000 BC, China
Cowrie shells are the first means of payment whose value stems primarily from their beauty.

Around 3000 BC, Mesopotamia
Grains as currency

DEPOSIT MONEY

War makes people inventive: The Knights Templar issue the first letters of credit in the 12th century and operate an international cashless payment system along the routes of the Crusades.

In the Arab world beginning in the 14th century, the Hawala finance system arises: money transfers over great distances via persons of trust.

15th century, Europe
The use of **deposit money** first spreads throughout Italy and the European centers of trade. Dealers increasingly exchange letters of credit directly, without intermediary payment in coins.

Bankers like the Medicis professionalize the banking industry, which becomes more international through global maritime trade.

VIRTUAL MONEY

In an online forum in 2009, someone known as Satoshi Nakamoto (a pseudonym) introduces the concept of the **cryptocurrency** Bitcoin: digital money without a central bank, managed by its users. To this day, the identity of the inventor remains mysterious.

2009
Bitcoin

20th century
Cashless payment becomes standard. Interbank trade emerges.

1950 USA
First credit card

**1990s
Electronic money**
becomes standard.

1980s
First online banking

Tenth century, China
First paper money (in the value of a coin deposit)

Fourteenth century, China
Official state banknotes (value per imperial decree)

1661, Sweden
The first official banknotes in Europe: The private Bank of Stockholm issues so-called *Credityf-Zedel*, which are secured by deposits of copper plate money. The concept of a central bank catches on throughout Europe in the 19th century.

**1718–1720
France**
John Law persuades King Louis XV to introduce **fiat money**. Initially a success, too much of the unsecured state paper money is printed. The project ends in disastrous inflation.

19th century
The banknote becomes the accepted means of payment.

1923, Germany
The peak of hyperinflation: The massive devaluation of money leads to citizens' financial ruin.

after 780, Western Europe
Charlemagne creates the first European monetary union, the Carolingian denarius, named for the ancient Roman denarius.

End of the 13th century
Europe learns about paper money through the travels of Marco Polo.

1620–1623, Europe
"Kipper und Wipper" period: the peak of a currency devaluation caused by the fraudulent addition of copper, tin, and lead

**After 1871,
German Empire**
The gold mark is the first uniform German currency after hundreds of small states had their own currencies.

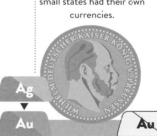

1944–1973
Bretton Woods system: New international monetary system with a gold exchange standard, fixed exchange rates, and the US dollar as primary currency

After the collapse, exchange rates are again deregulated in most countries.

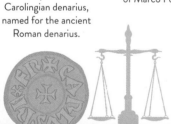

Middle Ages, Europe
Coinage rights are widely dispersed. There are many regional currencies. Uniform coins have been unable to establish themselves for the long term. Coins are no longer exchanged for their nominal value, but rather according to their weight.

In China, the cowrie snail remained in use as a form of payment—along with modern paper money, as a surprised Marco Polo noted.

End of the 18th century, post-revolutionary France
Coin supplies begin to run out. Trading in gold and silver coins is forbidden. Refusal to accept paper money is punishable by death.

19th century
England is the first country to depart from the **silver standard**, in 1816, and introduces the **gold standard**. Due to a silver shortage, it becomes an international standard in 1867.

First third of the 20th century
Suspension of the **gold standard** in many nations: unsecured **fiat money** is increasingly put into circulation because of the First World War's increasing financial demands.

Until the 19th century, cowrie money is in use in South Asia, and in Africa and the South Pacific until the 20th century.

Stone money from the Micronesian island of Yap is valid today as a (symbolic) means of payment.

HOW MUCH MONEY IS GOOD FOR US?

Central banks set the amount of money in circulation. That's a catch-22. They want to keep interest rates low to stimulate economic growth. For that they need to increase the money supply. But should supply exceed demand, inflation becomes a risk. The problem: Even central bankers know only afterward what the right decision would have been.

KEY INTEREST RATE

=

most important
monetary policy tool

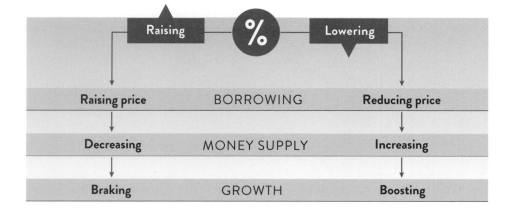

	%	
Raising		**Lowering**
Raising price	BORROWING	Reducing price
Decreasing	MONEY SUPPLY	Increasing
Braking	GROWTH	Boosting

IMPACT VECTORS

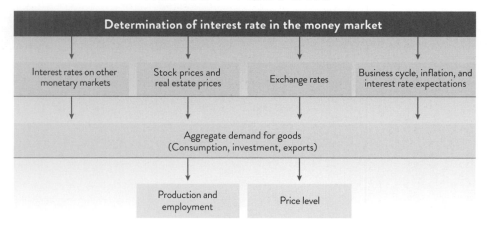

Determination of interest rate in the money market

Interest rates on other monetary markets	Stock prices and real estate prices	Exchange rates	Business cycle, inflation, and interest rate expectations

Aggregate demand for goods
(Consumption, investment, exports)

Production and employment	Price level

Changes in key interest rates

— Federal Reserve System   — European Central Bank   — Bank of England

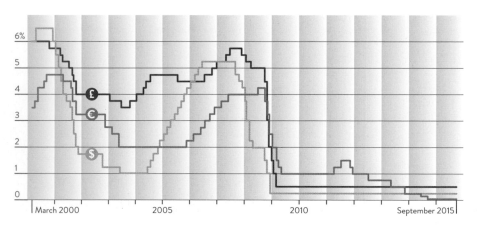

March 2000   2005   2010   September 2015

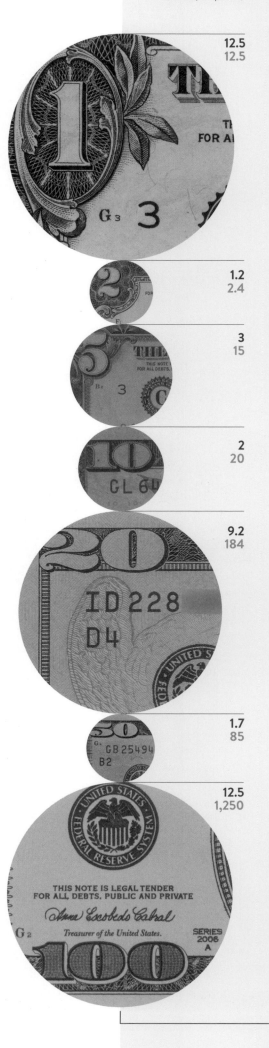

**Amount of Bills and
Value of US Currency**
(in US$ Bn, 2017)

12.5	12.5
1.2	2.4
3	15
2	20
9.2	184
1.7	85
12.5	1,250

The Fed
Federal Reserve System

The Fed was created on December 23, 1913 to control the monetary system of the USA. It sets its monetary policy and upholds the stability of the financial system.

TOTAL ASSETS
$4.29 Tn (July 2018)

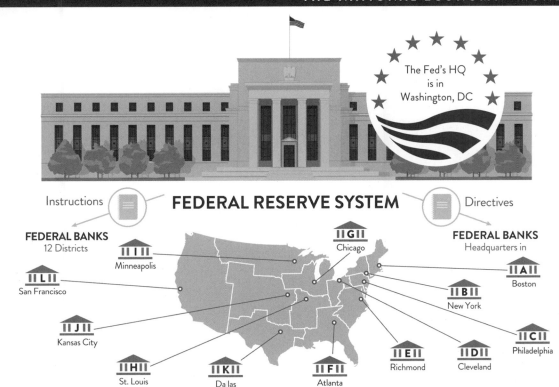

The Fed's HQ is in Washington, DC

Instructions

FEDERAL RESERVE SYSTEM

Directives

FEDERAL BANKS
12 Districts

Minneapolis
San Francisco
Kansas City
St. Louis
Dallas
Atlanta
Chicago
Richmond
Cleveland
Philadelphia
New York
Boston

FEDERAL BANKS
Headquarters in

Every dollar bill has a letter indicating which of the Federal Banks issued it.

KEY OBJECTIVES

Stabilizing the Financial System   ✛   Maximizing Employment
Stabilizing Prices
Moderating Interest Rates

ORGANIZATION

FED OPEN MARKET COMITTEE
Advisory body setting monetary policy
17 members, of which 12 vote
7 Board of Governors
5 Reserve Bank presidents

BOARD OF GOVERNORS
Central body of the Federal Reserve
7 members, 1 chairman, 1 vice chairman
Federal agency overseeing the banking system and the 12 Reserve Banks

FED RESERVE BANKS
Independent under Board of Gov.
Carry out the Fed's policies regionally
Place money in circulation
Not part of federal government

TASKS

Conducts the Nation's Monetary Policy

The discount rate is the Fed's most important instrument. It sets interest rates impacting credit, money supply, and therefore inflation.

TOOLS

 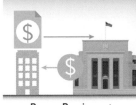 

Reserve Requirements
The Fed sets the portion of deposits banks must hold in cash. This impacts the funds available in the banking system.

Open Market Operations
Buying and selling US government securities. One of the main instruments of monetary policy.

Interests on Reserves
Sets interest rates for extra reserves of banks. Influences the amount of money banks lend.

Orchestrates Foreign Currencies Operations

Manages Currency Reserves

Maintains International Cooperation

Supervises and Regulates Financial Institutions

Safeguards Payment and Settlement System

Collects Data and Forecasting

Fosters Consumer Protection and Community Development

Currency Reserves

=

Gold Stock

+

Foreign Currencies

+

Reserve Positions in the International Monetary Fund

US Reserve Assets (in US$ Bn, 2005–2017)

Total Reserves

160,000
140,000
120,000
100,000
80,000
60,000
40,000
20,000
0   2005   2017

→ of which is **Gold Stock**   and **Foreign Currencies**

Au   €Y

2005   2017   2005   2017

Value of Total Dollar Bills in Circulation
in US$ Bn
2002–2017

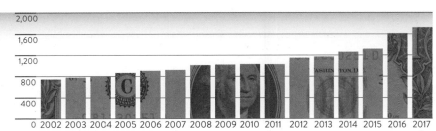

2,000
1,600
1,200
800
400
0   2002 2003 2004 2005 2006 2007 2008 2009 2010 2011 2012 2013 2014 2015 2016 2017

TYPES OF MONEY

The money supply is divided into categories classified as "M"s.
Here are the key Ms for the US money supply.

M0
all physical
currency

M1
M0 + demand
deposits and
other checkable
deposits

M2
M1 + savings accounts,
money market
accounts, retail money
market mutual funds,
and small time deposits

M3
M2 + large time deposits,
institutional money
market funds, repurchase
agreements, and larger
liquid assets

MB
(the monetary base):
M0 + Federal
Reserve deposits

HOW IS MONEY CREATED?

1 Money is not only printed by the Treasury. The majority of the money that we interact with economically is "created" by commercial banks. Simply put, this means that banks loan money that comes into existence only through the loan.

3 The size of the reserve requirement determines how many times an initial deposit can be "multiplied" through loans.

BANK A

CUSTOMER A

Suppose Customer A makes a deposit of $1,000 in Bank A.

$1,000

BORROWER A

$900

Less the 10% reserve requirement, that enables Bank A to loan $900 to Borrower A.

BANK B

CUSTOMER B

When Borrower A uses the loan to buy something from, say, Customer B, that $900 becomes a deposit in Bank B . . .

$900

BORROWER B

$810

. . . which enables Bank B to loan $810 to Borrower B.

BANK C

CUSTOMER C

When Borrower B uses that loan to buy something from Customer C . . .

$810

BORROWER C

$729

. . . Bank C can loan $729 to Borrower C, and so on . . .

4 Each new loan adds to the money supply—a smaller amount every time. Under the current 10% reserve requirement, an initial deposit of $1,000 creates an additional $9,000. Added to the initial deposit, that makes $10,000 in circulation. The ratio of $10,000 to $1,000 is 10—the same result you'll get if you divide 1 by the reserve requirement (0.1). Economists call this ratio the "money multiplier," and rightly so!

2 The Federal Reserve controls how much money can be "loaned into existence" by setting a reserve requirement.

COMMERCIAL BANK

DEPOSITORS' BANK ACCOUNTS

Most accounts in a commercial bank are in the form of **demand deposits**—for example, checking accounts—which allow a depositor to withdraw funds more or less immediately.

Demand deposits

BORROWERS' BANK ACCOUNTS

New deposits

The bank is allowed to loan out an amount equal to its **demand deposits** minus the reserve requirement. It does so by creating totally **new deposits** in the borrowers' accounts. Both the new deposits and the original demand deposits are available to be withdrawn. **Therefore, the bank has effectively added new money to the M1 money supply.**

The bank makes its profit when the loans are paid back—with interest.

FEDERAL RESERVE

COMMERCIAL BANK'S RESERVE

To ensure that there's enough money on hand to cover immediate withdrawals, the bank must keep a certain percentage of its demand deposits in reserve. This reserve requirement is set by the Federal Reserve—for large banks, it is currently 10%. The commercial bank can hold these funds either in its own vault or at the Federal Reserve.

Reserve requirement

A commercial bank can borrow money from other banks to meet its reserve requirement. That money is called **federal funds,** for which it pays the **fed funds rate**. Commercial banks can also borrow from the Federal Reserve. The rate charged is called the **discount rate,** which commercial banks use to set their loan rates. The **prime rate** is the interest rate commercial banks charge their best and most creditworthy customers.

THE MONETARY BASE

A measure of the most liquid money: currency in general circulation or in commercial bank deposits held in reserve at the Fed.

$4 trillion	
$3 trillion	
$2 trillion	
$1 trillion	

1959 1960 1961 1962 1963 1964 1965 1966 1967 1968 1969 1970 1971 1972 1973 1974 1975 1976 1977 1978 1979 1980 1981 1982 1983 1984 1985 1986 1987 1988 1989 1990 1991 1992 1993 1994 1995 1996 1997 1998 1999 2000 2001 2002 2003 2004 2005 2006 2007 2008 2009 2010 2011 2012 2013 2014 2015 2016 2017 2018

Finance and insurance
$3,636,114,357

Wholesale trade
$7,899,978,591

Accommodation and food services
$3,571,627,685

VALUE OF ECONOMIC SECTORS
(2012)

WHO DOES WHAT, AND IF SO, HOW MANY?

In 1900, 38% of the US workforce was still involved in agriculture. Today it's 2%. The arrival of mainframe computers in the 1960s marked the beginning of service providers' triumph at the expense of industrial workers. Robots are not yet counted as their own occupational group by the US Bureau of Labor Statistics. Today, people working in the following economic sectors create economic value in the following amounts:

Information and communication
$1,238,463,251

Real estate, rental, and leasing
$487,655,249

Health care, education, administration
$2,766,838,044

Retail trade, transport, and warehousing
$4,950,363,174

Manufacturing
$5,652,816,602

Construction
$3,994,199,491

Agriculture,
forestry, hunting
$136,672,000

Mining and utilities
$576,020,475

Primary industries
Agriculture, forestry, fishing, and hunting

Secondary industries
Manufacturing

Tertiary industries
Services and other industries

COMPARISON OF
ECONOMIC SECTORS
(2012)

LEGEND   Number of companies

Revenue in US$ Number of employees

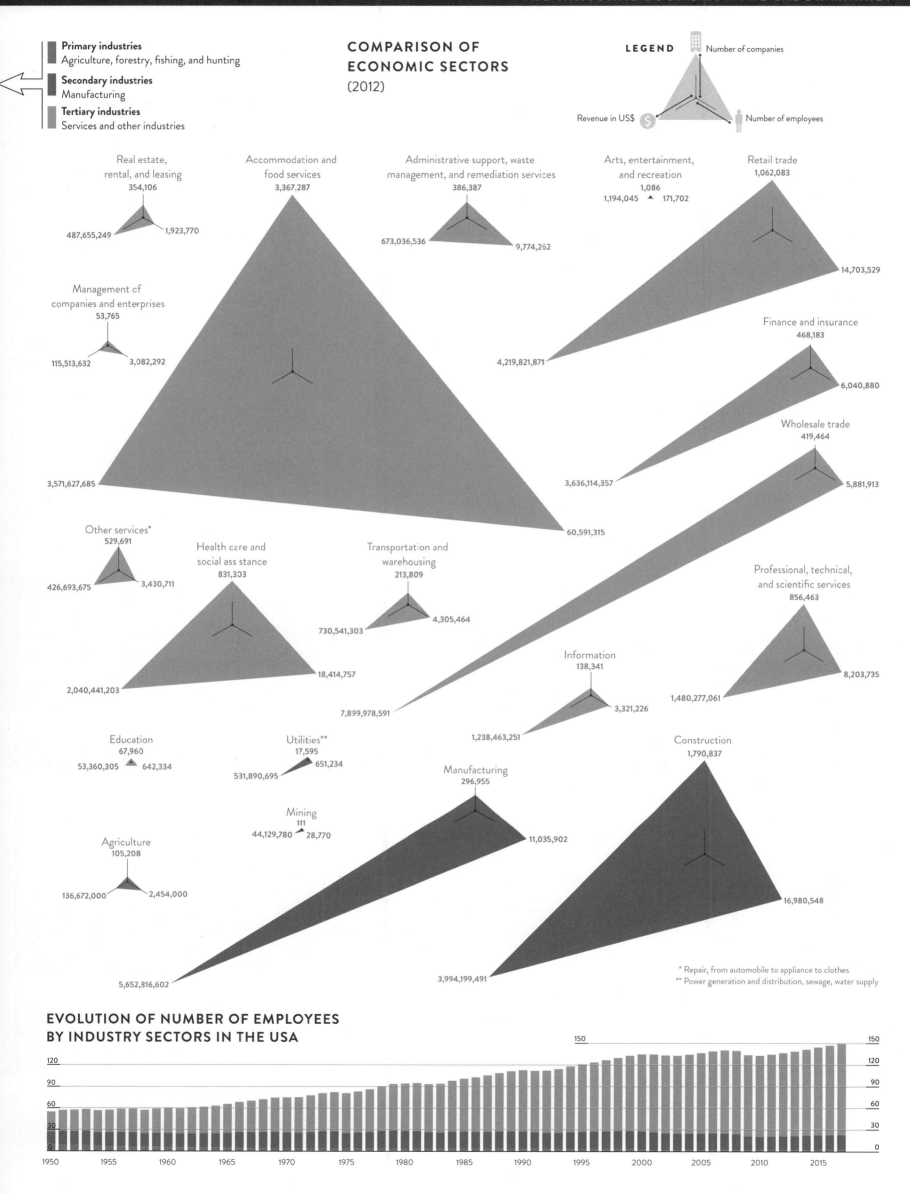

Real estate,
rental, and leasing
354,106

487,655,249   1,923,770

Accommodation and
food services
3,367,287

Administrative support, waste
management, and remediation services
386,387

673,036,536   9,774,262

Arts, entertainment,
and recreation
1,086
1,194,045   171,702

Retail trade
1,062,083

14,703,529

Management of
companies and enterprises
53,765

115,513,632   3,082,292

4,219,821,871

Finance and insurance
468,183

6,040,880

3,636,114,357

Wholesale trade
419,464

5,881,913

3,571,627,685

60,591,315

Other services*
529,691

426,693,675   3,430,711

Health care and
social assistance
831,303

2,040,441,203   18,414,757

Transportation and
warehousing
213,809

730,541,303   4,305,464

Professional, technical,
and scientific services
856,463

8,203,735

1,480,277,061

Information
138,341

1,238,463,251   3,321,226

7,899,978,591

Education
67,960
53,360,305   642,334

Utilities**
17,595
531,890,695   651,234

Manufacturing
296,955

11,035,902

Construction
1,790,837

16,980,548

Mining
111
44,129,780   28,770

Agriculture
105,208

136,672,000   2,454,000

5,652,816,602

3,994,199,491

* Repair, from automobile to appliance to clothes
** Power generation and distribution, sewage, water supply

EVOLUTION OF NUMBER OF EMPLOYEES
BY INDUSTRY SECTORS IN THE USA

150   150

120   120

90   90

60   60

30   30

1950   1955   1960   1965   1970   1975   1980   1985   1990   1995   2000   2005   2010   2015

HOW OLD IS OUR NATION?

In a few years, there will be as many US citizens over the age of 40 as under. In 2030 there will be as many people over 60 as under 20. With an aging population, our pension systems will become more and more difficult to finance. The figures from 1950 to 2017 allow a fairly reliable forecast.

In which country should you retire?

The Melbourne Mercer Global Pension Index ranks the pension systems of 30 countries along three main criteria: adequacy to meet the needs of retirees, sustainability, and integrity. The latter includes subcriteria like governance and regulation. A total of 40 indicators allow scores of up to 100 points, which can be summarized as school grades.

The marks for 2016: The only two pension systems to score an A were those of the Netherlands and Denmark. Australia comes in 3rd, the only country worldwide to earn a B+.

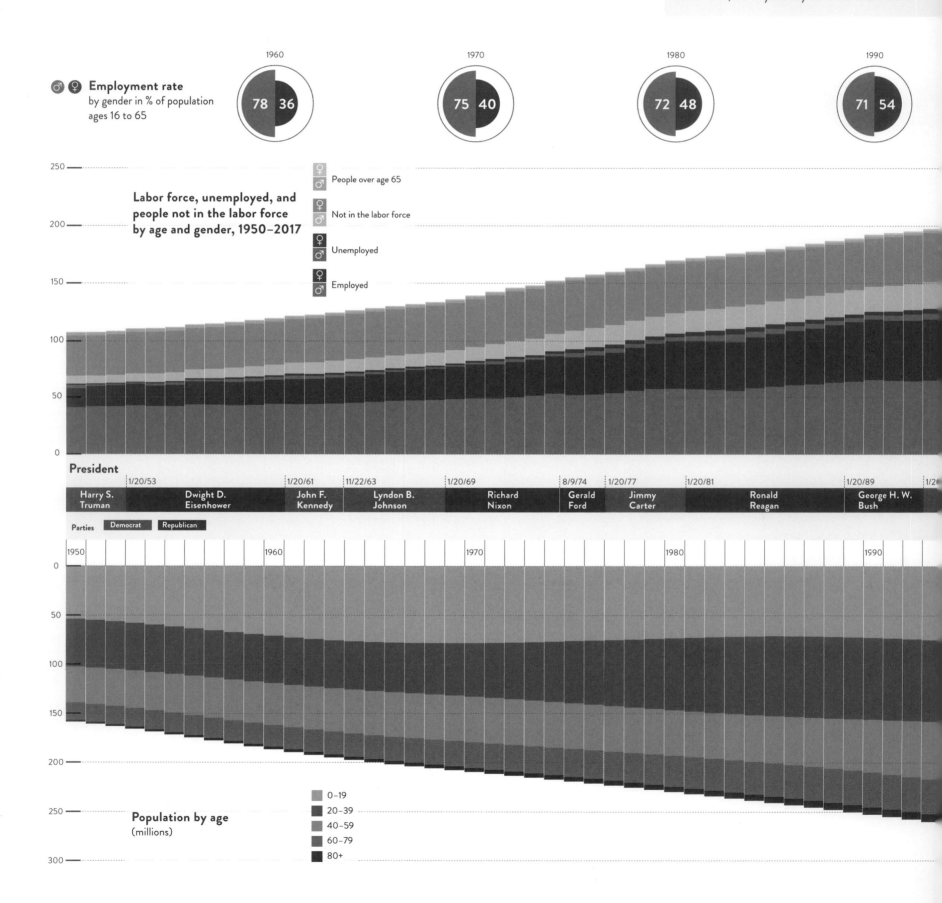

Employment rate
by gender in % of population
ages 16 to 65

1960: 78 36
1970: 75 40
1980: 72 48
1990: 71 54

Labor force, unemployed, and people not in the labor force by age and gender, 1950–2017

♀♂ People over age 65
♀♂ Not in the labor force
♀♂ Unemployed
♀♂ Employed

President

| 1/20/53 | 1/20/61 | 11/22/63 | 1/20/69 | 8/9/74 | 1/20/77 | 1/20/81 | 1/20/89 |

Harry S. Truman | Dwight D. Eisenhower | John F. Kennedy | Lyndon B. Johnson | Richard Nixon | Gerald Ford | Jimmy Carter | Ronald Reagan | George H. W. Bush

Parties Democrat Republican

Population by age
(millions)

0–19
20–39
40–59
60–79
80+

The US system gets a mediocre C, as do Germany, France, Brazil, and Malaysia: They're basically good systems, but have an uncertain future, as aging populations call into question their financing model.

A
Denmark, Netherlands

B
Australia (B+), Sweden, Finland, Switzerland, Singapore, Canada, Chile

C
Ireland (C+), United Kingdom (C+), Germany, **USA**, France, Malaysia, Brazil, Austria, Poland

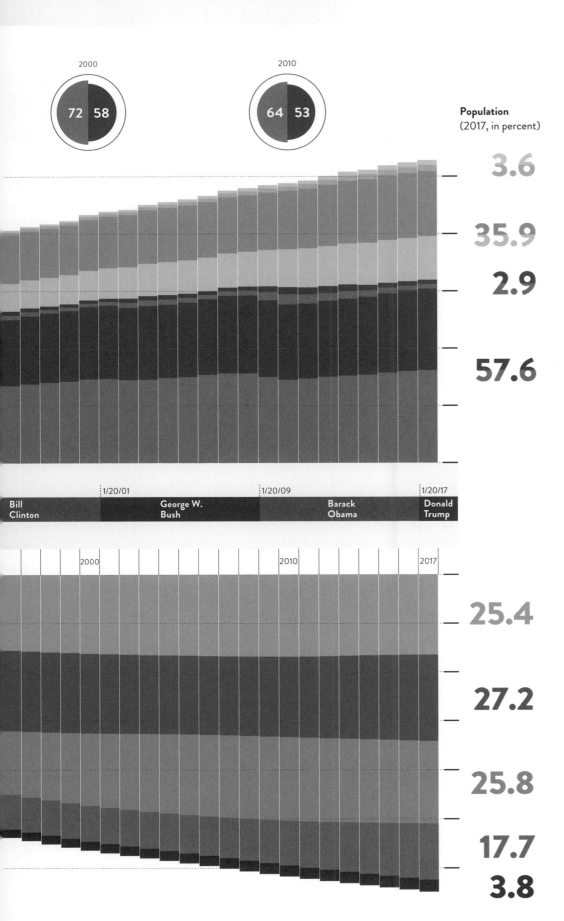

2000
72 58

2010
64 53

Population
(2017, in percent)

3.6

35.9

2.9

57.6

1/20/01   1/20/09   1/20/17

| Bill Clinton | George W. Bush | Barack Obama | Donald Trump |

2000   2010   2017

25.4

27.2

25.8

17.7

3.8

Projection of US population by age categories
in millions

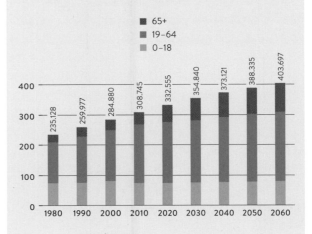

■ 65+
■ 19–64
■ 0–18

Year	Value
1980	235.128
1990	259.977
2000	284.880
2010	308.745
2020	332.555
2030	354.840
2040	373.121
2050	388.335
2060	403.697

Projection of US population by migration scenarios
in millions

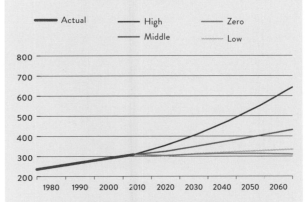

— Actual   — High   — Zero
— Middle   — Low

The different scenarios are based on assumptions of varying levels of childbearing, mortality, and migration. International migration varies over time, and is projected to reach higher levels after 2020. The zero-migration scenario is highly unlikely.

Projection of life expectancy

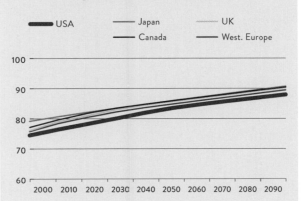

— USA   — Japan   — UK
— Canada   — West. Europe

MEASURING PROSPERITY

Who is doing well? According to which criteria? It's not easy to find universal criteria for the prosperity and well-being of a society. Money? Social mobility? A good health care system? Or is the best measure the greatest possible happiness of the greatest number of people?

HUMAN DEVELOPMENT INDEX, 2015

The United Nations' gauge of well-being (in use since 1990)

Criteria Per capita GNI*   Life expectancy   Education

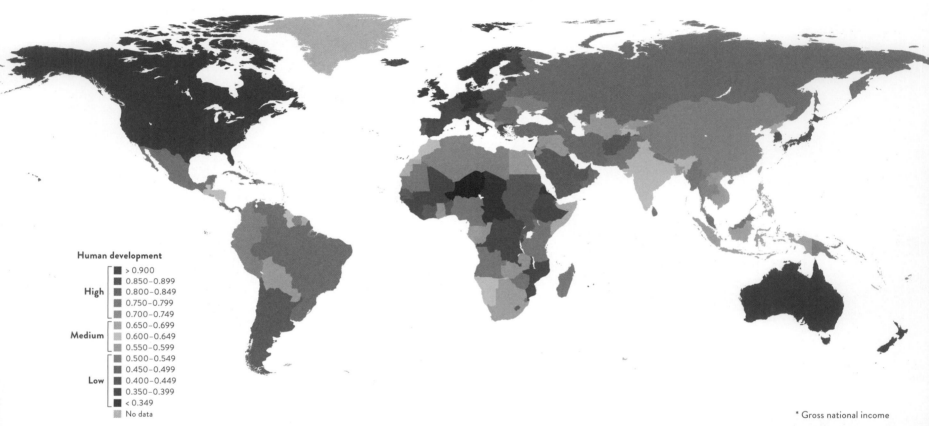

Human development

High
- \> 0.900
- 0.850–0.899
- 0.800–0.849
- 0.750–0.799
- 0.700–0.749

Medium
- 0.650–0.699
- 0.600–0.649
- 0.550–0.599

Low
- 0.500–0.549
- 0.450–0.499
- 0.400–0.449
- 0.350–0.399
- < 0.349
- No data

* Gross national income

HAPPINESS RANKING, 2015

From the *World Happiness Report* of the United Nations (in use since 2012)

 GDP per capita   Social bonds   Health/ life expectancy   Freedom in making life choices   Gener- osity   Corruption   Compared to dystopia** (benchmark)   I 95% confidence interval*** (benchmark)

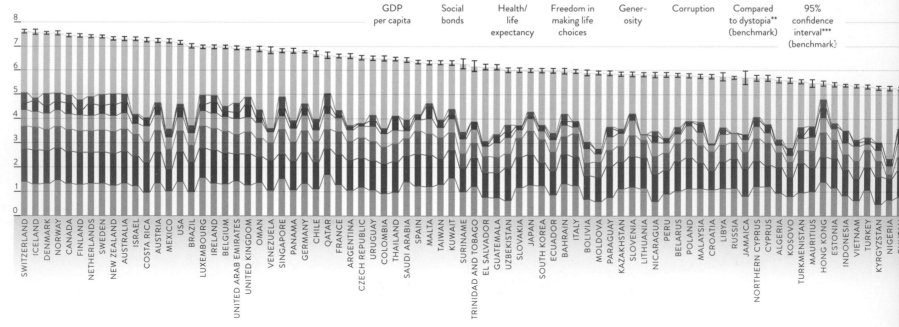

Health expenses

per capita 2013, in US$

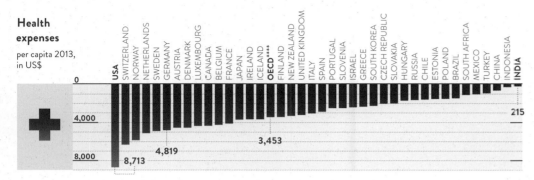

8,713
4,819
3,453
215

Median net worth of US households, 1989–2016

2016, in US$

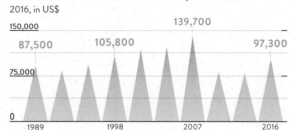

87,500   105,800   139,700   97,300

150,000
75,000
0

1989   1998   2007   2016

The median is the largest group with the same level of wealth, while the average is the total wealth divided by the total population.

Educational mobility in comparison

Percentage of college students (20–34 years old) whose parents did not graduate from high school

| 0 | GERMANY 2.2 | RUSSIA 6.1 | USA 8.2 | | | | | |

| 1.9 JAPAN | 3.5 UNITED KINGDOM | 6.9 DENMARK | 9.6 FRANCE | 13.3 NETHERLANDS | 24.5 ITALY | 33.3 SPAIN |

GINI COEFFICIENT

Measure of (in-)equality in income distribution

Maximum equality = 0

1 = Maximal inequal distribution

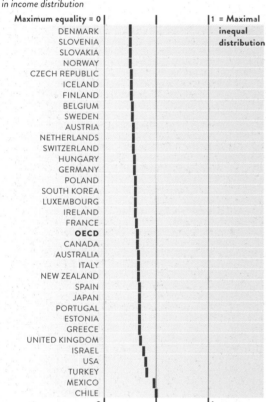

DENMARK
SLOVENIA
SLOVAKIA
NORWAY
CZECH REPUBLIC
ICELAND
FINLAND
BELGIUM
SWEDEN
AUSTRIA
NETHERLANDS
SWITZERLAND
HUNGARY
GERMANY
POLAND
SOUTH KOREA
LUXEMBOURG
IRELAND
FRANCE
OECD
CANADA
AUSTRALIA
ITALY
NEW ZEALAND
SPAIN
JAPAN
PORTUGAL
ESTONIA
GREECE
UNITED KINGDOM
ISRAEL
USA
TURKEY
MEXICO
CHILE

0   1

RELATIVE INCOME POVERTY

Survey by the OECD (in percentage of average income)

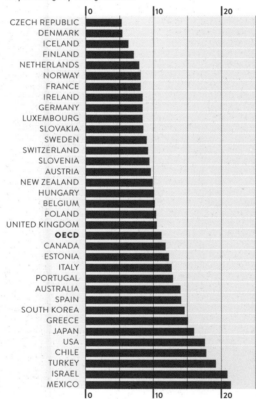

0   10   20

CZECH REPUBLIC
DENMARK
ICELAND
FINLAND
NETHERLANDS
NORWAY
FRANCE
IRELAND
GERMANY
LUXEMBOURG
SLOVAKIA
SWEDEN
SWITZERLAND
SLOVENIA
AUSTRIA
NEW ZEALAND
HUNGARY
BELGIUM
POLAND
UNITED KINGDOM
OECD
CANADA
ESTONIA
ITALY
PORTUGAL
AUSTRALIA
SPAIN
SOUTH KOREA
GREECE
JAPAN
USA
CHILE
TURKEY
ISRAEL
MEXICO

0   10   20

TOP 10% OF EARNERS VS. POOREST 10%

Income of the poorest 10%   → Income of the wealthiest 10%

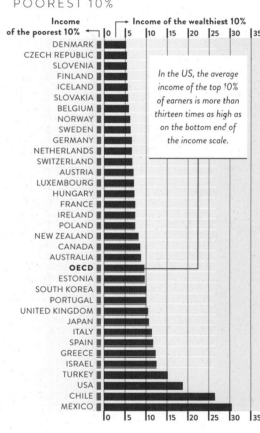

0   5   10   15   20   25   30   35

DENMARK
CZECH REPUBLIC
SLOVENIA
FINLAND
ICELAND
SLOVAKIA
BELGIUM
NORWAY
SWEDEN
GERMANY
NETHERLANDS
SWITZERLAND
AUSTRIA
LUXEMBOURG
HUNGARY
FRANCE
IRELAND
POLAND
NEW ZEALAND
CANADA
AUSTRALIA
OECD
ESTONIA
SOUTH KOREA
PORTUGAL
UNITED KINGDOM
JAPAN
ITALY
SPAIN
GREECE
ISRAEL
TURKEY
USA
CHILE
MEXICO

0   5   10   15   20   25   30   35

In the US, the average income of the top 10% of earners is more than thirteen times as high as on the bottom end of the income scale.

** Dystopia is a fictive land with the unhappiest people imaginable (as a negative point of comparison)

*** This value helps to compare how much the perception of happiness varies within a country

**** Organization for Economic Cooperation and Development

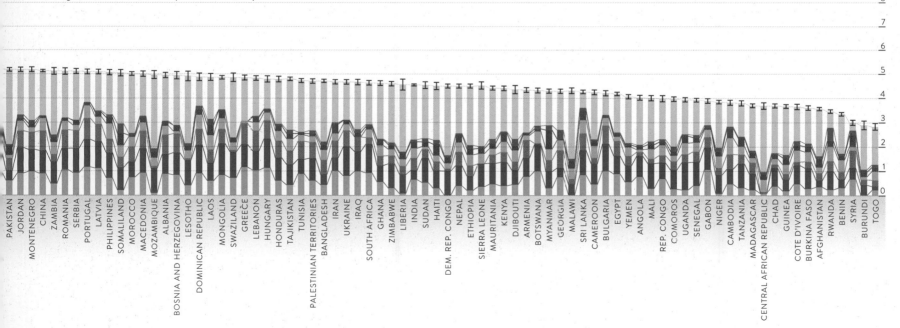

8
7
6
5
4
3
2
1
0

PAKISTAN
JORDAN
MONTENEGRO
CHINA
ZAMBIA
ROMANIA
SERBIA
PORTUGAL
LATVIA
PHILIPPINES
SOMALILAND
MOROCCO
MACEDONIA
MOZAMBIQUE
ALBANIA
BOSNIA AND HERZEGOVINA
LESOTHO
DOMINICAN REPUBLIC
LAOS
MONGOLIA
SWAZILAND
THAILAND
GREECE
LEBANON
HUNGARY
HONDURAS
TAJIKISTAN
TUNISIA
PALESTINIAN TERRITORIES
BANGLADESH
IRAN
UKRAINE
IRAQ
SOUTH AFRICA
GHANA
ZIMBABWE
LIBERIA
INDIA
SUDAN
HAITI
DEM. REP. CONGO
NEPAL
ETHIOPIA
SIERRA LEONE
MAURITANIA
KENYA
DJIBOUTI
ARMENIA
MYANMAR
GEORGIA
MALAWI
SRI LANKA
CAMEROON
BULGARIA
EGYPT
YEMEN
ANGOLA
MALI
REP. CONGO
COMOROS
UGANDA
SENEGAL
GABON
NIGER
CAMBODIA
TANZANIA
MADAGASCAR
CHAD
GUINEA
CENTRAL AFRICAN REPUBLIC
COTE D'IVOIRE
BURKINA FASO
AFGHANISTAN
RWANDA
BENIN
SYRIA
BURUNDI
TOGO

IV

THE GLOBAL ECONOMY

GLOBAL PRODUCTION
·
WORLD TRADE
·
ILLEGAL GLOBAL MARKETS
·
THE INSTITUTIONS
·
THE GLOBAL FINANCIAL MARKET
·
MULTINATIONALS AND BRAND NAMES
·
TALENT DISTRIBUTION AND LABOR MIGRATION

THE JEANS BUSINESS

In 1873, Levi Strauss and Jacob W. Davis patented "blue jeans." Even back then, the American jeans makers imported cloth from Europe. The rugged workman's trousers were pioneers of globalization. They became brand icons, the expression of an attitude toward life, and an example of a highly unequal global distribution of value creation.

WHAT DOES IT COST?

■ Bangladesh ■ Hong Kong ■ USA

Two examples (in US$)

Store-brand jeans from Walmart — Premium jeans from True Religion "Made in USA"

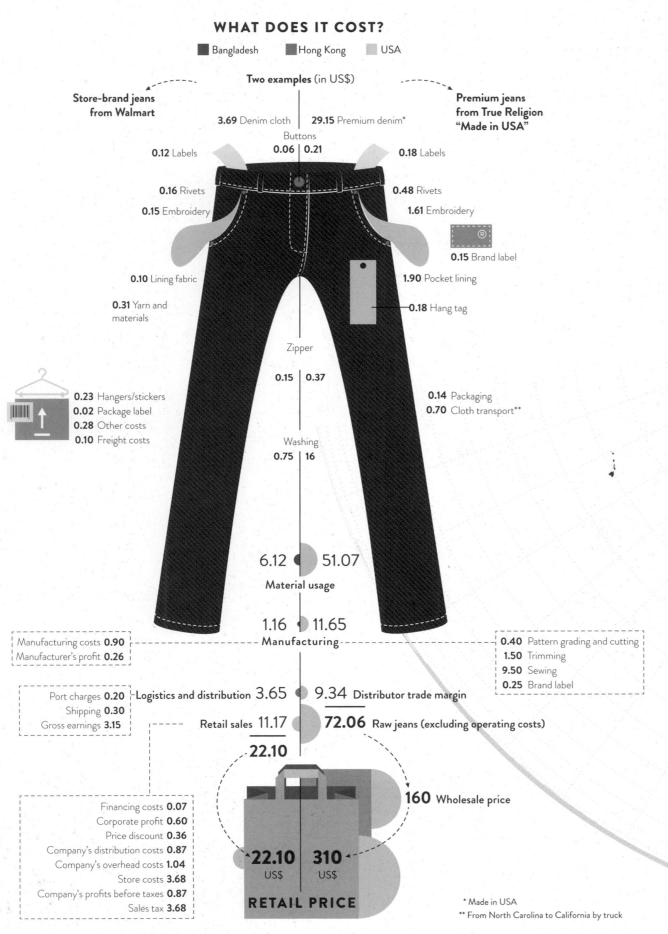

3.69 Denim cloth | 29.15 Premium denim*

Buttons
0.06 | 0.21

0.12 Labels | 0.18 Labels

0.16 Rivets | 0.48 Rivets
0.15 Embroidery | 1.61 Embroidery

0.15 Brand label

0.10 Lining fabric | 1.90 Pocket lining

0.31 Yarn and materials | 0.18 Hang tag

Zipper
0.15 | 0.37

0.23 Hangers/stickers
0.02 Package label
0.28 Other costs
0.10 Freight costs

0.14 Packaging
0.70 Cloth transport**

Washing
0.75 | 16

Material usage
6.12 | 51.07

Manufacturing
1.16 | 11.65

Manufacturing costs 0.90
Manufacturer's profit 0.26

0.40 Pattern grading and cutting
1.50 Trimming
9.50 Sewing
0.25 Brand label

Port charges 0.20
Shipping 0.30
Gross earnings 3.15

Logistics and distribution 3.65 | 9.34 Distributor trade margin

Retail sales 11.17 | 72.06 Raw jeans (excluding operating costs)

22.10

Financing costs 0.07
Corporate profit 0.60
Price discount 0.36
Company's distribution costs 0.87
Company's overhead costs 1.04
Store costs 3.68
Company's profits before taxes 0.87
Sales tax 3.68

160 Wholesale price

22.10 US$ | 310 US$

RETAIL PRICE

* Made in USA
** From North Carolina to California by truck

CEO of H&M

116,577
Annual bonus (after taxes)

?
Earnings unknown

4,641 Store manager | 1,293* Retail employee

Bangladesh 63 — Factory worker

India 24–61 — Spinning mill worker

India 44** | USA 3,013 — Cotton picker

WHO EARNS WHAT?

Monthly earnings in US$

* Lowest position, 38-hour workweek
** $1.75/day (25 workdays per month)

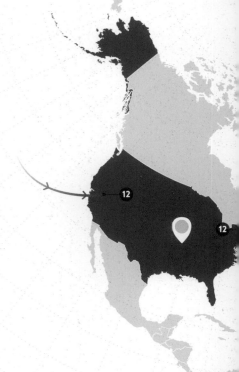

12
12

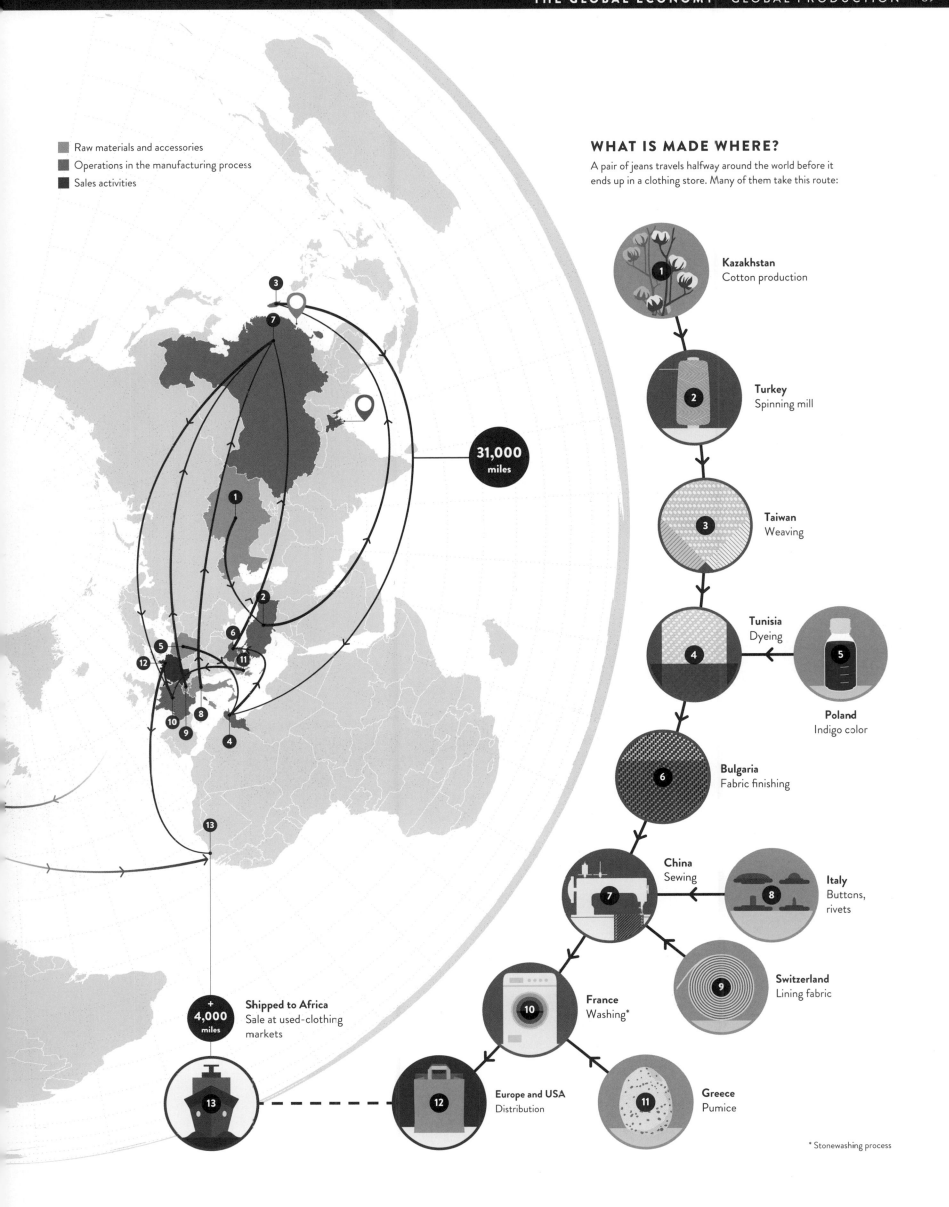

Raw materials and accessories
Operations in the manufacturing process
Sales activities

WHAT IS MADE WHERE?

A pair of jeans travels halfway around the world before it ends up in a clothing store. Many of them take this route:

Kazakhstan
Cotton production

Turkey
Spinning mill

Taiwan
Weaving

Tunisia
Dyeing

Poland
Indigo color

Bulgaria
Fabric finishing

China
Sewing

Italy
Buttons, rivets

Switzerland
Lining fabric

France
Washing*

Europe and USA
Distribution

Greece
Pumice

Shipped to Africa
Sale at used-clothing markets

31,000 miles

+ 4,000 miles

* Stonewashing process

WHO DELIVERS THE GOODS?
WHO EARNS THE MONEY?

Today, production and value creation are linked in global supply chains. The term "supply chain" can be misleading, however. It might be halfway accurate for bananas. For technologically complex products, networks of firms cooperate so that we can fly around the world safely—or bring the world to the screens of our smartphones.

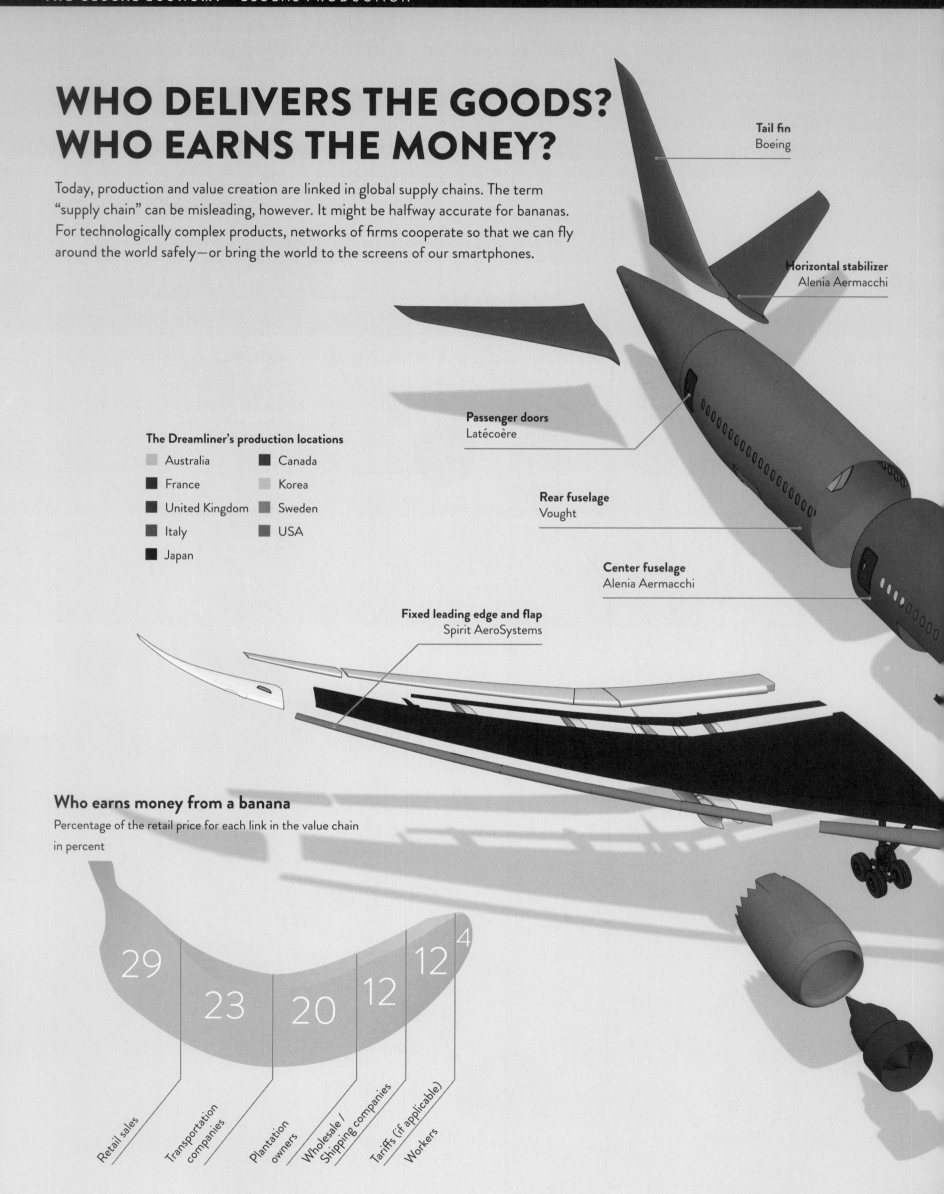

Tail fin
Boeing

Horizontal stabilizer
Alenia Aermacchi

Passenger doors
Latécoère

Rear fuselage
Vought

Center fuselage
Alenia Aermacchi

Fixed leading edge and flap
Spirit AeroSystems

The Dreamliner's production locations

- Australia
- France
- United Kingdom
- Italy
- Japan
- Canada
- Korea
- Sweden
- USA

Who earns money from a banana

Percentage of the retail price for each link in the value chain
in percent

29   23   20   12   12   4

Retail sales

Transportation companies

Plantation owners

Wholesale / Shipping companies

Tariffs (if applicable)

Workers

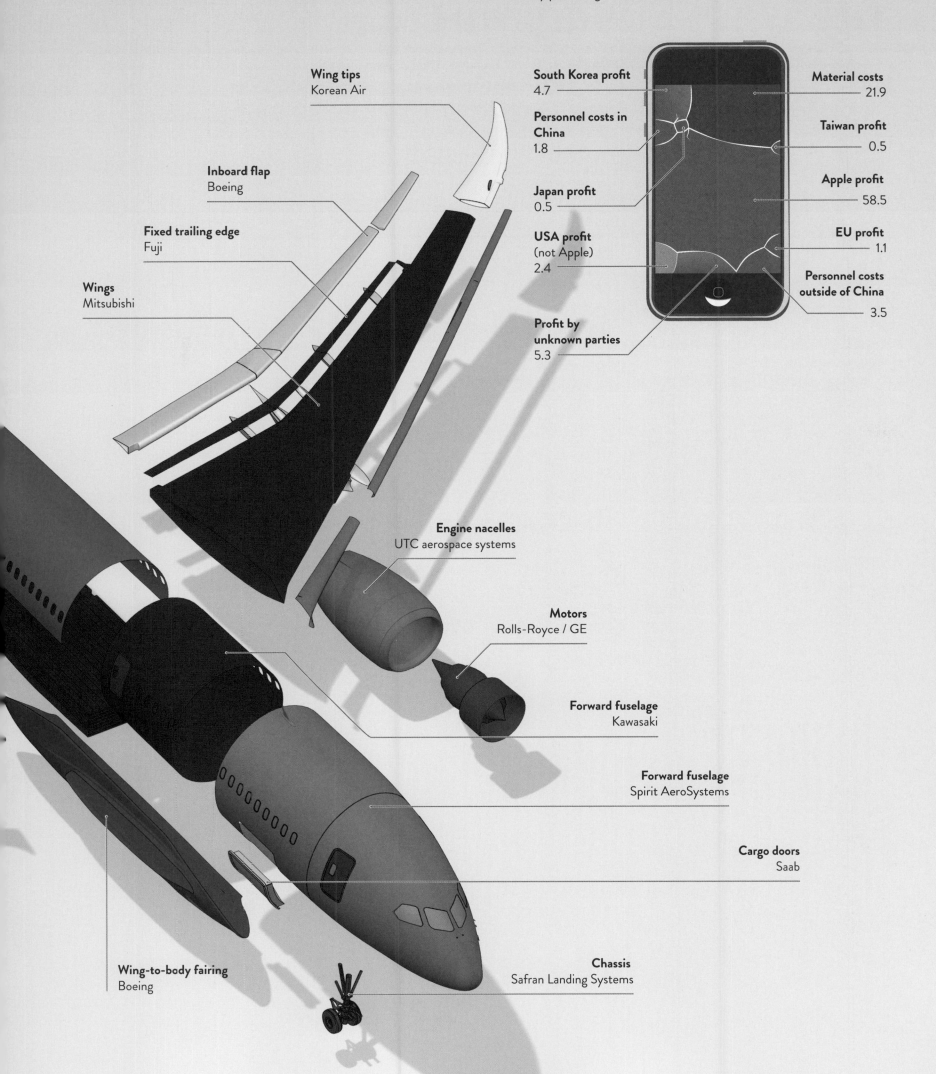

Wing tips
Korean Air

Inboard flap
Boeing

Fixed trailing edge
Fuji

Wings
Mitsubishi

Engine nacelles
UTC aerospace systems

Motors
Rolls-Royce / GE

Forward fuselage
Kawasaki

Forward fuselage
Spirit AeroSystems

Cargo doors
Saab

Wing-to-body fairing
Boeing

Chassis
Safran Landing Systems

Where the money for your iPhone goes
by percentages

South Korea profit
4.7

Personnel costs in China
1.8

Japan profit
0.5

USA profit
(not Apple)
2.4

Profit by unknown parties
5.3

Material costs
21.9

Taiwan profit
0.5

Apple profit
58.5

EU profit
1.1

Personnel costs outside of China
3.5

...AND IN THE END THE SWISS ALWAYS WIN

The more competitive a country is, the higher its productivity. The higher the productivity, the greater its economic prosperity. A prerequisite for this is entrepreneurial freedom based on a low level of regulation and a high degree of legal certainty. Those are the basic assumptions of rankings like the *Global Competitiveness Report* of the World Economic Forum and the *Index of Economic Freedom* from the conservative/libertarian Heritage Foundation think tank. And by the way, sometimes it's Hong Kong that wins.

COMPETITIVENESS

TWELVE PILLARS OF THE GLOBAL COMPETITIVENESS INDEX

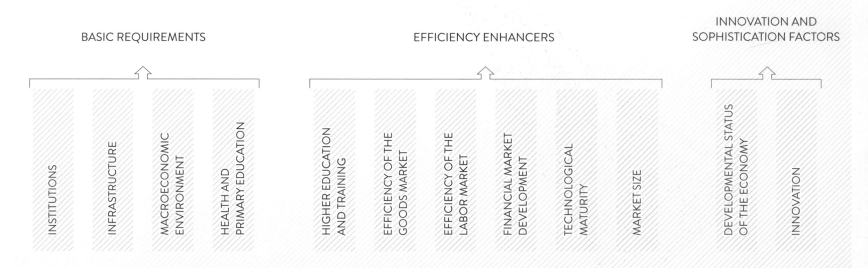

BASIC REQUIREMENTS

- INSTITUTIONS
- INFRASTRUCTURE
- MACROECONOMIC ENVIRONMENT
- HEALTH AND PRIMARY EDUCATION

EFFICIENCY ENHANCERS

- HIGHER EDUCATION AND TRAINING
- EFFICIENCY OF THE GOODS MARKET
- EFFICIENCY OF THE LABOR MARKET
- FINANCIAL MARKET DEVELOPMENT
- TECHNOLOGICAL MATURITY
- MARKET SIZE

INNOVATION AND SOPHISTICATION FACTORS

- DEVELOPMENTAL STATUS OF THE ECONOMY
- INNOVATION

THE WORLD'S MOST COMPETITIVE COUNTRIES
ACCORDING TO THE GLOBAL COMPETITIVENESS INDEX (GCI)

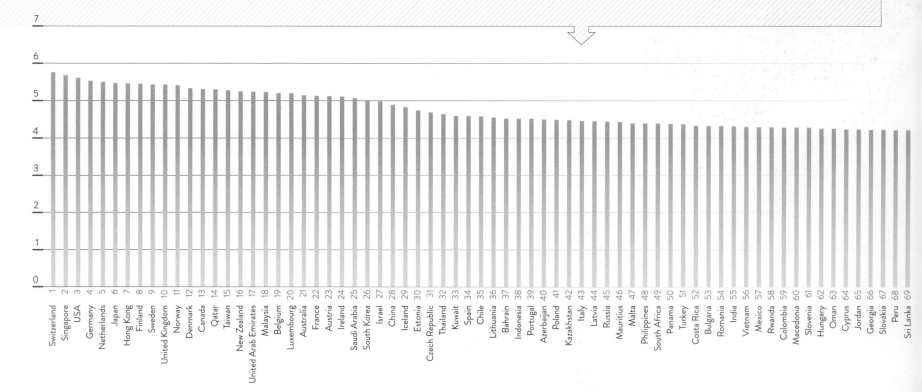

Switzerland 1, Singapore 2, USA 3, Germany 4, Netherlands 5, Japan 6, Hong Kong 7, Finland 8, Sweden 9, United Kingdom 10, Norway 11, Denmark 12, Canada 13, Qatar 14, Taiwan 15, New Zealand 16, United Arab Emirates 17, Malaysia 18, Belgium 19, Luxembourg 20, Australia 21, France 22, Austria 23, Ireland 24, Saudi Arabia 25, South Korea 26, Israel 27, China 28, Iceland 29, Estonia 30, Czech Republic 31, Thailand 32, Kuwait 33, Spain 34, Chile 35, Lithuania 36, Bahrain 37, Indonesia 38, Portugal 39, Azerbaijan 40, Poland 41, Kazakhstan 42, Italy 43, Latvia 44, Russia 45, Mauritius 46, Malta 47, Philippines 48, South Africa 49, Panama 50, Turkey 51, Costa Rica 52, Bulgaria 53, Romania 54, India 55, Vietnam 56, Mexico 57, Rwanda 58, Colombia 59, Macedonia 60, Slovenia 61, Hungary 62, Oman 63, Cyprus 64, Jordan 65, Georgia 66, Slovakia 67, Peru 68, Sri Lanka 69

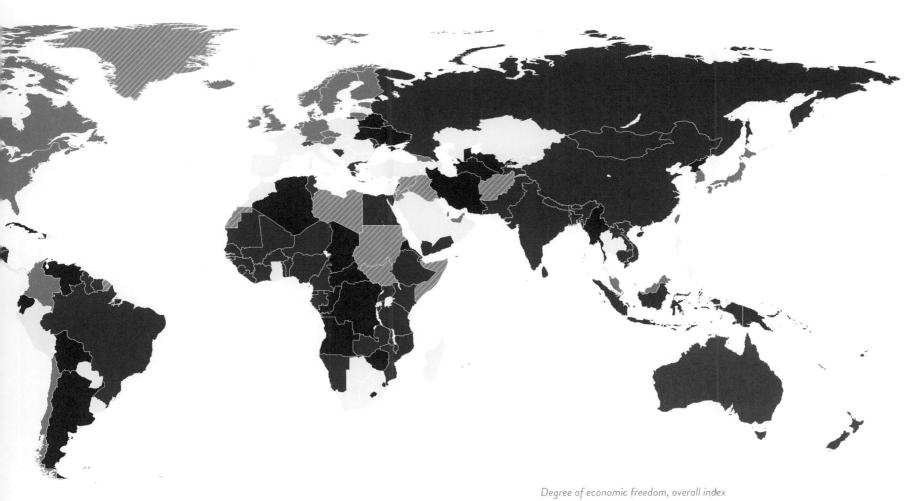

ECONOMIC FREEDOM

Degree of economic freedom, overall index

100–80	79.9–70	69.9–60	59.9–50	49.9–0	Not specified

Economically freest countries

Rank		Overall index
1	Hong Kong	88.6
2	Singapore	87.8
3	New Zealand	81.6
4	Switzerland	81.0
5	Australia	80.3
6	Canada	78.0
7	Chile	77.7
8	Ireland	77.3
9	Estonia	77.2
10	United Kingdom	76.4

Most repressed countries

Rank		Overall index
169	Argentina	43.8
170	Equatorial Guinea	43.7
171	Iran	43.5
172	Republic of the Congo	42.8
173	Eritrea	42.7
174	Turkmenistan	41.9
175	Zimbabwe	38.2
176	Venezuela	33.7
177	Cuba	29.8
178	North Korea	2.3

Factors for the calculation of the overall index

LEGAL CERTAINTY	EXTENT OF STATE REGULATION	REGULATORY EFFICIENCY	OPEN MARKETS
Property rights	Finance/financial market freedom	Freedom of business activity	Freedom of trade
Level of corruption	Level of state expenditures	Labor market regulation	Freedom of investment
	Monetary freedom		Tax freedom

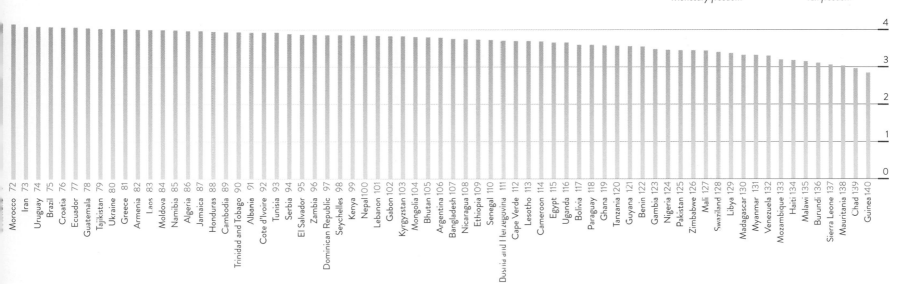

YEAR

WORLD TOTAL
CENTRAL AFRICAN REPUBLIC
UGANDA
TUNISIA
CHAD
TOGO
TANZANIA
SWAZILAND
SUDAN
SOUTH AFRICA (BEFORE 1910 CAPE COLONY)
SOMALIA
ZIMBABWE
SIERRA LEONE
SEYCHELLES
SENEGAL
SAO TOME AND PRINCIPE
ZAMBIA
RWANDA
NIGERIA
NIGER
NAMIBIA
MOZAMBIQUE
MALI
MAURITIUS
MAURITANIA
MOROCCO
MALAWI
MADAGASCAR
LIBYA
LIBERIA
LESOTHO
REPUBLIC OF THE CONGO
DEMOCRATIC REP. OF THE CONGO
COMOROS
KENYA
CAPE VERDE
CAMEROON
GUINEA
GUINEA-BISSAU
GHANA
GAMBIA
GABON
ERITREA AND ETHIOPIA
CÔTE D'IVOIRE
DJIBOUTI
BURUNDI
BURKINA FASO
BOTSWANA
BENIN
EQUATORIAL GUINEA
ANGOLA
ALGERIA
EGYPT
WEST BANK AND GAZA
UNITED ARAB EMIRATES
TURKEY (BEFORE 1923 OTTOMAN EMPIRE, BYZANTIUM)
SYRIA
SAUDI ARABIA
OMAN
LEBANON
KUWAIT
QATAR
JORDAN
YEMEN
ISRAEL
IRAQ
IRAN
BAHRAIN
VIETNAM
NORTH KOREA
MONGOLIA
LAOS
CAMBODIA
AFGHANISTAN
SRI LANKA
SINGAPORE
PAKISTAN
NEPAL
MYANMAR
MALAYSIA
HONG KONG
BANGLADESH
TAIWAN
THAILAND
SOUTH KOREA
PHILIPPINES
JAPAN
INDONESIA (BEFORE 1880 JAVA)
INDIA
CHINA
21 CARIBBEAN STATES
TRINIDAD AND TOBAGO
PUERTO RICO
PARAGUAY
PANAMA

2000s
1990s
1980s
1970s
1960s
1950s

1940

Today around forty times as many people are living
on Earth as in the year 1 AD. Since then, the per
capita gross domestic product has increased by a
factor of sixteen on a global average.

1913

x 16

1870

THE GDP TIME MACHINE

The Industrial Revolution does not enjoy an especially good reputation. But how
prosperous it made us can be clearly read in the data of the Maddison Project.
In meticulous detail, it reconstructed the per capita gross domestic product
since the birth of Christ. The data are inherently incomplete. It is also striking
that average wealth grew at a furious pace in Western industrialized nations
over the last fifty years. In oil-exporting countries, on the other hand, the
population grew much more rapidly than the gross domestic product.

1820

GDP per capita in international dollars*

▬▬▬	40,000
▬▬	30,000
▬	20,000
▬	10,000
–	7,500
▪	5,000
▪	2,500
ı	1,000

1775
1700
1600

1500
1450
1348
1280
1000

* The calculations of the Maddison Project are
based on the so-called **international dollar**, a
reference currency calculated by the World
Bank that reflects the purchasing-power parity
in the various countries. Maddison takes as its
basis the purchasing power of the int$ of 1990.

** and successor states

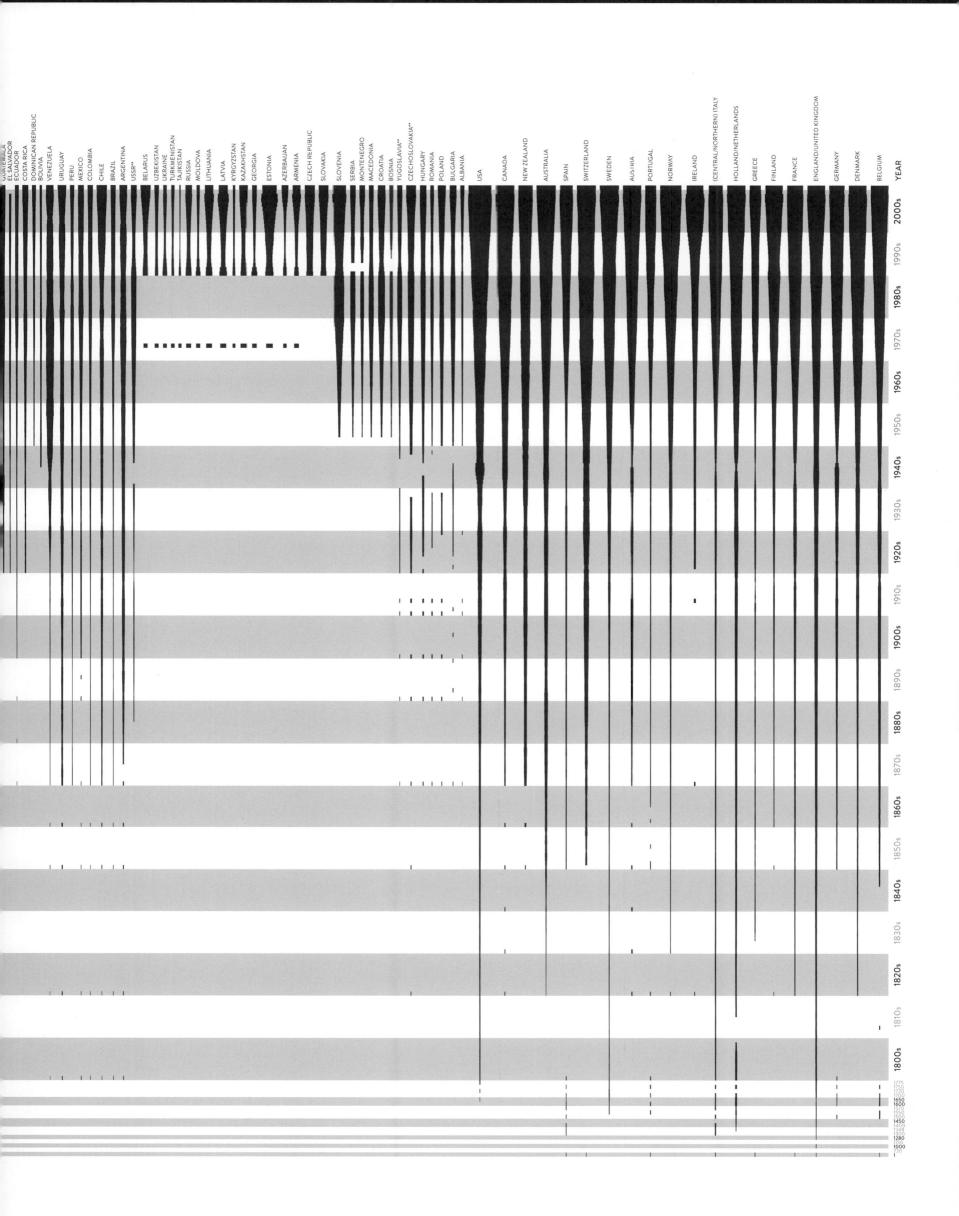

GUATEMALA
EL SALVADOR
ECUADOR
COSTA RICA
DOMINICAN REPUBLIC
BOLIVIA
VENEZUELA
URUGUAY
PERU
MEXICO
COLOMBIA
CHILE
BRAZIL
ARGENTINA
USSR**
BELARUS
UZBEKISTAN
UKRAINE
TURKMENISTAN
TAJIKISTAN
RUSSIA
MOLDOVA
LITHUANIA
LATVIA
KYRGYZSTAN
KAZAKHSTAN
GEORGIA
ESTONIA
AZERBAIJAN
ARMENIA
CZECH REPUBLIC
SLOVAKIA
SLOVENIA
SERBIA
MONTENEGRO
MACEDONIA
CROATIA
BOSNIA
YUGOSLAVIA**
CZECHOSLOVAKIA**
HUNGARY
ROMANIA
POLAND
BULGARIA
ALBANIA
USA
CANADA
NEW ZEALAND
AUSTRALIA
SPAIN
SWITZERLAND
SWEDEN
AUSTRIA
PORTUGAL
NORWAY
IRELAND
(CENTRAL/NORTHERN) ITALY
HOLLAND/NETHERLANDS
GREECE
FINLAND
FRANCE
ENGLAND/UNITED KINGDOM
GERMANY
DENMARK
BELGIUM
YEAR

2000s
1990s
1980s
1970s
1960s
1950s
1940s
1930s
1920s
1910s
1900s
1890s
1880s
1870s
1860s
1850s
1840s
1830s
1820s
1810s
1800s
1650
1600
1450
1280
1000

IT'S (TURNED INTO) A SMALL WORLD

Already in the second century BCE, the Silk Road connected Europe's traders with their counterparts in central and east Asia. Thirty years ago, globalization put the global movement of goods into overdrive. This is the flow of people and wares today.

Panama Canal

Legend for global trade routes

✗ Shipping routes
✗ Air routes
✗ Land routes
) Canals

The transport volume of the MSC Oscar is equivalent to 1,100 Boeing 747s.

BOEING 747-8F

MSC OSCAR
The world's largest container ship in terms of cargo capacity

19,224 TEU*

1,297.2 ft

Cargo transport in the US
Share in percent (2017)

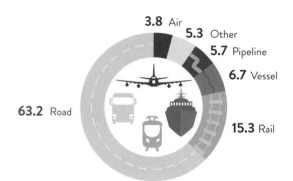

3.8 Air
5.3 Other
5.7 Pipeline
6.7 Vessel
63.2 Road
15.3 Rail

Transshipment volumes of the world's 10 largest container ports in 2016
in millions of TEU*

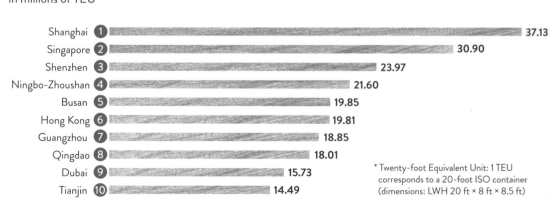

Port	Rank	Value
Shanghai	1	37.13
Singapore	2	30.90
Shenzhen	3	23.97
Ningbo-Zhoushan	4	21.60
Busan	5	19.85
Hong Kong	6	19.81
Guangzhou	7	18.85
Qingdao	8	18.01
Dubai	9	15.73
Tianjin	10	14.49

* Twenty-foot Equivalent Unit: 1 TEU corresponds to a 20-foot ISO container (dimensions: LWH 20 ft × 8 ft × 8.5 ft)

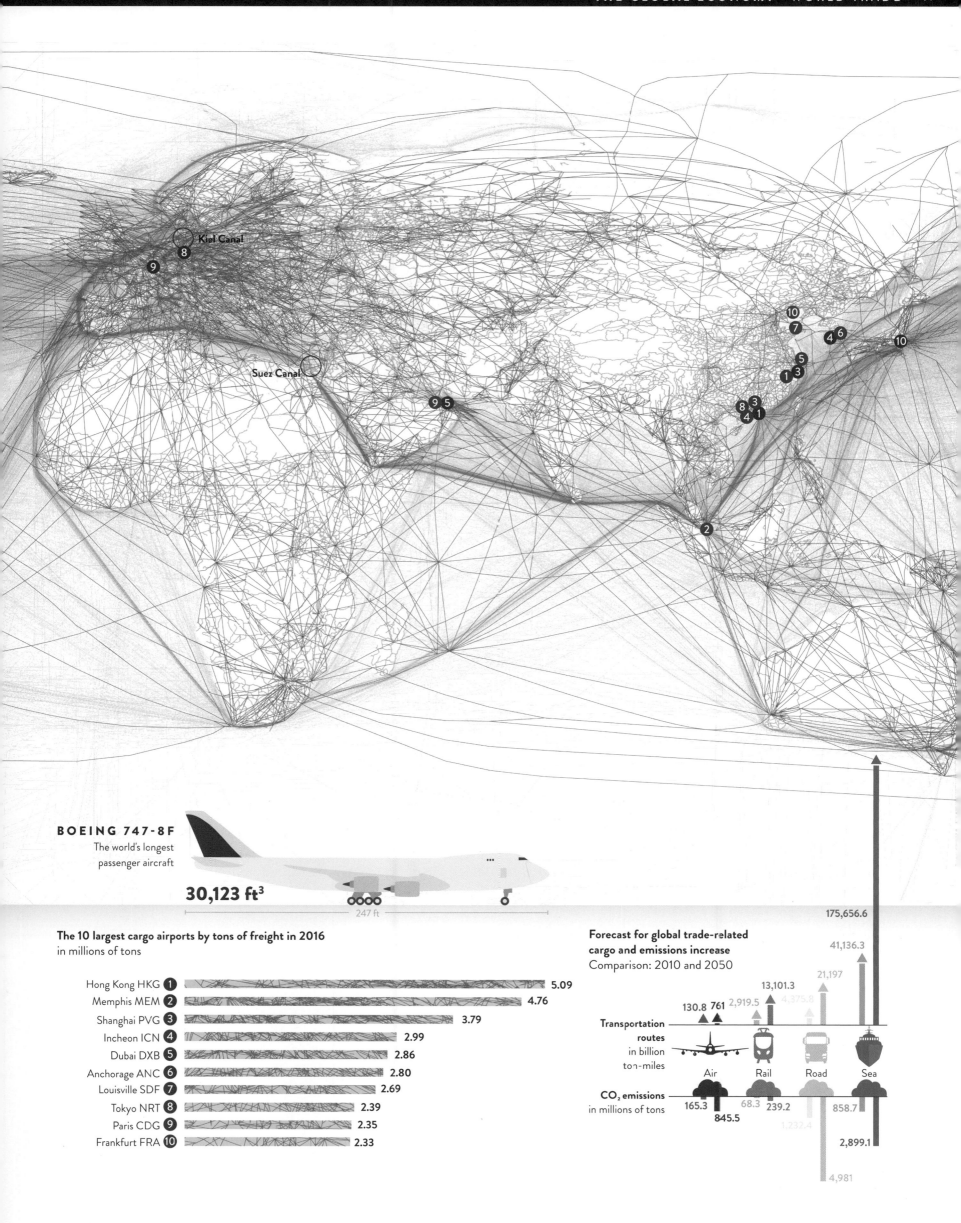

Kiel Canal ⑧
⑨

Suez Canal

⑨ ⑤

⑩
⑦
④ ⑥
⑤
① ③
⑧ ③
④ ①

②

⑩

BOEING 747-8F
The world's longest
passenger aircraft

30,123 ft³

247 ft

The 10 largest cargo airports by tons of freight in 2016
in millions of tons

Hong Kong HKG	①	5.09
Memphis MEM	②	4.76
Shanghai PVG	③	3.79
Incheon ICN	④	2.99
Dubai DXB	⑤	2.86
Anchorage ANC	⑥	2.80
Louisville SDF	⑦	2.69
Tokyo NRT	⑧	2.39
Paris CDG	⑨	2.35
Frankfurt FRA	⑩	2.33

Forecast for global trade-related cargo and emissions increase
Comparison: 2010 and 2050

175,656.6

41,136.3

21,197

13,101.3

4,375.8

2,919.5

130.8 761

Transportation routes
in billion
ton-miles

| Air | Rail | Road | Sea |

CO₂ emissions
in millions of tons

165.3   68.3 239.2   858.7
845.5   1,232.4

2,899.1

4,981

TPP

Major expansion of the free trade area between Australia, Brunei, Canada, Chile, Brunei Darussalam, Japan, Malaysia, Mexico, New Zealand, Peru, Singapore, and Vietnam. The agreement was signed in March 2018.

TTIP

The highly controversial Transatlantic Trade and Investment Partnership between the EU and the USA. Negotiations are still ongoing, but their outcome is uncertain.

FREE TRADE?

The freer the trade, the better for everyone. Trade barriers impede prosperity. That's how economic liberals see it. Critics of globalization, however, believe that free trade weakens local production and reinforces global exploitation. What's backed up by data is that trade is becoming freer almost everywhere—at least, that has been the trend for a long time. And prosperity is also increasing almost everywhere.

OTTAWA
WASHINGTON, D.C.
MEXICO CITY
NAFTA

GUATEMALA CITY
CACM

LIMA
Andean Community

MONTEVIDEO
MERCOSUR

Economic and monetary union
Economic union
Customs and currency union
Common market
Customs union
Multilateral free trade zone
WTO observer status (accession negotiations)
No WTO membership
Headquarters of the organization
-··- TTIP
····· TPP

WTO

Successor organization to GATT. The most important platform for global free trade policy. Mediator in many major trade disputes.

NAFTA

The North American response to the European Economic Community. It arrived on the scene very late. No ambitions for political integration.

MERCOSUR

The South American free trade area. The aim is a fully integrated internal market with around 300 million consumers.

Important free trade agreements (date of establishment)

EEC
European Economic Community

EFTA*
European Free Trade Association

ECCAS
Economic Community of Central African States

CAN
Andean Community

COMESA
Common Market for Eastern and Southern Africa

ECSC
European Coal and Steel Community (until 2002)

EURATOM
European Atomic Energy Community

GCC
Gulf Cooperation Council (for Arab states of the Persian Gulf)

WEU
Western European Union (until 2011)

CACM
Central American Common Market

ASEAN
Association of Southeast Asian Nations

ECOWAS
Economic Community of West African States

SADC
Southern African Development Community

GATT
General Agreement on Tariffs and Trade

1948   1950   1955   1960   1965   1970   1975   1980

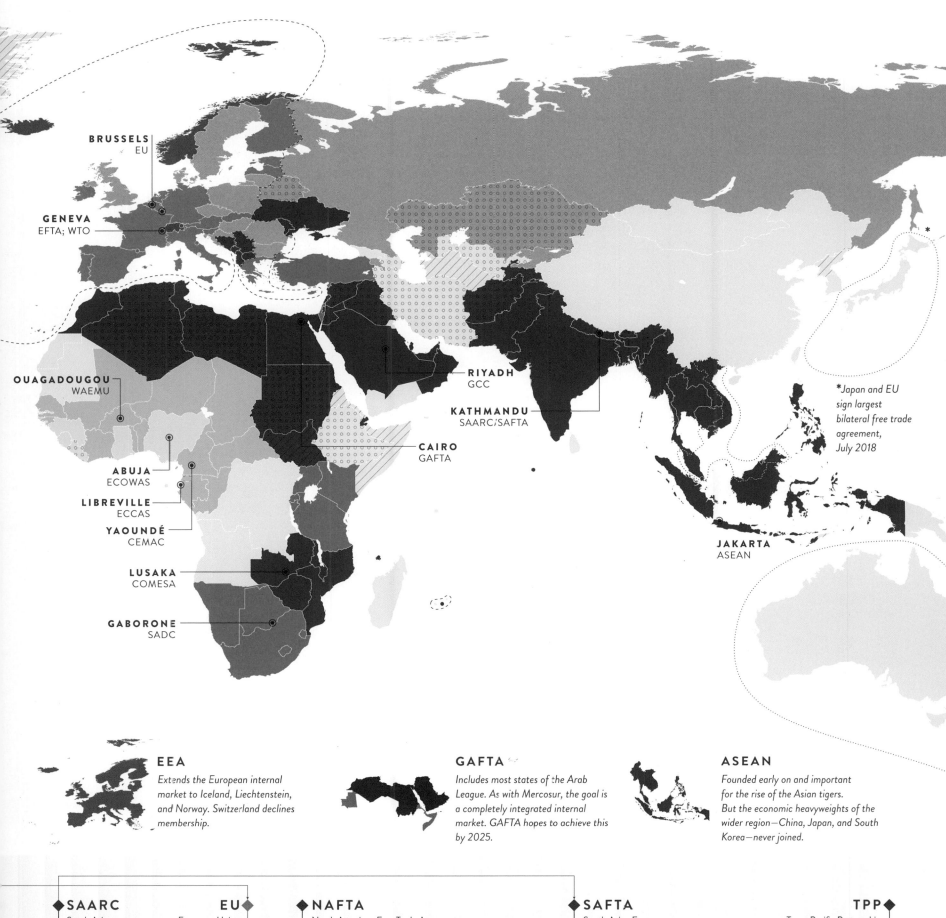

BRUSSELS
EU

GENEVA
EFTA; WTO

OUAGADOUGOU
WAEMU

ABUJA
ECOWAS

LIBREVILLE
ECCAS

YAOUNDÉ
CEMAC

LUSAKA
COMESA

GABORONE
SADC

RIYADH
GCC

KATHMANDU
SAARC/SAFTA

CAIRO
GAFTA

*Japan and EU
sign largest
bilateral free trade
agreement,
July 2018

JAKARTA
ASEAN

EEA

Extends the European internal market to Iceland, Liechtenstein, and Norway. Switzerland declines membership.

GAFTA

Includes most states of the Arab League. As with Mercosur, the goal is a completely integrated internal market. GAFTA hopes to achieve this by 2025.

ASEAN

Founded early on and important for the rise of the Asian tigers. But the economic heavyweights of the wider region—China, Japan, and South Korea—never joined.

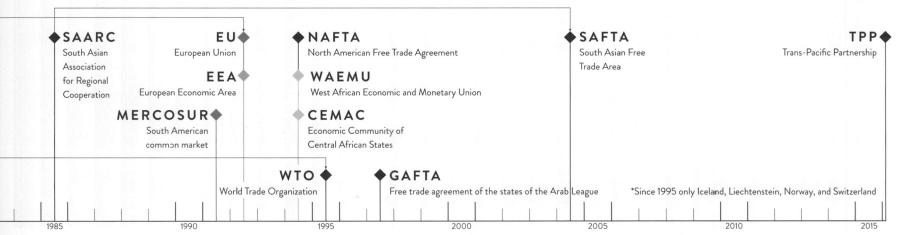

SAARC
South Asian Association for Regional Cooperation

EU
European Union

EEA
European Economic Area

MERCOSUR
South American common market

NAFTA
North American Free Trade Agreement

WAEMU
West African Economic and Monetary Union

CEMAC
Economic Community of Central African States

WTO
World Trade Organization

GAFTA
Free trade agreement of the states of the Arab League

SAFTA
South Asian Free Trade Area

TPP
Trans-Pacific Partnership

*Since 1995 only Iceland, Liechtenstein, Norway, and Switzerland

1985   1990   1995   2000   2005   2010   2015

Trade zones

- North America
- South and Central America
- Europe
- Africa
- Middle East
- Commonwealth of Independent States
- Asia

THE EXPORT GAMES

The US was the unrivaled exporting champion for decades. The first serious challenger was Germany, which went on to hold the title for a while. But then came longtime outsider China, crushing the waning champions. Luckily, regional alliances give little countries a better chance against big ones. In the regional class, the European Union comes first, teaching a key lesson: Economic and political integration brings growth.

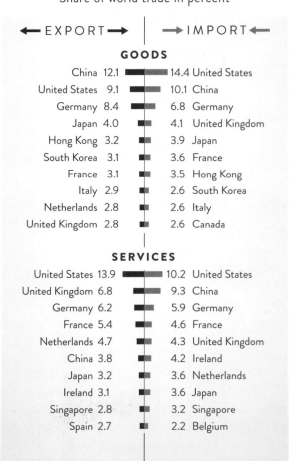

Leading trade nations 2016
Share of world trade in percent

←— EXPORT —→ →— IMPORT —←

GOODS

EXPORT		IMPORT	
China	12.1	14.4	United States
United States	9.1	10.1	China
Germany	8.4	6.8	Germany
Japan	4.0	4.1	United Kingdom
Hong Kong	3.2	3.9	Japan
South Korea	3.1	3.6	France
France	3.1	3.5	Hong Kong
Italy	2.9	2.6	South Korea
Netherlands	2.8	2.6	Italy
United Kingdom	2.8	2.6	Canada

SERVICES

EXPORT		IMPORT	
United States	13.9	10.2	United States
United Kingdom	6.8	9.3	China
Germany	6.2	5.9	Germany
France	5.4	4.6	France
Netherlands	4.7	4.3	United Kingdom
China	3.8	4.2	Ireland
Japan	3.2	3.6	Netherlands
Ireland	3.1	3.6	Japan
Singapore	2.8	3.2	Singapore
Spain	2.7	2.2	Belgium

Top three leading export nations over the course of time
Cumulative exports of goods in billions of US$

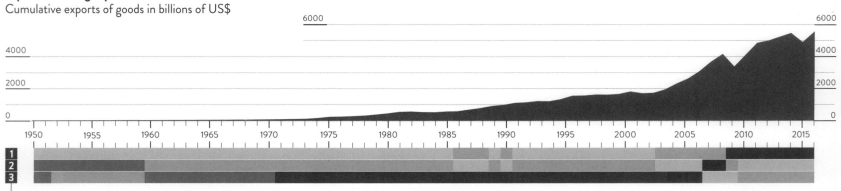

The top three places in the exports world championship ■ USA ■ CANADA ■ JAPAN ■ CHINA ■ FRANCE ■ UNITED KINGDOM ■ GERMANY

Intra- and interregional trade 2016
Flow of goods in billions of US$

LEGEND

1,028 ▭──────── 462 Trade between regions

2,745 ▭────────── Trade within a region

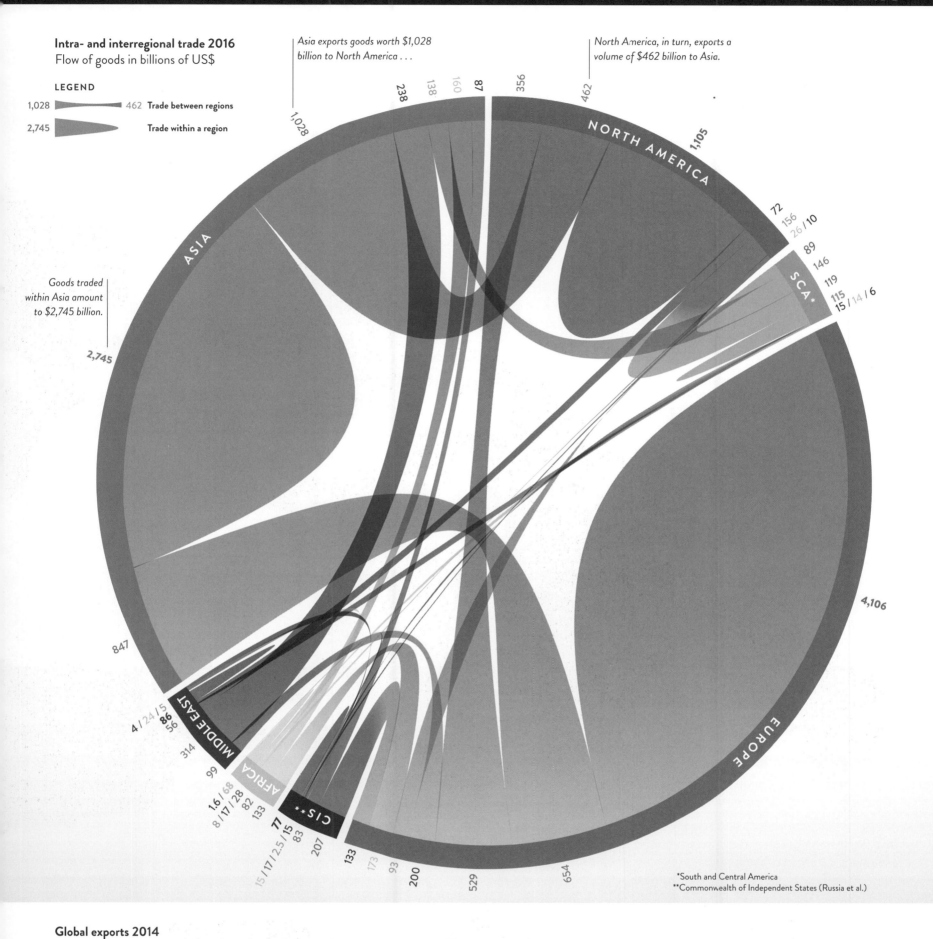

Asia exports goods worth $1,028 billion to North America . . .

North America, in turn, exports a volume of $462 billion to Asia.

Goods traded within Asia amount to $2,745 billion.

238 138 160 87 356 462

1,028

2,745

847

4/24/5 **86** 56

314

66

16/68

8/17/28 82 133

77

15/17/2.5/15 83

207 133 173 93 200 529 654

ASIA

NORTH AMERICA 1,105

72 156/10

26/10

89 146

119

115 15/14/6

SCA*

4,106

EUROPE

MIDDLE EAST

AFRICA

CIS**

*South and Central America
**Commonwealth of Independent States (Russia et al.)

Global exports 2014
Value in billions of US dollars

■ Services ■ Goods

2,585
Others

1,240
Travel

955
Transport

6,087
Machinery and
transportation equipment

3,783
Mining products
and fuels

2,057
Chemicals

1,623
Other
finished
products

1,486
Food

1,472
Other
goods

1,196
Other
semi-finished
products

503
Clothing

288
Agricultural
products
(others)

THE ILLEGAL GLOBAL MARKET

Organized criminal gangs are global players. The extent of the streams of illegal goods and their routes are inherently very difficult to determine. Two scholars from the Finnish Institute of International Affairs have collected facts and evidence that make possible at least a rough estimate and highlight particularly important routes of the world market in illegal goods. A depressing result of their study: Crime pays, probably to the tune of over $500 billion—with some estimates closer to $1 trillion.

SOUTHEAST EUROPE

WEST AND CENTRAL EUROPE

CARIBBEAN

USA

MEXICO

CENTRAL AMERICA

ANDES

Cocaine

The worldwide market for cocaine has been growing for decades. The number of users is growing especially fast in Europe. It's now almost as high as in the USA. The global cocaine business comes to around $90 billion.

Firearms

Illegal weapons are bought and sold around the world. But a particularly large number of them find their way from the former USSR to Africa, and from the USA across the Mexican border. The UN Office on Drugs and Crime estimates annual global sales as $170 million to $320 million.

Human smuggling

For a long time, Africans have made use of smugglers to get to Europe. In recent years, however, veritable smuggling industries have formed in Syria, Afghanistan, and Iraq.

JAPAN

SOUTHEAST ASIA

CHINA

RUSSIA

CENTRAL ASIA

MYANMAR

AFGHANISTAN

UKRAINE

INDIA

MIDDLE EAST

CENTRAL AFRICA

WESTERN
AFRICA

SOUTHERN AFRICA

BRAZIL

Heroin

Afghanistan is the largest producer
of heroin. Terrorists and the Taliban
take a hefty cut of the profits. The
Asian market frequently draws its
supply from Myanmar.

Counterfeit
goods

Copies of Gucci handbags are only
the tip of the counterfeit iceberg.
Counterfeiting gangs earn many times
more from cigarettes, alcohol, and
petroleum products with falsified
customs declarations than they earn
off of name-brand sneakers.

Phony
medicine

Fake medications are some of
the most sordid goods imaginable.
They often contain no active
ingredients, and sometimes even
contain poisonous substances.

Human trafficking

According to the study, Europe is
one of the most important destinations for human traffickers. Many of
the victims have been forced into
prostitution.

Wood

According to the Finnish
researchers, China is the main
supplier of protected trees
and wood.

Animals

The superstitious belief in potency
pills made from powdered rhino
horns is driving the beasts to the
brink of extinction. Rare birds are
smuggled alive around the world.
Asia is one of the largest importers.

COMPULSORY LABOR IN THE 21ST CENTURY

Slavery has been abolished all over the world—technically speaking. Unfortunately, it has not been vanquished. According to the International Labor Organization, around 24.9 million people are still exploited for compulsory labor using threats or acts of violence. That is more than at any previous point in history. Modern slaves are often abducted, toil in debt slavery in sweatshops or fields, are forced into prostitution, or have to fight as child soldiers in rebel armies. In Haiti, a girl costs $50. The extent of this disgrace in figures:

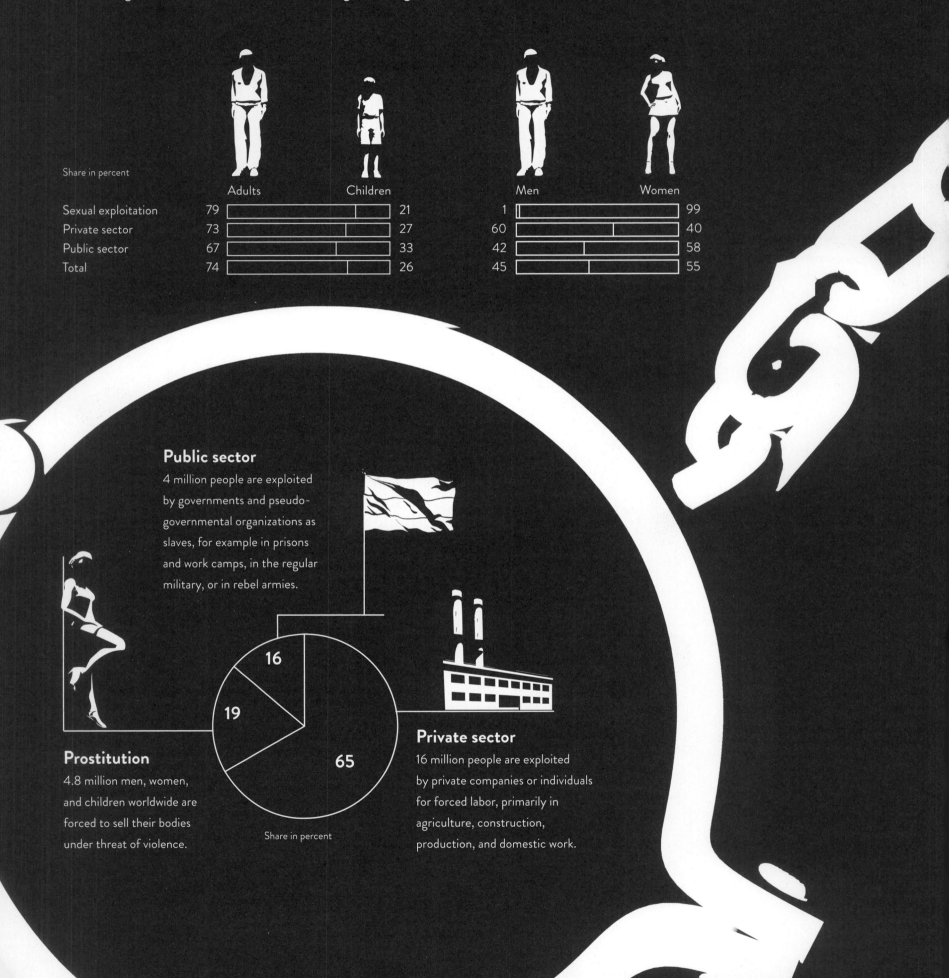

Share in percent	Adults		Children		Men		Women
Sexual exploitation	79		21		1		99
Private sector	73		27		60		40
Public sector	67		33		42		58
Total	74		26		45		55

Public sector

4 million people are exploited by governments and pseudo-governmental organizations as slaves, for example in prisons and work camps, in the regular military, or in rebel armies.

Prostitution

4.8 million men, women, and children worldwide are forced to sell their bodies under threat of violence.

16
19
65

Share in percent

Private sector

16 million people are exploited by private companies or individuals for forced labor, primarily in agriculture, construction, production, and domestic work.

How lucrative is forced labor for the perpetrators?

Annual profits	In billions of US$	In US$ per victim
Asia-Pacific region	51.8	5,000
Industrialized countries and EU	46.9	34,800
CIS* and East/Southeast Europe	18	12,900
Africa	13.1	3,900
Latin America and Caribbean	12	7,500
Middle East	8.5	15,000

People in forced labor

- Middle East
- Industrialized countries and EU
- CIS and East/Southeast Europe
- Latin America and Caribbean
- Africa
- Asia-Pacific region

1,500,000

1,600,000

600,000

11,700,000

3,700,000

1,800,000

*Commonwealth of Independent States

Some economists believe nothing and no one can restrain global capitalism. A network of international organizations and alliances believes otherwise—and has created an international regulatory framework whose powerful member organizations often mutually reinforce one another's power.

GLOBAL EC

Year of founding ·········	1945 ····· 1945
Seat ·····►	WASHINGTON WASHINGTON

IMF
International Monetary Fund

WBG
World Bank Group*

Mandate ·········

Currency policy—international cooperation
Supervision of monetary policy, exchange rate stabilization, international financial stability, growth of world trade

Combating global poverty
through
the financing of long-term development and construction projects

Instruments ·········

Extension of credit to countries experiencing difficulties with their balance of payments (functioning as a lender of last resort), advising, and economic policy requirements

Granting of loans, equity investments, guarantees, mediation of investment disputes, consulting
*Includes five organizations with their own legal identities

G7 + 12 + 1

The G20 is a rather loose grouping of the seven most important industrialized nations as well as twelve emerging economies. The EU has its own seat. The goal is to coordinate the international finance system—and thus to create the basis for the stable growth of the global economy.

The G7 nations are Germany, France, Italy, Japan, Canada, the USA, and the United Kingdom. The European Commission has observer status.

Members ·········

189 nations

Nonmembers include Cuba, North Korea, Andorra, Monaco, Nauru, and Liechtenstein

Quota system
(capital share of each nation)

	0	10	20%
USA			
JPN			
ITA			
GER			
IND			
RUS			
CAN			

Voting rights ◄·····
Largest voting shares

189 nations

Nonmembers include Cuba, North Korea, Andorra, Monaco, Nauru, and Liechtenstein

Quota system
(share ownership of each nation)

	5	15%
USA		
JPN		
CHN		
GER		
FRA		
GBR		
IND		

G7
1975

Informal association

Summit meetings of the heads of state and government

G8
1998–2014

G7 + Russia
(until the annexation of Crimea)

G20
1999

Expanded informal association*

*19 nations + EU

Structure ····

Board of Governors = supreme decision-making body (one representative per member state)

Consultation

International Monetary and Financial Committee (IMFC)

Development Committee

Managing Director

Executive Board
The Fund's day-to-day business (24 members)

IMF Administrative Tribunal

Board of Governors = highest decision-making body
(one governor and one alternate governor per member state). The Bank president directs ongoing business in accordance with the resolutions of the Boards of Directors (25 executive directors)

WBG

International Bank for Reconstruction and Development (IBRD)	International Development Association (IDA)
International Finance Corporation (IFC)	Multilateral Investment Guarantee Agency (MIGA)	International Center for Settlement of Investment Disputes (ICSID)

Budget ·····

204 billion SDR*
Capital (~$285 billion)
*SDR = Special Drawing Right (an independent accounting unit converted daily into the most important currencies)

2,600

Staff ◄·····
members

$61 billion
Loans to countries
$268.9 billion
capital

10,000

Foundation ·········

The founding of the IMF and the WBG at the Bretton Woods Conference in 1944 with the goal of creating the framework for a more stable, flourishing global economic order. These agencies, part of the UN, pursue similar goals with a complementary approach: The IMF is oriented toward macroeconomic affairs, while the WBG is oriented toward long-term economic development and reducing poverty.

Participants in the summits include, among others: heads of state and government from the **G20**, ministers of finance and central bank chairmen from the **G8** and 11 additional nations, the president of the European Central Bank, the EU president (if not held by a **G7** nation), the managing director of the **IMF**, and the president of the **World Bank**

Institutional cooperation ·········►

CONSULTING / COOPERATION ON ALL LEVELS   WBG – MEMBER OF VAR

EXTENSIVE EXCHANGE OF INFORMATION: IMF—MEMBER OR OBSERVER

COOPERATION: REGULAR CONSULTATION; MUT

NOMIC ADMINISTRATION

1961 — PARIS

OECD
Organization for Economic Cooperation and Development

Advancement of democracy and market economics
Forum for the sharing of experience and the development of collaborative solutions

Recommendations, standards and guidelines, agreements and occasionally legally binding treaties as well

34 nations* + European Commission

*The EU nations Bulgaria, Croatia, Cyprus, Latvia, Lithuania, Malta, and Romania do not have membership

One country, one vote

 = X

Decisions by mutual consent (except in isolated cases)

Council= decision-making body *Strategic direction and oversight*

Committees *Discussion and technical work*

Secretariat *Data collection, analysis, and proposals*

363 million euros
Budget and agenda are determined on a two-year basis.

2,500

Successor to the Organization for European Economic Cooperation and the 1948 Marshall Plan for the rebuilding of Europe

1995 — GENEVA

WTO
World Trade Organization

Global trade and economic relations
Liberalization of international trade and multilateral trade rules

General Agreement on Tariffs and Trade (GATT)

General Agreement on Trade in Services (GATS)

Trade Related Aspects of Intellectual Property Rights (TRIPS)

161 nations + EU

The EU is a member in its own right along with each EU member state.

One country, one vote

 = X

Although a simple majority is sufficient in actual fact, decisions are reached by consensus as a matter of principle.

Director-General

Secretariat

Ongoing business

General Council

General Council of economic and trade ministers = highest decision-making body (at least every two years)

The ambassadors and delegates meet regularly in Geneva.

General Council

Dispute Settlement Body

Trade Policy Review Body

197,500,000 Swiss francs

634

Successor organization of the General Agreement on Tariffs and Trade (GATT), which was intended to lower tariffs between trading partners and simplify trade after the Second World War

2009 — BASEL

FSB
Financial Stability Board

Global financial stability
Risk evaluation, formation and coordination of guidelines, monitoring of implementation, compendium of financial standards

Guidelines are not legally binding, but rather rely on moral persuasion and mutual pressure
Association under Swiss law

24 countries* + 12 organizations**

*G20 + Hong Kong, the Netherlands, Singapore, Spain, and Switzerland
**The ECB, European Commission, IMF, OECD, and World Bank, among others

No formal distribution of voting rights

Decisions by consensus

Plenary = decision-making body 69 representatives

Steering Committee: *Operational activity*

Assessment of Vulnerabilities (SCAV)

4 standing committees

Budget and Resources (SCBR)

Supervisory and Regulatory Cooperation (SRC)

Standards Implementation (SCSI)

12,285,000 Swiss francs
Majority of donations from the Bank for International Settlements (BIS)

24

Successor organization of the Financial Stability Forum (FSF), started by G20 nations at the peak of the financial crisis

---

...D COMMITTEES

...OUS OECD COMMITTEES

...ULAR CONSULTATION AND COOPERATION

...ERVER STATUS IN VARIOUS COMMITTEES; PARTICIPATION IN VARIOUS MEETINGS

OECD—INFLUENCE ON WTO NEGOTIATIONS

OECD—MEMBER OF FSB

·········· No substantive consultation or cooperation ··········

WBG—MEMBER OF FSB

IMF—MEMBER OF FSB

MULTIPLYING MONEY

Bill Gates once said that the world needs banking, but it does
not need banks. Really? Despite the skepticism, the old
moneymaking industry is still doing pretty well for itself.

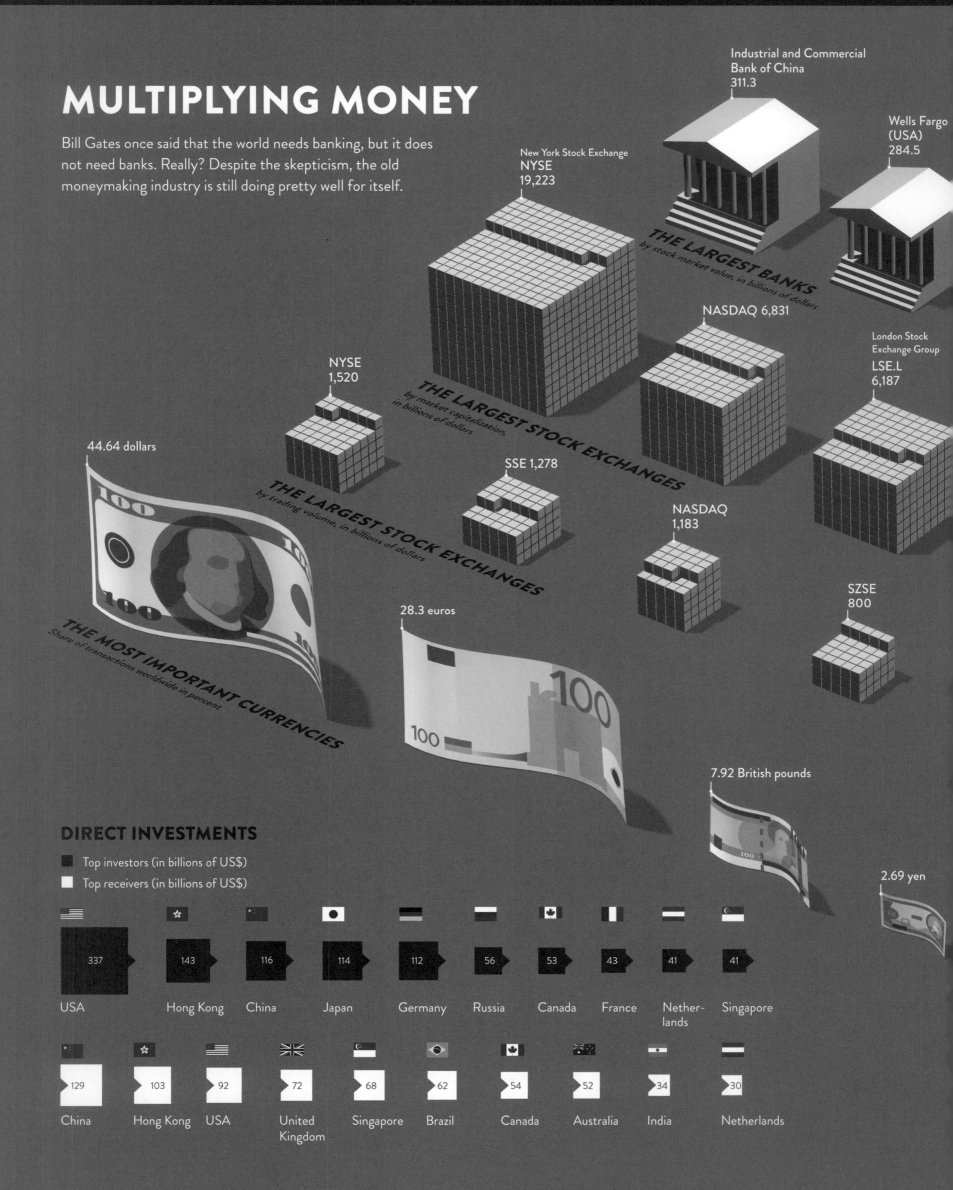

Industrial and Commercial
Bank of China
311.3

Wells Fargo
(USA)
284.5

New York Stock Exchange
**NYSE
19,223**

THE LARGEST BANKS
by stock market value, in billions of dollars

NASDAQ 6,831

London Stock
Exchange Group
**LSE.L
6,187**

**NYSE
1,520**

THE LARGEST STOCK EXCHANGES
by market capitalization,
in billions of dollars

SSE 1,278

NASDAQ
1,183

SZSE
800

44.64 dollars

THE LARGEST STOCK EXCHANGES
by trading volume, in billions of dollars

28.3 euros

THE MOST IMPORTANT CURRENCIES
Share of transactions worldwide in percent

7.92 British pounds

2.69 yen

DIRECT INVESTMENTS

■ Top investors (in billions of US$)
□ Top receivers (in billions of US$)

USA	Hong Kong	China	Japan	Germany	Russia	Canada	France	Nether-lands	Singapore
337	143	116	114	112	56	53	43	41	41

China	Hong Kong	USA	United Kingdom	Singapore	Brazil	Canada	Australia	India	Netherlands
129	103	92	72	68	62	54	52	34	30

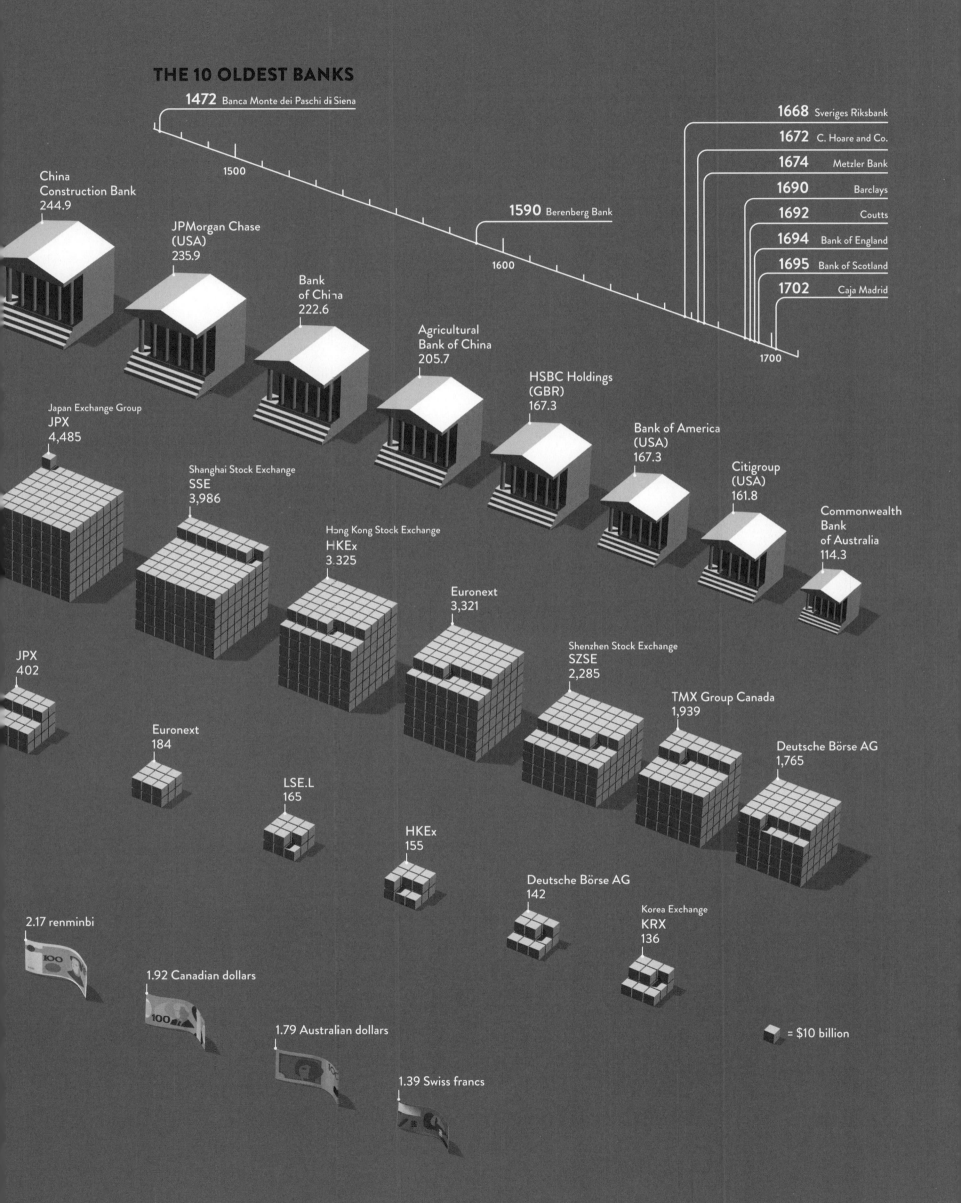

THE 10 OLDEST BANKS

1472 Banca Monte dei Paschi di Siena

1500

1590 Berenberg Bank

1600

1668 Sveriges Riksbank
1672 C. Hoare and Co.
1674 Metzler Bank
1690 Barclays
1692 Coutts
1694 Bank of England
1695 Bank of Scotland
1702 Caja Madrid

1700

China
Construction Bank
244.9

JPMorgan Chase
(USA)
235.9

Bank
of China
222.6

Agricultural
Bank of China
205.7

HSBC Holdings
(GBR)
167.3

Bank of America
(USA)
167.3

Citigroup
(USA)
161.8

Commonwealth
Bank
of Australia
114.3

Japan Exchange Group
JPX
4,485

Shanghai Stock Exchange
SSE
3,986

Hong Kong Stock Exchange
HKEx
3,325

Euronext
3,321

Shenzhen Stock Exchange
SZSE
2,285

TMX Group Canada
1,939

Deutsche Börse AG
1,765

JPX
402

Euronext
184

LSE.L
165

HKEx
155

Deutsche Börse AG
142

Korea Exchange
KRX
136

2.17 renminbi

1.92 Canadian dollars

1.79 Australian dollars

1.39 Swiss francs

= $10 billion

THE BIG MAC INDEX

How much is my money really worth in another country? And what does that say about the purchasing power of local currencies? The field of international economics has addressed this question since the 19th century through the concept of purchasing power parity. Theoretically, it's extremely complicated. The foundations were established by the British economist David Ricardo. In 1986, the *Economist* came up with the brilliant idea of simply comparing the prices of a highly standardized, globally available consumer product: the Big Mac. This approach is both highly simplistic and extremely enlightening.

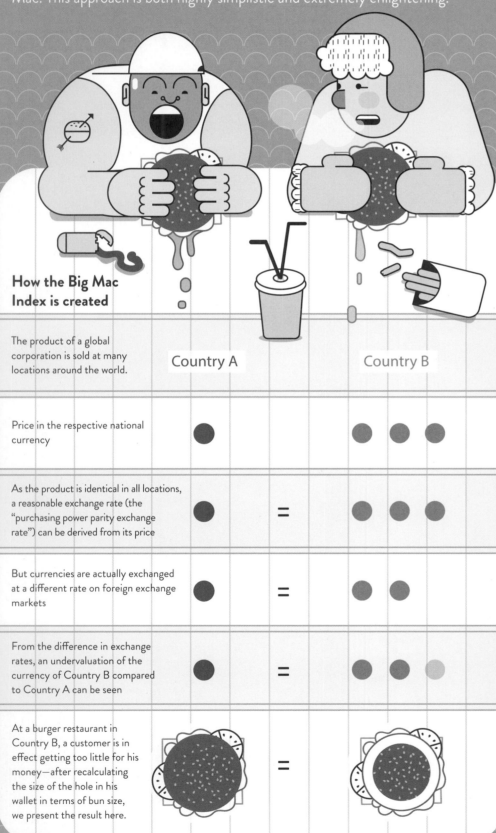

How the Big Mac Index is created

	Country A		Country B		
The product of a global corporation is sold at many locations around the world.					
Price in the respective national currency	●		● ● ●		
As the product is identical in all locations, a reasonable exchange rate (the "purchasing power parity exchange rate") can be derived from its price	●	=	● ● ●		
But currencies are actually exchanged at a different rate on foreign exchange markets	●	=	● ●		
From the difference in exchange rates, an undervaluation of the currency of Country B compared to Country A can be seen	●	=	● ● ●		
At a burger restaurant in Country B, a customer is in effect getting too little for his money—after recalculating the size of the hole in his wallet in terms of bun size, we present the result here.	🍔	=	🍔		

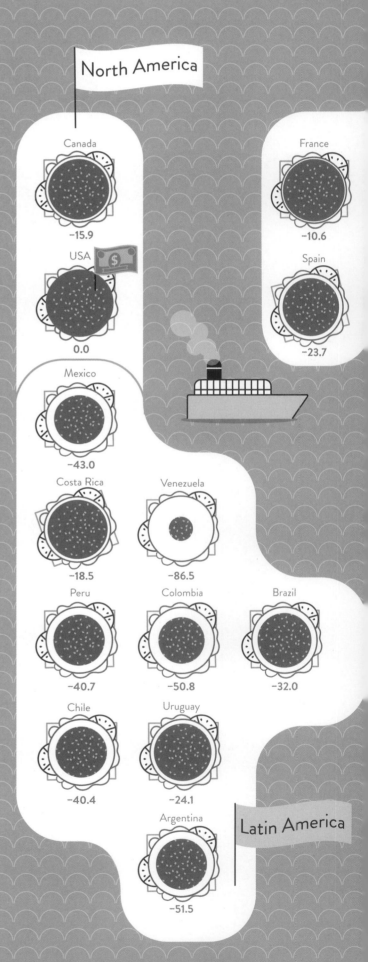

The Big Mac Index with an American "model burger": national currency in comparison to the dollar, over- and undervaluation in percent

North America

Canada −15.9

USA 0.0

Mexico −43.0

Costa Rica −18.5

Venezuela −86.5

Peru −40.7

Colombia −50.8

Brazil −32.0

Chile −40.4

Uruguay −24.1

Argentina −51.5

France −10.6

Spain −23.7

Latin America

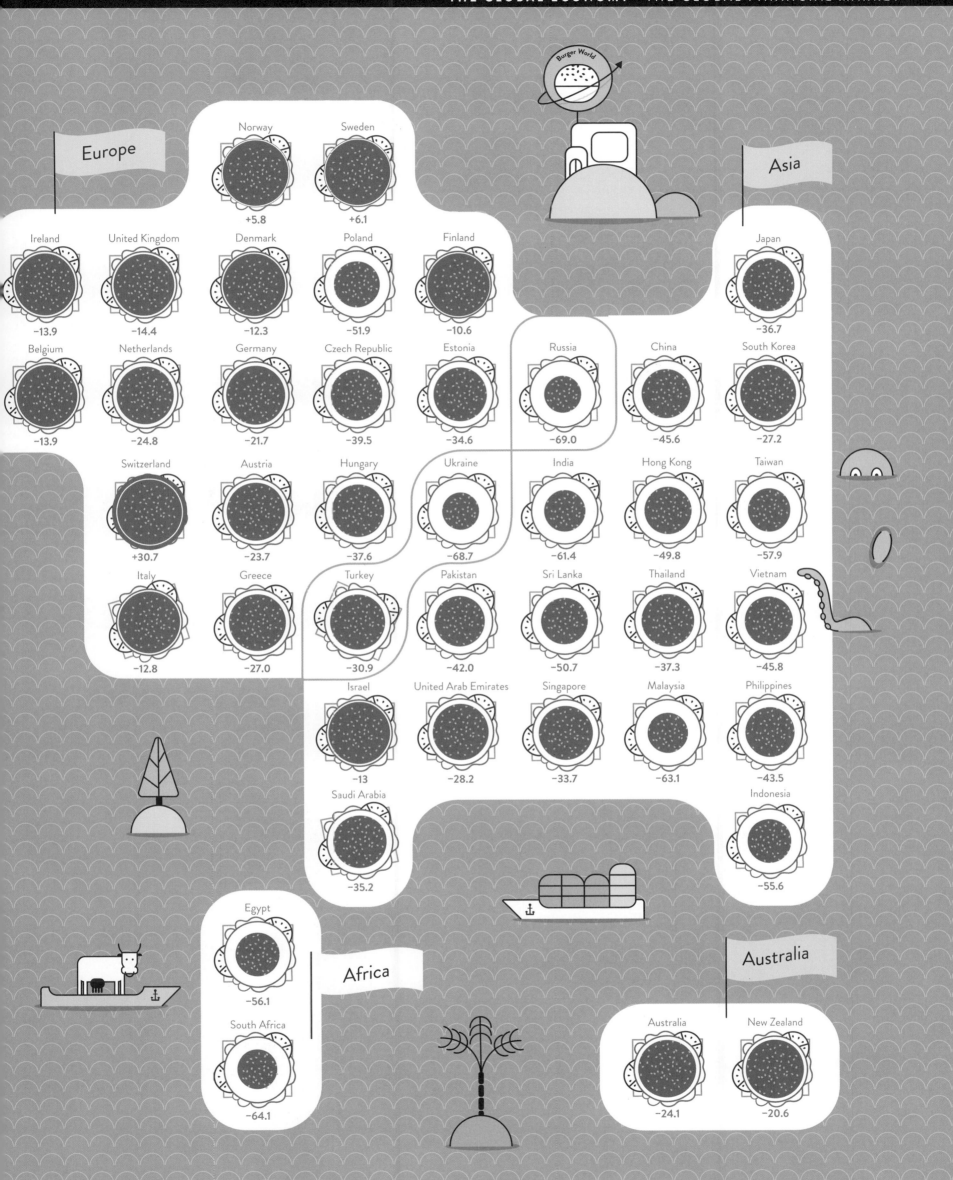

Europe

Asia

Norway +5.8

Sweden +6.1

Ireland −13.9

United Kingdom −14.4

Denmark −12.3

Poland −51.9

Finland −10.6

Japan −36.7

Belgium −13.9

Netherlands −24.8

Germany −21.7

Czech Republic −39.5

Estonia −34.6

Russia −69.0

China −45.6

South Korea −27.2

Switzerland +30.7

Austria −23.7

Hungary −37.6

Ukraine −68.7

India −61.4

Hong Kong −49.8

Taiwan −57.9

Italy −12.8

Greece −27.0

Turkey −30.9

Pakistan −42.0

Sri Lanka −50.7

Thailand −37.3

Vietnam −45.8

Israel −13

United Arab Emirates −28.2

Singapore −33.7

Malaysia −63.1

Philippines −43.5

Saudi Arabia −35.2

Indonesia −55.6

Egypt −56.1

Africa

South Africa −64.1

Australia

Australia −24.1

New Zealand −20.6

IS BIGGER REALLY BETTER?

Which one sells the most? Company managers and owners always have a burning interest in this question. But high sales don't say much about a company's value. Profit and future prospects have a greater effect on the stock price. So Amazon is worth more than Walmart, despite Walmart's mammoth sales. Still, sales provide some insight into a company's relative influence on the marketplace—and on our daily lives.

The ten largest companies worldwide per sector by revenue, in US$ Bn*
** Boldface text indicates US-based company

↑ Going up   → Unchanged   ↓ Going down   +1 Change compared to placement in 2015   • Not in the TOP 10 in 2015

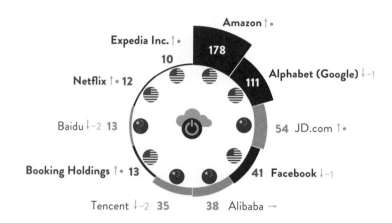

Amazon ↑ •   178
Expedia Inc. ↑ •   10
Alphabet (Google) ↓ –1   111
Netflix ↑ •   12
Baidu ↓ –2   13
JD.com ↑ •   54
Booking Holdings ↑ •   13
Facebook ↓ –1   41
Tencent ↓ –2   35
Alibaba →   38

INTERNET
Sales for internet companies are rising across the board, while Amazon becomes a global giant.

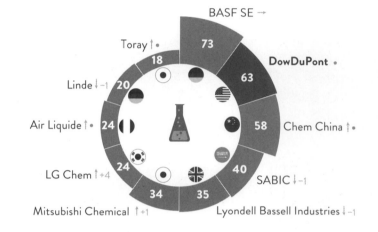

BASF SE →   73
Toray ↑ •   18
DowDuPont •   63
Linde ↓ –1   20
Air Liquide ↑ •   24
Chem China ↑ •   58
LG Chem ↑ +4   24
SABIC ↓ –1   40
Mitsubishi Chemical ↑ +1   34
Lyondell Bassell Industries ↓ –1   35

CHEMISTRY
BASF has long been the largest chemical company in the world. Their position is threatened due to an internal American merger.

* Revenues of publicly traded companies for their respective fiscal years ending on or before March 31, 2018

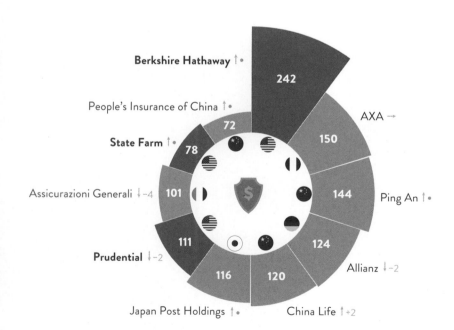

Berkshire Hathaway ↑ •   242
People's Insurance of China ↑ •   72
AXA →   150
State Farm ↑ •   78
Assicurazioni Generali ↓ –4   101
Ping An ↑ •   144
Prudential ↓ –2   111
Allianz ↓ –2   124
Japan Post Holdings ↑ •   116
China Life ↑ +2   120

INSURANCE
The conglomerate Berkshire Hathaway, which counts the auto insurer Geico as one of its subsidiaries, dominates this list.

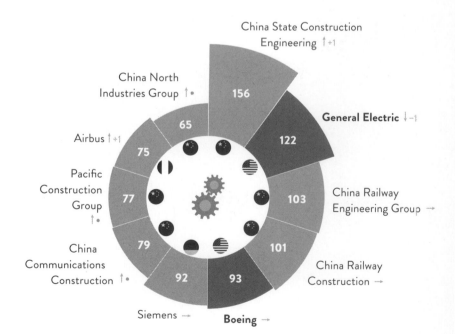

China State Construction Engineering ↑ +1   156
China North Industries Group ↑ •   65
General Electric ↓ –1   122
Airbus ↑ +1   75
Pacific Construction Group ↑ •   77
China Railway Engineering Group →   103
China Communications Construction ↑ •   79
China Railway Construction →   101
Siemens →   92
Boeing →   93

INDUSTRIAL GOODS
General Electric's largest business is the manufacture and maintenance of electricity companies' turbines. Orders have fallen, and so has its place at the top.

Number of top 10 global players per country

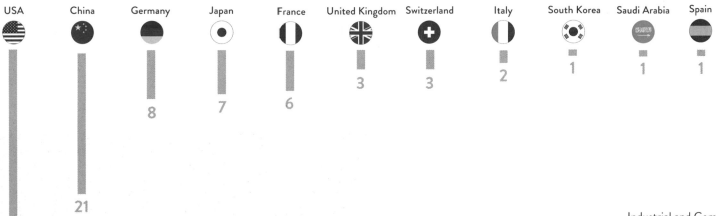

USA	China	Germany	Japan	France	United Kingdom	Switzerland	Italy	South Korea	Saudi Arabia	Spain
27	21	8	7	6	3	3	2	1	1	1

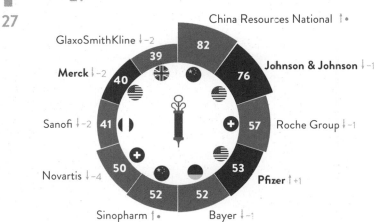

PHARMACEUTICALS

The Swiss have a reputation for innovative midsize drug companies as well as two giants. But a pair of Chinese newcomers are ascendant.

China Resources National ↑• 82
GlaxoSmithKline ↓−2 39
Johnson & Johnson ↓−1 76
Merck ↓−2 40
Roche Group ↓−1 57
Sanofi ↓−2 41
Pfizer ↑+1 53
Novartis ↓−4 50
Bayer ↓−1 52
Sinopharm ↑• 52

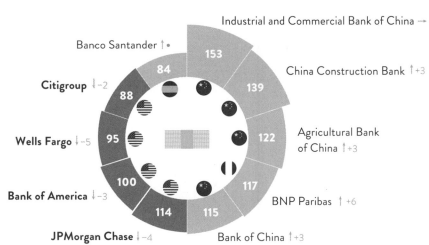

BANKS

It's the weight of numbers. Chinese banks are on the rise.

Industrial and Commercial Bank of China → 153
Banco Santander ↑• 84
China Construction Bank ↑+3 139
Citigroup ↓−2 88
Agricultural Bank of China ↑+3 122
Wells Fargo ↓−5 95
BNP Paribas ↑+6 117
Bank of America ↓−3 100
Bank of China ↑+3 115
JPMorgan Chase ↓−4 114

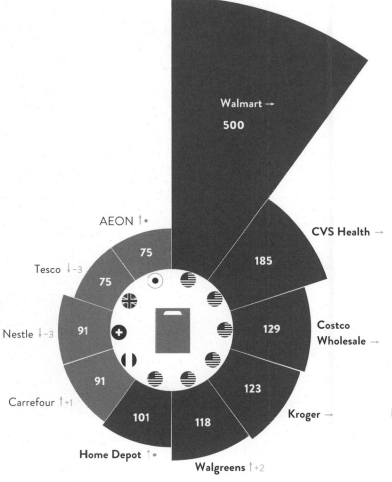

CONSUMER GOODS/TRADE

Walmart remains by far the multinational giant to beat.

Walmart → 500
AEON ↑• 75
CVS Health → 185
Tesco ↓−3 75
Costco Wholesale → 129
Nestlé ↓−3 91
Kroger → 123
Carrefour ↑+1 91
Walgreens ↑+2 118
Home Depot ↑• 101

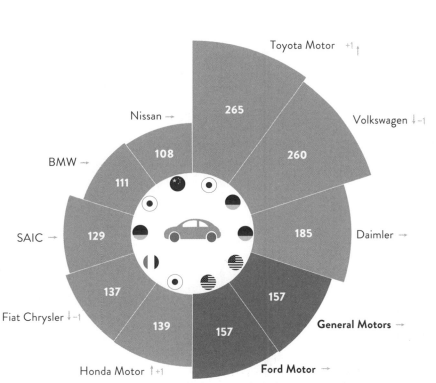

AUTOMOBILES

Have you ever seen a Maxus, Roewe, or Yuejin on the street? Just wait a few years. Those are brands of the first Chinese auto manufacturer (SAIC) to overtake BMW.

Toyota Motor +1 ↑ 265
Nissan → 108
Volkswagen ↓−1 260
BMW → 111
Daimler → 185
SAIC → 129
General Motors → 157
Fiat Chrysler ↓−1 137
Ford Motor → 157
Honda Motor ↑+1 139

BESTSELLERS

McDonald's showed how it's done: You can conquer the business world with franchises. Consumption is as global as production. And in many respects, the tastes of a Chinese customer are no longer so different from that of an Argentinean customer. Everyone likes Big Macs, Swedish furniture, electronics designed in California, and inexpensive clothes with simple designs from an expanding Japanese clothing corporation.

Distribution of branches

- ■ Europe
- ■ North America
- ■ South America
- ■ Asia
- ■ Australia
- ■ Africa
- ▨ Other nations of each continent

Uniqlo
has 1,920 stores worldwide

FRA	AUS	INA	RUS
GBR	SIN	THA	PHI
HKG	MAS	USA 44	
Taiwan	KOR 179		
CHN 555			
JPN 831			

Ikea
has 417 stores worldwide

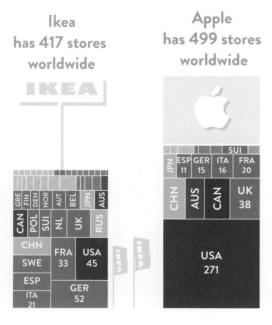

IKEA

CAN	GRE	FIN	DEN		
	POL	SUI	NOR	AUT	BEL
	NL	UK	JPN	AUS	
				RUS	
CHN	FRA 33	USA 45			
SWE					
ESP	GER 52				
ITA 21					

Apple
has 499 stores worldwide

JPN	ESP 11	GER 15	ITA 16	SUI	FRA 20
CHN	AUS	CAN	UK 38		
USA 271					

	NCA	HON	ESA	DOM	CRC	PAN	GUA

CAN
1,458

USA
14,036

McDonald's

has 37,241 restaurants worldwide

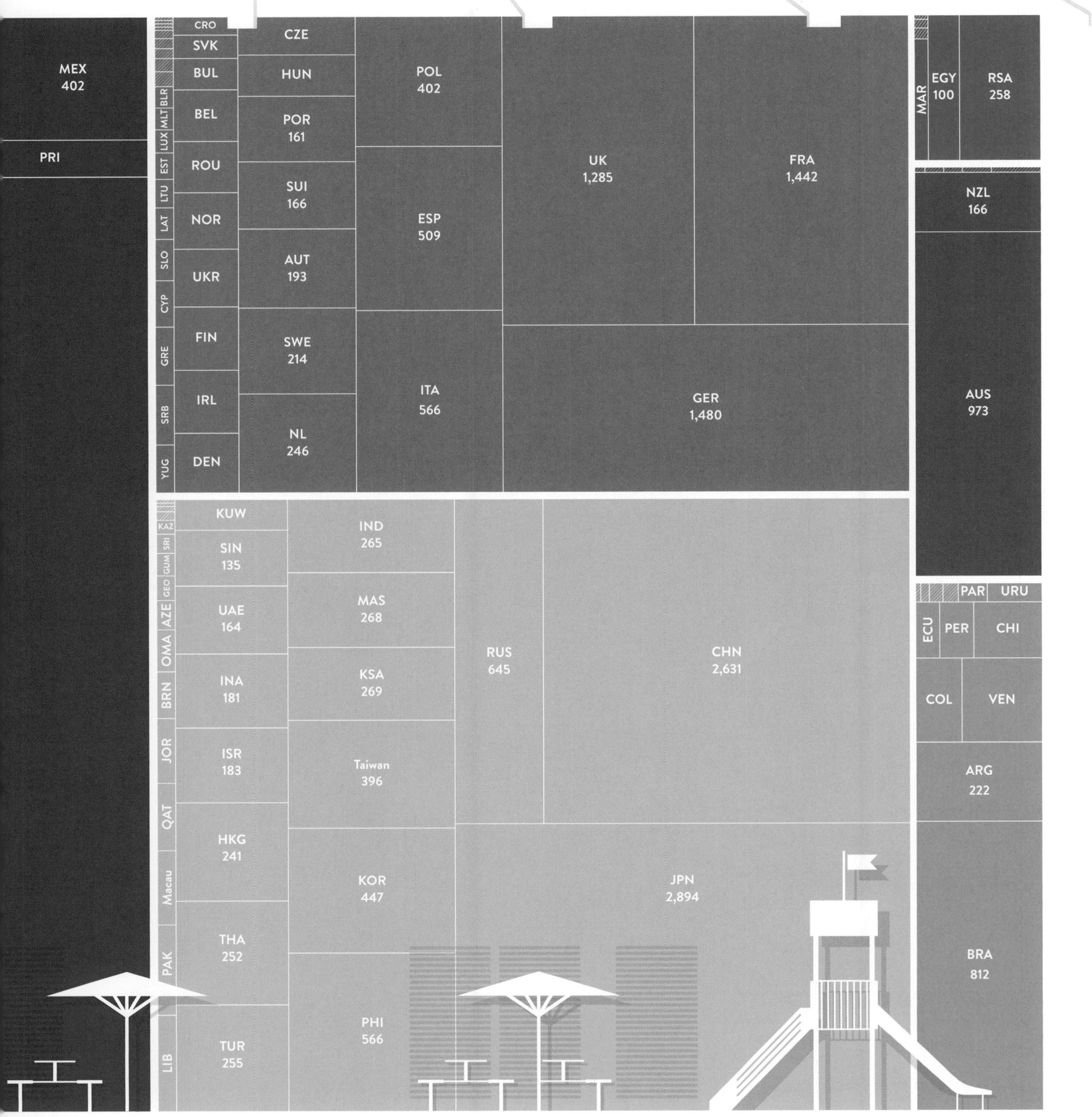

MEX
402

PRI

CRO
SVK
BUL
BLR
LUX MLT
BEL
EST
ROU
LTU
LAT
NOR
SLO
UKR
CYP
FIN
GRE
IRL
SRB
YUG
DEN

CZE
HUN
POR
161
SUI
166
AUT
193
SWE
214
NL
246

POL
402

ESP
509

ITA
566

UK
1,285

FRA
1,442

GER
1,480

MAR

EGY
100

RSA
258

NZL
166

AUS
973

KUW
KAZ
SIN
135
SRI
GUM
GEO
UAE
164
AZE
OMA
INA
181
BRN
ISR
183
JOR
QAT
HKG
241
Macau
KOR
447
PAK
THA
252
LIB
TUR
255

IND
265

MAS
268

KSA
269

Taiwan
396

PHI
566

RUS
645

CHN
2,631

JPN
2,894

ECU
PAR
URU
PER
CHI

COL
VEN

ARG
222

BRA
812

WATER WARS

In blind tests, practically no one can distinguish name-brand bottled water from tap water. That doesn't seem to be hurting the global water trade. Market leadership defeats taste buds—and consumers' rational judgment.

There are more than 4,000 brands of water worldwide. Around 200 billion liters of water are packaged in bottles and sold each year. Worldwide sales, 2017: $238.5 billion.

The size of the circles indicates the approximate market share of the companies in the global market in bottled water.

* Treated tap water

**Suntory has an alliance with PepsiCo in Vietnam

Beverage sales

Share of global beverage sales (2011–2016)

	%
Bottled water	18
Water jugs	18
Tea	15
Milk	12
Others	8
Juices	8
Beer	8
Iced tea	6
Carbonated beverages	6
Coffee	4

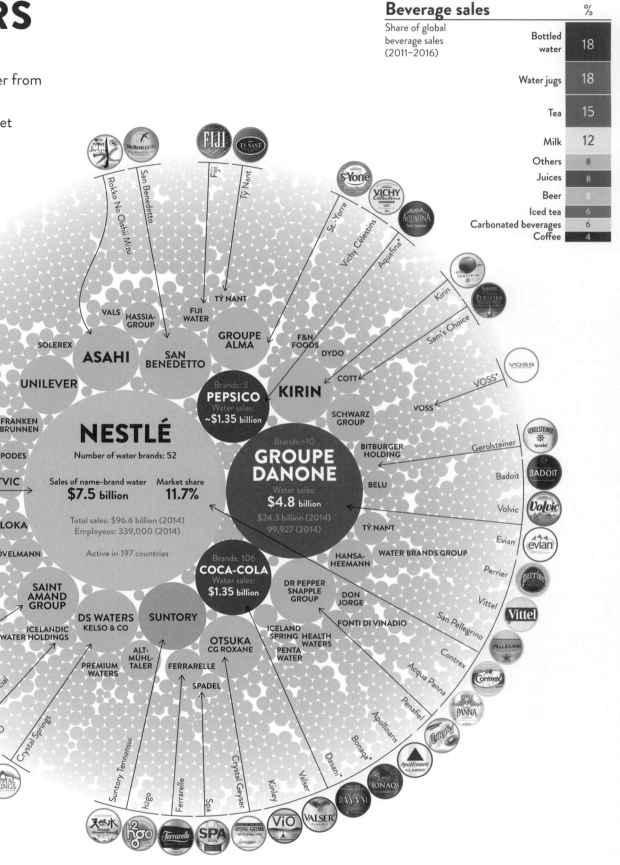

NESTLÉ
Number of water brands: 52
Sales of name-brand water **$7.5 billion** — Market share **11.7%**
Total sales: 96.6 billion (2014)
Employees: 339,000 (2014)
Active in 197 countries

PEPSICO Brands: 3 — Water sales: ~$1.35 billion

KIRIN

GROUPE DANONE Brands: ~10 — Water sales: $4.8 billion — $24.3 billion (2014) — 99,927 (2014)

COCA-COLA Brands: 106 — Water sales: $1.35 billion

SUNTORY

Companies/brands: ASAHI, UNILEVER, SAN BENEDETTO, GROUPE ALMA, SOLEREX, VALS, HASSIA-GROUP, FIJI WATER, F&N FOODS, DYDO, COTT, SCHWARZ GROUP, FRANKEN BRUNNEN, ANTIPODES, BRITVIC, BELOKA, HÖVELMANN, SAINT AMAND GROUP, DS WATERS KELSO & CO, OTSUKA CG ROXANE, ICELANDIC WATER HOLDINGS, PREMIUM WATERS, ALTMÜHLTALER, FERRARELLE, SPADEL, BITBURGER HOLDING, BELU, TÝ NANT, HANSA-HEEMANN, WATER BRANDS GROUP, DR PEPPER SNAPPLE GROUP, DON JORGE, FONTI DI VINADIO, ICELAND SPRING HEALTH WATERS, PENTA WATER

Brand labels: Rokko No Oishii Mizu, San Benedetto, Fiji, Tý Nant, S-Yorre, Vichy Célestins, Aquafina*, Kirin, Sam's Choice, VOSS*, VOSS, Gerolsteiner, Badoit, Volvic, Evian, Perrier, Vittel, San Pellegrino, Contrex, Acqua Panna, Peñafiel, Apollinaris, Bonaqa*, Valser, Dasani*, Kinley, Crystal Geyser, Spa, Ferrarelle, h2go, Suntory Tennensui, Crystal Springs, H2O, Icelandic Glacial, Saint Amand, Ozarka, Hépar, Levissima, Mountain Valley, Arrowhead, Pure Life, Poland Spring, Deer Park

Water consumption

Per capita consumption of bottled water in leading countries 2014, in gallons

Countries (left to right): MEXICO (~70), THAILAND (~66), ITALY (~53), BELGIUM-LUXEMBOURG, GERMANY (~40), UNITED ARAB EMIRATES, FRANCE, USA (~34), SPAIN, HONG KONG, LEBANON, CROATIA, SLOVENIA, HUNGARY, SAUDI ARABIA, SWITZERLAND, AUSTRIA, BRAZIL, POLAND, ROMANIA

Global consumption of bottled water, 2007 to 2017, in billions of liters

07	12	17
212	288	391*

Global drinking water needs, 1980 to 2030 (in cubic miles)

80	90	00	10	20	30
770	860	960	1,080	1,320*	1,520*

* Estimated

Daily US consumption of water for domestic use 1960–2015, in gallons

1960, 1965, 1970, 1975, 1980, 1985, 1990, 1995, 2000, 2005, 2010 (26.1), 2015

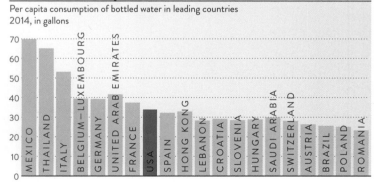

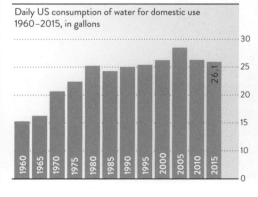

LEAVING ON A JET PLANE . . .

While many immigrants come to the US, many people also leave. In 2017, about 3 million people born in the US were living abroad. Compared to the close to 50 million people living in the US who were born elsewhere, that's not a huge number—by far, the US is a nation of immigrants. In fact, with the exception of Australia, there is no country where the American population is larger than that country's immigrant population in the US.

Most popular emigration destinations for Americans:

Most emigrants head to the borders: Mexico and Canada. About a quarter of American emigrants live in Mexico, but the majority tend to emigrate to anglophone countries such as Canada and the United Kingdom.

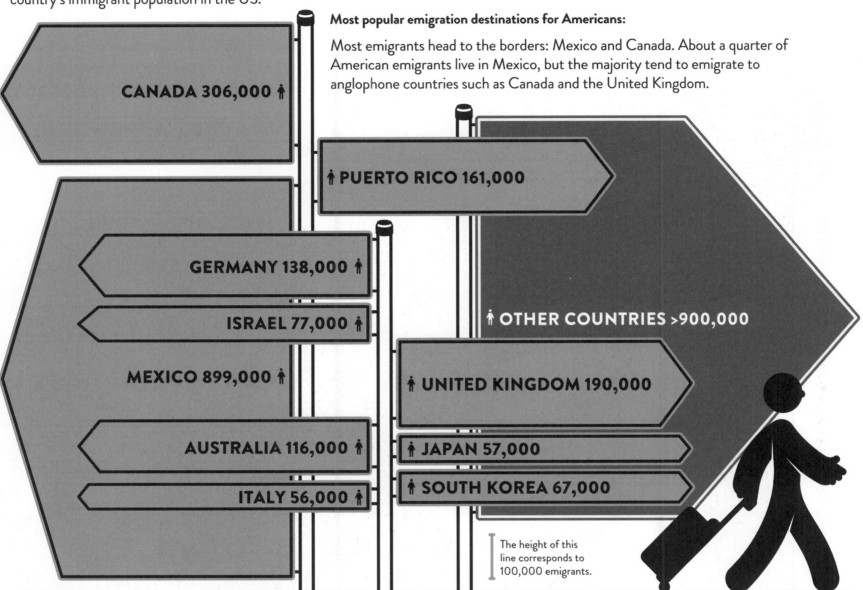

CANADA 306,000

PUERTO RICO 161,000

GERMANY 138,000

ISRAEL 77,000

OTHER COUNTRIES >900,000

MEXICO 899,000

UNITED KINGDOM 190,000

AUSTRALIA 116,000

JAPAN 57,000

ITALY 56,000

SOUTH KOREA 67,000

The height of this line corresponds to 100,000 emigrants.

A Nation of Immigrants

In the US, immigrants make up 13.4% of the population. Mexican immigrants account for about a quarter of them. But it's a common misconception that the majority of the nation's immigrants enter via the southern border; more Asian immigrants than Hispanic immigrants have immigrated into the US since 2010. In fact, Asians are projected to become the largest group among immigrants by 2055.

Top 4 countries of birth for immigrants in the US as of 2017 (in millions)

Mexico: **12.7**

China: **2.4**

India: **2.3**

Philippines: **2.1**

Top 3 metro areas with highest number of immigrants (2012–2016, in millions)

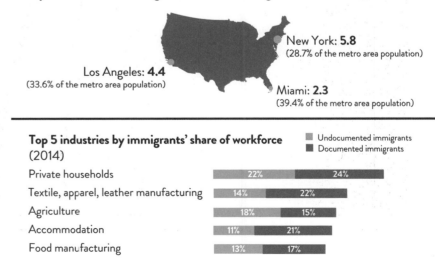

New York: **5.8**
(28.7% of the metro area population)

Los Angeles: **4.4**
(33.6% of the metro area population)

Miami: **2.3**
(39.4% of the metro area population)

Top 5 industries by immigrants' share of workforce (2014)

■ Undocumented immigrants
■ Documented immigrants

Industry	Undocumented	Documented
Private households	22%	24%
Textile, apparel, leather manufacturing	14%	22%
Agriculture	18%	15%
Accommodation	11%	21%
Food manufacturing	13%	17%

COMING AND GOING

Culturally, immigrants are often unwelcome. Economically, immigrants are almost always good business. Sociologists know the reason: It's the exceptionally ambitious who seek their fortunes abroad. In the year 2017, there were over 258 million of them.

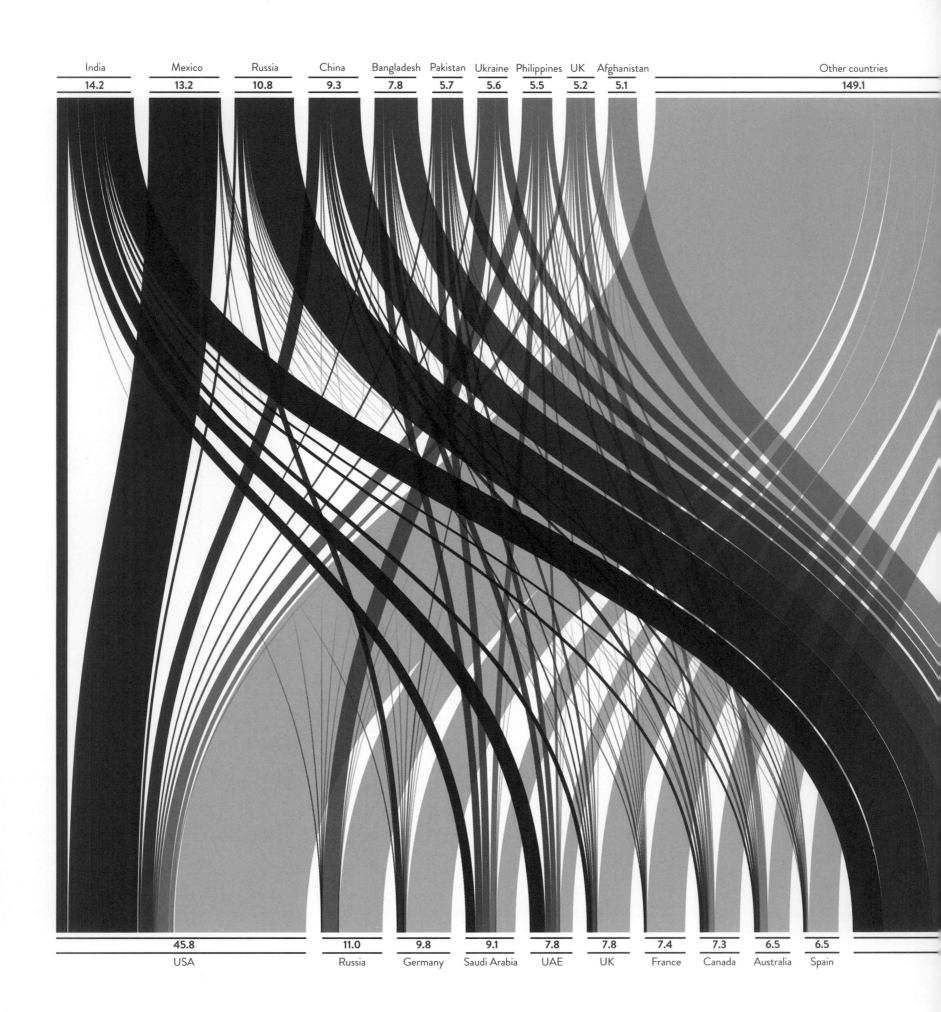

India	Mexico	Russia	China	Bangladesh	Pakistan	Ukraine	Philippines	UK	Afghanistan	Other countries
14.2	13.2	10.8	9.3	7.8	5.7	5.6	5.5	5.2	5.1	149.1

45.8	11.0	9.8	9.1	7.8	7.8	7.4	7.3	6.5	6.5
USA	Russia	Germany	Saudi Arabia	UAE	UK	France	Canada	Australia	Spain

LEGEND

Country of origin A

Total number of emigrants in millions

Country of origin B

Total number of emigrants in millions

Total number of immigrants in millions

Destination country A

Total number of immigrants in millions

Destination country B

112.5

Other countries

FACTS ABOUT MIGRATION

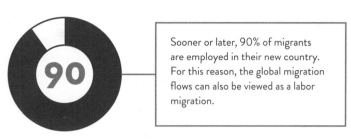

90

Sooner or later, 90% of migrants are employed in their new country. For this reason, the global migration flows can also be viewed as a labor migration.

NUMBER OF MIGRANTS IN OECD NATIONS

Migrants ages 15 and older. According to their region of origin.
Figures in millions (rounded)

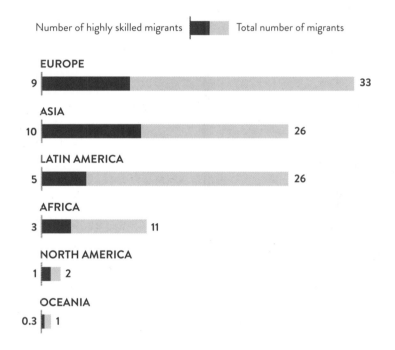

Number of highly skilled migrants ■□ Total number of migrants

EUROPE
9 — 33

ASIA
10 — 26

LATIN AMERICA
5 — 26

AFRICA
3 — 11

NORTH AMERICA
1 — 2

OCEANIA
0.3 — 1

WHICH DIRECTION?

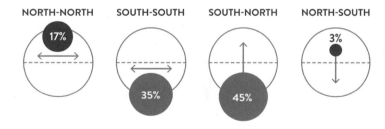

NORTH-NORTH 17%   SOUTH-SOUTH 35%   SOUTH-NORTH 45%   NORTH-SOUTH 3%

The World Bank and the United Nations collect information about the direction of migration flows. Unsurprisingly, the global north draws more migrants than the south. But many people also emigrate from one southern country to another. What's somewhat confusing is that for these large international organizations, Australia counts as the north, while Russia is part of the south.

● NORTH   ● SOUTH

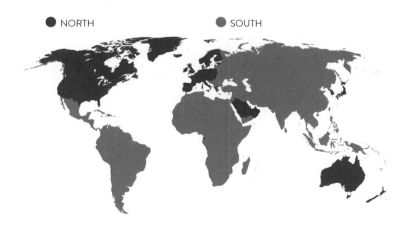

THEORY

ARISTOTLE
·
ADAM SMITH
·
KARL MARX
·
FREDERICK WINSLOW TAYLOR
·
JOHN MAYNARD KEYNES
·
MILTON FRIEDMAN
·
AMARTYA SEN

ARISTOTLE

"Oikonomia." That's what the Greek philosopher named his writings about organizing and leading a self-sufficient household. Only more than 2,000 years later, in the 18th century, did economics become an independent scholarly discipline. For some core topics, economic thinkers of the modern period were able to build on Aristotle, such as in how to use money to earn money, and in the role of private property.

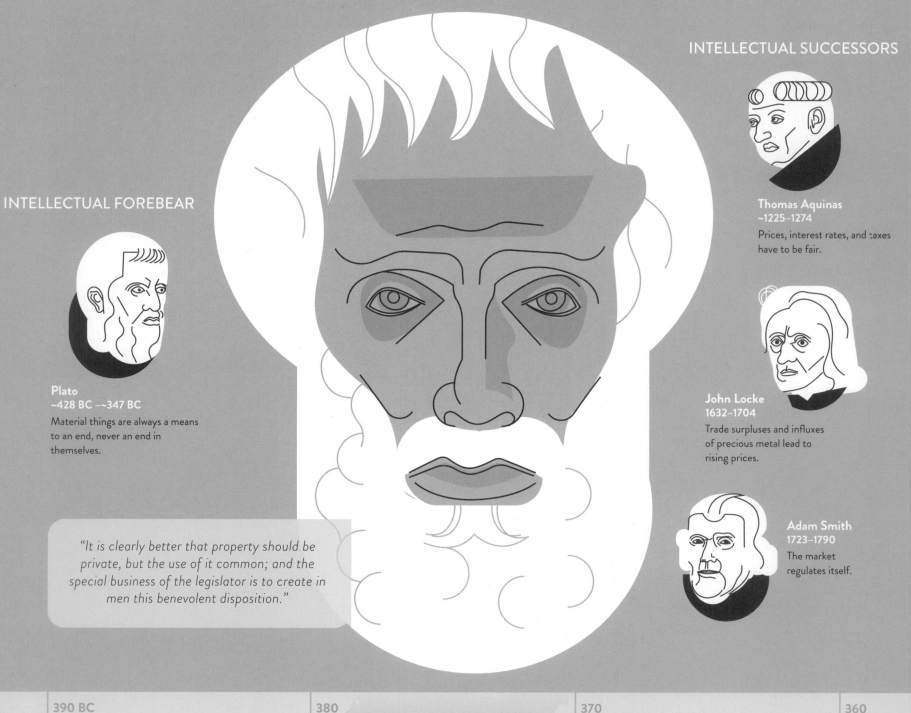

INTELLECTUAL FOREBEAR

Plato
~428 BC –~347 BC
Material things are always a means to an end, never an end in themselves.

INTELLECTUAL SUCCESSORS

Thomas Aquinas
~1225–1274
Prices, interest rates, and taxes have to be fair.

John Locke
1632–1704
Trade surpluses and influxes of precious metal lead to rising prices.

Adam Smith
1723–1790
The market regulates itself.

"It is clearly better that property should be private, but the use of it common; and the special business of the legislator is to create in men this benevolent disposition."

390 BC	380	370	360

384
Born on the Chalcidice peninsula in the Thracian town of Stagira. Father a doctor, mother from a medical family.

Stagira

Athens

Twenty years at the academy as student and teacher. **Lecture manuscripts** are written, the oldest of his surviving writings.

367
Entry at age 17 into **Plato's Academy** in Athens.

THREE IDEAS ABOUT ECONOMICS

Economics

"The art of managing a household" is for Aristotle the "natural art of acquisition."

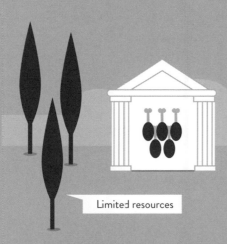

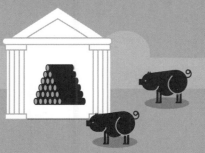

Meeting needs

Limited resources

Chrematistics

The philosopher sharply rejects the "art of acquiring money" as an "unnatural art of acquisition."

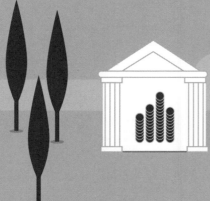

Gaining wealth . . .

often leads to poverty.

Private property

For Aristotle, private property is sensible, in contrast to his teacher Plato.

Under community ownership . . .

no one takes responsibility . . .

and no one preserves order.

350   340   330 BC

343
Called by King Philip II of Macedonia to the court as **tutor for Prince Alexander** (late- Alexander the Great).

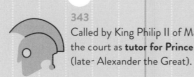

347
After Plato's death, goes to **Asia Minor** to the city ruler, Hermias, a former classmate. **Marriage** to Hermias's relative Pythias. **Birth** of their daughter.

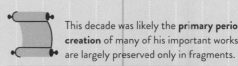

This decade was likely the **primary period of creation** of many of his important works, which are largely preserved only in fragments.

335
Lives in Athens again. Founds his own school at the **Lyceum**. His wife, Pythias, dies.

322
Due to political tensions, Aristotle flees from Athens to the country estate of his mother in Chalcis on Euboea. He **dies** at the age of 62.

ADAM SMITH

How does a market function? What roles do the individual and the state play in the economy? How are the division of labor, automation, and productivity related? Adam Smith was the first person to systematically investigate these questions. He thus became the founder of the classical school of economics. His thought has shaped economics up to the present—and explains why self-interest and the common good do not necessarily contradict each other in a market.

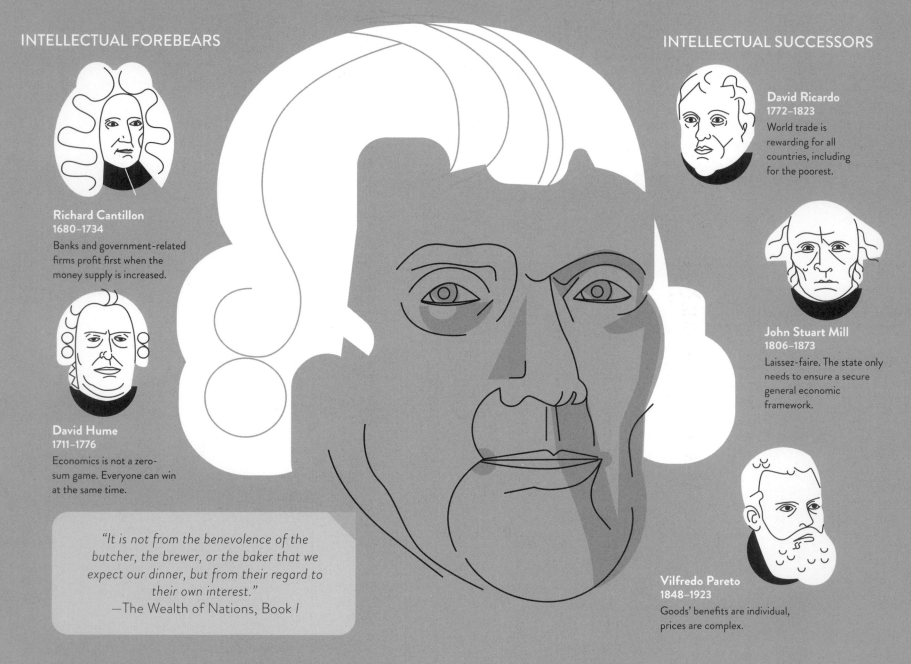

INTELLECTUAL FOREBEARS

Richard Cantillon
1680–1734
Banks and government-related firms profit first when the money supply is increased.

David Hume
1711–1776
Economics is not a zero-sum game. Everyone can win at the same time.

"It is not from the benevolence of the butcher, the brewer, or the baker that we expect our dinner, but from their regard to their own interest."
—The Wealth of Nations, Book I

INTELLECTUAL SUCCESSORS

David Ricardo
1772–1823
World trade is rewarding for all countries, including for the poorest.

John Stuart Mill
1806–1873
Laissez-faire. The state only needs to ensure a secure general economic framework.

Vilfredo Pareto
1848–1923
Goods' benefits are individual, prices are complex.

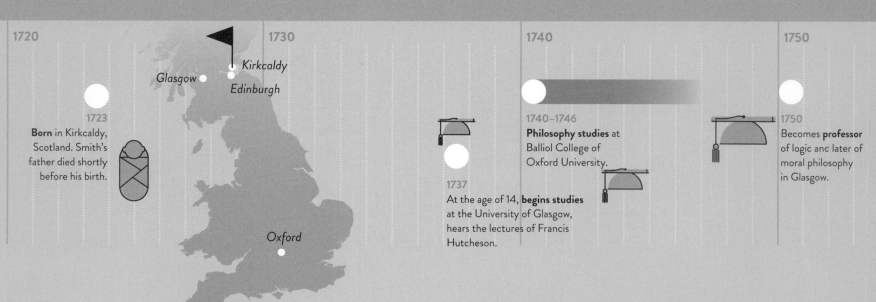

1720

1723
Born in Kirkcaldy, Scotland. Smith's father died shortly before his birth.

Glasgow
Kirkcaldy
Edinburgh

1730

Oxford

1740

1737
At the age of 14, **begins studies** at the University of Glasgow, hears the lectures of Francis Hutcheson.

1740–1746
Philosophy studies at Balliol College of Oxford University.

1750

1750
Becomes **professor** of logic and later of moral philosophy in Glasgow.

THE INVISIBLE HAND AND OTHER HANDS

Overcoming mercantilism
The absolutist state inhibits productivity and thus the welfare of its citizens.

A country's prosperity emerges from the gold and silver reserves of the potentate.

Prosperity on the basis of a country's productive forces, driven by the strength of individuals' selfishness

The more freedom that individuals have as economic actors, the more productive they become.

The self-regulating system
For Smith, freedom and individuals' personal interests and passions lead to a self-regulating system.

Self-interest (e.g., high prices) . . .

. . . leads to the public interest (prices aligned with demand).

In the long run, the "invisible hand of the market" leads to more productivity, appropriate prices, and fair wages. The market brings supply and demand into balance.

The functions of the state
In Smith's view, the state should intervene as little as possible and instead ensure that violence and fraud do not prevail in the marketplace.

Education

Infrastructure

Administration of justice

National defense

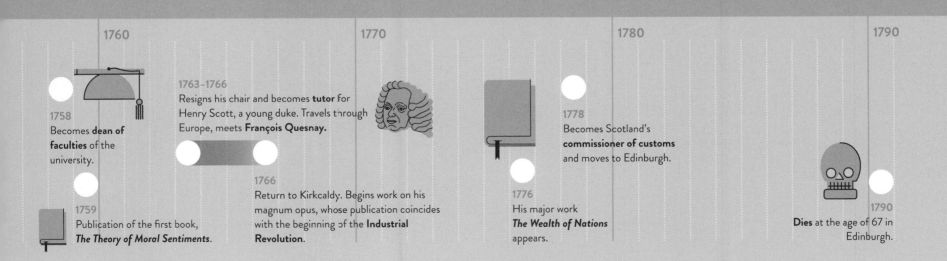

1760

1763–1766
Resigns his chair and becomes **tutor** for Henry Scott, a young duke. Travels through Europe, meets **François Quesnay**.

1770

1780

1790

1758
Becomes **dean of faculties** of the university.

1759
Publication of the first book, ***The Theory of Moral Sentiments***.

1766
Return to Kirkcaldy. Begins work on his magnum opus, whose publication coincides with the beginning of the **Industrial Revolution**.

1776
His major work ***The Wealth of Nations*** appears.

1778
Becomes Scotland's **commissioner of customs** and moves to Edinburgh.

1790
Dies at the age of 67 in Edinburgh.

KARL MARX

Marxism, as written on the back of a beer coaster, goes like this: Capitalism is a system with a built-in self-destruct mechanism. In terms of economic history, capital plays an important role. Capital sets large productive forces free. Thus capital unconsciously creates the material conditions for production methods on a higher level: socialism. The capitalist who tirelessly increases his profits doesn't notice that behind his back the revolution is brewing, which will turn the circumstances of production and ownership on their heads. As the antagonist of capitalism, Marxism shaped the history of the 20th century. And itself became history.

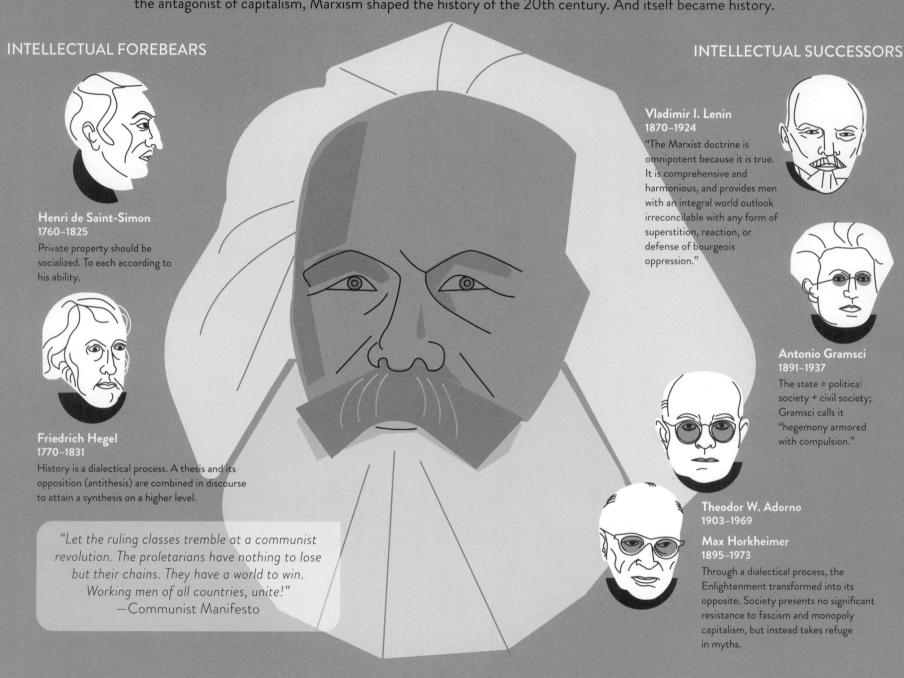

INTELLECTUAL FOREBEARS

Henri de Saint-Simon
1760–1825
Private property should be socialized. To each according to his ability.

Friedrich Hegel
1770–1831
History is a dialectical process. A thesis and its opposition (antithesis) are combined in discourse to attain a synthesis on a higher level.

"Let the ruling classes tremble at a communist revolution. The proletarians have nothing to lose but their chains. They have a world to win. Working men of all countries, unite!"
—Communist Manifesto

INTELLECTUAL SUCCESSORS

Vladimir I. Lenin
1870–1924
"The Marxist doctrine is omnipotent because it is true. It is comprehensive and harmonious, and provides men with an integral world outlook irreconcilable with any form of superstition, reaction, or defense of bourgeois oppression."

Antonio Gramsci
1891–1937
The state = political society + civil society; Gramsci calls it "hegemony armored with compulsion."

Theodor W. Adorno
1903–1969
Max Horkheimer
1895–1973
Through a dialectical process, the Enlightenment transformed into its opposite. Society presents no significant resistance to fascism and monopoly capitalism, but instead takes refuge in myths.

1820

1830

1840

Expulsion
from Paris
1845

1818
Born in Trier as the third of nine children. Just prior to this, his father converts from Judaism to Protestantism in order to continue his career as a lawyer.

1835–1841
Studies law and philosophy in Bonn and Berlin.

1842–1871
Works for various **newspapers**.

Founding of the **German Workers' Society** in 1847

Communist Manifesto
1848

London

Berlin

Bonn

Trier

1843
Marriage to Jenny von Westphalen. Seven children result from the marriage, of whom four die before the age of ten. Two adult daughters end their lives by suicide.

1844
Begins lifelong friendship and cooperation with **Friedrich Engels,** who supports Marx financially.

CLASSES AND CONFLICT

Historical materialism

Two classes with opposing interests confront each other. Tensions lead via class struggle and revolution to the next-higher form of society. The conflict ends in communism without private property.

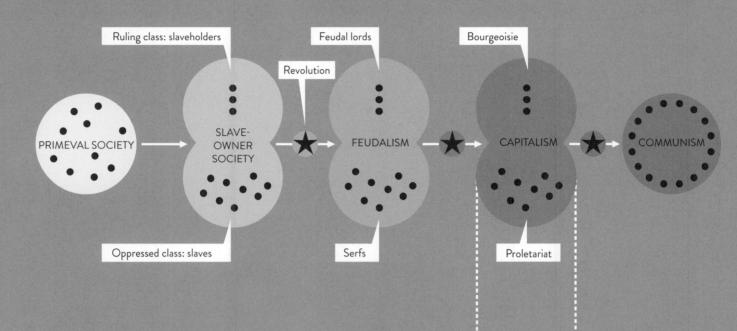

Ruling class: slaveholders

Feudal lords

Bourgeoisie

Revolution

PRIMEVAL SOCIETY

SLAVE-OWNER SOCIETY

FEUDALISM

CAPITALISM

COMMUNISM

Oppressed class: slaves

Serfs

Proletariat

Surplus value and accumulation

The proletarians create surplus value, while the capitalist skims it off. The lower the wages, the higher the surplus value. The capitalist is digging his own grave—according to the logic of Marx.

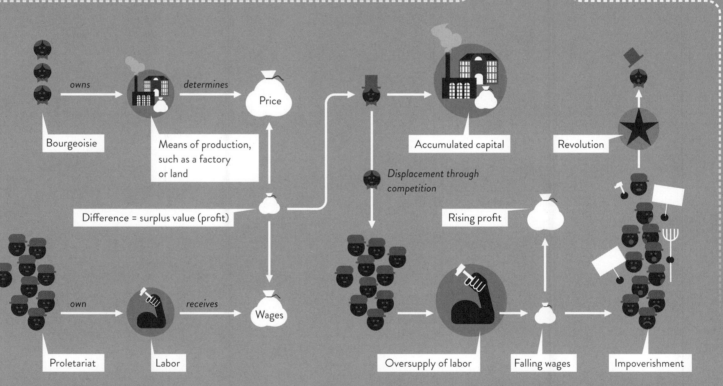

owns

determines

Price

Bourgeoisie

Means of production, such as a factory or land

Accumulated capital

Revolution

Difference = surplus value (profit)

Displacement through competition

Rising profit

own

receives

Wages

Proletariat

Labor

Oversupply of labor

Falling wages

Impoverishment

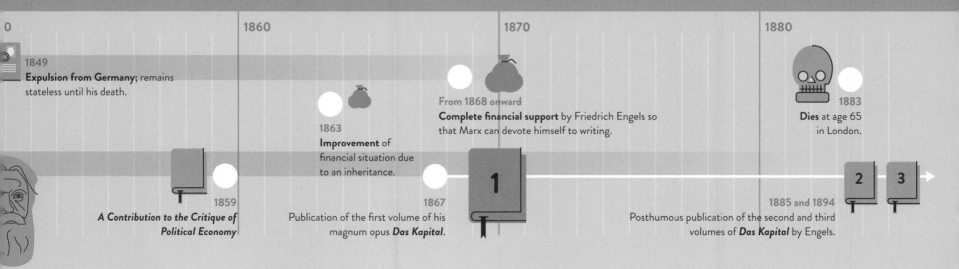

1860

1870

1880

1849
Expulsion from Germany; remains stateless until his death.

From 1868 onward
Complete financial support by Friedrich Engels so that Marx can devote himself to writing.

1883
Dies at age 65 in London.

1863
Improvement of financial situation due to an inheritance.

1859
A Contribution to the Critique of Political Economy

1867
Publication of the first volume of his magnum opus ***Das Kapital***.

1885 and 1894
Posthumous publication of the second and third volumes of ***Das Kapital*** by Engels.

FREDERICK WINSLOW TAYLOR

Faster! If you had to reduce the life, work, and thought of the inventor of management theory to one word, it would be "speed". Ironically, Taylor was little known during his lifetime for his theory of labor organization, with the help of which Ford later accelerated his production lines. As a young engineer, Taylor had invented a steel alloy, high-speed steel, that could be processed especially easily.

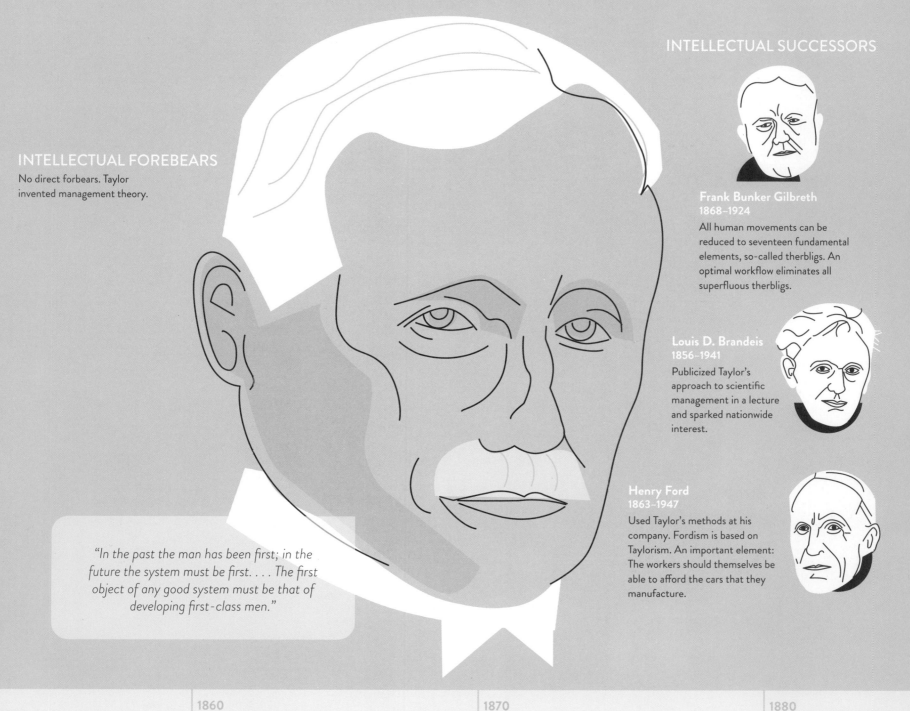

INTELLECTUAL SUCCESSORS

Frank Bunker Gilbreth
1868–1924
All human movements can be reduced to seventeen fundamental elements, so-called therbligs. An optimal workflow eliminates all superfluous therbligs.

Louis D. Brandeis
1856–1941
Publicized Taylor's approach to scientific management in a lecture and sparked nationwide interest.

Henry Ford
1863–1947
Used Taylor's methods at his company. Fordism is based on Taylorism. An important element: The workers should themselves be able to afford the cars that they manufacture.

INTELLECTUAL FOREBEARS

No direct forbears. Taylor invented management theory.

> "In the past the man has been first; in the future the system must be first. . . . The first object of any good system must be that of developing first-class men."

1860

1870

1880

1856
Born in Germantown, Philadelphia, as the son of a wealthy and respected Quaker family.

Philadelphia   *Cambridge*

1874
Passes the **entrance examination** for Harvard University in Cambridge, Massachusetts, with distinction, but does not enroll. Instead he begins an **apprenticeship** as a toolmaker and machinist.

1878–1893
Works at various companies in **senior positions**, but his attempts at increasing efficiency constantly lead to conflicts.

1880–1883
Correspondence-course degree in engineering.

1881
Wins first American tennis championship in men's doubles.

MEASURING AND MANAGING

Process optimization through scientific management

Taylor's credo: Work and production processes can be made much more efficient than what takes place in businesses. The management only needs to precisely observe, measure, monitor, and organize so that responsibilities are more clearly divided. For the individual, work often becomes more monotonous this way. But the increase in productivity is also supposed to benefit workers and employees—through shorter working hours, longer breaks, and higher wages, among other things.

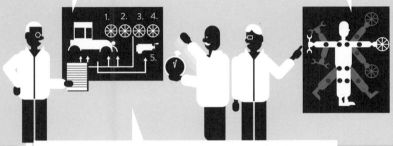

With scientific methods, it's possible to determine the best way to carry out each step in the work process.

Time and movement studies for process improvement and determining standard times.

Work can be divided into **planning** activities and **executing** them.

A company's processes, whether external (e.g., suppliers) or internal (e.g., workflows) can be calculated and governed.

Workers and machinery only fulfill specific functions (specialization) and can be centrally planned and directed (centralization).

But: Unpredictable events cause incalculable costs.

People only work to earn money. Structured activity satisfies them.

The process for the manufacture of a product consists of a certain and definable sequence of work functions.

Work in the smallest units, which are to be carried out quickly and repetitively.

Guidance and monitoring by specialized managers (functional managers).

Motivation to work through pay for performance (piece-rate wages).

1890

Independent business consultant, concentrating on efficiencies for reducing working time. Conducts extensive time studies and receives numerous patents.

1893–1901

1895
Lecture on the piecework system gains him attention in professional circles.

1900

1900
Gold medal of the Paris World Exposition for the Taylor-White process for increasing the strength of steel.

1903
Shop Management

Beginning in 1901
Supports himself solely by his numerous **patents** and **industry holdings**.

1910

1911
The Principles of Scientific Management

1909–1914
Lecturer in scientific management at Harvard University.

1915
Dies one day after his 59th birthday.

JOHN MAYNARD KEYNES

The free market-capitalist economic order is the best one known to man. But the state has to prevent capitalism from destroying itself through reasonable economic policy interventions. With these principles, Keynes, a Cambridge professor, became the most influential economist of the 20th century. Guiding demand in a national economy was for him the state's most important means of adjusting the economy's settings.

INTELLECTUAL FOREBEARS

Thomas Robert Malthus
1766–1834

If the population grows faster than the economy, a country becomes impoverished—and vice versa.

Michał Kalecki
1899–1970

Anticipated many of Keynes's theses (in Polish). Investments by the state increase national income and pay for themselves.

"In the long run we are all dead. Economists set themselves too easy, too useless a task if in tempestuous seasons they can only tell us that when the storm is long past the ocean is flat again."

INTELLECTUAL SUCCESSORS

Wesley C. Mitchell
1874–1948

Lends support to Keynes's theories with empirical research and accentuates the image of business cycles with the Burns-Mitchell diagram.

Gunnar Myrdal
1898–1987

The community of nations must intervene internationally to preserve public welfare, promote development, and combat poverty.

James Tobin
1918–2002

The world needs a global steering tax on international currency speculation — the Tobin tax.

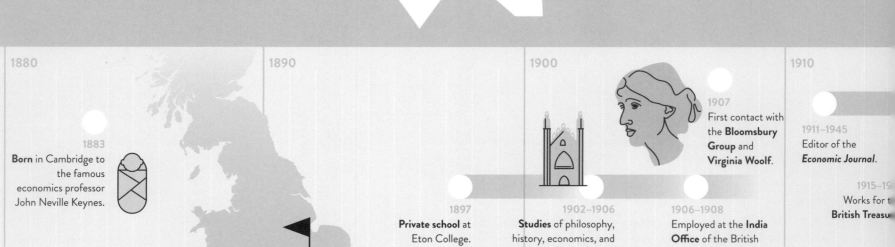

1880

1883
Born in Cambridge to the famous economics professor John Neville Keynes.

Cambridge

Eton London

1890

1897
Private school at Eton College.

1902–1906
Studies of philosophy, history, economics, and mathematics at King's College in Cambridge.

1900

1907
First contact with the **Bloomsbury Group** and **Virginia Woolf.**

1906–1908
Employed at the **India Office** of the British government.

1910

1911–1945
Editor of the *Economic Journal.*

1915–19
Works for t British Treasu

COUNTERCYCLICAL ECONOMIC POLICY

Demand guides the economy

Except during an economic boom, demand is fundamentally limited. But in the long term, demand determines how the economy grows and thus growth and prosperity as well.

ECONOMIC SLOWDOWN

ECONOMIC RECOVERY

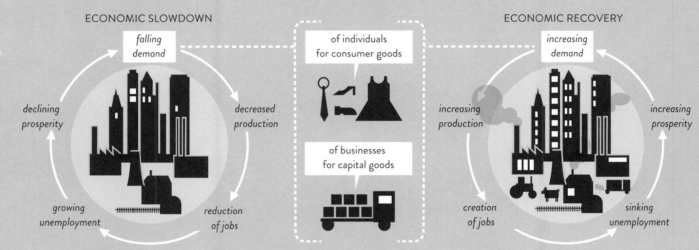

falling demand

declining prosperity

decreased production

growing unemployment

reduction of jobs

of individuals for consumer goods

of businesses for capital goods

increasing demand

increasing production

increasing prosperity

creation of jobs

sinking unemployment

The state is able to influence demand

Keynes sees several possibilities for states to intervene in a downward economic spiral if the private sector does not recover on its own. These state measures address the demand for capital goods.

1. SPURRING INVESTMENT THROUGH INTEREST RATE CUTS

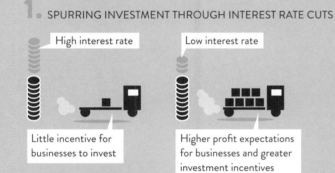

High interest rate

Low interest rate

Little incentive for businesses to invest

Higher profit expectations for businesses and greater investment incentives

2. REPLACING PRIVATE DEMAND WITH PUBLIC DEMAND

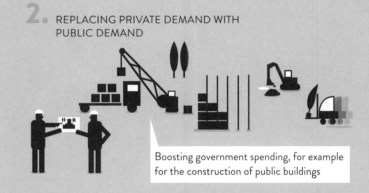

Boosting government spending, for example for the construction of public buildings

Counter-cyclical taxes

Rational economic policy thinks and acts counter-cyclically. During a boom, economic policy is frugal, while in a recession it spends liberally.

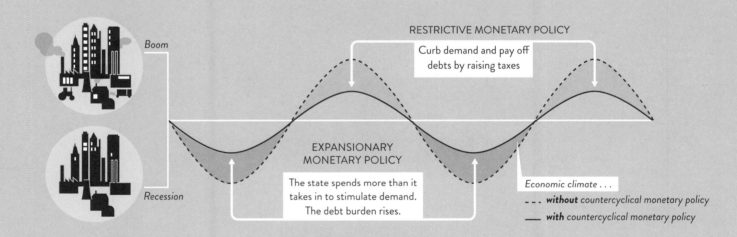

Boom

Recession

RESTRICTIVE MONETARY POLICY

Curb demand and pay off debts by raising taxes

EXPANSIONARY MONETARY POLICY

The state spends more than it takes in to stimulate demand. The debt burden rises.

Economic climate . . .
- - - *without* countercyclical monetary policy
—— *with* countercyclical monetary policy

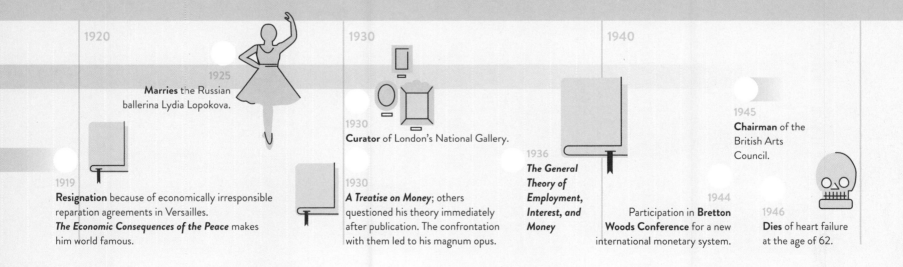

1920

1925
Marries the Russian ballerina Lydia Lopokova.

1930
Curator of London's National Gallery.

1940

1945
Chairman of the British Arts Council.

1919
Resignation because of economically irresponsible reparation agreements in Versailles. *The Economic Consequences of the Peace* makes him world famous.

1930
A Treatise on Money; others questioned his theory immediately after publication. The confrontation with them led to his magnum opus.

1936
The General Theory of Employment, Interest, and Money

1944
Participation in **Bretton Woods Conference** for a new international monetary system.

1946
Dies of heart failure at the age of 62.

MILTON FRIEDMAN

The more enemies, the greater the honor. Milton Friedman continues to polarize. For some, he was the founder of "monetarism," a hero of liberal economic policy whose theory established a counterbalance to the encroaching Keynesian welfare state and finally gave a voice to individual freedom again. For others, he was a trailblazer for social inequality in global capitalism and a pallbearer for a state capable of action. The core issue and linchpin of his theory is a money supply of the proper size.

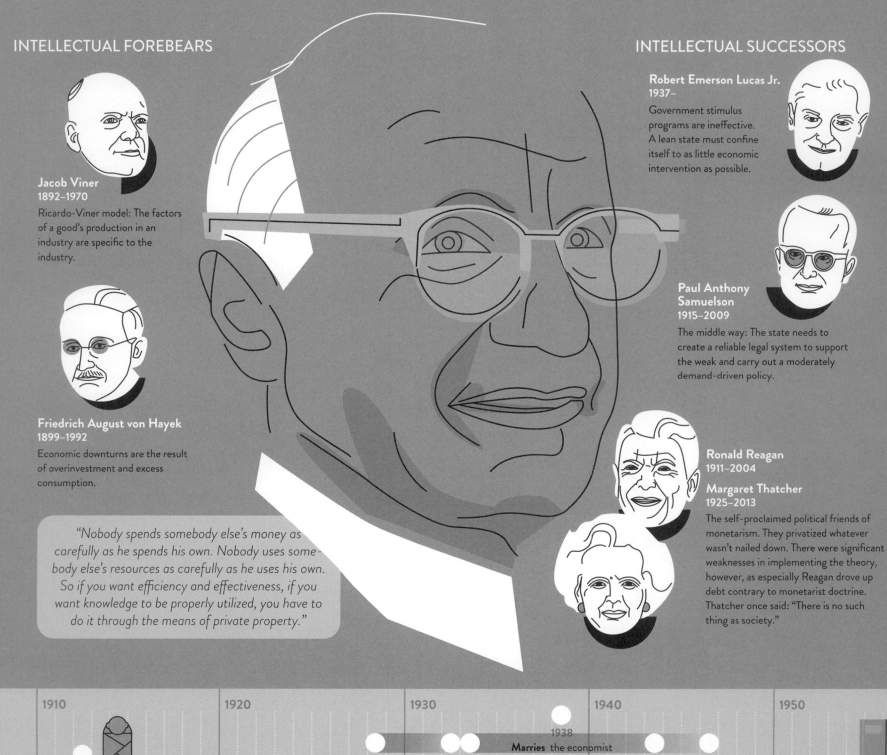

INTELLECTUAL FOREBEARS

Jacob Viner
1892–1970
Ricardo-Viner model: The factors of a good's production in an industry are specific to the industry.

Friedrich August von Hayek
1899–1992
Economic downturns are the result of overinvestment and excess consumption.

"Nobody spends somebody else's money as carefully as he spends his own. Nobody uses somebody else's resources as carefully as he uses his own. So if you want efficiency and effectiveness, if you want knowledge to be properly utilized, you have to do it through the means of private property."

INTELLECTUAL SUCCESSORS

Robert Emerson Lucas Jr.
1937–
Government stimulus programs are ineffective. A lean state must confine itself to as little economic intervention as possible.

Paul Anthony Samuelson
1915–2009
The middle way: The state needs to create a reliable legal system to support the weak and carry out a moderately demand-driven policy.

Ronald Reagan
1911–2004
Margaret Thatcher
1925–2013
The self-proclaimed political friends of monetarism. They privatized whatever wasn't nailed down. There were significant weaknesses in implementing the theory, however, as especially Reagan drove up debt contrary to monetarist doctrine. Thatcher once said: "There is no such thing as society."

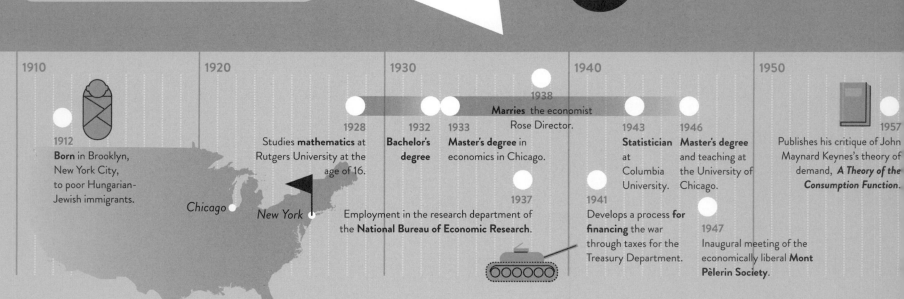

1912
Born in Brooklyn, New York City, to poor Hungarian-Jewish immigrants.

Chicago

New York

1928
Studies **mathematics** at Rutgers University at the age of 16.

1932
Bachelor's degree

1933
Master's degree in economics in Chicago.

1937
Employment in the research department of the **National Bureau of Economic Research**.

1938
Marries the economist Rose Director.

1941
Develops a process **for financing** the war through taxes for the Treasury Department.

1943
Statistician at Columbia University.

1946
Master's degree and teaching at the University of Chicago.

1947
Inaugural meeting of the economically liberal **Mont Pèlerin Society**.

1957
Publishes his critique of John Maynard Keynes's theory of demand, *A Theory of the Consumption Function*.

MONEY MATTERS

Critique of Keynesianism

Stimulus programs disrupt economic processes. Against Keynes, Friedman argued: More money from the central bank does not stimulate the economy. The average propensity to consume remains the same, and the additional money only feeds government bureaucracy and the consumer's piggy bank.

Friedman's measures

The money supply needs to grow slowly and according to fixed rules. Then the economy will also grow reliably. An independent central bank needs to determine the money supply, not elected politicians. Politicians should privatize state-owned enterprises.

(Social) policy demands

Friedman was thoroughly liberal not only economically, but also sociopolitically.

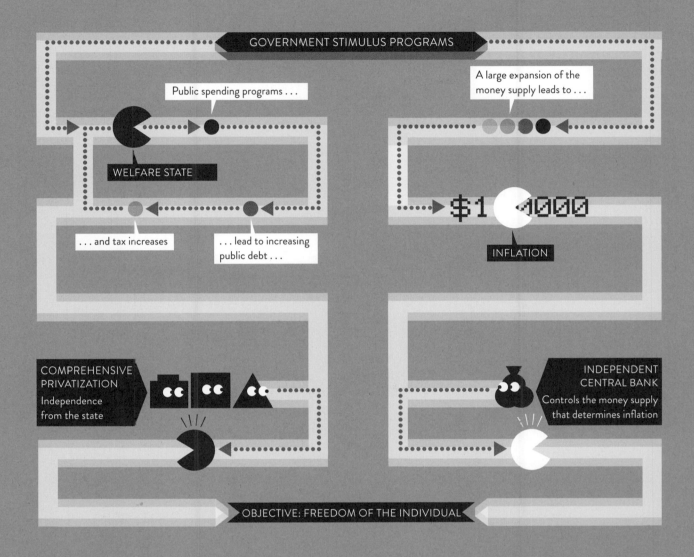

GOVERNMENT STIMULUS PROGRAMS

Public spending programs . . .

A large expansion of the money supply leads to . . .

WELFARE STATE

$1 000 000

. . . and tax increases

. . . lead to increasing public debt . . .

INFLATION

COMPREHENSIVE PRIVATIZATION
Independence from the state

INDEPENDENT CENTRAL BANK
Controls the money supply that determines inflation

OBJECTIVE: FREEDOM OF THE INDIVIDUAL

Education voucher

Negative income tax*

Free career choice

No compulsory military service

Legalization of prostitution and marijuana

*Above a fixed threshold one pays taxes, while below one is entitled to subsidies.

60

1962
The freedom of the individual is at the center of Friedman's argument in **Capitalism and Freedom**.

1963
His major work **A Monetary History of the United States, 1867–1960** disputes the Keynesian interpretation of the Great Depression.

1966–1984
Columnist for *Newsweek*.

1970

1969
A long-term relationship between money supply and inflation is the focus of **The Optimum Quantity of Money**.

1976
Alfred Nobel Memorial Prize for Economic Sciences.

1980

1980
In **Free to Choose**, he describes the welfare state and inflation as the economy's greatest enemies.

1990

2000

2005
He advocated for **legalizing marijuana**. Friedman thought the USA's war on drugs was not only economically inefficient, but also immoral.

2006
Dies at the age of 94.

AMARTYA SEN

What is the relationship between economic freedom and development, social opportunities and security, and poverty and democracy? This is the central question that has occupied this Indian-born Harvard professor for his entire life. His theory, located at the intersection of economics and philosophy, always had a clear practical goal: to combat poverty around the world.

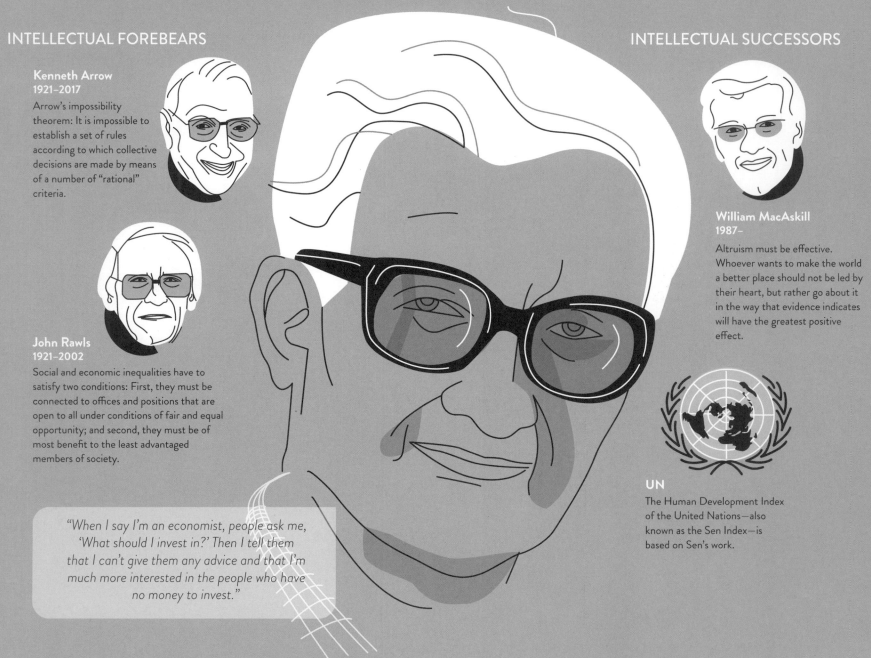

INTELLECTUAL FOREBEARS

Kenneth Arrow
1921–2017
Arrow's impossibility theorem: It is impossible to establish a set of rules according to which collective decisions are made by means of a number of "rational" criteria.

John Rawls
1921–2002
Social and economic inequalities have to satisfy two conditions: First, they must be connected to offices and positions that are open to all under conditions of fair and equal opportunity; and second, they must be of most benefit to the least advantaged members of society.

INTELLECTUAL SUCCESSORS

William MacAskill
1987–
Altruism must be effective. Whoever wants to make the world a better place should not be led by their heart, but rather go about it in the way that evidence indicates will have the greatest positive effect.

UN
The Human Development Index of the United Nations—also known as the Sen Index—is based on Sen's work.

"When I say I'm an economist, people ask me, 'What should I invest in?' Then I tell them that I can't give them any advice and that I'm much more interested in the people who have no money to invest."

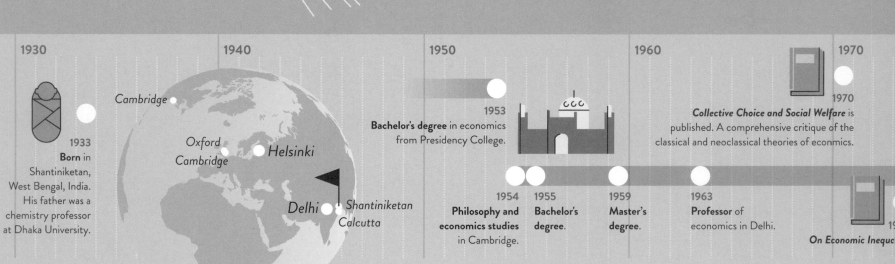

1930

Cambridge

1933
Born in Shantiniketan, West Bengal, India. His father was a chemistry professor at Dhaka University.

1940

Oxford
Cambridge   *Helsinki*

Delhi   *Shantiniketan*
Calcutta

1950

1953
Bachelor's degree in economics from Presidency College.

1954
Philosophy and economics studies in Cambridge.

1955
Bachelor's degree.

1959
Master's degree.

1960

1963
Professor of economics in Delhi.

Collective Choice and Social Welfare is published. A comprehensive critique of the classical and neoclassical theories of econmics.

1970

1970

On Economic Inequa

ECONOMY FOR HUMAN BEINGS

The human being

Individual skills and development opportunities are at the heart of Sen's thought. People strive for happiness and social recognition. In contrast, Sen calls the *"homo economicus"* of economic theory a "rational idiot."

Globalization and social opportunities

For Sen, development is more than a rise in the average per capita income. For him, it's more about an individual's freedoms and opportunities for self-realization. In the long term, democracy is the best form of government for attaining a (halfway) fair distribution of prosperity. Because in a democracy, the poor can at least vote and help determine society's values in public discourse.

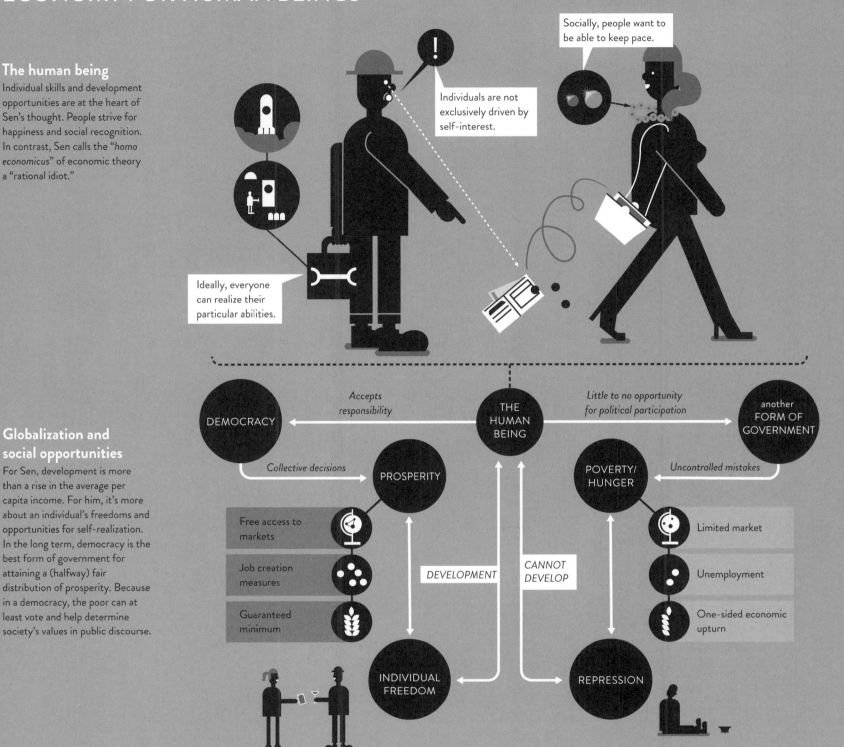

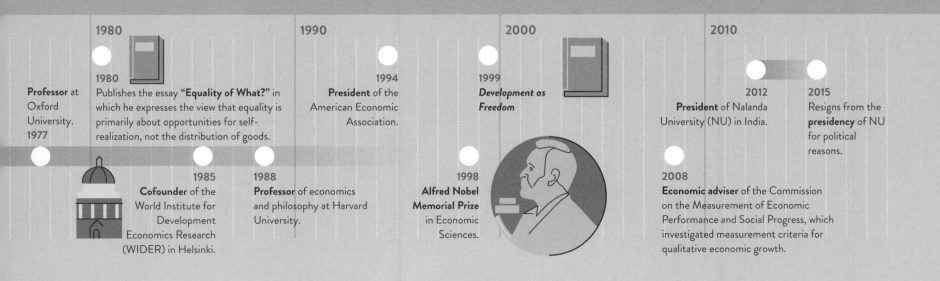

VI

ENVIRONMENT & RESOURCES

SUSTAINING SUSTAINABILITY

Corporations' PR departments aren't exactly sparing in their use of the term "sustainability." In recent years, its meaning has undergone inflationary expansion, which is a bit unfortunate. Because the devaluation of sustainability as a concept radically contradicts how important the basic idea of sustainability is in its three dimensions: Value creation needs to be brought into harmony with social development and the preservation of our planet.

PEOPLE!
Social dimension

PLANET!
Ecological dimension

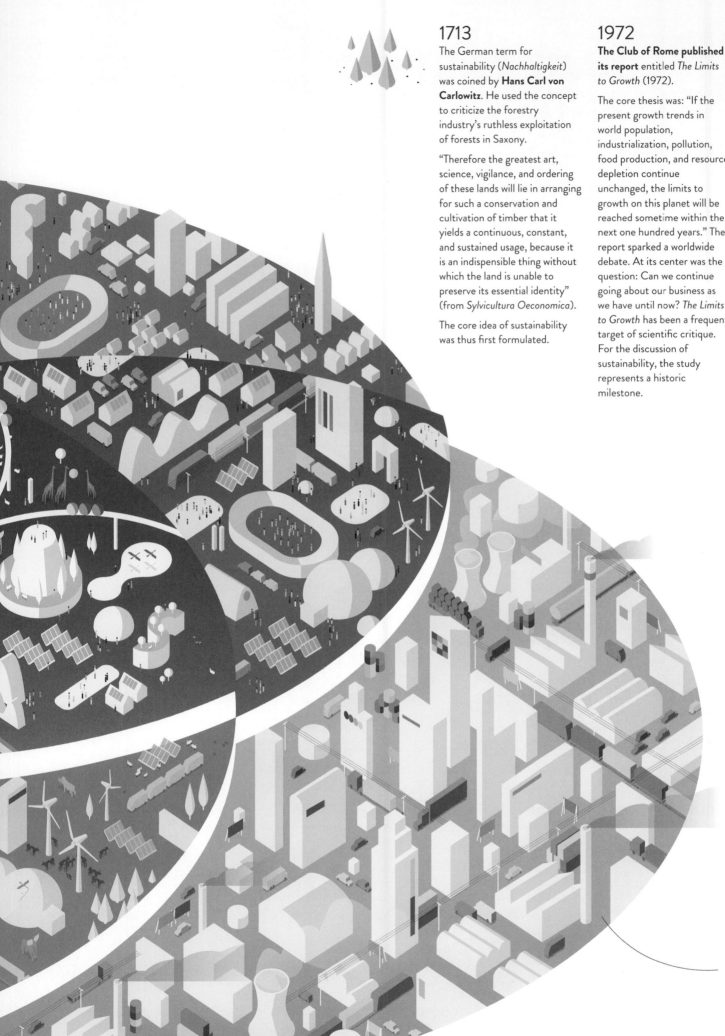

1713

The German term for sustainability (*Nachhaltigkeit*) was coined by **Hans Carl von Carlowitz**. He used the concept to criticize the forestry industry's ruthless exploitation of forests in Saxony.

"Therefore the greatest art, science, vigilance, and ordering of these lands will lie in arranging for such a conservation and cultivation of timber that it yields a continuous, constant, and sustained usage, because it is an indispensible thing without which the land is unable to preserve its essential identity" (from *Sylvicultura Oeconomica*).

The core idea of sustainability was thus first formulated.

1972

The Club of Rome published its report entitled *The Limits to Growth* (1972).

The core thesis was: "If the present growth trends in world population, industrialization, pollution, food production, and resource depletion continue unchanged, the limits to growth on this planet will be reached sometime within the next one hundred years." The report sparked a worldwide debate. At its center was the question: Can we continue going about our business as we have until now? *The Limits to Growth* has been a frequent target of scientific critique. For the discussion of sustainability, the study represents a historic milestone.

1987

The **Brundtland Commission of the United Nations** defined "sustainable development" from two perspectives:

1. "Sustainable development is development that meets the needs of the present without compromising the ability of future generations to meet their own needs."

2. "In essence, sustainable development is a process of change in which the exploitation of resources, the direction of investments, the orientation of technological development, and institutional change are all in harmony and enhance both current and future potential to meet human needs and aspirations."

Many national and international sustainability agreements adopted these perspectives and combined them with the three-pillar model shown here. These are often described as the three P's that must be brought into balance: People. Planet. Profit.

PROFIT!
Economic dimension

RARE EARTHS, AND COMMON ONES

Geologists and chemists have so far identified 5,000 different mineral resources. Here are the most important ones for manufacturing and production arranged according to the quantity mined. Incidentally, the global economy consumes 410 million times as much cement as the expensive metalloid tellurium, which is used for improving steel, copper, and lead alloys.

Te — Tellurium

D — Diamond*

Re — Rhenium

Ge — Germanium

Pt — Platinum

Pa — Palladium

Be — Beryllium

Ga — Gallium

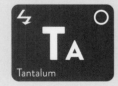
In — Indium

Ta — Tantalum

Zr — Zirconium

Au — Gold

Y — Yttrium

Bi — Bismuth

As — Arsenic

Cd — Cadmium

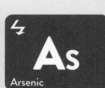
Nb — Niobium

Ag — Silver

Al — Aluminum

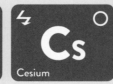
I — Iodine

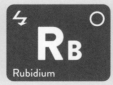
V — Vanadium

Li — Lithium

W — Tungsten

See — Rare earths

Sb — Antimony

Mo — Molybdenum

Sn — Tin

Sr — Strontium

Br — Bromine

Ve — Vermiculite

Cy — Kyanite

Wo — Wollastonite

Mg — Magnesium

Sic — Silicon carbide

Mi — Mica

Ek — Aluminum oxide

G — Garnet*

Ab — Asbestos

Di — Diatomite

Ni — Nickel

Co — Cobalt

Hg — Mercury

Hf — Hafnium

Sc — Scandium

S+S — Gravel + stones

Cs — Cesium

Rb — Rubidium

Se — Selenium

Th — Thorium

Production volume
in tons in 2015

All non-elements are *italicized*.

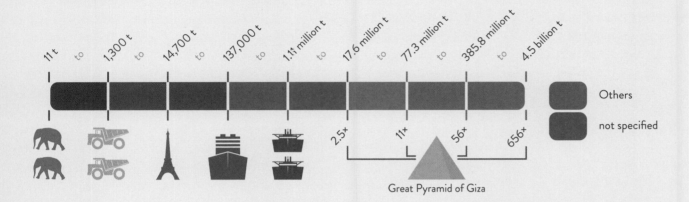

11 t to 1,300 t to 14,700 t to 137,000 t to 1.1 million t to 17.6 million t to 77.3 million t to 385.8 million t to 4.5 billion t

2.5×   11×   56×   656×

Great Pyramid of Giza

Others

not specified

Main use

🝪 Chemistry
⚡ Electronics
🏭 Industry
▽ Ceramics
☢ Nuclear energy
⚓ Construction
▨ Alloys
⚙ Machinery
🔫 Ammunition/firearms
◉ Optics
♲ Plastics
▽ Jewelry
○ Other

*Industrially produced

P — Perlite

Tı — Titanium

Z — Zeolite

Fʟs — Fluorspar

Bt — Bentonite

Cr — Chrome

Bʟe — Bleaching earth

T — Talc

Bs — Pumice

Kaʟ — Potash

Pb — Lead

Ba — Barium

Mn — Manganese

S — Sulfur

Am — Ammonia

Re — Cast iron

Iʟ — Ilmenite

Sı — Silicon

Cu — Copper

Ko — Kaolin

S+K — Sand and gravel

Sa — Salt

Rs — Raw steel

Rt — Rutile

Mgv — Magnesium compounds

Fes — Feldspar

Gra — Graphite

Ph — Phosphorite

Bx — Bauxite

Ee — Iron ore

B — Boron

Zn — Zinc

To — Peat

Nac — Sodium carbonate

Gi — Plaster

Kk — Lime

Ze — Cement

Sʟ — Slag

Tʟ — Thallium

Qk — Quartz crystal*

Fep — Iron oxide pigments

Am — Scrap metal

He — Helium 168 million m³

Es — Gemstones $71.3 billion

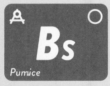

IT BURNS!

Fossil fuels made the Industrial Revolution—and today's mobile society—possible. Nuclear power once had the reputation of a futuristic source of clean energy. Today coal, gas, oil, and uranium satisfy over 90% of the global hunger for energy. And now we know: Along with the blessings of economic growth and prosperity, they brought the curse of climate change, meltdowns, and long-term storage of toxic waste. Taking stock of the situation is necessary before a turn to alternative energy sources is possible.

Energy resources by region, 2015
in exajoules (EJ)

Production
2015, in EJ

Consumption
2015, in EJ

Resources
2015, in EJ

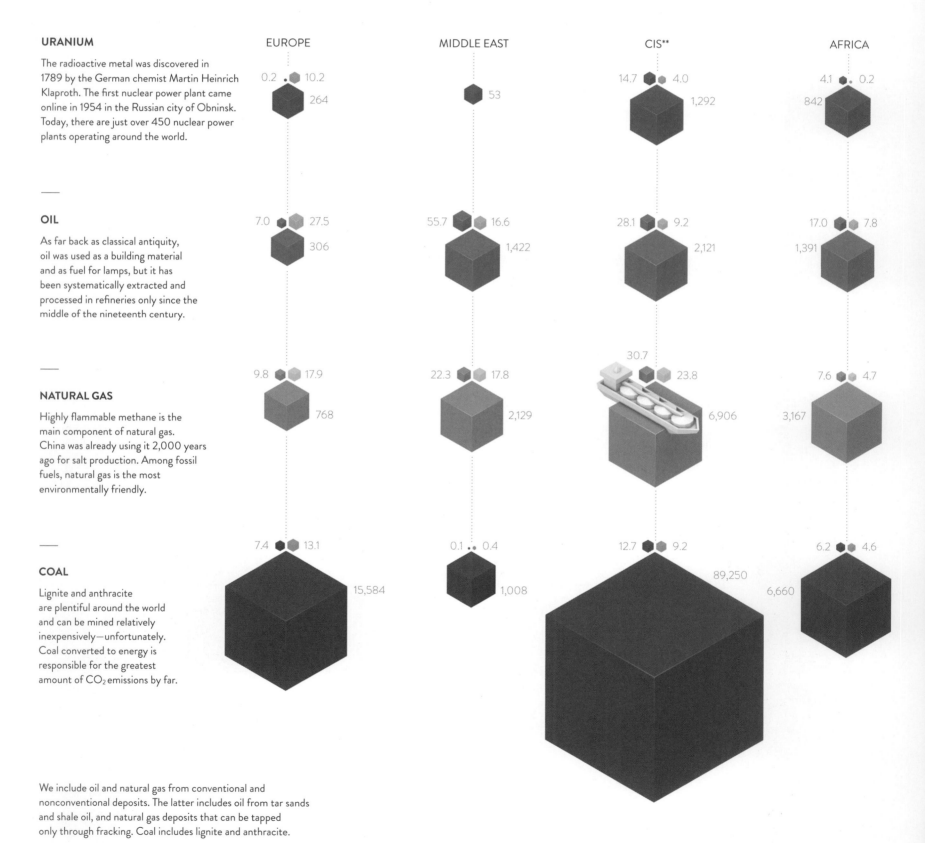

URANIUM

The radioactive metal was discovered in 1789 by the German chemist Martin Heinrich Klaproth. The first nuclear power plant came online in 1954 in the Russian city of Obninsk. Today, there are just over 450 nuclear power plants operating around the world.

OIL

As far back as classical antiquity, oil was used as a building material and as fuel for lamps, but it has been systematically extracted and processed in refineries only since the middle of the nineteenth century.

NATURAL GAS

Highly flammable methane is the main component of natural gas. China was already using it 2,000 years ago for salt production. Among fossil fuels, natural gas is the most environmentally friendly.

COAL

Lignite and anthracite are plentiful around the world and can be mined relatively inexpensively—unfortunately. Coal converted to energy is responsible for the greatest amount of CO_2 emissions by far.

EUROPE   MIDDLE EAST   CIS**   AFRICA

URANIUM
Europe: 0.2 · 10.2 · 264
Middle East: 53
CIS: 14.7 · 4.0 · 1,292
Africa: 4.1 · 0.2 · 842

OIL
Europe: 7.0 · 27.5 · 306
Middle East: 55.7 · 16.6 · 1,422
CIS: 28.1 · 9.2 · 2,121
Africa: 17.0 · 7.8 · 1,391

NATURAL GAS
Europe: 9.8 · 17.9 · 768
Middle East: 22.3 · 17.8 · 2,129
CIS: 30.7 · 23.8 · 6,906
Africa: 7.6 · 4.7 · 3,167

COAL
Europe: 7.4 · 13.1 · 15,584
Middle East: 0.1 · 0.4 · 1,008
CIS: 12.7 · 9.2 · 89,250
Africa: 6.2 · 4.6 · 6,660

We include oil and natural gas from conventional and nonconventional deposits. The latter includes oil from tar sands and shale oil, and natural gas deposits that can be tapped only through fracking. Coal includes lignite and anthracite.

* Preliminary values; rounding differences are possible
** Commonwealth of Independent States (Russia et al.)

The world's primary energy consumption in 2013 was **567.5 exajoules.**

The US had a primary energy consumption of **102.9 exajoules.***

What is primary energy consumption?

Strictly speaking, according to physics, energy cannot be consumed, but only transformed. Nevertheless, economists use this definition: The primary energy consumption of an economy is derived from the final energy consumption and the losses incurred in the production of the energy used (that is, transformed).

How much energy is in an exajoule?

In order to be able to compare the depicted fossil fuels, we illustrate their energy content in exajoules. A joule is equivalent to the work performed by a human heartbeat. An exajoule, in turn, corresponds to a quintillion joules (a one followed by eighteen zeroes)—the work of 340 million human hearts over a lifetime.

US Energy Consumption by Energy Source 2017, in percent

Petroleum	Natural gas	Coal	Renewables	Nuclear power
37	29	14	11	9

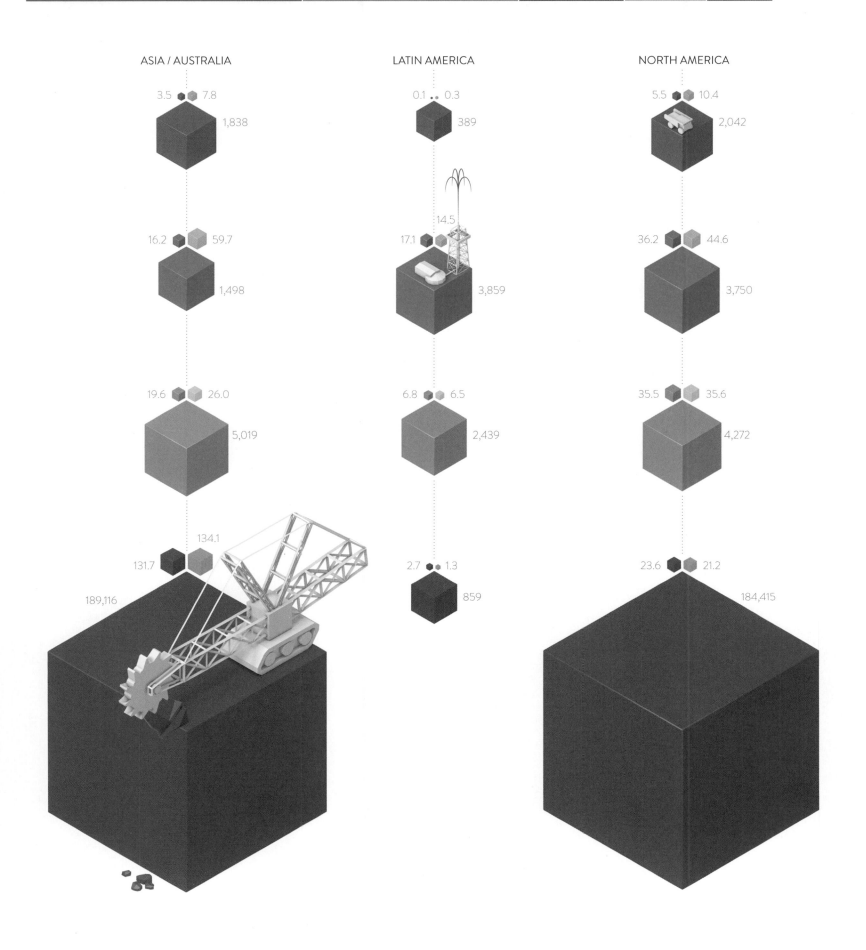

ASIA / AUSTRALIA

3.5 ●● 7.8   1,838

16.2 ■ 59.7   1,498

19.6 ■ 26.0   5,019

131.7   134.1   189,116

LATIN AMERICA

0.1 ●● 0.3   389

14.5
17.1 ●● 3,859

6.8 ●● 6.5   2,439

2.7 ●● 1.3   859

NORTH AMERICA

5.5 ■ 10.4   2,042

36.2 ■ 44.6   3,750

35.5 ■ 35.6   4,272

23.6 ■ 21.2   184,415

Canada

15,000 gallons

USA

**NORTH AND
SOUTH AMERICA**

6,300 gallons

EUROPE

Atlantic Ocean

Brazil

Argentina

Volume of the entire Earth:
259,902,236,843 miles³

WATER VOLUME
Volume of all the water on Earth:
332,519,083,390 mi³

salt water
96.5%   fresh water
                         3.5%

bound in ice (5,800,000 mi³)
in groundwater (5,600,000 mi³)
in lakes and rivers (43,000 mi³)
bound in the soil (4,000 mi³)
in the atmosphere (3,000 mi³)
in all living organisms (240 mi³)

Water resources worldwide

■ Renewable freshwater resources
Gallons per person per day

◆ Surplus water

◆ Adequate water resources

◆ Increasing water shortage

◆ Water shortage

THE VALUE
OF WATER

Water is the source of life. And it's a valuable
economic asset that people have been fighting
over for millennia. Without water, there would
be no agriculture, no fishing, no rivers for
transportation, no waterwheels to drive mills,
no steel industry, no sewage systems, no
radiators, and no cooling systems for server
farms. Without water, nothing happens. People
especially notice how valuable it is when there's
not enough of it.

**Estimated water use
in the USA by category**
2015, in billion of gallons per day and percent

Billion gallons/day
▼

133	■	Thermoelectric power
118	■	Irrigation
39	■	Public supply
14.8	■	Industrial
7.6	■	Aquaculture
4	■	Mining
3.3	■	Domestic
2	■	Livestock

0.6 1.0 1.2 2.4 4.6

12.1

41.3

%

36.7

Percent

**Per capita water consumption per year,
international comparison**
in cubic feet

USA	55,800
Estonia	43,400
New Zealand	42,000
Canada	36,400
Spain	28,600
Mexico	24,400
Turkey	22,600
Netherlands	22,600
Japan	22,600
Australia	630

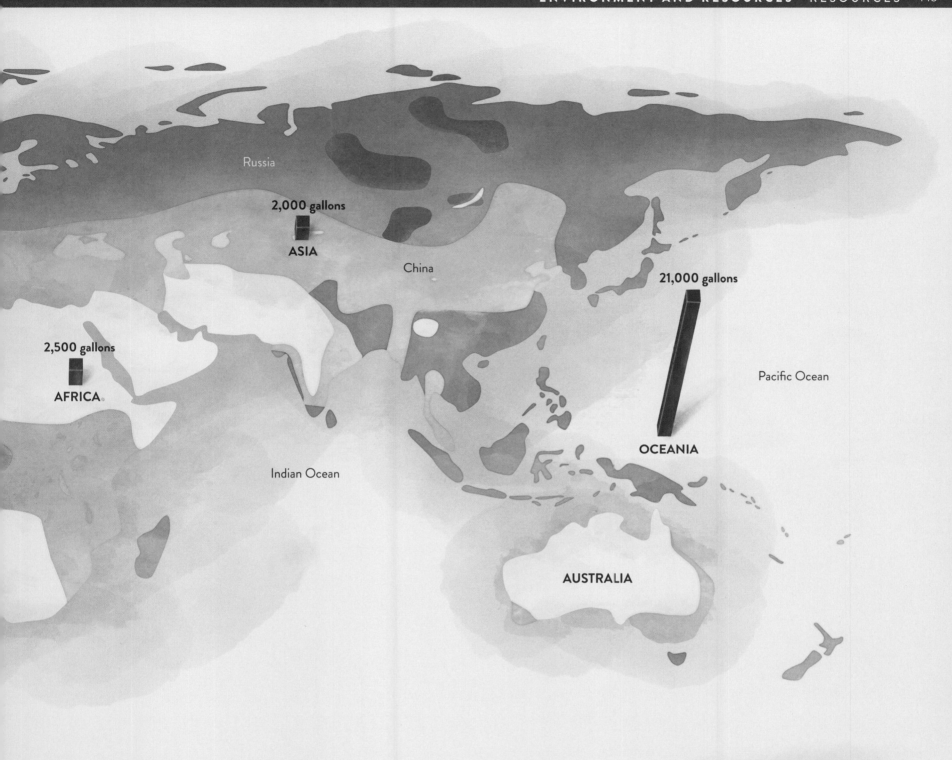

Russia

2,000 gallons

ASIA

China

21,000 gallons

OCEANIA

Pacific Ocean

2,500 gallons

AFRICA

Indian Ocean

AUSTRALIA

Virtual water consumption of everyday objects

The technical term "virtual water" (sometimes latent water) describes the total amount of water that is actually used in the manufacturing of a product.

1,110 gallons
Average consumption of virtual water by one person in a day

33 gallons
Real average water consumption at home per inhabitant per day

106,000 gallons

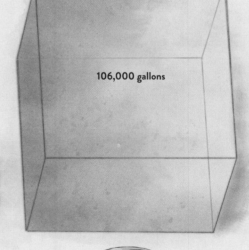

49 gallons

79 gallons

251 gallons

264 gallons

872 gallons

1,321 gallons

2,906 gallons

4,083 gallons

5,283 gallons

35 oz toma-toes

4.2 cups beer

4.2 cups apple juice

4.2 cups milk

35 oz eggs

35 oz cheese

35 oz cotton or 1 pair of jeans

35 oz beef

↓
35 oz pork: 1,268 gallons

1 personal computer

↓
1 microchip: 8.5 gallons

1 car (around 3,300 lbs.)

WHAT FILLS THE MOST BELLIES

According to a popular saying, the dumbest farmer harvests the biggest potatoes. First of all, that's nonsense, and second, it wouldn't be all that relevant even if it were true. Milk, rice, soy, and many other vegetable raw materials play much larger roles in the global agricultural industry.

The most important agricultural commodities worldwide
Raw materials produced in millions of tons and value in billions of US$

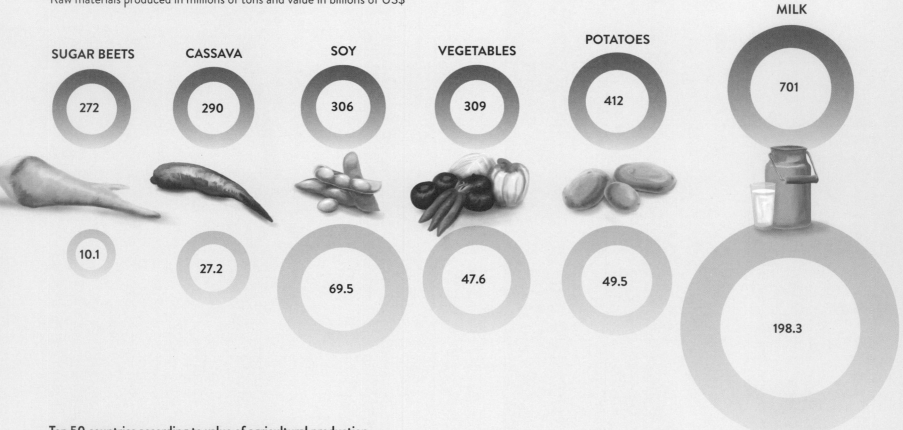

SUGAR BEETS — 272 — 10.1
CASSAVA — 290 — 27.2
SOY — 306 — 69.5
VEGETABLES — 309 — 47.6
POTATOES — 412 — 49.5
MILK — 701 — 198.3

Top 50 countries according to value of agricultural production
Gross production value in billions of US$

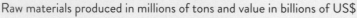

9.2	9.2	9.2	9.7	11	11	11.1	11.2	12.3	12.6	13.3	14	14.1	14.2	14.3	15.7	17.3	20.3	20.9	22.1	23.2	23.5	26.1	26.8	28.6
Kazakhstan	Mozambique	Cote d'Ivoire	Paraguay	Ghana	Kenya	New Zealand	Denmark	Saudi Arabia	Ethiopia	Netherlands	Chile	Peru	Morocco	Sudan	Greece	Bangladesh	Romania	South Africa	Colombia	Poland	Algeria	Malaysia	Pakistan	Venezuela

Share of gross domestic product from agricultural production
Values by percentage, 1970 to 2013

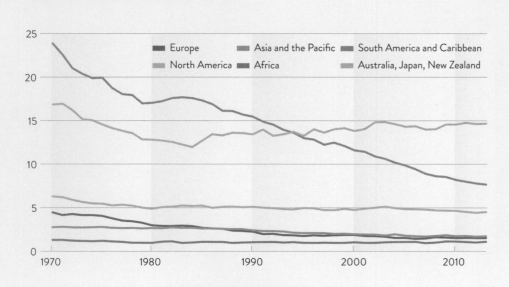

- Europe
- North America
- Asia and the Pacific
- Africa
- South America and Caribbean
- Australia, Japan, New Zealand

Top exporters and importers of agricultural commodities
in billions of US$

Top exporters 2013			Top importers 2013
USA	148	115	China
Netherlands	91	114	USA
Germany	84	94	Germany
Brazil	84	63	United Kingdom
France	75	61	Japan
China	46	59	Netherlands
Spain	46	57	France
Canada	45	48	Italy
Belgium	44	40	Russia

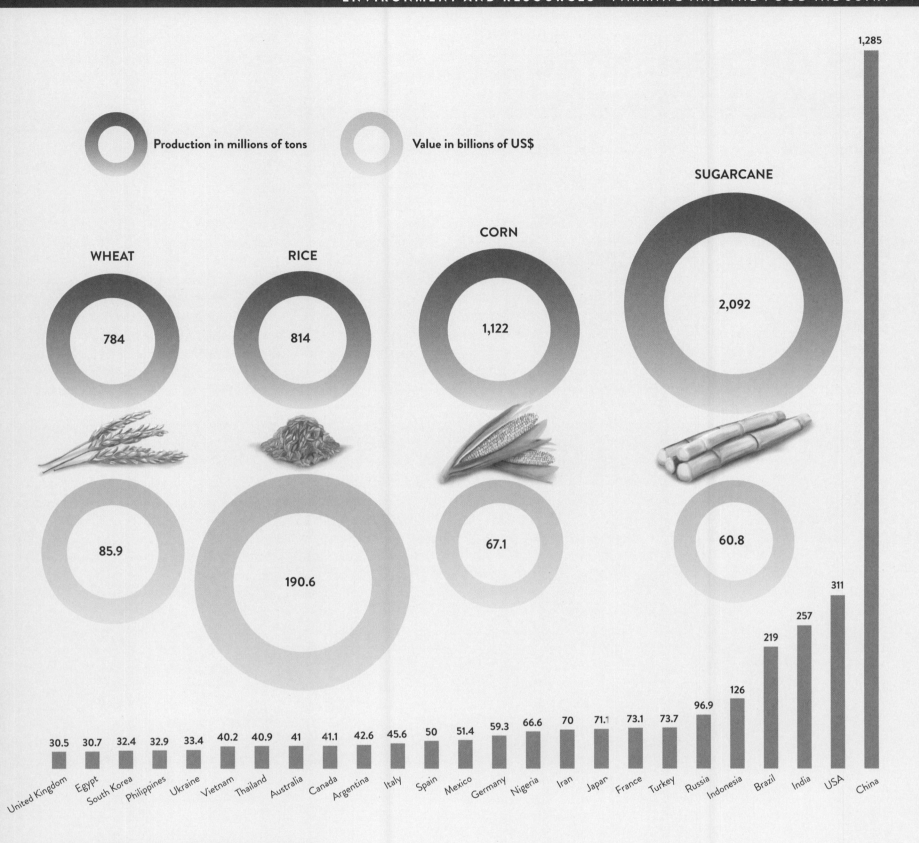

Production in millions of tons   **Value in billions of US$**

WHEAT
784
85.9

RICE
814
190.6

CORN
1,122
67.1

SUGARCANE
2,092
60.8

United Kingdom 30.5
Egypt 30.7
South Korea 32.4
Philippines 32.9
Ukraine 33.4
Vietnam 40.2
Thailand 40.9
Australia 41
Canada 41.1
Argentina 42.6
Italy 45.6
Spain 50
Mexico 51.4
Germany 59.3
Nigeria 66.6
Iran 70
Japan 71.1
France 73.1
Turkey 73.7
Russia 96.9
Indonesia 126
Brazil 219
India 257
USA 311
China 1,285

Price fluctuations of foodstuffs by product group

100 = Index 2002 to 2004

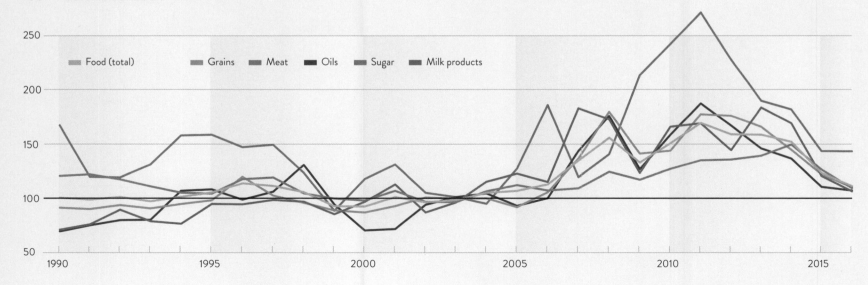

Food (total)   Grains   Meat   Oils   Sugar   Milk products

250
200
150
100
50

1990   1995   2000   2005   2010   2015

ENVIRONMENTAL CONSCIOUSNESS

The key economic indicators for organic farming have been on an upward trend for decades. Today, organic practically sells itself. For many consumers, the price hardly matters. Only the minimal increase in organically cultivated cropland is constraining growth.

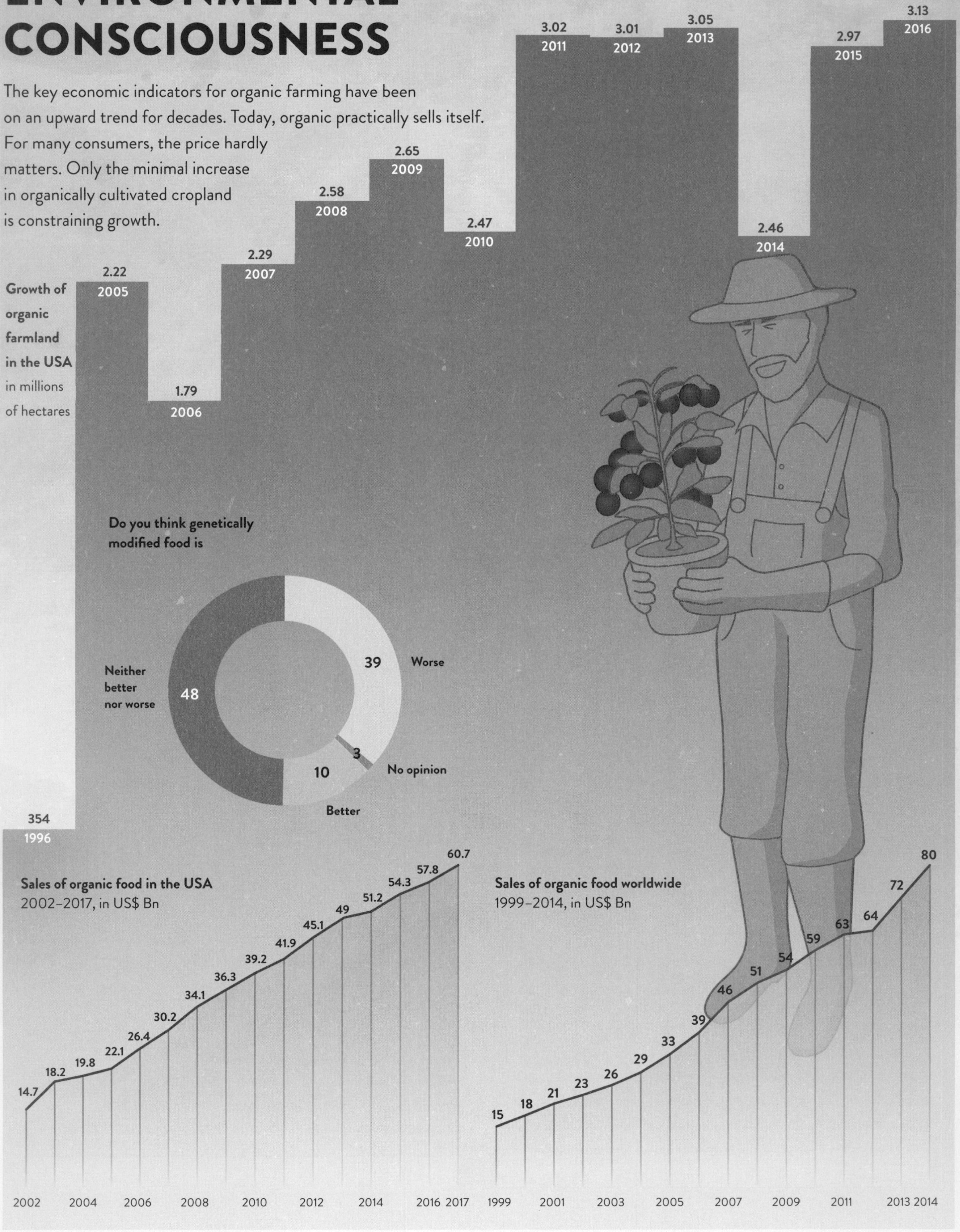

Growth of organic farmland in the USA in millions of hectares

3.02 2011
3.01 2012
3.05 2013
2.97 2015
3.13 2016
2.65 2009
2.58 2008
2.47 2010
2.46 2014
2.29 2007
2.22 2005
1.79 2006

Do you think genetically modified food is

Neither better nor worse 48
39 Worse
3 No opinion
10 Better

Sales of organic food in the USA
2002–2017, in US$ Bn

354 1996

14.7
18.2
19.8
22.1
26.4
30.2
34.1
36.3
39.2
41.9
45.1
49
51.2
54.3
57.8
60.7

2002 2004 2006 2008 2010 2012 2014 2016 2017

Sales of organic food worldwide
1999–2014, in US$ Bn

15
18
21
23
26
29
33
39
46
51
54
59
63
64
72
80

1999 2001 2003 2005 2007 2009 2011 2013 2014

GREEN GENETIC ENGINEERING

Genetically engineered plants don't have an especially good reputation. Risks to people and to the ecosystem are perceived as strongly outweighing the opportunities resulting from innovation in agricultural technology. People see things differently in places where there's not enough food for everybody.

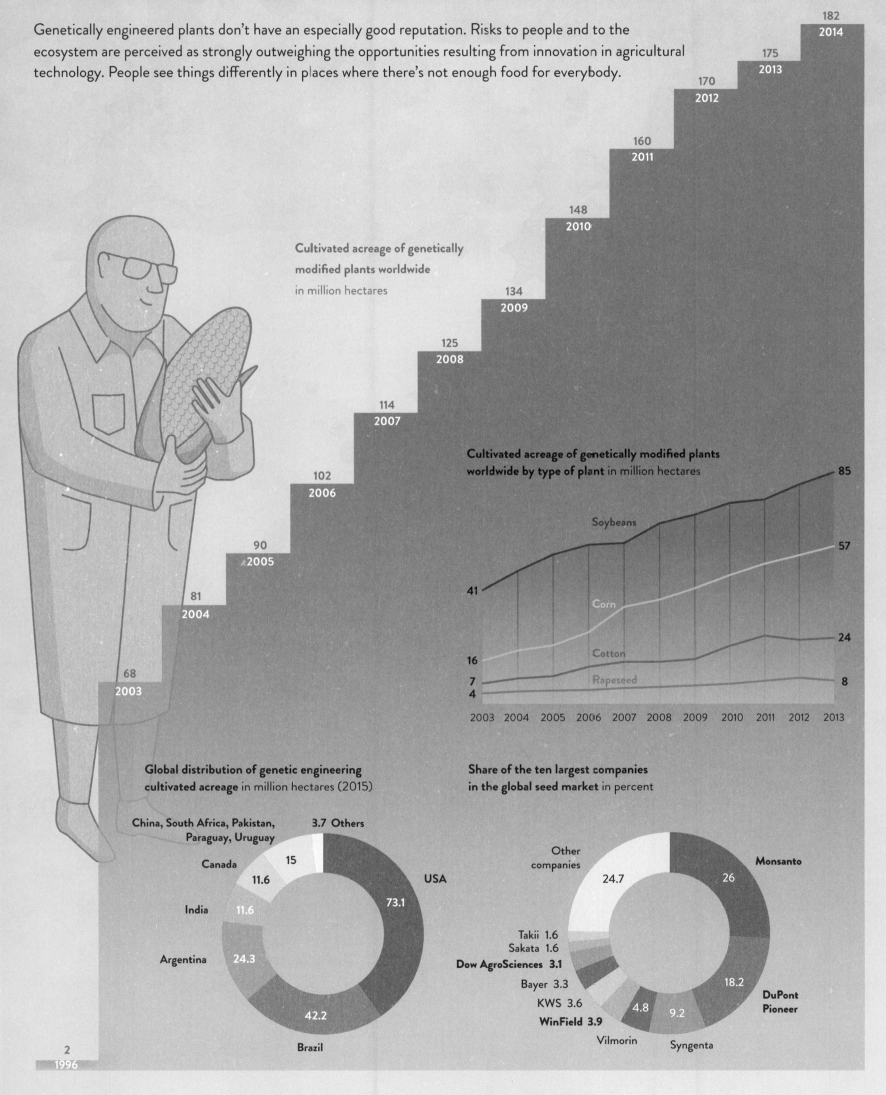

Cultivated acreage of genetically modified plants worldwide
in million hectares

182 · 2014
175 · 2013
170 · 2012
160 · 2011
148 · 2010
134 · 2009
125 · 2008
114 · 2007
102 · 2006
90 · 2005
81 · 2004
68 · 2003
2 · 1996

Cultivated acreage of genetically modified plants worldwide by type of plant in million hectares

Soybeans 41 → 85
Corn 16 → 57
Cotton 7 → 24
Rapeseed 4 → 8

2003 2004 2005 2006 2007 2008 2009 2010 2011 2012 2013

Global distribution of genetic engineering cultivated acreage in million hectares (2015)

China, South Africa, Pakistan, Paraguay, Uruguay 15
3.7 Others
Canada 11.6
USA 73.1
India 11.6
Argentina 24.3
Brazil 42.2

Share of the ten largest companies in the global seed market in percent

Other companies 24.7
Monsanto 26
Takii 1.6
Sakata 1.6
Dow AgroSciences 3.1
Bayer 3.3
KWS 3.6
WinField 3.9
DuPont Pioneer 18.2
Vilmorin 4.8
Syngenta 9.2

TRANSPARENCY

Large corporations have a large influence on the welfare of many people. Because of this, they bear a large responsibility. Responsible companies report where, how, and with whom they do business, how they support political parties, and in which countries they pay taxes. It's unfortunate that sharing information isn't exactly a high priority for the world's 124 largest publicly traded companies, as a report by Transparency International about corporate reporting strikingly demonstrates.

Which company is the most transparent?

Overall index

Anti-corruption programs in %

7.3

96

22

100

Organizational transparency in %

Country-specific reporting in %

The overall index rates transparency on a scale from 0 to 10 (0 = lowest, 10 = highest transparency). It is calculated by taking the average from the categories of anti-corruption programs, organizational transparency, and country-specific reporting.

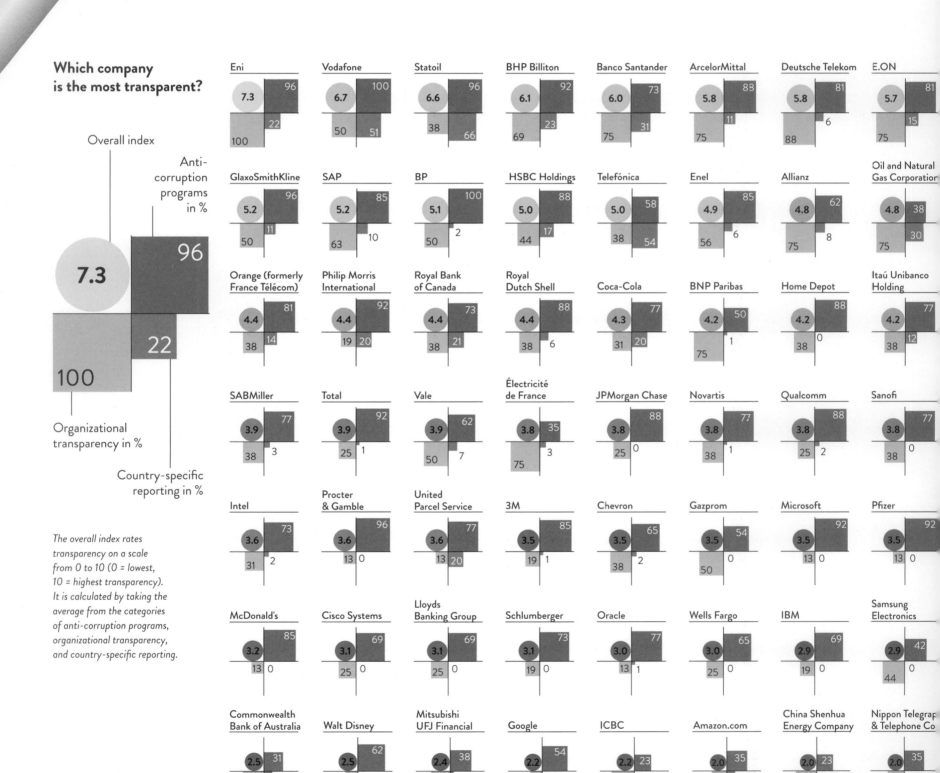

Company	Overall	Anti-corruption	Org. transparency	Country-specific
Eni	7.3	96	100	22
Vodafone	6.7	100	50	51
Statoil	6.6	96	38	66
BHP Billiton	6.1	92	69	23
Banco Santander	6.0	73	75	31
ArcelorMittal	5.8	88	75	11
Deutsche Telekom	5.8	81	88	6
E.ON	5.7	81	75	15
GlaxoSmithKline	5.2	96	50	11
SAP	5.2	85	63	10
BP	5.1	100	50	2
HSBC Holdings	5.0	88	44	17
Telefónica	5.0	58	38	54
Enel	4.9	85	56	6
Allianz	4.8	62	75	8
Oil and Natural Gas Corporation	4.8	38	75	30
Orange (formerly France Télécom)	4.4	81	38	14
Philip Morris International	4.4	92	19	20
Royal Bank of Canada	4.4	73	38	21
Royal Dutch Shell	4.4	88	38	6
Coca-Cola	4.3	77	31	20
BNP Paribas	4.2	50	75	1
Home Depot	4.2	88	38	0
Itaú Unibanco Holding	4.2	77	38	12
SABMiller	3.9	77	38	3
Total	3.9	92	25	1
Vale	3.9	62	50	7
Électricité de France	3.8	35	75	3
JPMorgan Chase	3.8	88	25	0
Novartis	3.8	77	25	1
Qualcomm	3.8	88	25	2
Sanofi	3.8	77	38	0
Intel	3.6	73	31	2
Procter & Gamble	3.6	96	13	0
United Parcel Service	3.6	77	13	20
3M	3.5	85	19	1
Chevron	3.5	65	38	2
Gazprom	3.5	54	50	0
Microsoft	3.5	92	13	0
Pfizer	3.5	92	13	0
McDonald's	3.2	85	13	0
Cisco Systems	3.1	69	25	0
Lloyds Banking Group	3.1	69	25	0
Schlumberger	3.1	73	19	0
Oracle	3.0	77	13	1
Wells Fargo	3.0	65	25	0
IBM	2.9	69	19	0
Samsung Electronics	2.9	42	44	0
Commonwealth Bank of Australia	2.5	31	38	6
Walt Disney	2.5	62	13	0
Mitsubishi UFJ Financial	2.4	38	31	1
Google	2.2	54	13	0
ICBC	2.2	23	44	0
Amazon.com	2.0	35	19	6
China Shenhua Energy Company	2.0	23	38	0
Nippon Telegraph & Telephone Co	2.0	35	25	0

NO CHINESE COMPANY

. . . publishes its financial data in any of the 59 countries in which they operate.

90 COMPANIES
. . . provide no information about tax payments abroad.

SECRECY

Amazon, Apple, Google, and IBM did not publish a complete list of the countries in which their subsidiaries operate.

Eight of the ten least transparent companies are from Asia.

THE ONLY COMPANY
. . . that reached at least 50% in all categories was Vodafone.

101 COMPANIES
. . . received less than half the total number of points.

70%
. . . of the most transparent companies are European.

65 COMPANIES
. . . did not publish their political contributions.

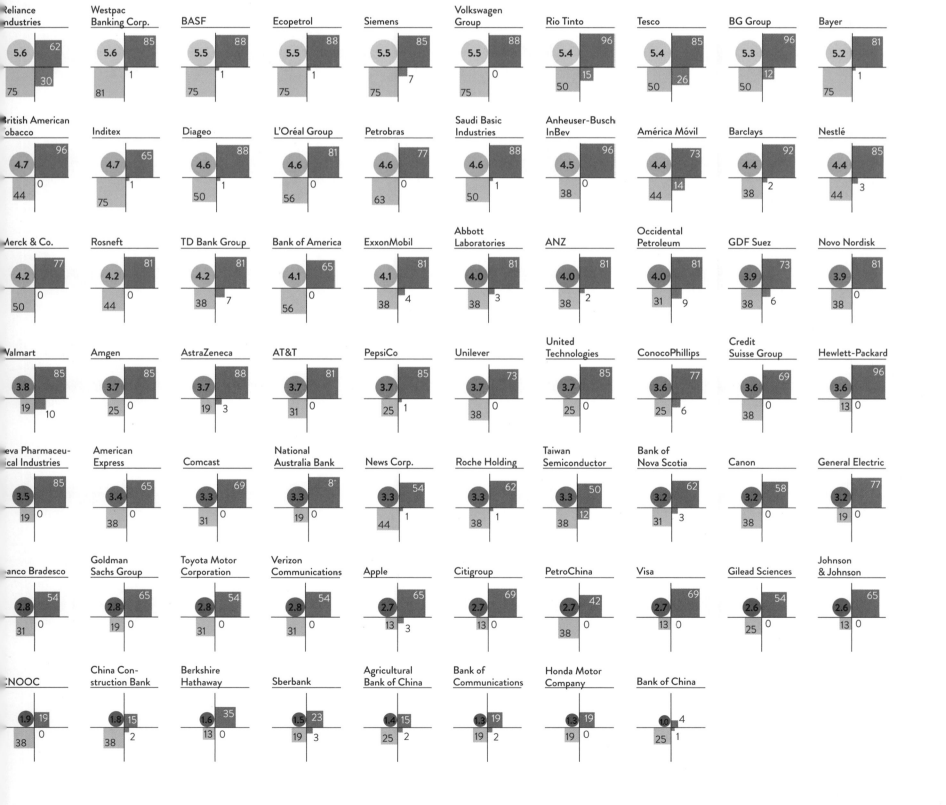

Company	Score			
Reliance Industries	5.6	62	75	30
Westpac Banking Corp.	5.6	85	81	1
BASF	5.5	88	75	1
Ecopetrol	5.5	88	75	1
Siemens	5.5	85	75	1
Volkswagen Group	5.5	88	75	7 / 0
Rio Tinto	5.4	96	50	15
Tesco	5.4	85	50	26
BG Group	5.3	96	50	12
Bayer	5.2	81	75	1
British American Tobacco	4.7	96	44	0
Inditex	4.7	65	75	1
Diageo	4.6	88	50	1
L'Oréal Group	4.6	81	56	0
Petrobras	4.6	77	63	0
Saudi Basic Industries	4.6	88	50	1
Anheuser-Busch InBev	4.5	96	38	0
América Móvil	4.4	73	44	14
Barclays	4.4	92	38	2
Nestlé	4.4	85	44	3
Merck & Co.	4.2	77	50	0
Rosneft	4.2	81	44	0
TD Bank Group	4.2	81	38	7
Bank of America	4.1	65	56	0
ExxonMobil	4.1	81	38	4
Abbott Laboratories	4.0	81	38	3
ANZ	4.0	81	38	2
Occidental Petroleum	4.0	81	31	9
GDF Suez	3.9	73	38	6
Novo Nordisk	3.9	81	38	0
Walmart	3.8	85	19	10
Amgen	3.7	85	25	0
AstraZeneca	3.7	88	19	3
AT&T	3.7	81	31	0
PepsiCo	3.7	85	25	1
Unilever	3.7	73	38	0
United Technologies	3.7	85	25	0
ConocoPhillips	3.6	77	25	6
Credit Suisse Group	3.6	69	38	0
Hewlett-Packard	3.6	96	13	0
Teva Pharmaceutical Industries	3.5	85	19	0
American Express	3.4	65	38	0
Comcast	3.3	69	31	0
National Australia Bank	3.3	81	19	0
News Corp.	3.3	54	44	1
Roche Holding	3.3	62	38	1
Taiwan Semiconductor	3.3	50	38	12
Bank of Nova Scotia	3.2	62	31	3
Canon	3.2	58	38	0
General Electric	3.2	77	19	0
Banco Bradesco	2.8	54	31	0
Goldman Sachs Group	2.8	65	19	0
Toyota Motor Corporation	2.8	54	31	0
Verizon Communications	2.8	54	31	0
Apple	2.7	65	13	3
Citigroup	2.7	69	13	0
PetroChina	2.7	42	38	0
Visa	2.7	69	13	0
Gilead Sciences	2.6	54	25	0
Johnson & Johnson	2.6	65	13	0
CNOOC	1.9	19	38	0
China Construction Bank	1.8	15	38	2
Berkshire Hathaway	1.6	35	13	0
Sberbank	1.5	23	19	3
Agricultural Bank of China	1.4	15	25	2
Bank of Communications	1.3	19	19	2
Honda Motor Company	1.3	19	19	0
Bank of China	1.0	4	25	1

GREENWASHING

1 Redesign your label. Use the color green, leaves, trees, or the recycling symbol. If your product has anything to do with water or the ocean, you can use light blue and a happy fish as alternatives.

2 Change the product name. It should include the words "organic," "environmental," "green," "natural," or "fair." Occasionally it's possible to use several of these words at the same time.

3 Look for some international organization that passes out pleasant-sounding environmental certifications that have especially lax or confusing criteria. The organization's reputability is not particularly important. What's critical is that compliance with the criteria is difficult to verify.

International Organization for Eco-Labels

4 Print "CFC-free" on your product, and not only on hair spray, refrigerators, and air conditioners. There are also CFC-free mattresses. Incidentally, most consumers don't know that CFCs have been forbidden since 1991 in any case.

5 Compare your environmentally questionable product with one that pollutes the environment even more. Additionally, you can equip your product with supplemental technology that a) makes it substantially more expensive, and b) makes it appear greener in comparison to the model without this added technology. On the environmental balance sheet, it can even c) end up on the noxious side for most uses. For car manufacturers, it often helps to call the whole thing a hybrid.

1×   1×   1×   1×   1×   1×   >1000×   1×   **AS MANY AS POSSIBLE**

8

Issue a sustainability report. The CEO's opening remarks should begin with the formulation: "As a company, we are aware of our important responsibility." The magazine section at the front should include many large-format photographs with environmental motifs and coverage of fabulous employees from all levels of the company hierarchy who are making the world a better place. The part with the facts and figures about environmental and social responsibility isn't as important. It should stay at the back and remain as short as possible.

9

Advertise your product in outlets where environmentally conscious brands (that is, the ones that actually take it seriously) also advertise. There's a halo effect. But don't advertise on online platforms where hypercritical consumers tend to congregate. They'll quickly turn up with multi-paragraph comments that accuse you of greenwashing, and may even back up their criticisms with facts if any doubt is expressed.

7

When it comes to lobbying in Washington or Brussels, the kid gloves come off. Your goal is to lower legal limits so that your products can just barely be classified as environmentally friendly. Internally, they call it "deep greenwashing."

6

Participate in programs to compensate for harming the environment whose effectiveness is difficult to verify. Or to put it another way: Sell your customers a clean conscience to go along with their poor consumption choices. It's what they want!

10

Launch expensive campaigns with vague statements in which children and grandparents are prominently featured and that somehow contain the message that we have to tackle problems together in order to make the world a better place.

THE WASTE SYSTEM

We love our new smartphone, our new smart TV, our new automatic coffee maker. Manufacturers and dealers love us for loving new things. Which has led to whatever's new in electronics becoming old faster and faster, and to the mountains of electronic waste that are growing three times faster than waste in general. We tell ourselves it's only half as bad as it looks because of recycling. But with electronic waste, the global recycling quota is well under 20%. And because industrialized nations' recycling capacity is exhausted, electronic waste is often exported to developing countries illegally, mostly declared as used electronic devices. In 2016, every American contributed 42 pounds of e-waste to the 6.9 million tons generated overall in the US, of which 750,000 tons are exported annually.

WORLDWIDE

46.2

MILLION TONS
ELECTRONIC WASTE IN 2014

consisting of:

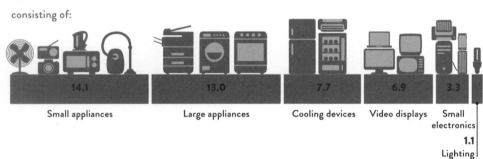

14.1	13.0	7.7	6.9	3.3
Small appliances	Large appliances	Cooling devices	Video displays	Small electronics

1.1
Lighting

MAIN ROUTES OF WASTE EXPORT

Proper disposal comes at a high cost in industrialized countries, so the export business is lucrative for unscrupulous waste traders. Threats to human beings and environmental hazards are just part of the bargain.

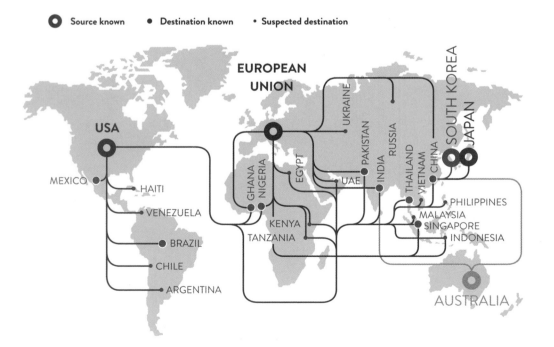

● Source known   • Destination known   • Suspected destination

USA · MEXICO · HAITI · VENEZUELA · BRAZIL · CHILE · ARGENTINA · EUROPEAN UNION · GHANA · NIGERIA · EGYPT · KENYA · TANZANIA · UAE · UKRAINE · PAKISTAN · INDIA · RUSSIA · THAILAND · VIETNAM · CHINA · SOUTH KOREA · JAPAN · PHILIPPINES · MALAYSIA · SINGAPORE · INDONESIA · AUSTRALIA

THE CELL PHONE MARKET

The ongoing triumph of the cell phone began in 1984 in Europe, Japan, and the USA. Developing and emerging nations quickly caught up.

Registered cell phones per 100 inhabitants

■ Industrialized countries   ■ Developing countries   — World

120
90
60
30
0
2001 — 2015

Percentage of the world's population with access to the wireless network

95% with access
(2015, according to the UN)

③ CONSUMPTION

Unsold goods

② DISTRIBUTION

COMPETITION

Short product cycles are good for sales and profits. They're bad for the environment, unfortunately.

MINING

Companies go to great lengths to access valuable metal ores. That has significant consequences for nature and the environment. In order to obtain a ton of copper, more than 100 tons of ore have to be mined.

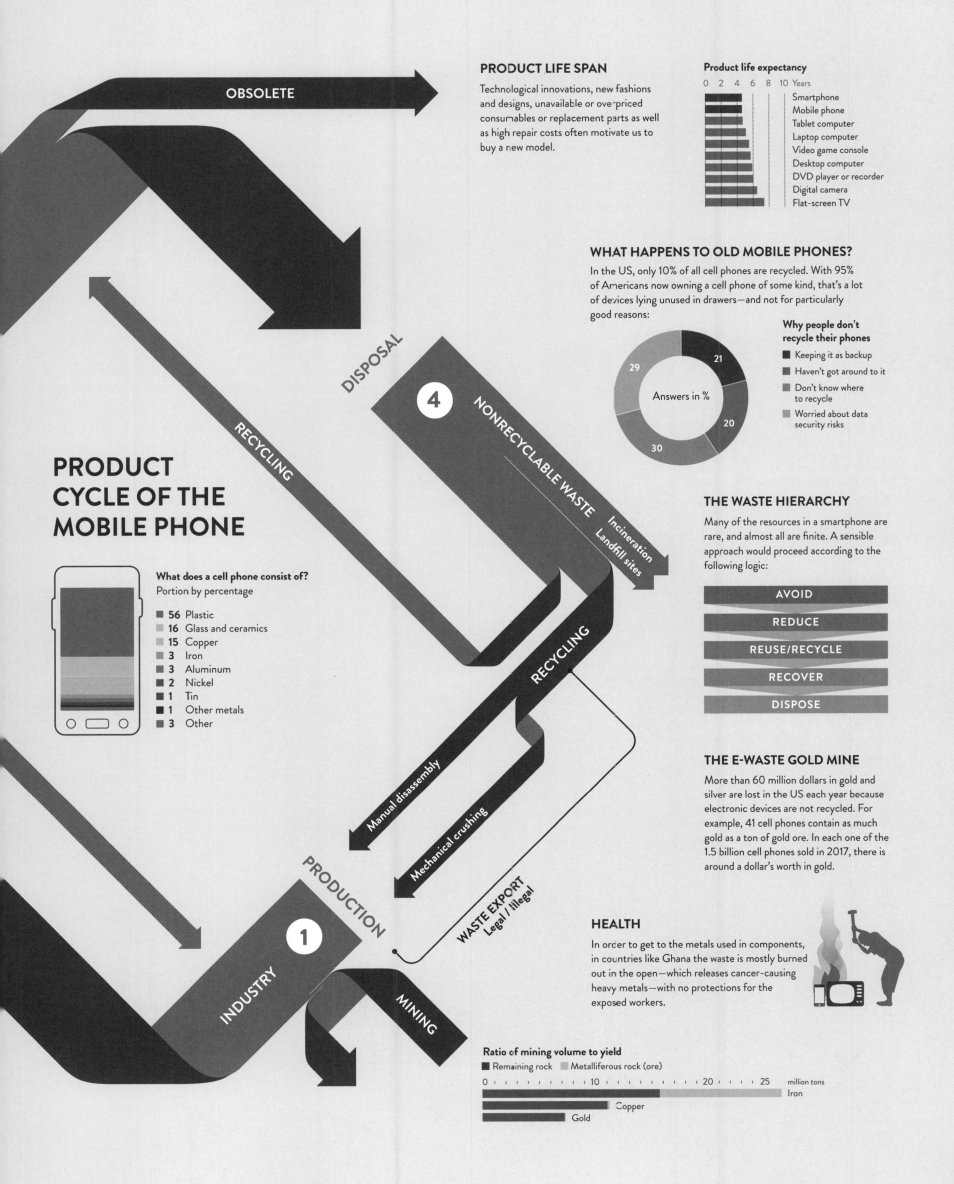

PRODUCT CYCLE OF THE MOBILE PHONE

OBSOLETE

DISPOSAL

RECYCLING

NONRECYCLABLE WASTE — Incineration — Landfill sites

RECYCLING

Manual disassembly

Mechanical crushing

WASTE EXPORT Legal / Illegal

PRODUCTION

INDUSTRY

MINING

1

4

What does a cell phone consist of?
Portion by percentage

- **56** Plastic
- **16** Glass and ceramics
- **15** Copper
- **3** Iron
- **3** Aluminum
- **2** Nickel
- **1** Tin
- **1** Other metals
- **3** Other

PRODUCT LIFE SPAN

Technological innovations, new fashions and designs, unavailable or over-priced consumables or replacement parts as well as high repair costs often motivate us to buy a new model.

Product life expectancy

0 2 4 6 8 10 Years

- Smartphone
- Mobile phone
- Tablet computer
- Laptop computer
- Video game console
- Desktop computer
- DVD player or recorder
- Digital camera
- Flat-screen TV

WHAT HAPPENS TO OLD MOBILE PHONES?

In the US, only 10% of all cell phones are recycled. With 95% of Americans now owning a cell phone of some kind, that's a lot of devices lying unused in drawers—and not for particularly good reasons:

Why people don't recycle their phones

- Keeping it as backup
- Haven't got around to it
- Don't know where to recycle
- Worried about data security risks

Answers in %

21
20
30
29

THE WASTE HIERARCHY

Many of the resources in a smartphone are rare, and almost all are finite. A sensible approach would proceed according to the following logic:

- **AVOID**
- **REDUCE**
- **REUSE/RECYCLE**
- **RECOVER**
- **DISPOSE**

THE E-WASTE GOLD MINE

More than 60 million dollars in gold and silver are lost in the US each year because electronic devices are not recycled. For example, 41 cell phones contain as much gold as a ton of gold ore. In each one of the 1.5 billion cell phones sold in 2017, there is around a dollar's worth in gold.

HEALTH

In order to get to the metals used in components, in countries like Ghana the waste is mostly burned out in the open—which releases cancer-causing heavy metals—with no protections for the exposed workers.

Ratio of mining volume to yield

- Remaining rock
- Metalliferous rock (ore)

0 10 20 25 million tons

Iron

Copper

Gold

EMISSIONS TRADING

How do we reduce air pollution as quickly as possible at the lowest possible cost? A doctoral student at the University of Wisconsin had a brilliant answer in 1966: emissions trading. He suggested a government-regulated market for pollution rights. According to the basic idea, market mechanisms would allow market actors to enact environmental protection measures at the lowest price. In 2005, the Kyoto Protocol (whose negotiation process the US dropped out of in 2001) implemented the idea on a large scale for the first time for reduction of CO_2 emissions. Success to this point has been modest, however, as too many certificates were issued.

How does emissions trading work?

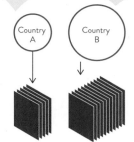

I LIMITS

Politicians agree on climate goals.

II CERTIFICATES

One nation or a community of nations first determines the total amount of permitted greenhouse gas emissions — the so-called "cap." This is then issued to companies ("emitters") in the form of emission permits or purchased by them at auction. One emission allowance thus makes permissible the emission of one ton of CO_2 or CO_2-equivalent within a specified commitment period.

III TRADE

Depending on their needs, governments and business can buy or sell emission rights. If the emission rights values are exceeded, rights of equivalent value must be purchased to compensate—otherwise, penalty fees loom.

IV RREDUCTION TARGETS

In each commitment period, the number of emission permits decreases according to internationally agreed quotas, and the share of fee-based emission rights to be bought at auction rises. The principle of "reduce or pay" is intended to increase the incentives for companies to invest in more efficient and environmentally friendly technologies so they can meet or remain under future limits.

V THE KEY FEATURE

Every company is not required to reduce pollution by the same amount. What counts is only the total result for everyone involved. The companies with the lowest reduction costs can acquire the emission reductions of those businesses for whom reducing emissions would be very expensive. By doing so, they earn more than reducing emissions costs them. In the end, this means that a desired reduction of CO_2 can be attained very cost-effectively (economic minimalist principle), or, at a desired cost, emissions can be reduced to the greatest degree possible (maximal principle).

CRITICISM

The European Union has the world's largest greenhouse gases trading program. The higher the price for a CO_2 certificate, the higher the incentive for all companies to invest in energy-efficient technologies. Environmental groups have criticized the EU for issuing too many certificates from the start, so a price drop was predictable. They demand an additional tightening or a minimum price of 20 euros.

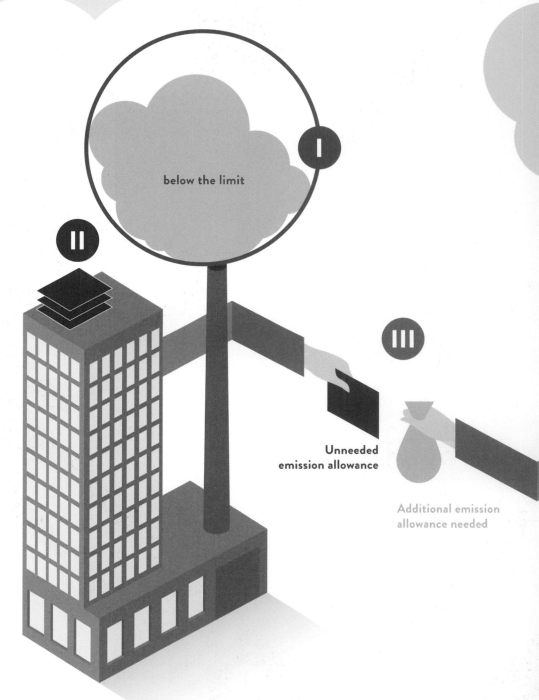

below the limit

Unneeded emission allowance

Additional emission allowance needed

Price history in EU emissions trading (European Union Emissions Trading System, EU ETS) in euros

—EUA (European Union Allowance) spot price— CER (Certified Emission Reduction)

PHASE 1 2005–2007

PHASE 2 2008–2012

PHASE 3 2013–2020

2005 2006 2007 2008 2009 2010 2011 2012 2013 2014 2015

Greenhouse gases and their main causes

CO_2 is the best-known greenhouse gas, but other gases also have a substantial greenhouse warming potential (GWP). Methane, fo-example, contributes 25 times as much to the greenhouse effect within 100 years after its release as CO_2 does, while the effect of nitrous oxide is 298 times higher.

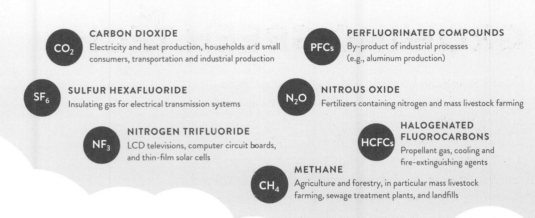

CARBON DIOXIDE CO_2
Electricity and heat production, households and small consumers, transportation and industrial production

SULFUR HEXAFLUORIDE SF_6
Insulating gas for electrical transmission systems

NITROGEN TRIFLUORIDE NF_3
LCD televisions, computer circuit boards, and thin-film solar cells

PERFLUORINATED COMPOUNDS PFCs
By-product of industrial processes (e.g., aluminum production)

NITROUS OXIDE N_2O
Fertilizers containing nitrogen and mass livestock farming

HALOGENATED FLUOROCARBONS HCFCs
Propellant gas, cooling and fire-extinguishing agents

METHANE CH_4
Agriculture and forestry, in particular mass livestock farming, sewage treatment plants, and landfills

Who's taking part?

As the first multinational system, the European Emissions Trading System could be a model for a unified global carbon market. To this point, only a few countries have implemented emissions trading — but the club is growing: Even some large countries, including Brazil and Russia, are now considering their own systems. Here you can see a snapshot of the national and regional systems implemented as of 2015.

Limit exceeded

As an alternative, governments and companies in industrialized nations can purchase "certified emission reductions" for climate-protection projects in developing countries.

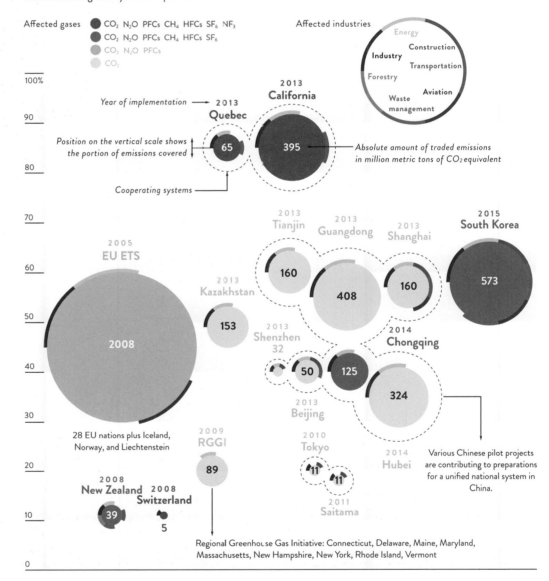

How much of a reduction is needed to reach the goal of 2.7°F?

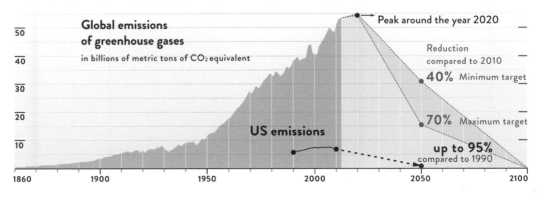

GROWING GREEN TECH

Good money can be made with a good conscience. Providers of environmental technologies have been proving that for many years, and according to the calculations of the consulting firm Roland Berger, it will remain that way for a long time. Three important reasons: Environmental requirements are rising around the world; more and more consumers are prepared to pay extra for environmentally friendly technology; and investments in green tech offer solid returns, thanks to energy saving and other perks.

MATERIAL EFFICIENCY

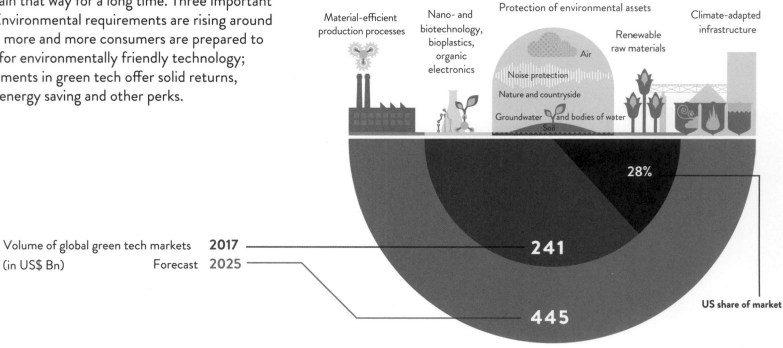

Material-efficient production processes

Nano- and biotechnology, bioplastics, organic electronics

Protection of environmental assets

Air
Noise protection
Nature and countryside
Groundwater and bodies of water
Soil

Renewable raw materials

Climate-adapted infrastructure

28%

Volume of global green tech markets (in US$ Bn)

2017

Forecast 2025

241

445

US share of market

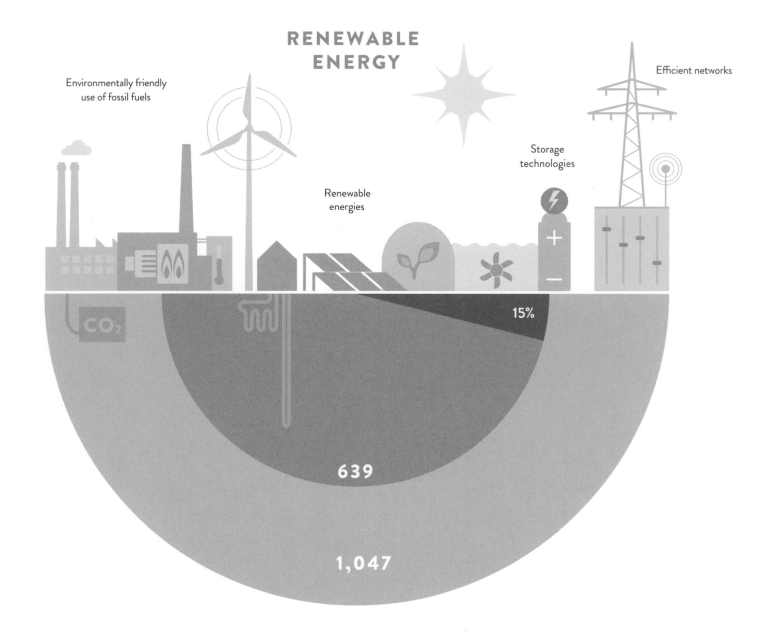

RENEWABLE ENERGY

Environmentally friendly use of fossil fuels

Efficient networks

Storage technologies

Renewable energies

CO₂

15%

639

1,047

SMART WATER MANAGEMENT

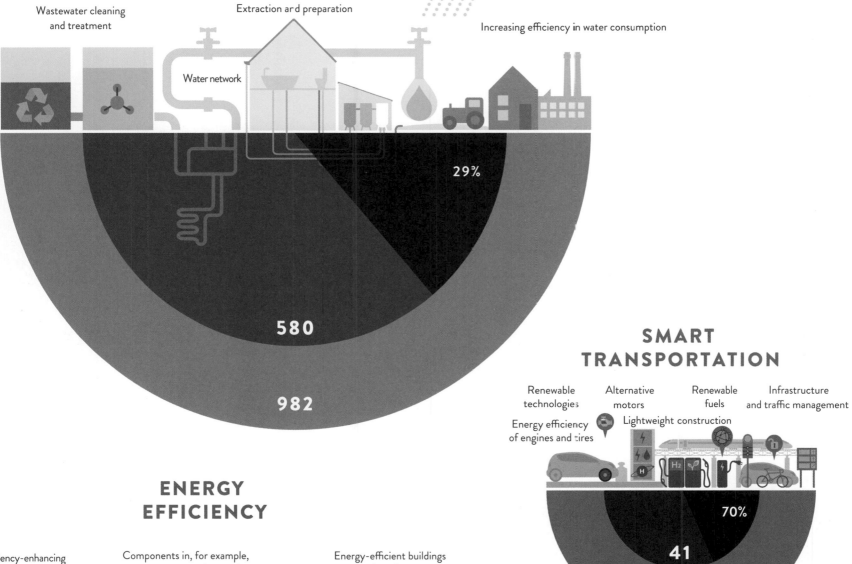

Wastewater cleaning
and treatment

Extraction and preparation

Water network

Increasing efficiency in water consumption

29%

580

982

SMART
TRANSPORTATION

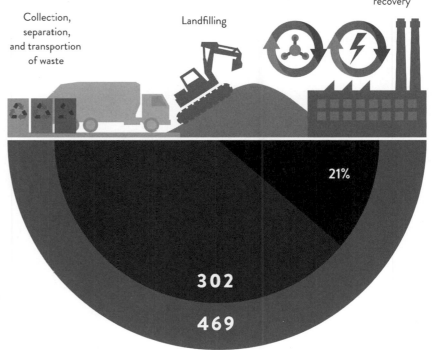

Renewable
technologies

Alternative
motors

Renewable
fuels

Infrastructure
and traffic management

Energy efficiency
of engines and tires

Lightweight construction

70%

41

156

ENERGY
EFFICIENCY

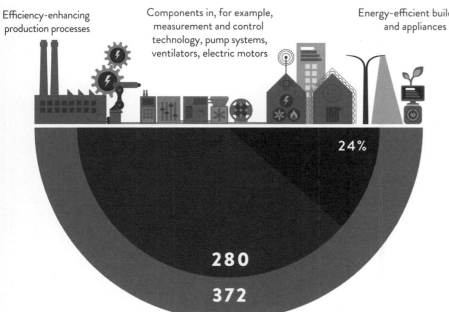

Efficiency-enhancing
production processes

Components in, for example,
measurement and control
technology, pump systems,
ventilators, electric motors

Energy-efficient buildings
and appliances

24%

280

372

WASTE
MANAGEMENT

Collection,
separation,
and transportation
of waste

Landfilling

Material and energy
recovery

21%

302

469

VII

THE
FUTURE

EXPLORING THE FUTURE

What is going to happen? If we can predict it, we can prepare for it. That is the primary focus of futurologists and trend researchers. But even they don't have crystal balls. Futurology attempts to derive probable scenarios for the future from historical developments and contemporary data. As an academic discipline, peering into the future is in its infancy. American universities made pioneering efforts in the 1960s, but it wasn't one of the field's experts who brought about its big breakthrough, but rather the entrepreneur John Naisbitt. In 1982, he published the book *Megatrends*, which held first place on the *New York Times* bestsellers list for two years and sold over 15 million copies. Naisbitt had found a way to make the field accessible to a general audience. With ten simple concepts, he showed how easy reading tea leaves could be. . . .

From centralization to decentralization

From hierarchies to networks

From either/or to diverse options

From an industrial society to an information society

From the national economy to the global economy

From compulsory adoption of technology to high tech/high touch

From short term to long term

From Northern Hemisphere to Southern

From institutional assistance to self-help

From representative to participatory democracy

Naisbitt's 10 megatrends
Classification by relevance

Largely relevant

Partially relevant

Of only limited relevance

1982
Naisbitt's
Megatrends
published

The history of the word "megatrends" according to Google Ngram:
(occurrences per year)

Google's Ngram Viewer analyzes word sequences (so-called ngrams) from 5.2 million books published between 1500 and 2008. For a given search term, the result tells you how often a word appeared, given as a percentage of the entire word inventory in each year.

0.00000140%

0.00000120%

0.00000100%

0.00000080%

0.00000060%

0.00000040%

0.00000020%

1975   1980   1985   1990   1995   2000   2005

WRITTEN IN THE STARS

Trends are developments in the present that are highly likely to be perpetuated in the future. Megatrends are the ultimate trends. Their effects are especially far-reaching, long-lasting, and world-spanning. Strategy departments everywhere breathlessly debate until they're blue in the face about how they can incorporate some megatrend or another into their business development, product portfolio, or marketing. Commercially oriented trend researchers are always in the state of having just identified the next big trend. It's not always scientific, but it's usually entertaining.

DEMOGRAPHICS

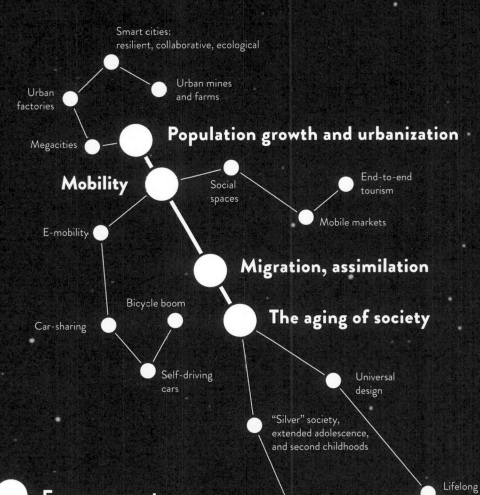

Smart cities: resilient, collaborative, ecological
Urban mines and farms
Urban factories
Megacities
Population growth and urbanization
Mobility
Social spaces
End-to-end tourism
Mobile markets
E-mobility
Migration, assimilation
Bicycle boom
The aging of society
Car-sharing
Self-driving cars
Universal design
"Silver" society, extended adolescence, and second childhoods
Lifelong learning
Slow culture

GEOPOLITICAL DEVELOPMENTS

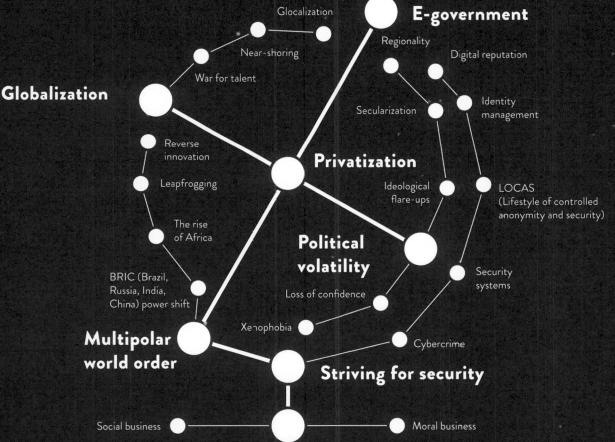

Glocalization
Near-shoring
War for talent
E-government
Regionality
Digital reputation
Globalization
Secularization
Identity management
Reverse innovation
Privatization
Leapfrogging
Ideological flare-ups
LOCAS (Lifestyle of controlled anonymity and security)
The rise of Africa
Political volatility
Security systems
BRIC (Brazil, Russia, India, China) power shift
Loss of confidence
Xenophobia
Cybercrime
Multipolar world order
Striving for security
Social business
Moral business
Citizen and NGO engagement

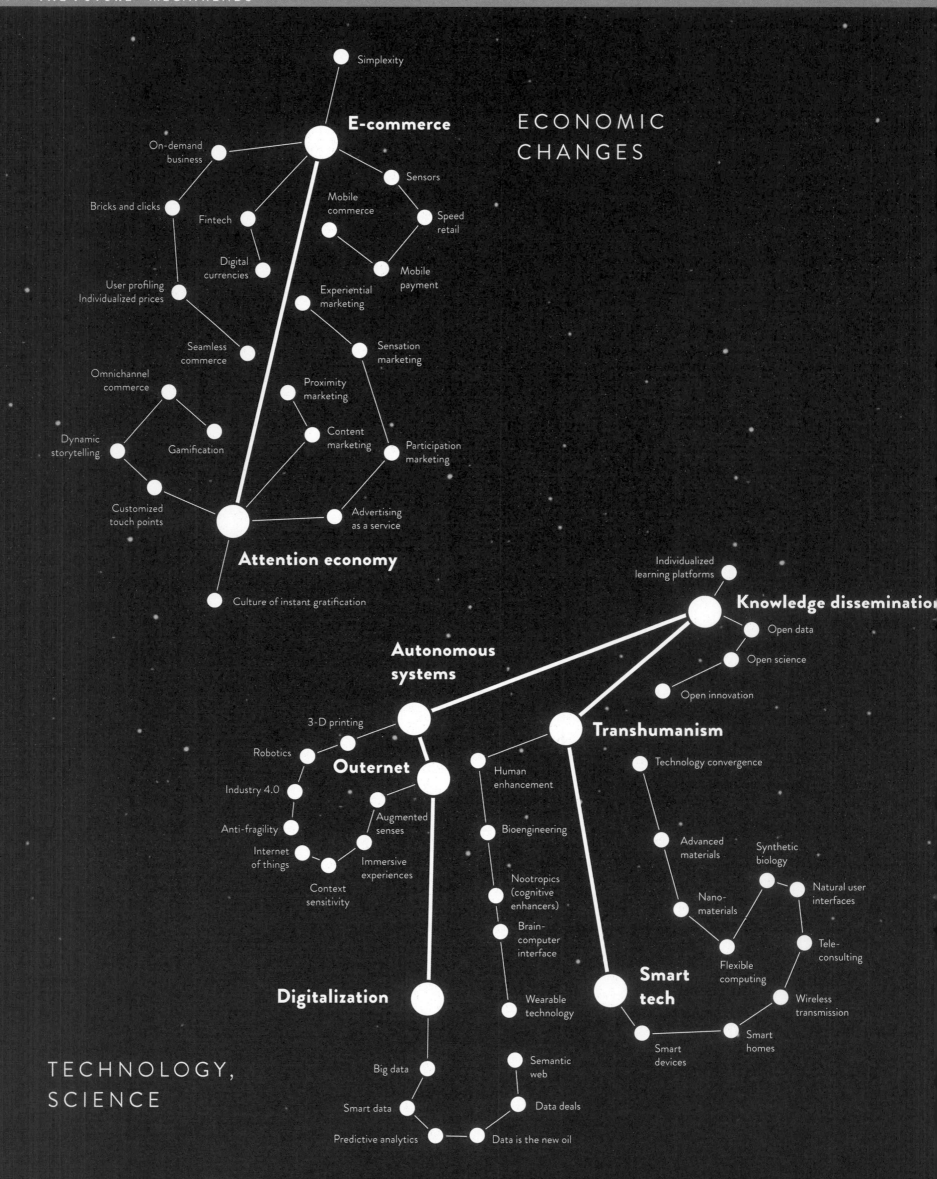

ECONOMIC
CHANGES

Simplexity

E-commerce

On-demand
business

Sensors

Bricks and clicks

Mobile
commerce

Fintech

Speed
retail

Digital
currencies

Mobile
payment

User profiling
Individualized prices

Experiential
marketing

Seamless
commerce

Sensation
marketing

Omnichannel
commerce

Proximity
marketing

Dynamic
storytelling

Gamification

Content
marketing

Participation
marketing

Customized
touch points

Advertising
as a service

Attention economy

Culture of instant gratification

Individualized
learning platforms

Knowledge dissemination

Open data

**Autonomous
systems**

Open science

Open innovation

3-D printing

Transhumanism

Robotics

Outernet

Human
enhancement

Technology convergence

Industry 4.0

Anti-fragility

Augmented
senses

Bioengineering

Advanced
materials

Synthetic
biology

Internet
of things

Immersive
experiences

Nano-
materials

Natural user
interfaces

Context
sensitivity

Nootropics
(cognitive
enhancers)

Flexible
computing

Tele-
consulting

Brain-
computer
interface

**Smart
tech**

Wireless
transmission

Digitalization

Wearable
technology

Smart
homes

Smart
devices

Semantic
web

Big data

TECHNOLOGY,
SCIENCE

Smart data

Data deals

Predictive analytics

Data is the new oil

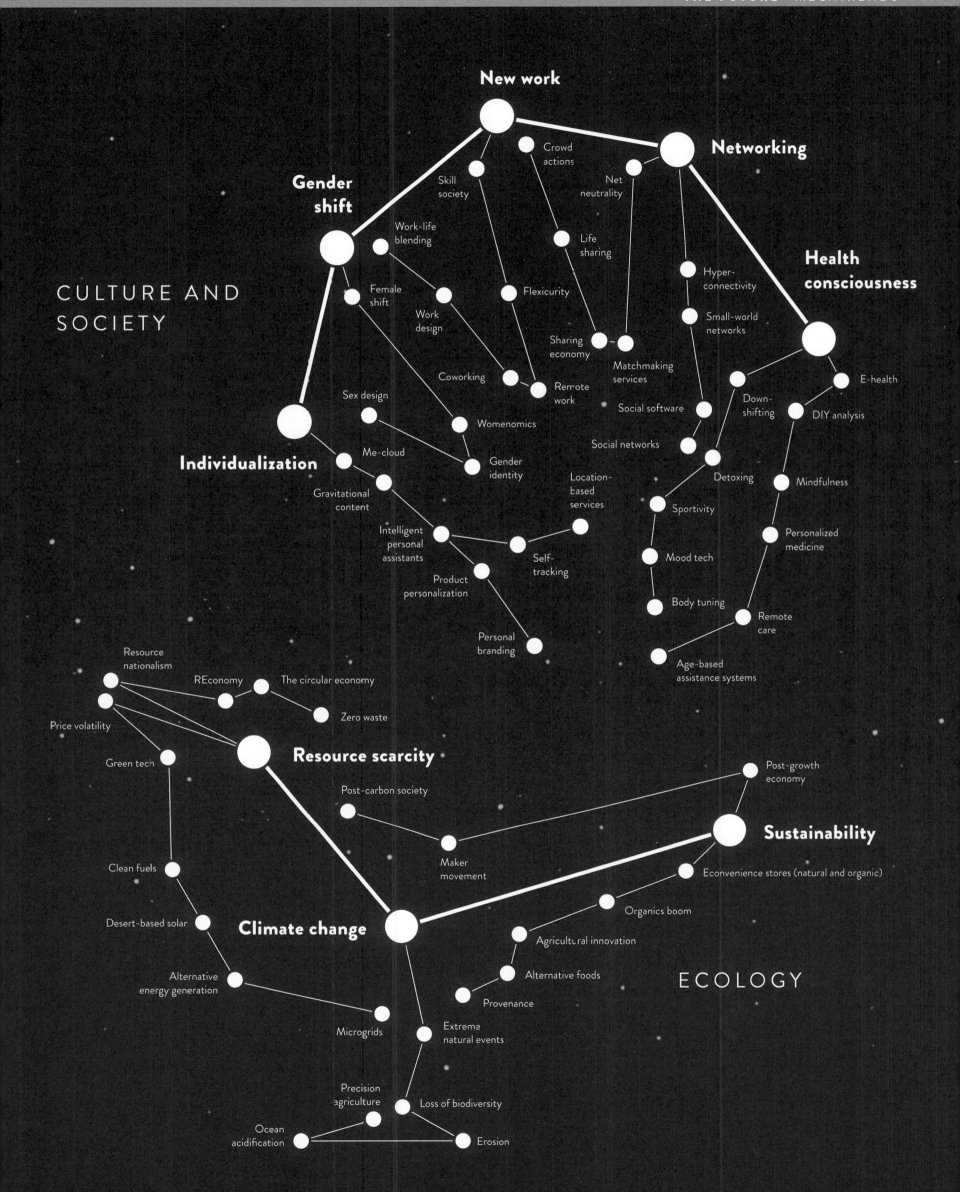

New work

Crowd actions

Networking

Gender shift

Skill society

Net neutrality

Work-life blending

Life sharing

Health consciousness

CULTURE AND SOCIETY

Female shift

Flexicurity

Hyper-connectivity

Work design

Sharing economy

Small-world networks

E-health

Coworking

Remote work

Matchmaking services

Down-shifting

DIY analysis

Sex design

Social software

Individualization

Me-cloud

Womenomics

Social networks

Detoxing

Mindfulness

Gravitational content

Gender identity

Location-based services

Sportivity

Personalized medicine

Intelligent personal assistants

Self-tracking

Mood tech

Product personalization

Body tuning

Remote care

Personal branding

Age-based assistance systems

Resource nationalism

REconomy

The circular economy

Price volatility

Zero waste

Green tech

Resource scarcity

Post-growth economy

Post-carbon society

Sustainability

Clean fuels

Maker movement

Econvenience stores (natural and organic)

Organics boom

Desert-based solar

Climate change

Agricultural innovation

Alternative energy generation

Alternative foods

ECOLOGY

Provenance

Microgrids

Extreme natural events

Precision agriculture

Loss of biodiversity

Ocean acidification

Erosion

4000 BC	3000 BC	2000 BC	1000 BC	500 BC	0	500	1000	1500	1700	1800

YESTERDAY'S FUTURE

Which major innovations truly moved humanity forward? A group of twelve scientists commissioned by the *Atlantic* magazine created and categorized a list of the fifty most important breakthroughs since the invention of the wheel. The result of twelve subjective opinions does not yield an objective view—but it does yield an interesting one.

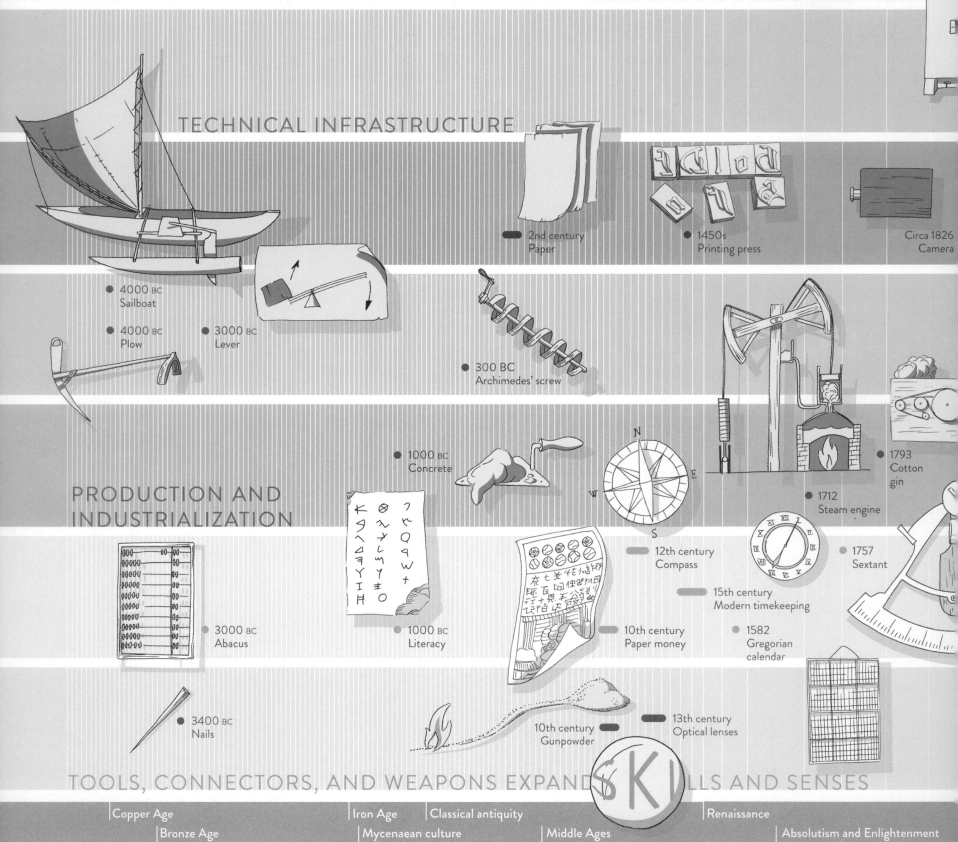

● 1796
Vaccinations

HEALTH AND NUTRITION

REAL-TIME COMMUNICATION

TECHNICAL INFRASTRUCTURE

■ 2nd century
Paper

● 1450s
Printing press

Circa 1826
Camera

● 4000 BC
Sailboat

● 4000 BC
Plow

● 3000 BC
Lever

● 300 BC
Archimedes' screw

● 1000 BC
Concrete

● 1793
Cotton gin

● 1712
Steam engine

PRODUCTION AND INDUSTRIALIZATION

■ 12th century
Compass

● 1757
Sextant

■ 15th century
Modern timekeeping

● 3000 BC
Abacus

● 1000 BC
Literacy

■ 10th century
Paper money

● 1582
Gregorian calendar

● 3400 BC
Nails

10th century
Gunpowder

■ 13th century
Optical lenses

TOOLS, CONNECTORS, AND WEAPONS EXPAND SKILLS AND SENSES

| Copper Age | | Iron Age | Classical antiquity | | Renaissance | |
| Bronze Age | | Mycenaean culture | | Middle Ages | | Absolutism and Enlightenment |

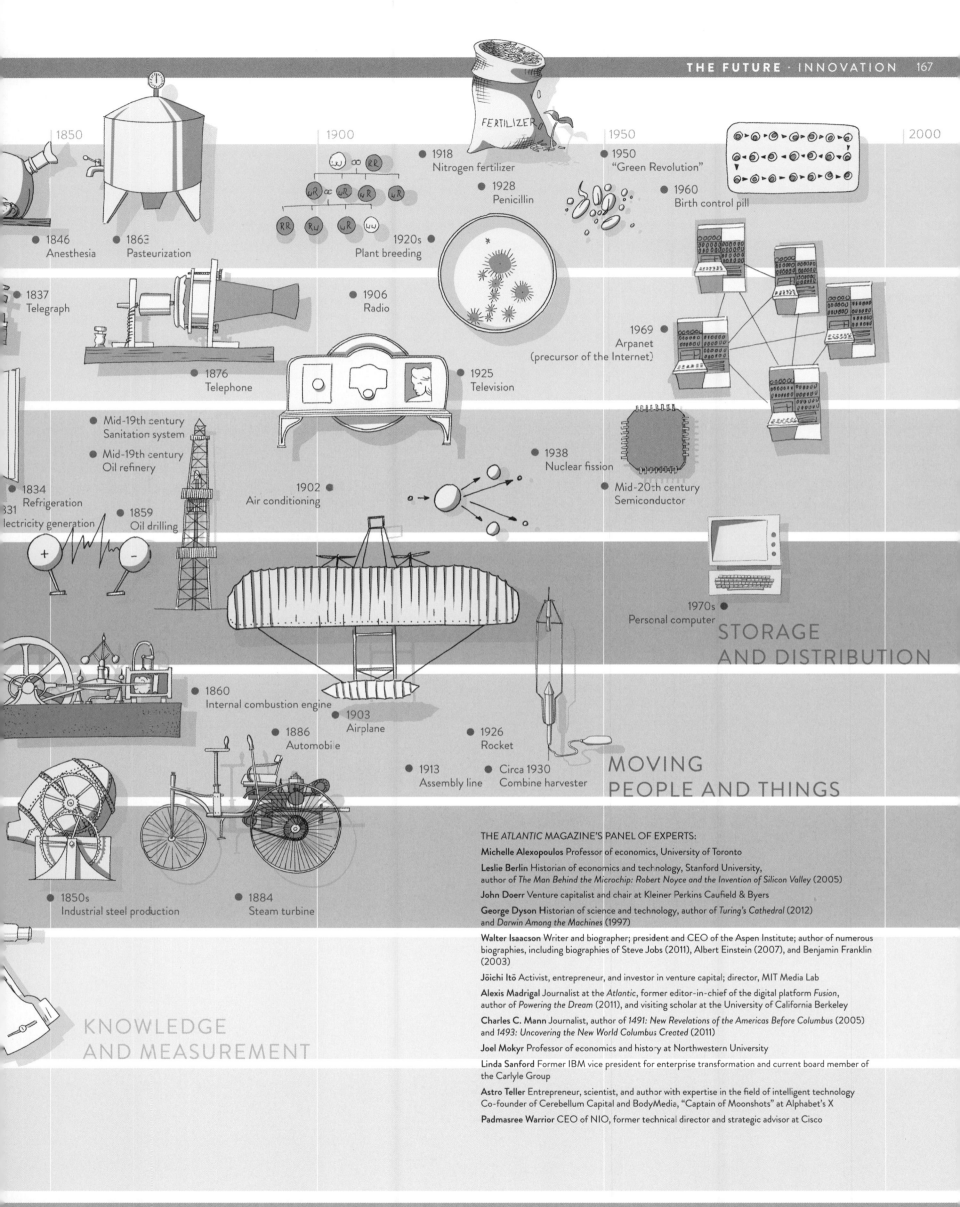

1850

1900

1950

2000

● 1918
Nitrogen fertilizer

● 1950
"Green Revolution"

● 1928
Penicillin

● 1960
Birth control pill

● 1846
Anesthesia

● 1863
Pasteurization

● 1920s
Plant breeding

● 1837
Telegraph

● 1906
Radio

● 1969
Arpanet
(precursor of the Internet)

● 1876
Telephone

● 1925
Television

● Mid-19th century
Sanitation system

● Mid-19th century
Oil refinery

● 1938
Nuclear fission

● 1902
Air conditioning

● Mid-20th century
Semiconductor

● 1834
Refrigeration

●31
electricity generation

● 1859
Oil drilling

1970s
Personal computer

STORAGE
AND DISTRIBUTION

● 1860
Internal combustion engine

● 1903
Airplane

● 1886
Automobile

● 1926
Rocket

● 1913
Assembly line

● Circa 1930
Combine harvester

MOVING
PEOPLE AND THINGS

● 1850s
Industrial steel production

● 1884
Steam turbine

KNOWLEDGE
AND MEASUREMENT

THE *ATLANTIC* MAGAZINE'S PANEL OF EXPERTS:

Michelle Alexopoulos Professor of economics, University of Toronto

Leslie Berlin Historian of economics and technology, Stanford University,
author of *The Man Behind the Microchip: Robert Noyce and the Invention of Silicon Valley* (2005)

John Doerr Venture capitalist and chair at Kleiner Perkins Caufield & Byers

George Dyson Historian of science and technology, author of *Turing's Cathedral* (2012)
and *Darwin Among the Machines* (1997)

Walter Isaacson Writer and biographer; president and CEO of the Aspen Institute; author of numerous
biographies, including biographies of Steve Jobs (2011), Albert Einstein (2007), and Benjamin Franklin
(2003)

Jōichi Itō Activist, entrepreneur, and investor in venture capital; director, MIT Media Lab

Alexis Madrigal Journalist at the *Atlantic*, former editor-in-chief of the digital platform *Fusion*,
author of *Powering the Dream* (2011), and visiting scholar at the University of California Berkeley

Charles C. Mann Journalist, author of *1491: New Revelations of the Americas Before Columbus* (2005)
and *1493: Uncovering the New World Columbus Created* (2011)

Joel Mokyr Professor of economics and history at Northwestern University

Linda Sanford Former IBM vice president for enterprise transformation and current board member of
the Carlyle Group

Astro Teller Entrepreneur, scientist, and author with expertise in the field of intelligent technology
Co-founder of Cerebellum Capital and BodyMedia, "Captain of Moonshots" at Alphabet's X

Padmasree Warrior CEO of NIO, former technical director and strategic advisor at Cisco

dustrialization

Recent history

HOW DO NEW THINGS ENTER THE WORLD?

It's very simple. Non-innovative companies disappear from the market, because another company will offer better products or services, or offer them at a cheaper price, or replace them with new products or services that better meet customers' needs. The economists Joseph Schumpeter and Peter F. Drucker examined the process a bit more closely. And it turns out that it's not quite so simple after all. . . .

PATENT OFFICE

"Innovation is change that creates a new dimension of performance."

Application for trademark registration	1

Fax in advance to

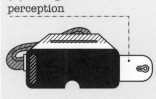

PETER F. DRUCKER 1909–2005	American **economist** of Austrian origin	Frames **innovations** as the key to success for businesses	Best-known work: *The Practice of Management* (1954)
Intellectual forebear Economist Joseph Alois Schumpeter 1883–1950	**Definition** of innovation according to Schumpeter: Continuous renewal/creative destruction. The true entrepreneurs are those who achieve a new combination.	**Stages** of innovation (1) Idea (2) Prototype (3) Implementation (4) Market penetration	**Features** of innovation (1) Novelty or renewal (2) Change or alteration

7 POSSIBILITIES FOR INNOVATION according to Drucker

(1) The unexpected

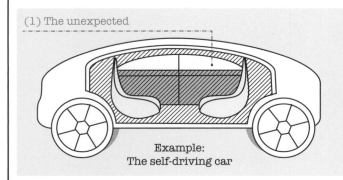

Example: The self-driving car

(2) The (apparently) contradictory

Example: The $100 laptop

(3) The necessity

Example: Large batteries for energy storage

(4) Change in the market

Example: Health apps

(5) Change in demographics

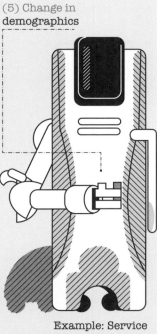

Example: Service robots for senior citizens

(7) New knowledge

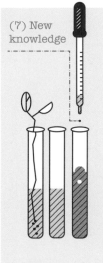

Example: Biotechnology

(6) Change in perception

Example: Augmented reality

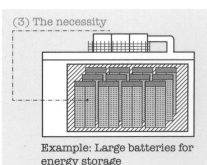

CHECKLIST FOR INNOVATION according to Drucker

- ☐ Thought through all possibilities for innovation
- ☐ Tested the market
- ☐ The innovation is simple, yet effective
- ☐ The innovation is specific
- ☐ The innovation aims at market leadership

THAT WAS MY IDEA!

Whoever improves the (technological) world with an invention can have their idea protected. For that, they have to go to the patent office. It verifies that the invention is truly new and does not infringe upon the patent rights of other inventors. In the United States, patents are valid for 20 years. During that time, no one is allowed to use the invention without asking the patent owner and obtaining a license. The economic idea behind protecting ideas: No one would invest in research and development if everyone could copy the idea. And then the (technological) world wouldn't be improved.

The largest companies in leading technology sectors by patent applications, 2014

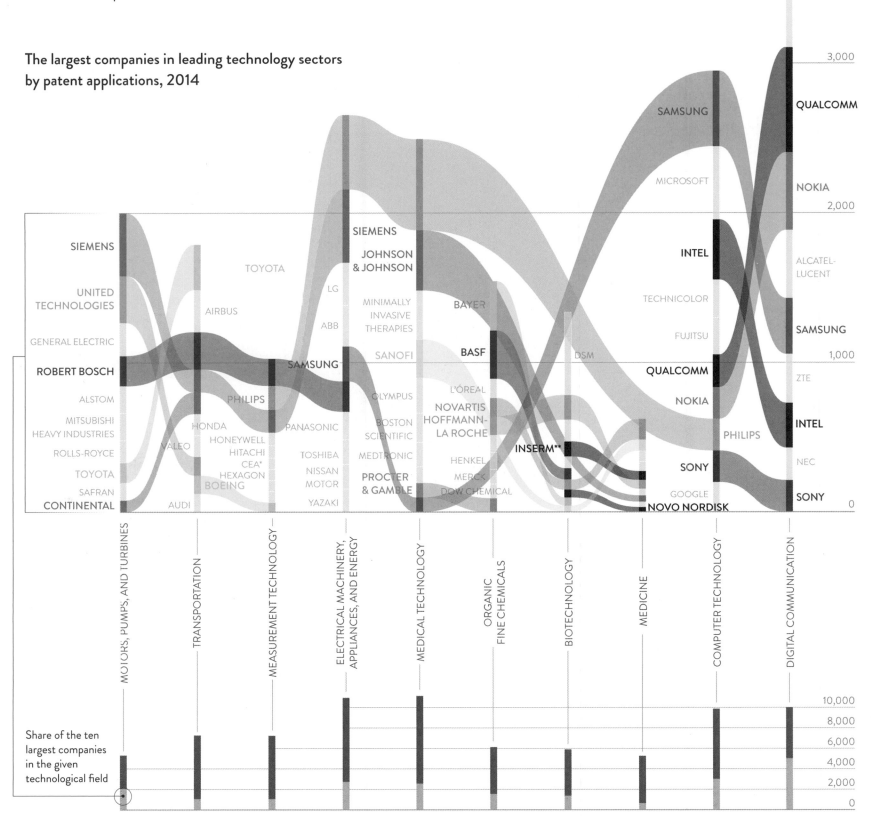

Share of the ten largest companies in the given technological field

Total number of patent applications in the leading technology sectors, 2014

* French Alternative Energies and Atomic Energy Commission
** French National Institute of Health and Medical Research

HOW DO YOU MEASURE INNOVATION?

Innovation is the key to competitiveness for most companies and industries. People use various indicators to measure the innovation of each nation. The scoreboard shown here uses relative parameters to assess the innovativeness of a country, independent of its size—thus the innovation potential and scores can be compared between countries.

INNOVATION SCOREBOARD

The innovation scoreboard is compiled by the Fraunhofer Institute for Systems and Innovation Research (ISI) in Karlsruhe, Germany, in cooperation with the Center for European Economic Research (ZEW) in Mannheim. The overall score (measured on a scale from 1 to 100) is calculated from data from five segments: economy, science, education, government, and society. In turn, thirty-eight subindicators feed into the calculation, with some indicators feeding into multiple segments. The innovation scoreboard includes data from thirty-five nations. Listed here are thirty nations including the US. In international comparison, the US—with 51 points—is around eighth place in the overall ranking.

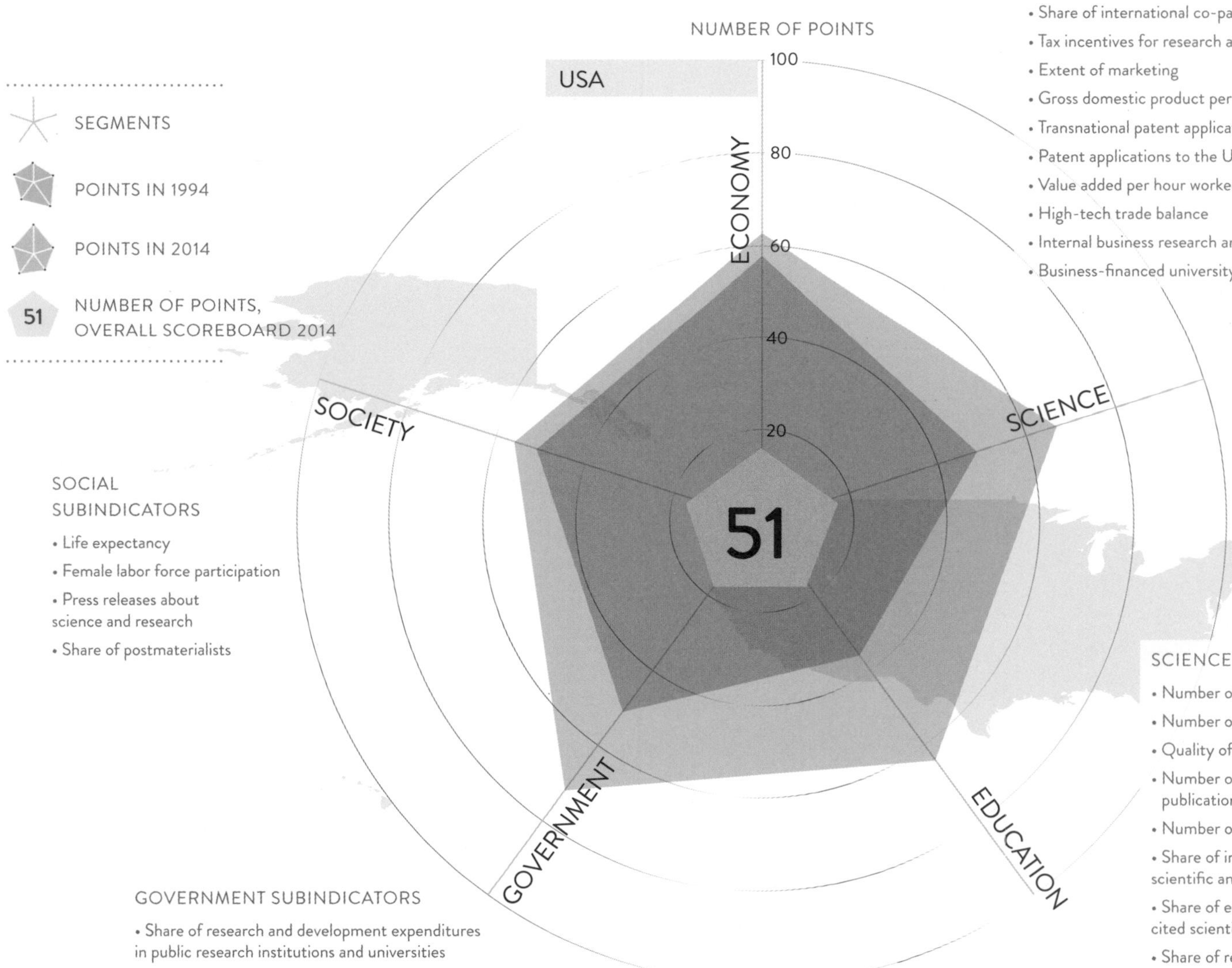

ECONOMIC SUBINDICATORS

- Companies' demand for technological products
- Venture capital invested in the early phase
- Publicly financed business research and development expenses
- Employees in knowledge-intensive services
- High-tech share of value added
- Intensity of local competition
- Share of international co-patents
- Tax incentives for research and development
- Extent of marketing
- Gross domestic product per capita
- Transnational patent applications
- Patent applications to the USPTO*
- Value added per hour worked
- High-tech trade balance
- Internal business research and development expenses
- Business-financed university research and development expenses

SEGMENTS

POINTS IN 1994

POINTS IN 2014

51   NUMBER OF POINTS, OVERALL SCOREBOARD 2014

NUMBER OF POINTS

USA

100

80

60

40

20

51

ECONOMY

SCIENCE

SOCIETY

EDUCATION

GOVERNMENT

SOCIAL SUBINDICATORS

- Life expectancy
- Female labor force participation
- Press releases about science and research
- Share of postmaterialists

SCIENCE-RELATED SUBINDICATORS

- Number of researchers
- Number of scientific and technical articles published
- Quality of scientific research institutions
- Number of citations per scientific or technical publication in relation to the global average
- Number of patents from public research
- Share of international copublications from all scientific and technical articles
- Share of each country in the top 10% of the most commonly cited scientific and technical publications
- Share of research and development expenditures in public research institutions and universities

GOVERNMENT SUBINDICATORS

- Share of research and development expenditures in public research institutions and universities
- Governmental demand for advanced technological products
- Tax incentives for research and development
- Publicly financed business research and development expenses
- Education expenditures per student
- Quality of the education system
- Quality of education in mathematics and science
- PISA Index scores: science, reading, and mathematics

EDUCATION SUBINDICATORS

- Share of population holding a PhD
- Share of employees with postsecondary education
- Share of foreign students
- College graduates in relation to highly qualified employees ages 55 and older
- Employees with at least high school but no college degree
- Education expenditures per student
- Quality of the education system
- Quality of education in mathematics and science
- PISA Index scores: science, reading, and mathematics

* United States Patent and Trademark Office

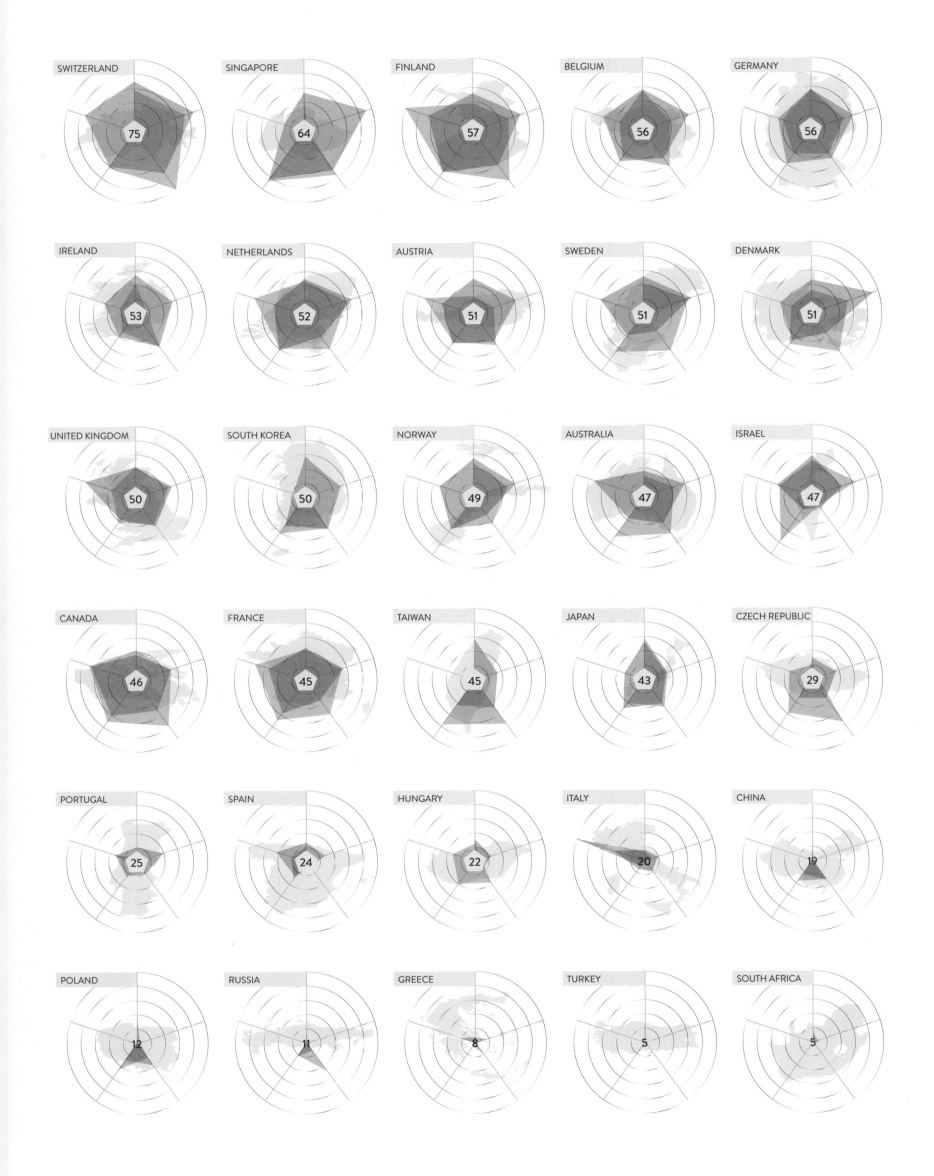

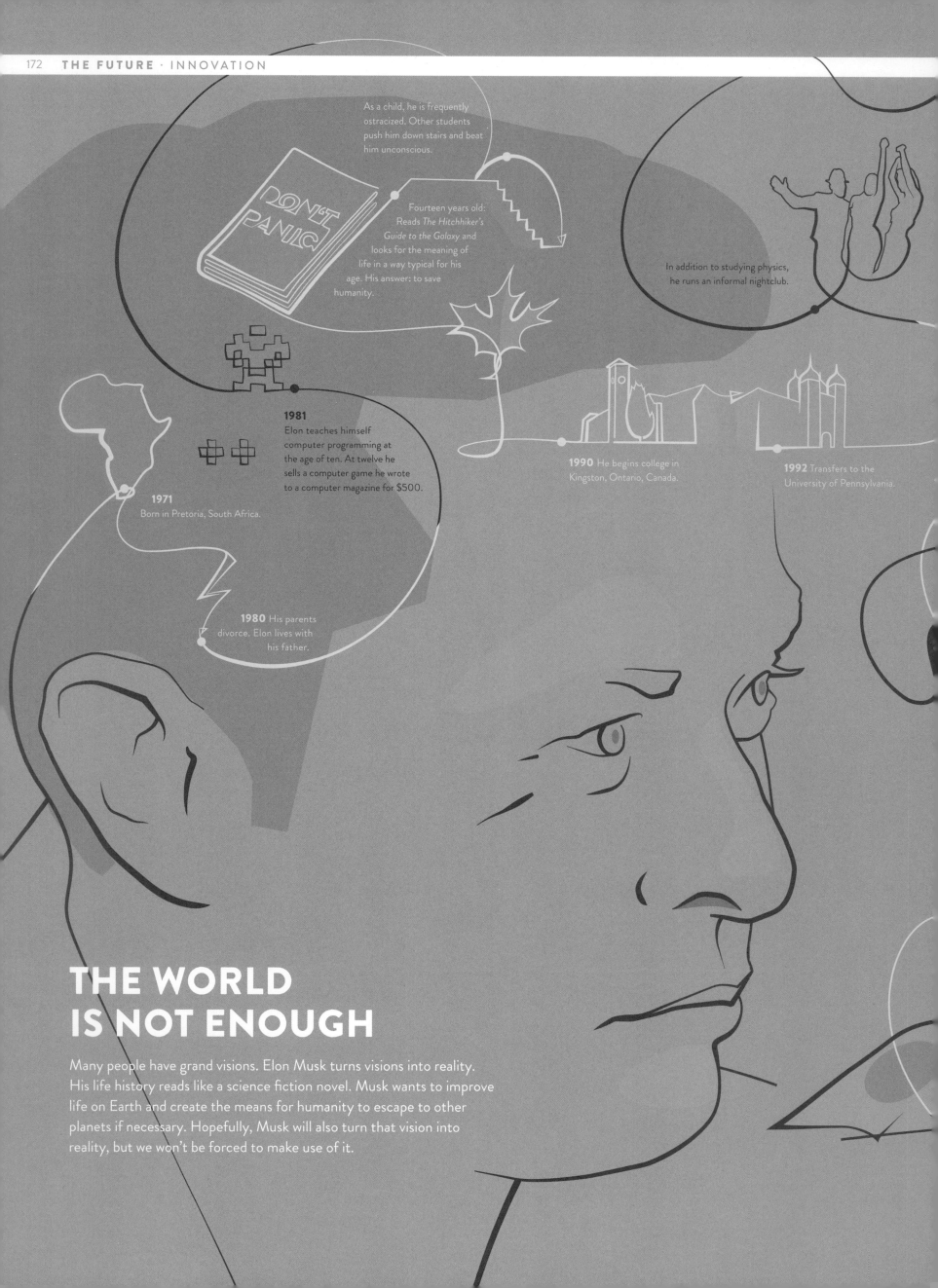

As a child, he is frequently ostracized. Other students push him down stairs and beat him unconscious.

Fourteen years old: Reads *The Hitchhiker's Guide to the Galaxy* and looks for the meaning of life in a way typical for his age. His answer: to save humanity.

In addition to studying physics, he runs an informal nightclub.

1981
Elon teaches himself computer programming at the age of ten. At twelve he sells a computer game he wrote to a computer magazine for $500.

1971
Born in Pretoria, South Africa.

1990 He begins college in Kingston, Ontario, Canada.

1992 Transfers to the University of Pennsylvania.

1980 His parents divorce. Elon lives with his father.

THE WORLD IS NOT ENOUGH

Many people have grand visions. Elon Musk turns visions into reality. His life history reads like a science fiction novel. Musk wants to improve life on Earth and create the means for humanity to escape to other planets if necessary. Hopefully, Musk will also turn that vision into reality, but we won't be forced to make use of it.

zip2

1995 Together with his brother, he founds a software company. Compaq buys the company four years later for $300 million. Elon owns 7% of the shares.

X.COM + CONFINITY

1999 Musk recognizes that convenient and secure payment over the Internet has a bright future.

Pay Pal

RIP

2002 His first son dies at the age of 10 weeks.

SPACEX

2001 The idea occurs to him that it would be possible to grow plants in a tent on Mars. His actual goal: to revive space travel. One year later, the idea has grown into a company. Musk invests $100 million.

2000 Marriage to Justine Wilson.

2004 Musk becomes the father of twins.

TESLA

2003 Musk declares war on the gasoline-fixated automobile industry. For him, electricity is the better fuel.

2006 With two cousins, he founds a company that manufactures and installs solar cells. They are meant to provide clean energy for the Tesla.

SolarCity

2006 Musk's triplets are born.

2010 Marriage to Talulah Riley.

2012 Second divorce.

2008 First divorce.

2013 Musk and Talulah Riley remarry.

OpenAI

2015 Musk founds a nonprofit organization to promote artificial intelligence and make it accessible to everyone.

RIP

Musk wants humanity to spread itself across several planets. He thinks it would be "fantastic" to die on Mars.

2013 Musk introduces the concept for a giant pneumatic tube system. The idea is to shoot capsules with people inside them from Los Angeles to San Francisco.

hyperloop

THE EVERYTHING COMPANY

Amazon's unlike other tech companies; it got its start not by creating a new product or service but by selling books online, because they were easy to ship and already digitally cataloged. Amazon soon crossed into new product categories and later into new services, reinvesting all of its earnings—as well as the capital it accrues from its skyrocketing stock price, which has risen 9,300% since going public—to fuel its meteoric growth. Today, what was once nicknamed "The Everything Store" is fast becoming "The Everything Company"—it's hard to think of anything Amazon doesn't offer.

606 Mn Available Products

Analyzing the Biggest Online Retailer

Net sales by division, 2017

NET SALES 2017

$177.86 Bn

Online Stores
$108.35 Bn 2016: $91.43 Bn
Percent change: +18%

Core business of Amazon, biggest segment of all.
Made $3.06 Bn losses worldwide in 2017.

Marketplace
$31.88 Bn 2016: $22.99 Bn
Percent change: +38%

Services to third-party sellers.
Represented half of Amazon's
online sales in 2017.

Amazon Web Services
$17.45 Bn 2016: $12.21 Bn
Percent change: +43%

Cloud computing.
In 2017, AWS was the undisputed
leader with a market share of 47.1%.

Subscription Services
$9.72 Bn 2016: $6.39 Bn
Percent change: +52%

Prime Membership, ebooks,
audiobooks, Amazon music,
and Amazon Prime video.

Physical Stores
$5.79 Bn

All brick-and-mortar
stores of Amazon,
including Whole Foods.

EARNINGS

North America (consumer products & subscriptions)	$2.84 Bn
Amazon Web Services	$4.33 Bn

Total: $7.17 Bn

LOSSES

International (consumer products & subscriptions)	$3.06 Bn
Tax Provisions	$0.77 Bn
Other Expenses	$0.30 Bn

Total: $4.14 Bn

⬤ **Amazon's Biggest Fan**
★★★★★

The strategy behind Amazon's breakneck growth is the
"flywheel" philosophy, as CEO Jeff Bezos calls it. In a new
market, they offer steep discounts until they have the size
to influence prices, benefitting from economies of scale.
Amazon's announcement of plans to enter a new market
sends the stocks of established players tumbling—five
stars for sure.

⬤ **. . . And Its Worst Critic**
★☆☆☆☆

Aggressive tax avoidance, monopolistic tendencies,
questionable ethics at times, alleged patent infringement
and intellectual property violations, and dubious
authenticity of customer reviews (not this one, of course).
All this makes one star far too generous.

*Stocks can be split to make share prices more
affordable. Amazon has split its stock three times, so
first-hour stockholders now hold twelve times as
many units. Splitting increases trade volume, and is
therefore a source of Amazon's liquidity.*

Split: 2 for 1
06/02/1998

Split: 3 for 1
01/05/1999

Split: 2 for 1
01/05/1999

$18.00
5/16/1997

$63.22
5/16/2007

**Amazon
Stock Price**
In US$

Product Introduction

Toys,
Electronics

Amazon Web Storage
(Cloud Computing)

Books

Year	1995	1996	1997	1998	1999	2000	2001	2002	2003	2004	2005	2006	2007
Net Sales in US$ Mn	1	16	146	610	1,640	2,762	3,122	3,922	5,264	6,921	8,490	10,711	14,83
Employees	1	256	614	2,100	7,600	9,000	7,800	7,500	7,800	9,000	12,000	13,900	17,000

Acquisitions
Price in US$ Mn

Alexa Internet
Search Engine Optimization Analysis
250

Exchange
Antique Books
645

Mobipocket.com
Ebook software
N/A

**Brilliance
Audio**
Audioboc
N/A

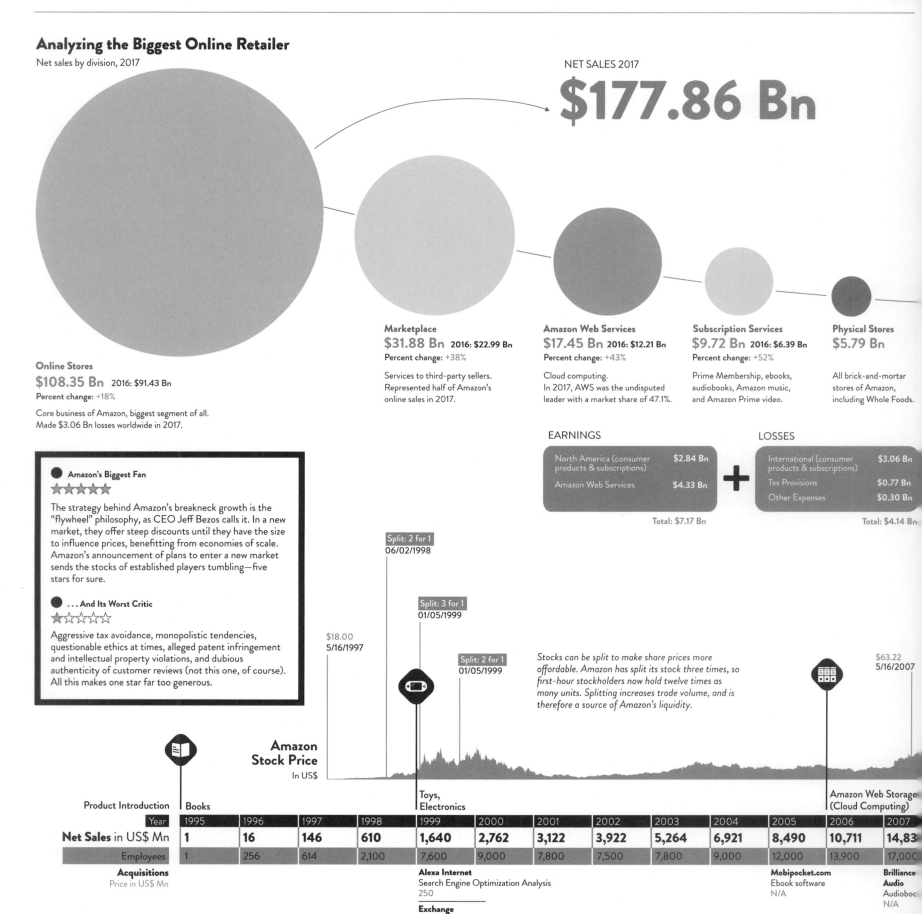

Amazon's Footprint

Square footage covered by Amazon's facilities

All US Facilities:

Fulfillment Centers	155
Food Distribution Centers	31
Prime Now Hubs	51
Inbound Sortation Centers	9
Outbound Sortation Centers	39
Delivery Stations	73

Total area US: **123,159,646 sq ft**
Total area World: **194,310,306 sq ft**

Midwest & Great Lakes
Total Area
44,070,600 sq ft
Total Units
78

New England & East Coast
Total Area
38,896,500 sq ft
Total Units
71

Southeast
Total Area
38,896,500 sq ft
Total Units
57

West Coast
Total Area
38,896,500 sq ft
Total Units
104

South Central
Total Area
32,129,600 sq ft
Total Units
48

Other
$4.66 Bn 2016: **$2.95 Bn**
Percent change: +58%

Includes advertisement sales and co-branded credit card agreements.

NET PROFIT 2017
= **$3.03 Bn**

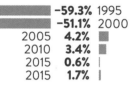

$1,000,000,000,000
AMAZON'S STOCK MARKET VALUE 2017

Founded in 1994 in a garage in Seattle, Amazon is on track to reach $1 trillion in market capitalization at the turn of 2019, making it the most valuable company in the world.

Stock was issued at $18 in 1997. It cost $1,699 by the end of June 2018, a rise of 9,300% in just one decade. Sluggish for years, growth became exponential from 2015 onwards. When the stock hits $2,061.45, Amazon will be the first trillion-dollar company in history.

Amazon disregards profitability to invest earnings in its expansion. Its profit margin in 2017 was a modest 1.7%. Morgan Stanley sees Amazon focusing on profits around 2022–2023. It would then likely reap net profits of several tens of billions per year.

WHO NEEDS PROFITS?
NET PROFIT MARGINS OF AMAZON

−59.3%	1995
−51.1%	2000
2005	**4.2%**
2010	**3.4%**
2015	**0.6%**
2015	**1.7%**

IF YOU PAY LOW TAX ...

0.005%

is the part of its revenue Amazon sets aside to pay taxes. Maximizing tax avoidance plays a key role in keeping profit margins low.

21%

is the corporate tax rate in the US since 2018.

THE AMAZON EFFECT
DEATH OF RETAIL

AMAZON MARKET SHARE IN US RETAIL 2016

E-Commerce
44

Total Retail
4

Year-over-year e-commerce market share growth: +6%

US RETAILER CLOSURES 2017

Sears	42
Guess	60
Abercrombie & Fitch	60
Macy's	66
Staples	70
Kmart	108
American Apparel	110
JCPenney	138
Family Christian	240
RadioShack	582

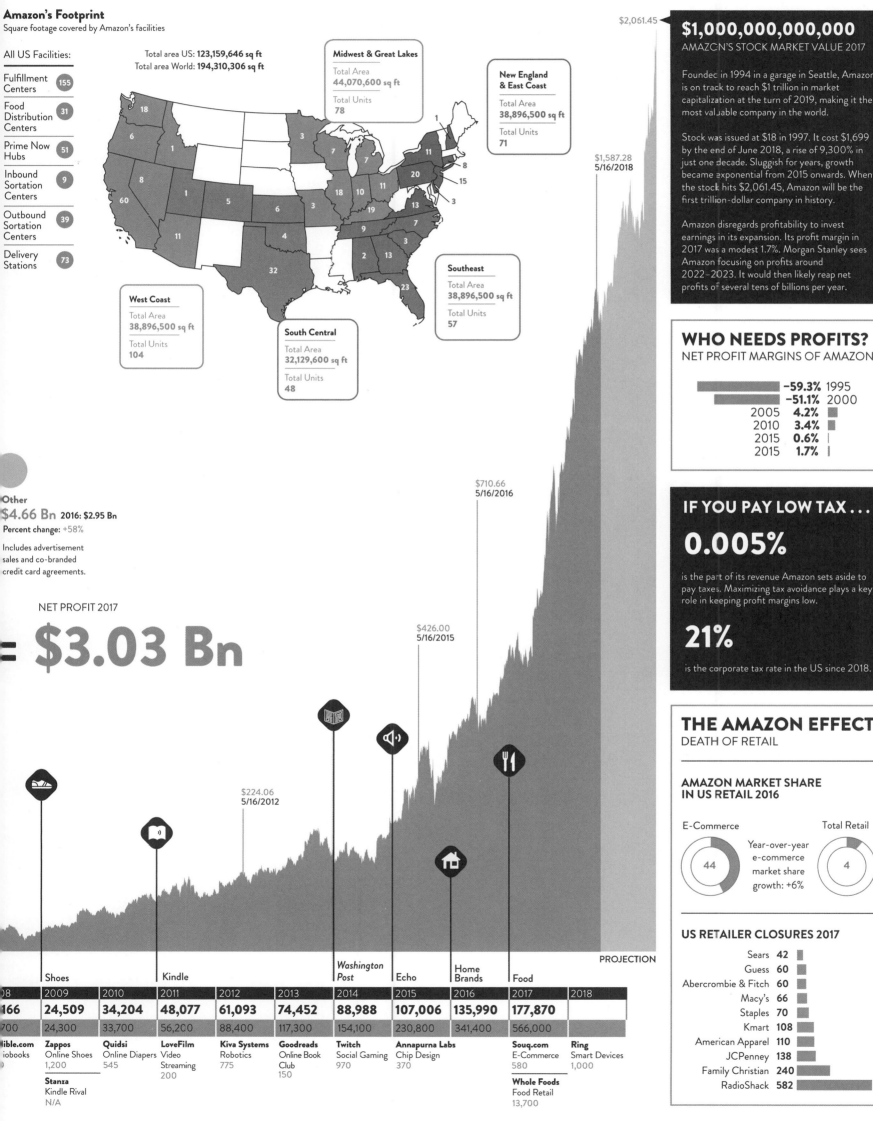

$2,061.45
$1,587.28 5/16/2018
$710.66 5/16/2016
$426.00 5/16/2015
$224.06 5/16/2012

PROJECTION

	Shoes		Kindle				Washington Post	Echo	Home Brands	Food	
08	**2009**	**2010**	**2011**	**2012**	**2013**	**2014**	**2015**	**2016**	**2017**	**2018**	
166	**24,509**	**34,204**	**48,077**	**61,093**	**74,452**	**88,988**	**107,006**	**135,990**	**177,870**		
700	24,300	33,700	56,200	88,400	117,300	154,100	230,800	341,400	566,000		
dible.com iobooks	**Zappos** Online Shoes 1,200	**Quidsi** Online Diapers 545	**LoveFilm** Video Streaming 200	**Kiva Systems** Robotics 775	**Goodreads** Online Book Club 150	**Twitch** Social Gaming 970	**Annapurna Labs** Chip Design 370		**Souq.com** E-Commerce 580	**Ring** Smart Devices 1,000	
	Stanza Kindle Rival N/A								**Whole Foods** Food Retail 13,700		

THE NEXT UNICORN

In literature, unicorns are mythical creatures. Most people don't believe they exist. In the world of start-ups, unicorns are companies that are supposed to be worth fabulous sums of money: more than $1 billion. Their investors believe in them. Or at least they believe they will more often win than lose risky bets on potential profits in the distant future.

VANCOUVER

ANN ARBOR

FREMONT

WASHINGTON, DC

EMERYVILLE

PROVO

CAMBRIDGE

BOSTON

SAN
FRANCISCO

CHICAGO

Uber

HAYWARD

CHARLOTTE

NEW YORK

SAN MATEO

ATLANTA

HOBOKEN

Airbnb

REDWOOD CITY

AMERICAN
FORK

AUSTIN

PLANTATION

Palantir

IRVINE

MIAMI

PALO ALTO

JACKSONVILLE

LOS
ANGELES
COUNTY

MENLO PARK

**SILICON
VALLEY**

CULVER CITY

MOUNTAIN VIEW

SANTA MONICA

LOS ANGELES

$150 billion

SUNNYVALE

SpaceX   HAWTHORNE

$62 billion

$40 billion

$20 billion

$10 billion

$1 billion

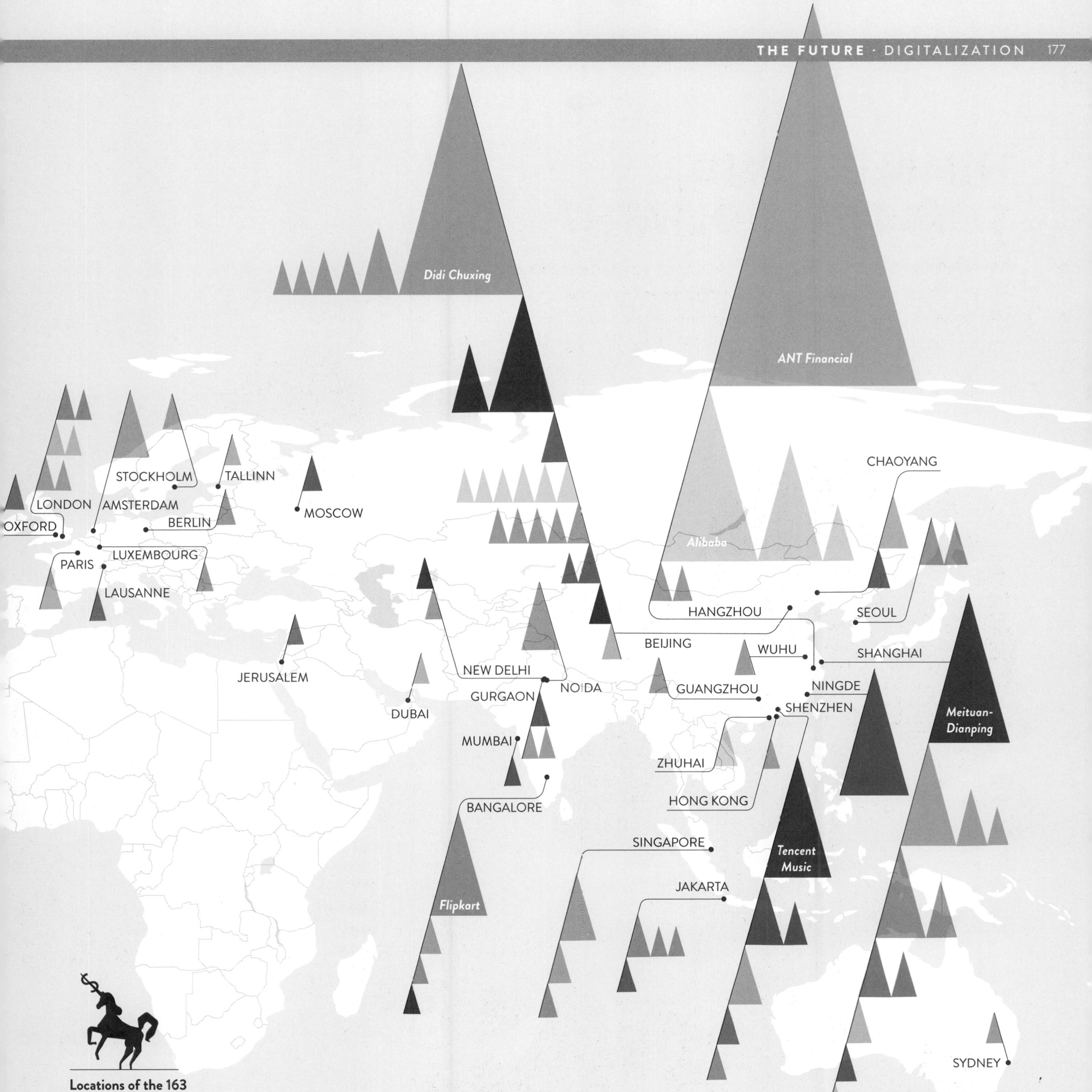

Didi Chuxing

ANT Financial

CHAOYANG

Alibaba

STOCKHOLM TALLINN
LONDON AMSTERDAM MOSCOW
OXFORD BERLIN
PARIS LUXEMBOURG
LAUSANNE
JERUSALEM
DUBAI
NEW DELHI HANGZHOU SEOUL
GURGAON NOIDA BEIJING WUHU SHANGHAI
MUMBAI GUANGZHOU NINGDE
SHENZHEN *Meituan-Dianping*
ZHUHAI
HONG KONG
BANGALORE
SINGAPORE *Tencent Music*
JAKARTA
Flipkart

SYDNEY

Locations of the 163 unicorns worldwide by category (in 2018) . . .

	Number	Total category value in US$ billion	. . . and value
Business services & software	38		154.29
Consumer goods & retail	37		107.43
Financial services	22		262.35
Transportation	18		208.55
Media	14		115.02
Health	13		40.65
Real estate	8		36.27
Manufacturing	4		37
Travel	4		36.5
Energy	3		6.63
Education	2		4.0

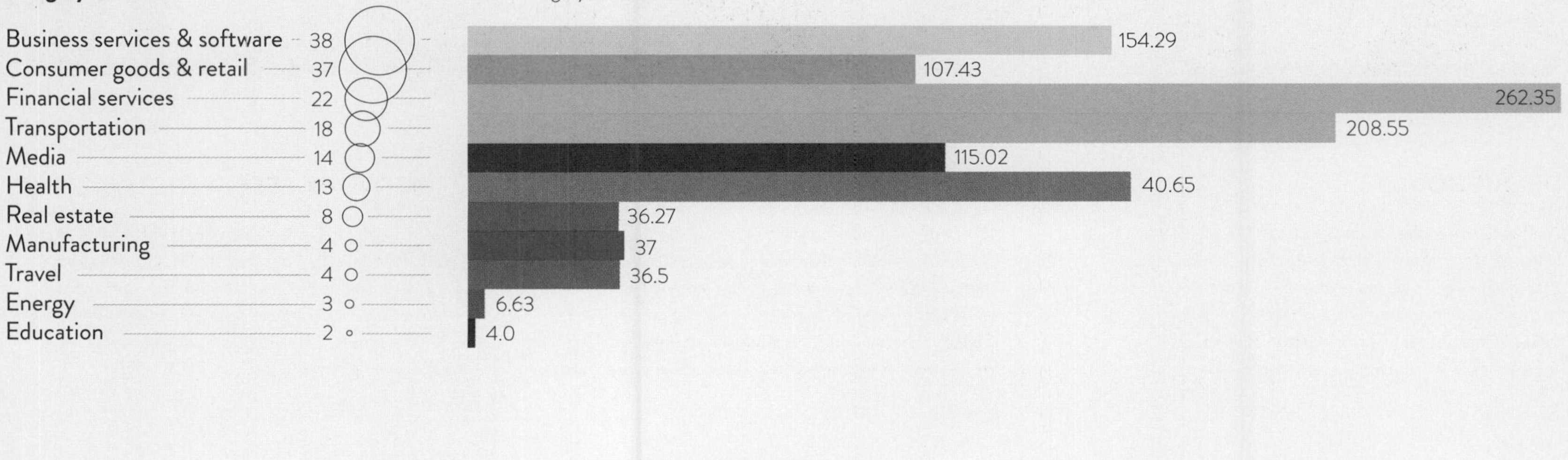

NIMBLE DAVID, SLUGGISH GOLIATH?

Disruption is Silicon Valley's favorite concept. Start-up founders like to see themselves as clever Davids who are attacking the business models of lumbering market leaders with their digital slings. Sometimes that even works—but much less often than claimed. The watchful Goliaths also learn new things—and then they call it digital transformation.

DISRUPTION

The Harvard economist **Clayton Christensen** is the theory-hero of the digital start-up scene because he says that every large company is trapped in a dilemma— it has to satisfy existing customers and therefore cannot be radically innovative. Every successful company will at some point be disrupted by a new company.

PLATFORMS

(Almost) all successful start-ups build digital platforms. The platforms push their way in between manufacturers and customers and in doing so eliminate the old middlemen. A good example: Streaming services like **Spotify** that have wormed their way in between musicians and listeners at the expense of record stores.

NETWORK EFFECT

On platforms, self-reinforcing network effects come into play. That means: The more market players are in the game on a platform, the more attractive it becomes for others. Network effects, for example, ensured that **Facebook** was able to become so large so quickly.

THE VANITY OF THE PRESENT

Do we overestimate how quickly progress is moving in the present because we all want to live in eventful times? It seems so. For example, are **Google**, **Amazon**, or **Twitter** really as helpful as flush toilets, penicillin, or the bicycle?

GOOD VS. BAD MANAGEMENT

Is disruption by outsiders truly a law of nature, as Christensen claims? The **iPhone** was a disruptive device. But who prevented Nokia from building smartphones as good as Samsung's?

WHAT IS DISRUPTIVE?

Amazon founder **Jeff Bezos** found a simple definition, explaining that anything that customers like more than whatever they knew before is disruptive. With this attitude, Bezos turned a start-up into a Goliath that's still growing.

SMART FACTORY

What role will people play in manufacturing in the future? What's fairly certain is that in the smart factory, they won't perform heavy physical labor and will only need to intervene to provide guidance from time to time. Intelligent machines that communicate with each other will perform most of the work. With increasing frequency, products will be fashioned according to customers' wishes. In short: Only a few highly qualified people will work at an intelligent factory, and custom manufacturing will become standard.

4 **Data analytics** enables better decision-making at all stages of production.

5 **IT-security standards are extremely high**, including the use of encryption.

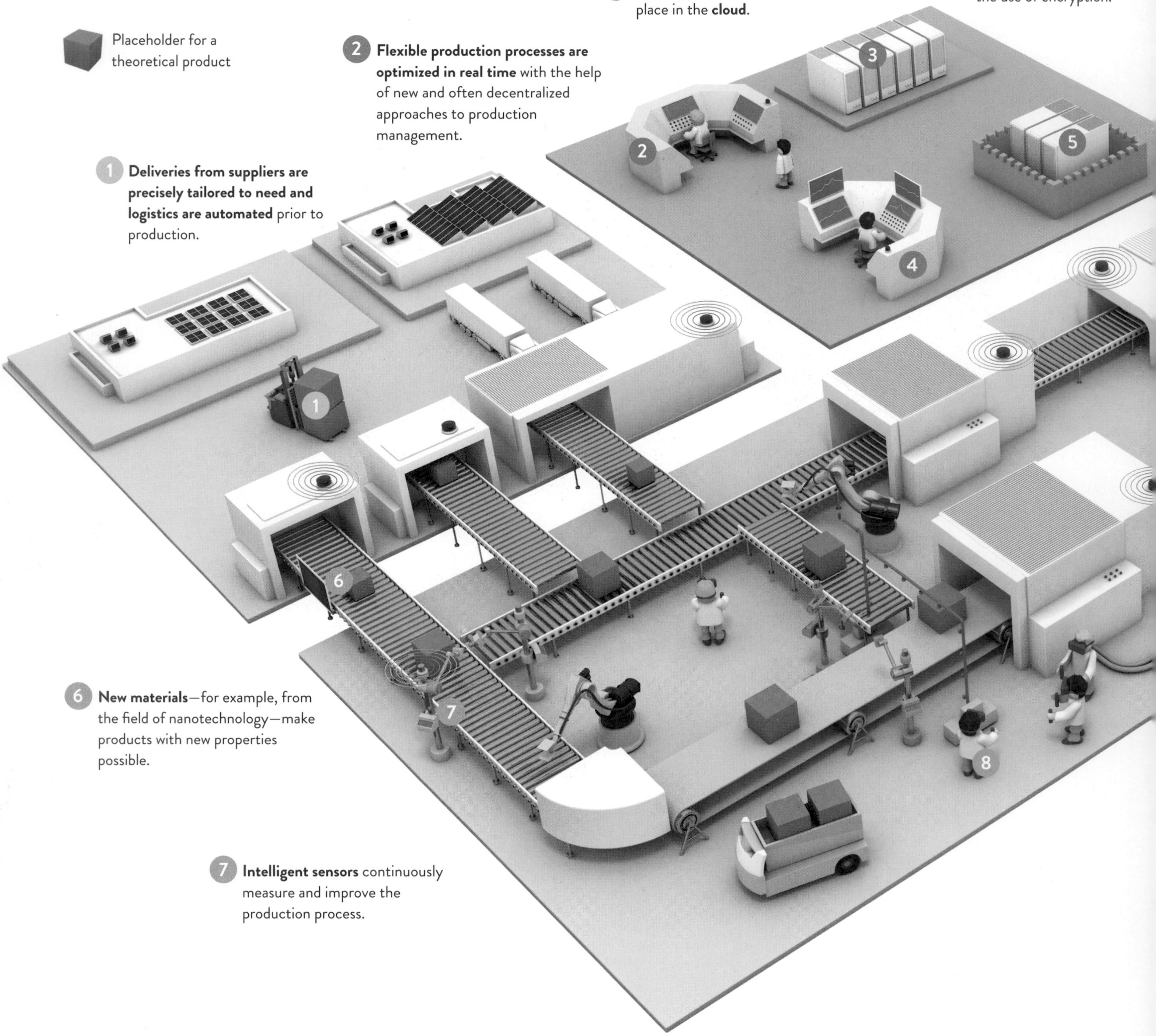

3 IT processes take place in the **cloud**.

Placeholder for a theoretical product

2 **Flexible production processes are optimized in real time** with the help of new and often decentralized approaches to production management.

1 **Deliveries from suppliers are precisely tailored to need and logistics are automated** prior to production.

6 **New materials**—for example, from the field of nanotechnology—make products with new properties possible.

7 **Intelligent sensors** continuously measure and improve the production process.

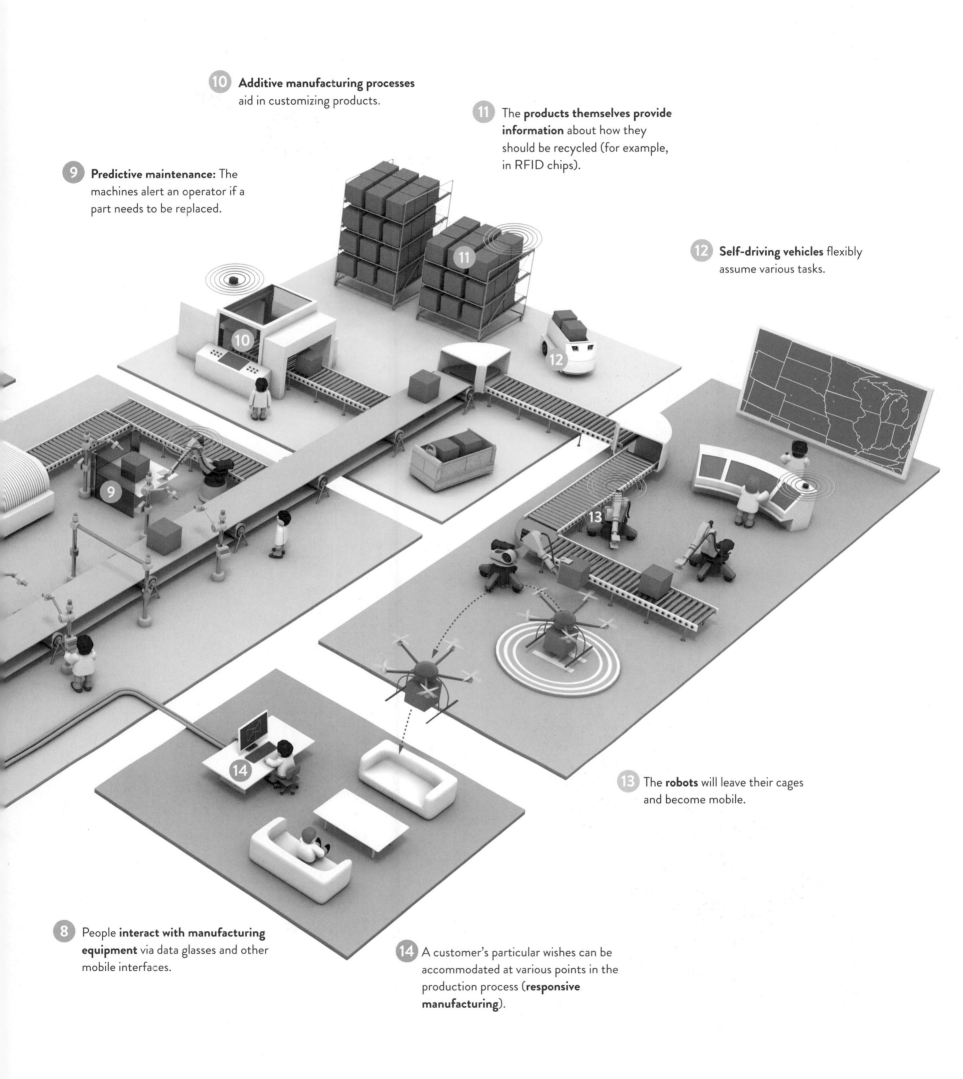

10 Additive manufacturing processes aid in customizing products.

11 The **products themselves provide information** about how they should be recycled (for example, in RFID chips).

9 **Predictive maintenance:** The machines alert an operator if a part needs to be replaced.

12 **Self-driving vehicles** flexibly assume various tasks.

13 The **robots** will leave their cages and become mobile.

8 People **interact with manufacturing equipment** via data glasses and other mobile interfaces.

14 A customer's particular wishes can be accommodated at various points in the production process (**responsive manufacturing**).

INDUSTRY 1.0 TO 4.0

Industrial progress takes place in developmental leaps. Businesses have to be ready to jump when trailblazers use a technical innovation to do things in a fundamentally different way. Industrial history teaches that after every technological paradigm shift, there are winners and losers. Industry 4.0 is a provocative term used in politics and by trade associations for leaping as high and as far as possible in digitally interconnected manufacturing. This time, the companies who missed the start of the Internet don't want to be caught napping like they were about 25 years ago.

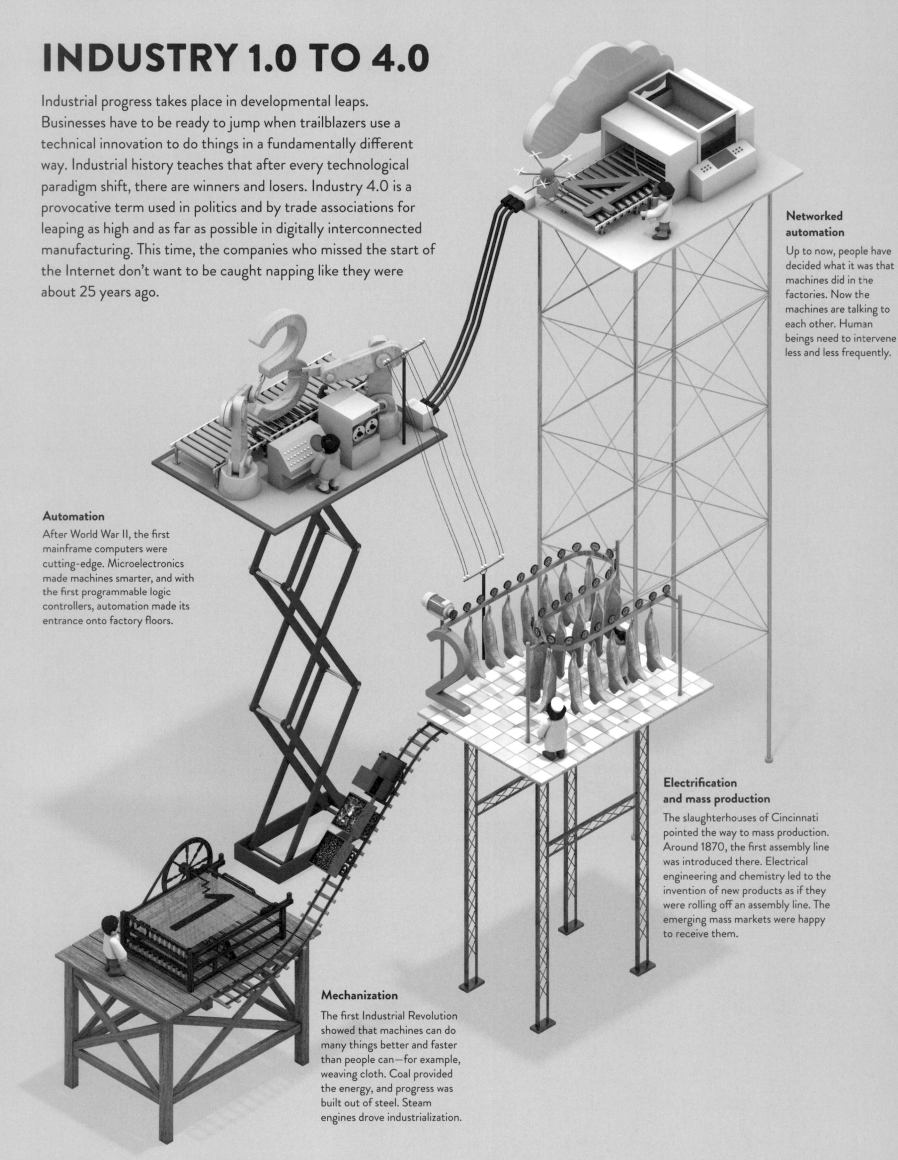

Networked automation

Up to now, people have decided what it was that machines did in the factories. Now the machines are talking to each other. Human beings need to intervene less and less frequently.

Automation

After World War II, the first mainframe computers were cutting-edge. Microelectronics made machines smarter, and with the first programmable logic controllers, automation made its entrance onto factory floors.

Electrification and mass production

The slaughterhouses of Cincinnati pointed the way to mass production. Around 1870, the first assembly line was introduced there. Electrical engineering and chemistry led to the invention of new products as if they were rolling off an assembly line. The emerging mass markets were happy to receive them.

Mechanization

The first Industrial Revolution showed that machines can do many things better and faster than people can—for example, weaving cloth. Coal provided the energy, and progress was built out of steel. Steam engines drove industrialization.

STRONG AI

Machines that think and act like human beings: Artificial intelligence (AI for short) has inspired the human imagination since the Enlightenment. With the rise of computers, a vague idea turned into a plausible technical concept. Research distinguishes between strong and weak AI. The goal of strong AI is to teach machines to think creatively and independently. In doing so, machines might develop (self-)consciousness and even feelings under some circumstances. As of today, such machines are only theoretical—except in the imaginations of science-fiction authors and game developers. But that's nothing new, after all. . . .

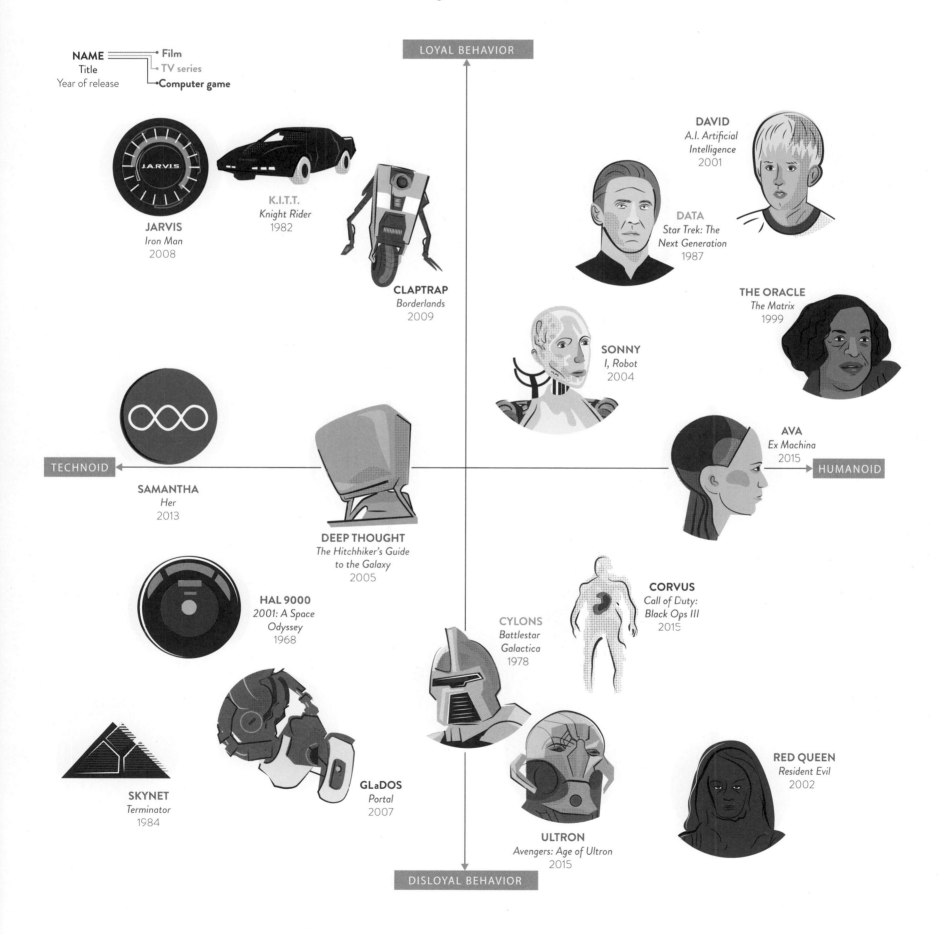

NAME ──── Film
Title ──── TV series
Year of release ──── Computer game

LOYAL BEHAVIOR

JARVIS
Iron Man
2008

K.I.T.T.
Knight Rider
1982

CLAPTRAP
Borderlands
2009

DAVID
A.I. Artificial Intelligence
2001

DATA
Star Trek: The Next Generation
1987

THE ORACLE
The Matrix
1999

SONNY
I, Robot
2004

AVA
Ex Machina
2015

TECHNOID ←──────────────────────→ HUMANOID

SAMANTHA
Her
2013

DEEP THOUGHT
The Hitchhiker's Guide to the Galaxy
2005

HAL 9000
2001: A Space Odyssey
1968

CYLONS
Battlestar Galactica
1978

CORVUS
Call of Duty: Black Ops III
2015

SKYNET
Terminator
1984

GLaDOS
Portal
2007

ULTRON
Avengers: Age of Ultron
2015

RED QUEEN
Resident Evil
2002

DISLOYAL BEHAVIOR

WEAK AI

Strong AI is science fiction, but weak AI is already fairly strong today. It's taking on more and more tasks that only human beings could have done just a few years ago. The concept of artificial intelligence is slightly misleading. Mostly it involves automation of complex but routine tasks.

Analysis of stock prices

0 or 1?

Question
Question mark
Question of the day
Question of time

Search engines

Medical diagnoses

Hello | 你好

Machine translation

AI

Self-driving vehicles

Robots with their own decision routines

"HELLO?"

Textbots

With two weeks to go in the season, the Yankees are only a game behind the Red Sox for the final wildcard spot. The race for the playoffs is far from over. |

Group simulations

Speech recognition for mobile phones

Optical character recognition

Scan
For automated postal sorting, the system needs to recognize the zip code. The envelope is scanned.

Rasters
The recognized zip codes are divided into raster images of the individual digits and converted into a mathematical vector.

= ...1000110101...

Compare
The mathematical vector is compared to the information gathered during the learning phase.

8   = ...1000110101...
7   = ...111110101...
6   = ...11110101...
5   = ...101110111...
4   = ...1110000101...
3   = ...11100110101...
2   = ...110011001...
1   = ...1100110000...
    = ...1010110001...

Learning phase and output of results
The prototypical digit with the least deviation is chosen as the recognized digit. The prototypical digit is simultaneously modified by the new information.

= 8 = 0b1000*

* Binary code for further processing in the system

SMARTER AND SMARTER

Since the end of World War II, scientists have been systematically trying to teach machines to think. The first large-scale research programs began in the mid-1950s. But machines stubbornly remained stupider than expected. They struggle to understand human language and carry out routine mental activities. A phase of disappointment ensues. Many research programs are frozen beginning in the mid-1970s due to their lack of success. With the digital networking of the world, AI receives a new boost. For some years now, weak artificial intelligence has been registering breakthroughs on several fronts. It appears that this technology has had its Kitty Hawk moment—the Wright brothers made the first motorized flight at Kitty Hawk, North Carolina, and then aviation developed quickly. With artificial intelligence, things might turn out the same way.

1945 Vannevar Bush's essay "As We May Think" is published in the *Atlantic* magazine. In it, Bush describes the concept of a universal knowledge machine, the memex.

1966 ELIZA, a computer program developed by Joseph Weizenbaum, is capable of holding seemingly human conversations. ELIZA will later become famous for its simulation of psychotherapy sessions.

1959 The AI Laboratory is founded at the Massachusetts Institute of Technology (MIT) by John McCarthy and Marvin Minsky.

1956 At the Dartmouth conference (Dartmouth Summer Research Project on Artificial Intelligence), the term "artificial intelligence" is coined.

1955 Work begins on Logic Theorist. The first AI computer program will go on to solve 38 of the 52 theorems found in *Principia Mathematica*.

1950 Alan Turing devises a test to determine if a machine possesses intelligence comparable to a human being's. The computer is supposed to answer like a human being.

1970 The expert system MYCIN analyzes blood infections and recommends treatments.

1971 The first self-driving vehicle is presented by Stanford University.

1982 The first commercially usable speech recognition system comes onto the market. It answers to the name of Dragon Dictate.

1993 The robot Polly gives tours through the MIT AI lab and interacts with visitors.

1996 The IBM computer Deep Blue wins two of six chess games against the reigning chess world champion Garry Kasparov. A year later, the Russian no longer stood a chance against the American computer.

1997 The first official world championship in robot soccer, RoboCup, is held. 40 teams participate.

1998 27 million Furbies are sold. The small robot with fake fur is able to learn languages.

2016 The Google program AlphaGo wins against one of the best Go players in the world. To do so, the program trained by playing against itself. The process is called "machine learning."

2009 Wolfram Alpha, the first semantic search engine, enlivens the Internet.

2004 The DARPA Grand Challenge has cars drive autonomously through the Mojave Desert. The victor only makes it 7.4 miles.

2014 Facebook announces its investment in strong AI.

2012 Opening kickoff for the DARPA Robotics Challenge, funded with over $30 million. Semi-autonomous robots are supposed to complete complex tasks in the dangerous ruins of man-made environments.

2011 Google announces that its test fleet of self-driving cars has driven almost 160,000 miles.

IBM's supercomputer Watson wins against two former grand champions in the game show *Jeopardy!*.

Milestones of AI development

VISIBILITY ▲

TIME ►

EXAGGERATED EXPECTATIONS | **EUPHORIA** | DISILLUSIONMENT | **ENLIGHTENMENT** | **PROFITABILITY**

| 1950 | 1960 | 1970 | 1980 | 1990 | 2000 | 2010

The Turing test

A person (A) chats without visual contact (using a keyboard) with another person (B) and a computer (C). B and C both try to convince A that they are the human partner and not a machine. If after intensive questioning A doesn't know which one is the human being, the computer passes the Turing test. Under rigorous experimental conditions, no computer program has passed the test yet.

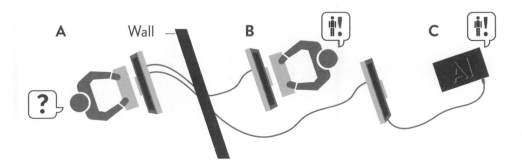

THE DON'T-BE-EVIL EMPIRE

Organizing the world's information and making it accessible to everyone: That was the mission of the Google founders. A simple but highly profitable business model was added to the big-picture concept: Anyone who searches for information using Google would see individualized advertisements. A complex enterprise arose from this mission and business model. It's involved in almost all future-oriented topics that have anything to do with data.

2005 **2010** **2015**

SMART CONTACT LENS ▸ CLIPS
CHROMECAST
PROJECT LOON
GOOGLE GLASS
CHROMEBOOK ▸ PIXELBOOK
GOOGLE TV
WAYMO (DRIVERLESS CAR)
GOOGLE FIBER
NEXUS ONE ▸ HOME
GOOGLE SEARCH APPLIANCE ▸ DAYDREAM VIEW
CALICO
GOOGLE CLOUD PLATFORM
GOOGLE VENTURES
GOOGLE FLU TRENDS
DOCS AND SHEETS ▸ GOOGLE DOCS ▸ GOOGLE DRIVE
G SUITE
GOOGLE FINANCE
GOOGLE ANALYTICS
GOOGLE.ORG
GOOGLE SCHOLAR
GOOGLE AD GRANTS
GOOGLE ADSENSE
GOOGLE LAB
GOOGLE APIs ▸ GOOGLE CODE
GOOGLE ZEITGEIST ▸ GOOGLE TRENDS
GOOGLE ADWORDS

GOOGLE NOW
HANGOUTS
GOOGLE+
ART PROJECT
GOOGLE CRISIS RESPONSE
ANDROID MARKET ▸ GOOGLE PLAY
GOOGLE CHROME
GOOGLE POLITICS
GOOGLE VOICE
YOUTUBE
GOOGLE CHECKOUT ▸ GOOGLE PAY
GOOGLE TRANSLATE
GOOGLE CALENDAR
TALKS AT GOOGLE
GOOGLE EARTH
PICASA
GMAIL
GOOGLE LOCAL ▸ GOOGLE MAPS
GOOGLE CLOUD PRINT ▸ GOOGLE BOOKS ▸ LENS
BLOGGER ▸ DUO
FROOGLE ▸ GOOGLE SHOPPING ▸ ALLO
GOOGLE NEWS
GOOGLE IMAGES
GOOGLE GROUPS
GOOGLE FRIENDS NEWSLETTER
BACKRUB ▸ GOOGLE.COM

Google Inc. Timeline

- ■ Products
- ■ Organization
- ■ Services
- ■ Acquisitions
- — Employees
- ■ Sales in US$ Bn

DEJA.COM
PYRA LABS
APPLIED SEMANTICS
PICASA
KEYHOLE
URCHIN SOFTWARE CORPORATION
ANDROID
YOUTUBE
DOUBLECLICK
GRANDCENTRAL
APIGEE
ZAGAT (FOUNDED IN 1979) HTC
MOTOROLA MOBILITY
MEEBO
QUICKOFFICE
WAZE
NEST

■ 1999
Move to Palo Alto
with eight employees

■ 1998
Application for registration in the commercial
register and first employee of Google Inc.

■ 1997
Registration of the domain name Google.com

■ 1996
Development of the BackRub search engine

■ 1995
Larry Page and Sergey Brin meet at Stanford.

80,000
61,184
60,000
40,000
20,000

1995 **2000** 0.4 1.5 3.2 6.1 10.6 16.6 21.8 23.7 29.3 37.9 50.2 55.5 65.7 74.5 90 110.8
2005 **2010** **2015**

October 2015
Restructured under the umbrella
of the new parent company,

ALPHABET INC.

G
GOOGLE INC.

Google Inc. remains the largest and
most profitable part of the group by
far. The flagship helps finance many
ideas in the larger corporate group.

X

The group's most important
development lab for big ideas,
so-called "moon shots." This is
where the self-driving car and the
(failed) Google Glass were born.

VERILY LIFE SCIENCES
Research lab for applications
related to the human body.

NEST LABS
The company for innovation and
services related to smart homes.

CALICO
Research center for combatting
major diseases.

GOOGLE VENTURES
The group's venture capital company (primarily
early investment with strategic technological goals).

CAPITALG
The group's investment company (primarily
active during growth phases; strong profit focus).

JIGSAW
Tech incubator based in New York.

FLUX
Laboratory for development of sustainable architecture.

SIDEWALK LABS
Innovation center for urban infrastructure.

ACCESS AND ENERGY
The broadband and cable TV service (formerly Fiber)
from Google, expanded to include energy services.

Promising future PROJECTS

LUNAR XPRIZE
Competition to
promote private
moon missions

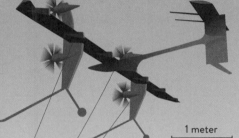

MAKANI
Flying wind turbine
1 meter

GOOGLE PAY
Electronic wallet
(so far unsuccessful)

1 meter
LOON
Internet access everywhere
through the use of helium balloons

SINGULARITY UNIVERSITY
Think tank for future technologies

**SMART
CONTACT LENS**
For blood sugar
measurement

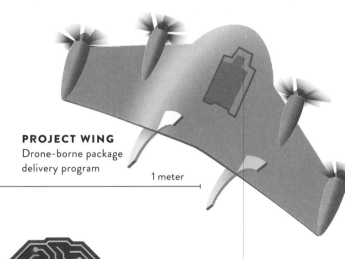

PROJECT WING
Drone-borne package
delivery program
1 meter

GOOGLE BRAIN
Simulation of neuron connections
in the human brain for AI research

GOOGLE VR
Solutions for virtual reality

1 meter
**GOOGLE
WAYMO**
Self-driving car

HOW BIG IS BIG DATA?

More and more intelligent algorithms are analyzing larger and larger volumes of data and can thus predict the future more and more exactly. At least that's the promise of Big Data. At the moment, it doesn't function quite as well as is claimed. But it is actually getting better.

THE 4 Vs OF BIG DATA
The quality of analyzing data on a massive scale is determined by:

VOLUME
The quantity of data from which conclusions can be drawn

VARIETY
The ability to work with different types of data
(for example text, geographic, image, and video data)

VELOCITY
The speed with which data can be obtained and analyzed
(for example, in real time)

VARIABILITY
The reliability/accuracy of data and the ability to recognize which data are deceptive

THE FOUR GOALS OF MASS DATA ANALYSIS

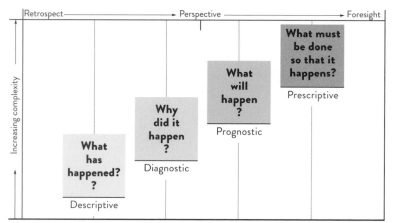

Retrospect — Perspective — Foresight

Increasing complexity

What has happened??
Descriptive

Why did it happen?
Diagnostic

What will happen?
Prognostic

What must be done so that it happens?
Prescriptive

ADOPTION OF BIG DATA BY VERTICAL INDUSTRY
(Survey among US companies, 2017)

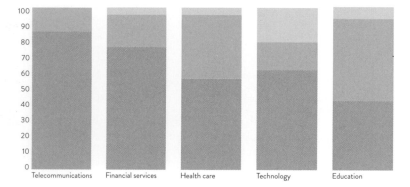

Telecommunications   Financial services   Health care   Technology   Education

- No. We have no plans to use Big Data at all.
- We may use Big Data in the future.
- Yes, we use Big Data today.

Source: bigdataanalyticsreport.com, 2017

Processing of data from weather satellites and other scientific sensors as well as access to and analysis of spatial-temporal raster data in science and industry

SMART DATA APPLICATIONS

Forecasting epidemics and recognizing medical correlations in diagnosis

Cross- and up-selling* in real time and individualized online advertising in local stores and in e-commerce

Route optimization for vehicle fleets

Predictive maintenance of machines

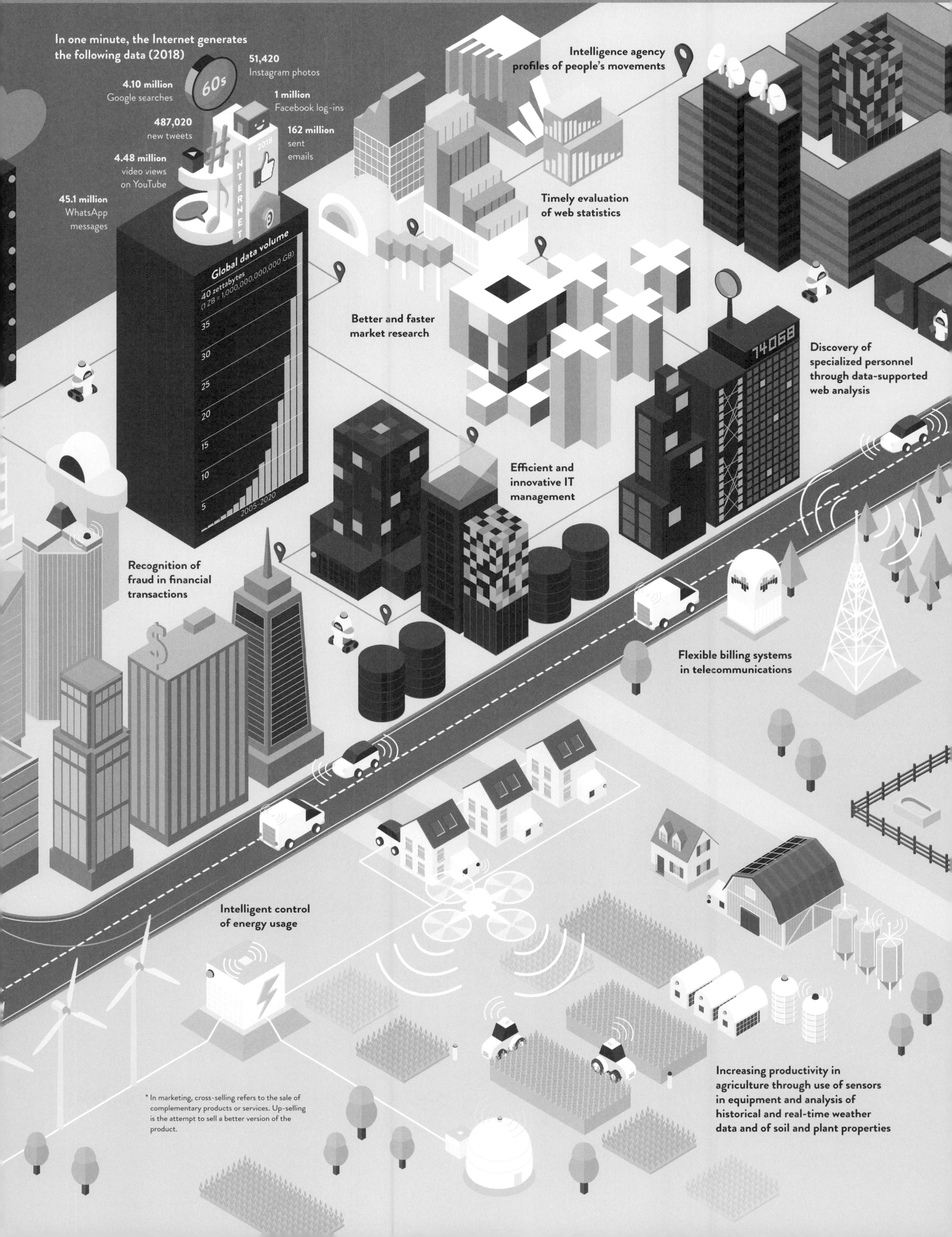

In one minute, the Internet generates
the following data (2018)

60s

4.10 million
Google searches

487,020
new tweets

4.48 million
video views
on YouTube

45.1 million
WhatsApp
messages

51,420
Instagram photos

1 million
Facebook log-ins

162 million
sent
emails

Global data volume
40 zettabytes
(1 ZB = 1,000,000,000,000 GB)

35

30

25

20

15

10

5

2005–2020

Intelligence agency
profiles of people's movements

Timely evaluation
of web statistics

Better and faster
market research

Discovery of
specialized personnel
through data-supported
web analysis

Efficient and
innovative IT
management

Recognition of
fraud in financial
transactions

Flexible billing systems
in telecommunications

Intelligent control
of energy usage

Increasing productivity in
agriculture through use of sensors
in equipment and analysis of
historical and real-time weather
data and of soil and plant properties

* In marketing, cross-selling refers to the sale of
complementary products or services. Up-selling
is the attempt to sell a better version of the
product.

THE FUTURE OF WORK

How will we work? And what must we do to succeed professionally? Of course we don't know the precise answer, but it's apparent that we should continue to educate ourselves about math and technology in order to be able to work more effectively with intelligent machines. But at the same time, we need to strengthen social competence, because working in teams with very different personalities is also becoming more important.

Future personnel strategies, all industries (strategy's share in percent)

65	Investment in retraining of current employees
39	Support for mobility and internal job changes
25	Cooperation with educational institutions
25	Targeted search for female workers
22	Hiring of foreign workers
22	Creation of trainee positions
14	Cooperation with other companies across industries
12	Cooperation with other companies in the same industry
12	Hiring of minority workers
11	Hiring of more short-term workers

Effects on employment by drivers of change according to industry (aggregate growth rate, 2015–2020, by percentage)

POSITIVE   NEGATIVE

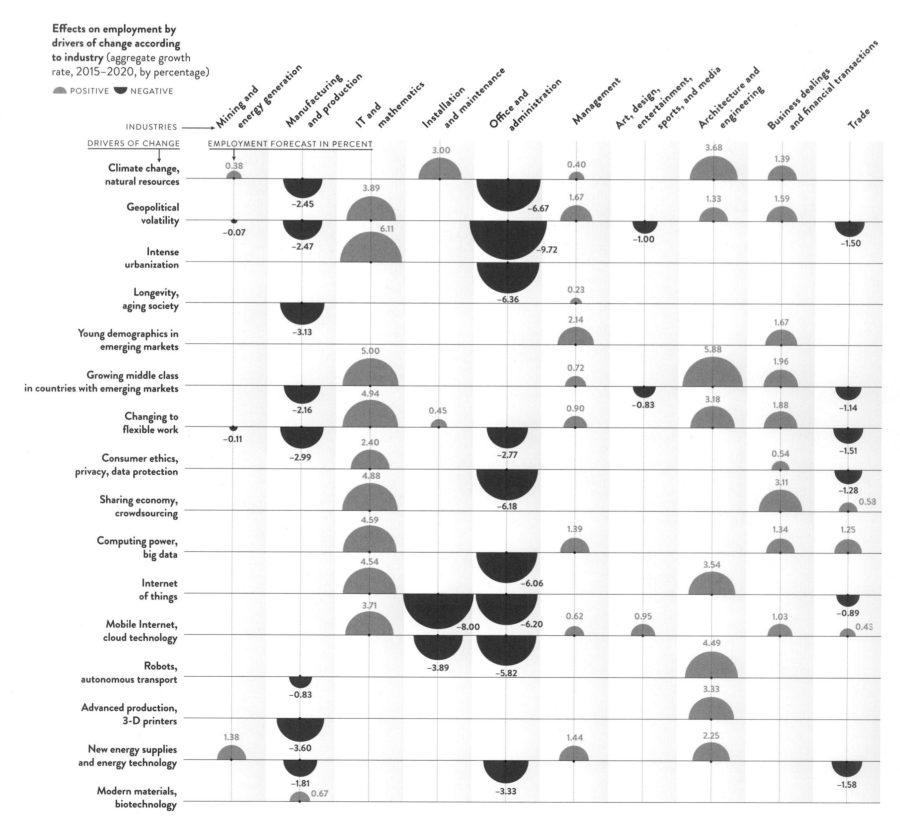

CORE COMPETENCIES
FOR THE WORK OF THE FUTURE

Recognition of deeper relationships

The ability to recognize deeper meanings and assess relevance

Interdisciplinarity

The ability to connect the modes of thinking of different scholarly disciplines

Innovative and flexible thinking

The ability to find solutions beyond the well-known ones

Thinking like a data scientist

The ability to convert great amounts of data into abstract concepts and to understand data-based logic

Social intelligence

The ability to form deep and direct connections and to perceive and generate reactions and the desired interactions

Competency for new media

The ability to critically question content and use new media for compelling communication

Intercultural competence

The ability to act appropriately in different cultural contexts

Information selection and management

The ability to differentiate, filter, and understand information according to its importance

Virtual collaboration

The ability to work productively and actively in interconnected digital teams and make one's presence felt

Design mind-set

The ability to visualize and develop functions and work processes to achieve a desired result

DRIVERS OF CHANGE

INTELLIGENT MACHINES

Robots and artificial intelligence replace people in routine jobs.

COMPUTER-AIDED WORLD

A sharp increase in sensors and computing power turns the world into a programmable system.

NEW MEDIA ENVIRONMENT

New communications tools require new media skills beyond what's needed for text.

SUPERSTRUCTURED ORGANIZATIONS

Social technologies create new forms of production and value creation.

GLOBALLY NETWORKED WORLD

Growing global interconnectedness makes diversity and adaptability central to organizational activities.

LIFE SPAN EXTENSION

Higher life expectancy changes the nature of career paths and continuing education.

BANKING WITHOUT BANKS?

Banks are old, unwieldy companies. Start-ups in the financial technology sector that aren't weighed down by history are able to offer many banking services cheaper, faster, and in a more customer-friendly way. This is the credo of fintech founders. For more than ten years, they have been trying to break off or conquer parts of the traditional bank business. Up to now, they've had limited success. But fintech investors remain optimistic.

Banking and stock exchange applications

Payment and bank transfer

Insurance/reinsurance

Wealth creation and management

Other

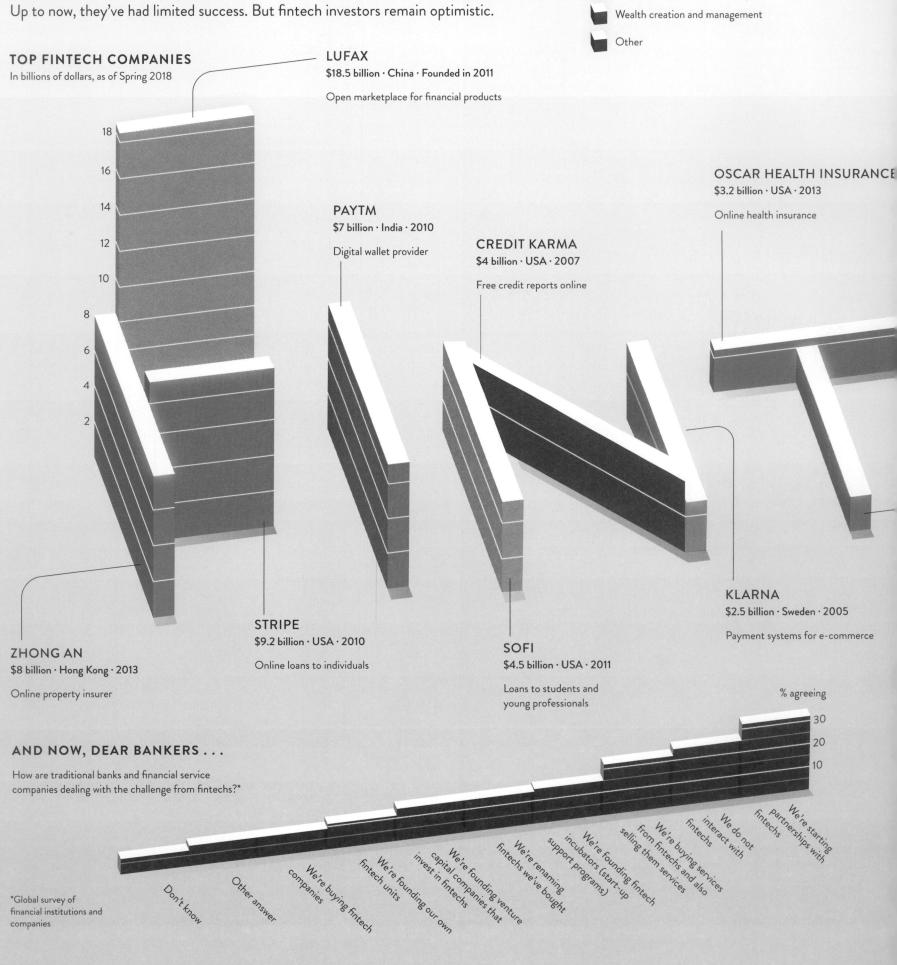

TOP FINTECH COMPANIES

In billions of dollars, as of Spring 2018

LUFAX
$18.5 billion · China · Founded in 2011

Open marketplace for financial products

PAYTM
$7 billion · India · 2010

Digital wallet provider

CREDIT KARMA
$4 billion · USA · 2007

Free credit reports online

OSCAR HEALTH INSURANCE
$3.2 billion · USA · 2013

Online health insurance

ZHONG AN
$8 billion · Hong Kong · 2013

Online property insurer

STRIPE
$9.2 billion · USA · 2010

Online loans to individuals

SOFI
$4.5 billion · USA · 2011

Loans to students and young professionals

KLARNA
$2.5 billion · Sweden · 2005

Payment systems for e-commerce

AND NOW, DEAR BANKERS . . .

How are traditional banks and financial service companies dealing with the challenge from fintechs?*

% agreeing

*Global survey of financial institutions and companies

Don't know

Other answer

We're buying fintech companies

We're founding our own fintech units

We're founding venture capital companies that invest in fintechs

We're renaming fintechs we've bought

We're founding incubators (start-up support programs)

We're buying services from fintechs and also selling them services

We do not interact with fintechs

We're starting partnerships with fintechs

ANT FINANCIAL
$150 billion · China · 2014

The biggest fintech firm is Ant Financial, the largest online payment platform in China. Alipay, its online payments business, boasts 870 million users.

PAYPAL
$94 billion · USA · 1998

One of the largest fintech companies in the world is the online payment service PayPal. The eBay spinoff went public in 2015. Today it's apparently too large to be perceived as a fintech. It usually doesn't appear at all in popular lists of fintech companies.

FINTECH

AVANT
$2 billion · USA · 2012

Online marketplace for loans

ZENEFITS
$2 billion · USA · 2013

HR, payroll, benefits and compliance management for small and mid-sized businesses

NUBANK
$1–2 billion · Brazil · 2013

Digital bank and credit card services

FUNDING CIRCLE
$1 billion · United Kingdom · 2009

Financial services for small businesses

KABBAGE
$1 billion · USA · 2009

Fully automated lending to small businesses

TRANSFERWISE
$1.6 billion · United Kingdom · 2010

Global money transfers

AFFIRM
$1.8 billion · USA · 2012

Hire-purchase provider that makes it possible to pay for purchased products in installments

ADYEN
$2.3 billion · Netherlands · 2006

Global payment processing

REVOLUT
$1.7 billion · United Kingdom · 2015

Currency exchange and other banking services

AND TOMORROW, DEAR BANKERS . . .

In which market segments will fintechs likely be successful with breakthrough innovations in the next five years?*

% agreeing
80
60
40
20

Reinsurance
Investment banking
Funds
Operation of trading platforms
Insurance brokerage
Commercial banks
Property and life insurance
Broker services
Services for small and mid-sized companies
Investment and asset management
Payment systems
Financial services for consumers

BITCOIN

1

Payer transfers money to receiver. All that's required is for both to know the Bitcoin addresses.

Only central banks can create money? Hardly! A parallel digital currency was created in 2009 in the form of Bitcoin. Money can be transferred anonymously from one user to another. There is no central authority that issues Bitcoins. They are created in controlled amounts through computing capacity provided by so-called "miners." The transactions are managed by the network.

5

The receiver is credited with Bitcoins after verification by the network. On special exchanges, the user can exchange them for official currencies. The exchange rate fluctuates.

PAYER

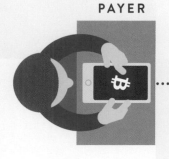

RECIPIENT

DATABASE

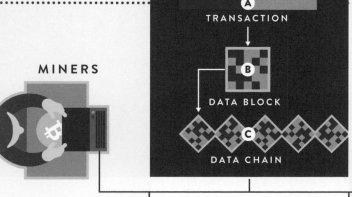

A — TRANSACTION

B — DATA BLOCK

C — DATA CHAIN

MINERS

2

"Miners" provide computing capacity and maintain the database. The transaction is recorded in an encrypted block of data.

BITCOIN NETWORK

3

The anonymous transaction is stored on all computers in the network every ten minutes.

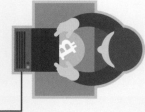

4

"Miners" are credited with small amounts in Bitcoin for computational work. The money supply increases according to controlled rules to prevent inflation.

RISKS FOR USERS

Losses caused by malware, data manipulation, or thefts from online stock exchanges

Overloading the system's capacity; transactions today are often slow and expensive

Large fluctuations in exchange rates and exaggerated expectations for commercial use

Government prohibitions and usage restrictions to fight money laundering and illicit transactions

THE EVOLUTION OF BITCOIN

 Total number of Bitcoins in circulation

— Number of transactions per day

— Market price (in US$)

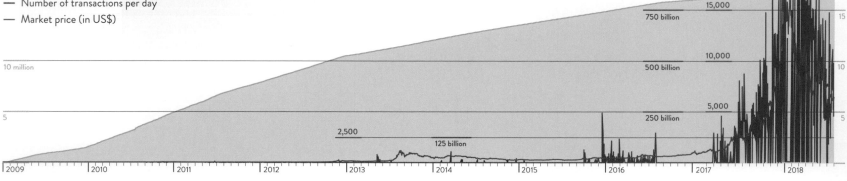

US$ 20,000 (market price)
1,000 billion (transactions)
20 million (coins)

15,000
15
750 billion

10,000
500 billion

5,000
250 billion

10 million

5

2,500
5
125 billion

2009 2010 2011 2012 2013 2014 2015 2016 2017 2018

BLOCKCHAIN

The technology behind Bitcoin is known as blockchain. It can do more than manage cryptocurrencies. A blockchain is an incorruptible bookkeeping system that exists on many computers at the same time and constantly updates itself. An unlimited number of strangers can conduct business directly with each other on a large scale. Blockchain could thus become the backbone of a sharing economy worthy of the name.

SAMPLE APPLICATIONS

CERTIFICATES OF AUTHENTICITY

Diamonds are often counterfeited. A blockchain could guarantee one's authenticity even if it has passed through many hands.

THE END OF MIDDLEMEN?

Trustworthy persons or institutions record each major transaction. Our economic system is based on this principle. Blockchain challenges this assumption. The community of users takes on the brokering and supervisory function of banks or land registry offices. Accountants and notaries are automated out of existence.

LAND REGISTRATION

In many countries there are no land registration offices. Blockchain would be able to reliably document property rights.

SUPPLY CHAIN CONTROL

Does the sausage really come from an organic farm? With a supply chain-blockchain, each production step can be precisely reconstructed down to the name of the pig that was processed.

SMART CONTRACTS

Smart contracts can be built into blockchains. For example, it could be established that an electric car would no longer start if the lease was not paid.

ACCOUNTING LOGS

In the Internet of things, many small services have to be accounted for. For example, how much electricity a private solar power system feeds into the electric grid. Blockchain is a good technical solution for this.

ADVANTAGES OF BLOCKCHAIN

Blockchain is . . .
an innovative way to store data in a decentralized way.

Blockchain has . . .
a high security standard thanks to sophisticated encryption techniques.

Blockchain is . . .
anonymous and transparent, as it is visible at every instant for all network participants.

Blockchain makes possible . . .
network effects on platforms that have no owner. So Uber without Uber, for example.

Blockchain creates . . .
trust between people who are connected to each other in a digital network. It is also referred to as a "trust protocol."

MAKE SOMETHING . . .

Since the invention of the wheel, human beings have been looking for technical solutions to make their work easier. Until now, more machines have always meant more work—and more prosperity. But one fundamental principle hasn't changed in centuries: People receive wages for work. They have to pay part of it to the state as taxes. From the remainder, they finance the rest of their lives and are able to buy nice things now and then, including goods that they themselves produced.

PAYROLL DEPARTMENT

... MR. ROBOT!

What would it be like if the machines were able to do all the work? A group of British utopians is hoping for a fully automated luxury communism. The robots work, and the state levies a tax on machines and then distributes it to the citizens—perhaps through a guaranteed Universal Basic Income (UBI). That's not only convenient for all the humans involved, but also an economic necessity. Because if people no longer work and receive no pay, they can't buy the things that the robots produce.

DEPARTMENT OF MACHINE TAX REDISTRIBUTION

APPENDIX

I. THE INDIVIDUAL

Pages 2–3

US Department of Labor, Bureau of Labor Statistics: bls.gov

Pages 4–5

Sprenger, Reinhard K., *Mythos Motivation* (20th edition), 2014, Frankfurt am Main: Campus Verlag • de.wikipedia.org • terrihughes.com

Pages 6–7

Federal Statistical Office of Germany: de.statista.com • Bureau of Labor Statistics • forbes.com • timeshighereducation.com • spiegel.de/wirtschaft/ • de.wikipedia.org • abendblatt.de • handelsblatt.com • gehalt.de • gehaltsvergleich.com/gehalt

Pages 10–11

US Census Bureau: census.gov • Bureau of Labor Statistics

Pages 12–13

Bittner, Gerhard, and Elke Schwarz, *Emotion Selling* (2nd edition), 2015, Wiesbaden: Springer Gabler

Pages 14–15

International Journal of Social, Behavioral, Educational, Economic, Business and Industrial Engineering (World Academy of Science, Engineering and Technology), 2013 • bonappetit.com • businessinsider.com • thefunambulist.net

Pages 16–17

Organization for Economic Co-operation and Development (OECD): oecd.org • United Nations Human Rights Office of the High Commissioner: ohchr.org • Human Development Report: dgvn.de • Worldbank: data.worldbank.org • Central Intelligence Agency: cia.gov • US Census Bureau • Federal Statistical Office of Germany • nationmaster.com • hg.org/bankrpt.html • en.wikipedia.org • nolo.com • arringtonlegal.com • diakonie.de • wirtschaftslexikon.gabler.de • laenderdaten.info • handelsblatt.com

Pages 18–19

German Federal Foreign Office: auswaertiges-amt.de/en • Wealth-X; World Ultra Wealth Report: wealthx.com • UBS Wealth Management: ubs.com • forbes.com • time.com • faz.net • ap.org • blogs.wsj.com/wealth • de.wikipedia.org

Pages 20–21

US Department of Labor: dol.gov • German Trade Union Confederation: en.dgb.de • Techniker Krankenkasse Health Report: tk.de/techniker • compsych.com • statista.de • de.wikipedia.org

Pages 22–23

de.wikipedia.org

II. THE COMPANY

Pages 26–27

Volkswagen AG, Annual Report: volkswagenag.com • qz.com • dw.com • spiegel.de/auto • manager-magazin.de

Pages 28–29

City of Wolfsburg Population Report: wolfsburg.de • Volkswagen AG, Annual Report • volkswagen-media-services.com • waz-online.de/Wolfsburg • faz.net/aktuell/technik-motor • www.bezreg-arnsberg.nrw.de • ndr.de/kultur

Pages 32–33

American Bankruptcy Institute: abi.org • Apple Inc., Annual Report: investor.apple.com • bloomberg.com • japan.go.jp • forbes.com • en.wikipedia.org • de.wikipedia.org

Pages 34–35

LinkedIn State of Salary Report: linkedin.com • Federal Statistical Office of Germany • ft.com • basf.com • siemens.com • finance.yahoo.com • time.com • forbes.com • thomsonreuters.com • ard.de • stepstone.de/gehaltsreport • wiwo.de/unternehmen • archined.nl • n-tv.de/wirtschaft • chinamobileltd.com • finanzen.net • futuresmag.com • creditreform.de • faz.net • handelsblatt.com • de.wikipedia.org

Pages 36–37

Model based on the work of Michael Eugene Porter: de.wikipedia.org/wiki/Wertkette • Wiedemann, Arnd, *Value Chains in Upheaval*, 2007, University of Siegen • www.wiwi.uni-muenster.de • henkel.de/nachhaltigkeit/wertschoepfungskette

Pages 38–39

en.wikipedia.org/wiki/Business_Model_Canvas

Pages 40–41

nytimes.com • statista.com • the-numbers.com • vgchartz.com • packagedfacts.com • lifewire.com • cheatsheet.com • eetimes.com • safran-group.com

Pages 42–43

US Patent and Trademark Office: uspto.gov • Grant, Robert M., *Contemporary Strategy Analysis* (5th edition), 2004, Malden: Blackwell • six-sigma-deutschland.de • ferdinandgrah.de/design-thinking • mt08a.wordpress.com • saiglobal.com • de.wikipedia.org

Pages 44–45

Reichwald, Ralf, and Kathrin Möslein, *Organization: Structures and Design*, Technical University of Munich • Zöllner, Christine, *General Business Studies*, 2012, University of Hamburg • Schrader, Inka, and Michael Treutler, *Organization in Multinational Companies*, 2002, Weimar: Bauhaus University • Schlachtet, Marion, *Basic Models of Organizational Structure in the Company*, Frankfurt University of Applied Sciences • www.iwk-svk-dresden.de • economics.phil.fau.de • pqrst.at • de.wikipedia.org

Pages 46–47

Rademacher, Ute, *Leading and Making Decisions Easier*, 2014, Wiesbaden: Springer Gabler • Tuckman, Bruce W., and Mary Ann Jensen, *Stages of Small-Group Development Revisited*, 1977 • focus.de/finanzen • humanresources.about.com • de.wikipedia.org

Pages 48–49

de.wikipedia.org

Pages 50–51

International Advertising Association: iaaglobal.com • nielsen.com • brandeins.de • de.wikipedia.org

Pages 52–53

torok.com • wiwo.de • grey.colorado.edu

Pages 54–55

Zenith Media: zenithmedia.com • Insurance Auto Auctions Corporation: iaai.com • reuters.com

III. THE NATIONAL ECONOMY

Pages 58–59

Federal Reserve Bank of St. Louis: fred.stlouisfed.org • Federal Statistical Office of Germany • de.wikipedia.org

Pages 60–61

Federal Reserve Bank of Minneapolis: minneapolisfed.org • Federal Reserve Bank of St. Louis

Pages 62–63

Böker, Jürgen, *Economic Policy Workbook/Economic Order* (3rd edition), 2005, Darmstadt: Winklers Verlag • de.wikipedia.org

Pages 64–65

Office of Management and Budget, Historical Tables: whitehouse.gov/omb/historical-tables/

Pages 66–67

Weidmann, Jens, *Money and Monetary Policy*, 2015 • Sperber, Herbert, *Understanding the Economy* (4th edition), 2012, Stuttgart: Schäffer-Poeschel • bundesbank.de

Pages 68–69

The World Bank: data.worldbank.org • OECD

Pages 70–71

Federal Agency for Civic Education, Germany: bpb.de • de.wikipedia.org

Pages 72–73

European Commission: ec.europa.eu • Federal Network Agency, Germany: bundesnetzagentur.de • Association of Telecommunications, Germany: vatm.de • Network of European Railways: netzwerk-bahnen.de • Federal Ministry of Finance, Germany: bundesfinanzministerium.de • Rasch, Benjamin, *Competition Through Network Access*, 2009, Wiesbaden: Gabler • Federal Agency for Civic Education • latimes.com • bloomberg.com • wsj.com • reuters.com • zoll.de • zuhause.de • tagesspiegel.de • de.wikipedia.org

Pages 74–75

finanzen-heute.de • muenzenwoche.de • bundesbank.de • faz.net • de.wikipedia.org

Pages 76–77

US Federal Reserve: federalreserve.gov • Sperber, Herbert, *Understanding the Economy* (4th edition), 2012, Stuttgart: Schäffer-Poeschel • Federal Statistical Office of Germany

Pages 78–79

Federal Reserve Bank of New York: newyorkfed.org • thebalance.com • investopedia.com • Federal Reserve Bank of St. Louis • US Federal Reserve

Pages 80–81

US Department of Agriculture: usda.gov

Pages 82–83

Melbourne Mercer Global Pension Index: australiancentre.com.au • United Nations: un.org • US Census Bureau • Bureau of Labor Statistics

Pages 84–85

American Consumers Newsletter, New Strategist Press: newstrategist.com • Peter G. Peterson Foundation: pgpf.org • United Nations Development Programme, Human Development Reports: hdr.undp.org • World Happiness Report: worldhappiness.report • OECD-iLibrary.org • OECD • Bureau of Labor Statistics • Federal Statistical Office of Germany

IV. THE GLOBAL ECONOMY

Pages 88–89

Friedrich Ebert Foundation: fes-online-akademie.de • Clean Clothes Campaign: cleanclothes.org • Birnbaum, David, *Birnbaum's Global Guide to Winning the Great Garment War*, 2005, New York: Fashiondex • bloomberg.com • wsj.com

Pages 90–91

Breuhaus, Rich, *787 Dreamliner: A New Airplane for a New World*, 2008, Airports Council International: aci-na.org • Kraemer, Kenneth L., Greg Linden, and Jason Dedrick, *Capturing Value in Global Networks*, 2007, Information Technology & Innovation Foundation: itif.org • Make Fruit Fair: makefruitfair.org • German Trade Union Confederation

Pages 92–93

World Economic Forum, Global Competitiveness Report: weforum.org • The Heritage Foundation: heritage.org

Pages 94–95

University of Groningen, Growth and Development Center: ggdc.net • US Census Bureau

Pages 96–97

US Department of Transportation, Bureau of Transportation Statistics: www.bts.gov • World Shipping Council: worldshipping.org • National Oceanic and Atmospheric Administration: noaa.gov • OECD, International Transport Forum: www.itf-oecd.org • Airports Council International: aci.aero • aircargoworld.com • wikimedia.de • Federal Statistical Office of Germany

Pages 98–99

South Asian Association for Regional Cooperation: saarc-sec.org • npr.org • de.wikipedia.org

Pages 100–101

World Bank Group: worldbank.org • World Trade Organization: wto.org • Federal Statistical Office of Germany • de.wikipedia.org

Pages 102–103

Lallerstedt, Karl, and Michael Wigell, *Briefing Paper*, 2014, Finnish Institute of International Affairs: fiia.fi

Pages 104–105

International Labour Organization: ilo.org

Pages 106–107

International Monetary Fund: imf.org • Financial Stability Board: fsb.org • Wouters, Jan, and Jed Odermatt, *Comparing the "Four Pillars" of Global Economic Governance*, 2013, Leuven Centre for Global Governance Studies • OECD • World Bank • World Trade Organization • de.wikipedia.org

Pages 108–109

Federal Statistical Office of Germany • spiegel.de • handelszeitung.ch • de.wikipedia.org

Pages 110–111

economist.com • mba-mondays-illustrated.com • de.wikipedia.org

Pages 112–113

fortune.com • marketwatch.com • wiwo.de • handelsblatt.com

Pages 114–115

Annual reports: Apple Inc., investor.apple.com; Uniqlo, fastretailing.com; McDonald's, corporate.mcdonalds.com; Ikea, inter.ikea.com • en.wikipedia.org

Page 116

US Geological Survey: usgs.gov • Office of Water Information: owi.usgs.gov • Beverage Marketing Corporation: beveragemarketing.com • International Bottled Water Association: bottledwater.org • Euromonitor International: euromonitor.com • marketresearch.com • zenithglobal.com • wafg.de • Federal Statistical Office of Germany

Page 117

Pew Research Center: pewglobal.org • Migration Policy Institute: migrationpolicy.org • medium.com/migration-issues

Pages 118–119

International Organization for Migration, World Migration Report: publications.iom.int • OECD • un.org

V. THEORY

Pages 122–123

de.wikipedia.org

Pages 124–125

whoswho.de • de.wikipedia.org

Pages 126–127

Lebendiges Museum Online: dhm.de • World Bank • International Monetary Fund • investopedia.com • agso.uni-graz.at/lexikon/klassiker • wirtschaftslexikon.gabler.de • doener235.wordpress.com • de.wikipedia.org

Pages 128–129

wirtschaftslexikon.gabler.de • de.wikipedia.org

Pages 130–131

keynes-gesellschaft.de • de.wikipedia.org

Pages 132–133

Economy: Compact Classics (Financial Times Deutschland) • de.wikipedia.org

Pages 134–135

Globalization: Compact Knowledge (Financial Times Deutschland) • *Economy: Compact Classics* • de.wikipedia.org

VI. ENVIRONMENT AND RESOURCES

Pages 138–139

nachhaltigkeit.info

Pages 140–141

US Department of the Interior: doi.gov • US Geological Survey, Mineral Commodity Summary: minerals.usgs.gov/minerals • de.wikipedia.org

Pages 142–143

Federal Institute for Geosciences and Natural Resources, Germany: bgr.bund.de • Federal Ministry for Economic Affairs and Technology, Germany: bmwi.de

Pages 144–145

Food and Agriculture Organization of the United Nations: fao.org • UNESCO: unesco.org • Federal Association of the Energy and Water Industries, Germany: bdew.de • Association of German Water Protection: vdg-online.de and virtuelles-wasser.de • US Geological Survey • Office of Water Information • OECD • Federal Statistical Office of Germany

Pages 146–147

Food and Agriculture Organization of the United Nations

Page 148

Federal Ministry of Food and Agriculture, Germany: bmel.de • gfk-verein.org • US Department of Agriculture • Pew Research Center • Federal Statistical Office of Germany

Page 149

International Service for the Acquisition of Agri-biotech Applications: isaaa.org • Federal Statistical Office of Germany

Pages 150–151

Transparency International: transparency.org

Pages 154–155

World Ocean Review: worldoceanreveiw.com • US International Trade Commission: usitc.gov • US Environmental Protection Agency: epa.gov • Pew Research Center • Baldé, C.P., F. Wang, R. Kuehr, and J. Huisman, *Global E-waste Monitor*, United Nations University, Institute for the Advanced Study of Sustainability: ias.unu.edu • International Telecommunication Union, ICT Data and Statistics Division, Telecommunication Development Sector: itu.int • Consumer Technology Association: cta.tech • Mobile Information Center, Germany: izmf.de • e-cycle.com • dosomething.org • gartner.com • socialmediaweek.org • bitkom.org

Pages 156–157

International Carbon Action Partnership: icapcarbonaction.com • European Environment Agency: eea.europa.eu • Federal Environment Agency, Germany: umweltbundesamt.de • United Nations Association of Germany: nachhaltig-entwickeln.dgvn.de • dehst.de • de.wikipedia.org

Pages 158–159

US Energy Information Administration: eia.gov • Federal Ministry for the Environment, Nature Conservation and Nuclear Safety: bmu.de • Greentech: greentech-made-in-germany.de • European Commission

VII. THE FUTURE

Pages 162–163

Naisbitt, John, *Megatrends: Ten New Directions Transforming Our Lives* (6th edition), 1982, London: Warner Books

Pages 164–165

nowandnext.com • trendone.com • rolandberger.de • zukunftsinstitut.de • pwc.com • weiterdenken.ch • mba13-group8.weebly.com

Pages 166–167

US Department of Energy, Office of Scientific and Technical Information: osti.gov • National Bank of Belgium Museum: nbbmuseum.be • Pallaske, Christoph, *Timeline: Important Events and Epochs of History*, 2010 • theatlantic.com

Page 168

Schumpeter, Joseph A., *Capitalism, Socialism, and Democracy* (8th edition), 2005, Tübingen and Basel: UTB/A • Federal Agency for Civic Education, Germany • druckerinstitute.com • wirtschaftslexikon.gabler.de • de.wikipedia.org

Page 169

European Patent Office: epo.org

Pages 170–171

National Academy of Science and Engineering, Germany, Innovation Indicator: innovationsindikator.de

Pages 172–173

Vance, Ashlee, *Elon Musk*, 2015, New York: Ecco • cnet.com • t3n.de

Pages 174–175

Amazon, Annual Report: business.nasdaq.com • MWPVL International: mwpvl.com • bloomberg.com/businessweek • bloomberg.com • forbes.com • economist.com • reuters.com • fortune.com • morganstanley.com • guardian.co.uk • zeit.de • stocksplithistory.com • authorearnings.com • ebookfriendly.com • allthingsdistributed.com

Pages 176–177

fortune.com/unicorns • crunchbase.com • en.wikipedia.org

Pages 180–181

iot-analytics.com

Page 182

Federal Ministry for Transport, Innovation and Technology, Austria: bmvit.gv.at

Page 183

de.wikipedia.org

Page 184

chip.de • de.wikipedia.org

Page 185

bbc.com • smithsonianmag.com • wired.com • chip.de • de.wikipedia.org

Pages 186–187

Alphabet (Google), Annual Report: abc.xyz/investor • commons.wikimedia.org • koozai.com • arstechnica.com • Federal Statistical Office of Germany

Pages 188–189

United Nations Economic Commission for Europe: unece.org • Bloching, Björn, Lars Luck, and Thomas Ramge, *Data User: Customer Data Revolutionizing the Economy*, 2012, Munich: Redline Verlag • Federal Statistical Office of Germany • forbes.com • businessinsider.com • internetlivestats.com • zephoria.com • ibmbigdatahub.com/infographics • research.ibm.com • miprofs.com • n-news.de

Pages 190–191

World Economic Forum, Global Challenge Insight Report: weforum.org • Institute for the Future: iftf.org

Pages 192–193

PricewaterhouseCoopers, Global Fintech Report: pwc.com • cnbc.com • bloomberg.com • fortune.com

Pages 194–195

Common Market for Eastern and Southern Africa: www.comesa.int • Heuer, Steffan, and Thomas Ramge, *Transparent Shops*, 2016: brandeins.de • blockchain.info • economist.com • ft.com • de.wikipedia.org

Pages 196–197

guardian.co.uk

IDEA AND CONCEPT

Thomas Ramge writes for the *Economist* and is the technology correspondent of the German business magazine *brand eins*. He's the author of one novel and twelve nonfiction books, for which he's received numerous awards, including the *Financial Times* Business Book Award.

Jan Schwochow, an infographic specialist, was the art director of *Stern* magazine's infographics and today is the founder and CEO of the Infographics Group, which has received numerous awards. He's the author of the bestsellers *Understanding Germany* and the *100 + 1 Facts* series.

TEXT
Thomas Ramge

ART DIRECTION
Klaas Neumann

PROJECT MANAGEMENT
Annemarie Kurz

RESEARCH & DOCUMENTATION
Katja Ploch, Victoria Strathon, René Kohl, Heike Barnitzke

INFOGRAPHICS
Annick Ehmann, Klaas Neumann, Anton Delchmann, Jan Schwochow, Katharina Schwochow, Verena Muckel, Nick Oelschlägel, Jakub Chrobok, Daniela Scharffenberg, Henning Trenkamp, Christian Eisenberg, Jonas Parnow, Christophorus Halsch, Jaroslaw Kaschtalinski

ACKNOWLEDGMENTS FOR THIS ENGLISH-LANGUAGE EDITION

Adapting a book of infographics into another language and for another culture is a massive undertaking that requires an enormous amount of time and effort. We are deeply grateful and very honored that The Experiment made a US edition with global outreach possible.

We first want to thank our American editor, Nicholas Cizek, who believed in the global dimension of our German book since he first saw it, and championed it against all of our warnings as to how much work a US edition would be.

We are extremely thankful to the whole The Experiment team, which burned the midnight oil making this edition possible, including Karen Giangreco, Pamela Schechter, Sophie Appel, Zach Pace, Liana Willis, Jeanne Tao, Sarah Smith, Sarah Schneider, Jennifer Hergenroeder, Ashley Yepsen, Angel Rodriguez, Dan O'Connor, and Matthew Lore.

Adrian Garcia-Landa brought in all the experience he had gathered while adapting the book for the French edition. Thanks once again, Adrian!

Jonathan Green, the translator we know and highly regard from other book projects, is a cross-cultural superstar with a deep understanding of the nuances of the German language. In this edition, he not only translated but helped facilitate the placement of his new text, a process neither easy nor straightforward.

We highly appreciate the work of and do warmly thank Nancy Elgin, who had to sift through heaps of sources for her outstanding fact-checking and copyediting of the new material.

We are also very grateful to Annemarie Blumenhagen of Econ Verlag and our German agent Thomas Hölzl for taking care of the complex legal work that all transatlantic projects come along with.

In times of difficult international relations on the highest political level, we need to strengthen the global ties in our daily work. Maybe the making of this edition can serve as a modest example. *Danke!*

—Thomas and Jan